Herbal Treasures

INSPIRING MONTH-BY-MONTH PROJECTS
FOR GARDENING,
COOKING, AND CRAFTS

by
Phyllis V. Shaudys

A Garden Way Publishing Book

STOREY

Storey Communications, Inc.
Schoolhouse Road
Pownal, VT 05261

Cover, interior design, and production by Cynthia McFarland
Edited by Gwen W. Steege

Illustrated by Brigita Fuhrmann, except herb drawings on pages 12, 15, 33, 59, 62, 98, 102, 106, 113, 222-23, 228, and 250 which are by Charles Joslin
Heart wreath pictured on front cover was made by Betsy Williams/ The Proper Season, Andover, MA; photo by Bruce Anderson
Back cover photo by Derek Fell
Production assistance by Kelly Madden

Printed in the United States by R. R. Donnelley
First Printing, October 1990

Library of Congress Cataloging-in-Publication data

Shaudys, Phyllis
    Herbal treasures : inspiring month-by-month projects for gardening, cooking, and crafts / by Phyllis V. Shaudys.
       p.   cm
    "A Garden Way Publishing Book."
    Includes bibliographical references
    Includes index.
    ISBN 0-88266-618-5 (pbk) : -- ISBN 0-88266-619-3 (hc)

    1. Herbs. 2. Herb gardening. 3. Cookery (Herbs) 4. Herbs-- Utilization. 5. Nature craft. I. Title.
SB351.H5S48 1990
635' .7--dc20

                                              90-10145
                                                CIP

♥

This book is lovingly dedicated

to

all four generations of my so-supportive family —
from my husband Hugh and our children Kirk, Karen, and Kim,
and their spouses, to our so-patient octogenarian parents and
our first grandchild, Danny —
all of whom allowed

Herbal Treasures

to be my first priority for almost two years, without guilt.

ABOUT THE AUTHOR

Phyllis Vandenbergh Shaudys is a homemaker, publisher, and author who specializes in herbs as a result of a hobby she started in 1960 when her children were preschoolers. She has lived in Pennsylvania since her graduation from Bucknell University and her marriage to Hugh Kirkbright Shaudys. For many years her hobby "paid for itself" with earnings from fragrant products she sold in over a dozen local stores. In 1978, Mrs. Shaudys established a home-based publishing business in order to share her love of herbs with others through booklets and a newsletter covering all facets of herbs. Called *Potpourri from Herbal Acres,* this networking newsletter is now the longest-surviving herbal newsletter available to the public in the United States, and put the author in touch with herb experts all over the country who also wanted to share their experiences and favorite projects. These combined writings in the newsletter have led to the publication of both *The Pleasure of Herbs: A Month-by-Month Guide to Growing, Using, and Enjoying Herbs* (1986, Storey Communications, Pownal, VT) and its sequel, *Herbal Treasures: Inspiring Month-by-Month Projects for Gardening, Cooking, and Crafts* (1990, Storey Communications, Pownal, VT).

The author has also co-authored *The Vegetable Spaghetti Cookbook* with Derek Fell (Pine Row Publications, Washington Crossing, PA 1982), and her work has been published in *Woman's Day, Whitechappel's Herbal, Flower & Garden, The Mother Earth News, The Brooklyn Botanic Garden Record, Creative Ideas for Living, Baer's Agricultural Almanac, The Joy of Herbs,* and *The Herb Companion.* She is a member of The Herb Society of America, The International Herb Growers & Marketers Association, and The Garden Writers Association of America.

Contents

Introduction

It is incredible how much has happened in the world of herbs in the 5 years since I wrote The Pleasure of Herbs, *an introductory guide to growing, using, and enjoying herbs at home. So much has occurred so fast, that it is time to share the newest developments to update herb enthusiasts. This book will not repeat the very basic information about herbs given in my first book, but in many ways it picks up where that one leaves off.*

The number of American households growing their own herbs is escalating at a rapid pace each year. In 1986, five million gardeners spent $39 million growing herbs. In 1987, six million households spent $46 million on their herb gardens. And, for those who don't grow their own, fresh herbs are now available year-round in the major supermarkets across the land. In 1989, pricey herb-flavored vinegars and oils were the best-selling culinary items in gift shops.

Herb groups and herb businesses are organizing on the local, state, and national levels at a fast clip, often merging with university and state Cooperative Extension personnel and offering conferences, seminars, and newsletters to the public. Major cosmetic industries are flooding the marketplace with fragrance products that simulate traditional potpourri or that promise the virtues bestowed by herbs. Fragrances to scent the home and simmering potpourri products are big business today.

Five years ago, I had never heard of the word "aromatherapy." Now, it is one of the fastest growing forms of self-help therapy in the country. The Victorian Age was seldom referred to in the early part of the 1980s. Today, the romantic and fragrant crafts of Victoriana have replaced "country" in the gift and decorative fields, and the language of herbs and flowers is becoming a popular part of gift-giving. Edible flowers are the new rage in every fancy restaurant and gourmet kitchen. Cellulose fiber was unheard of in 1985; it's now the latest fixative on the market (see the September chapter). In the early 1980s, we added cedar or sandalwood shavings to potpourri; now, garish, painted wood shavings of all kinds are used to add bulk and color to commercial potpourri.

The Pleasure of Herbs *is a compilation in month-by-month form of the information from the first 5 years of my newsletter,* Potpourri from Herbal Acres. Herbal Treasures *includes crafts, recipes, and information from the 6 years of the newsletter published after* The Pleasure of Herbs. *My newsletter continues to expand on the themes of both books.*

A funny thing happened to me on my way to the typewriter. As I began to write about herbs in order to share my enchantment with others — and my writing and publishing tasks skyrocketed into a full-time career — I had less and less time to actually do the enjoyable things I was writing about — less time to garden, to experiment, to create crafts and recipes, to blend fragrant potpourris and prod-

ucts. So, I started hiring those who were *doing it all to write articles for my newsletter. So much excellent material from the experts crossed my desk, that I had to increase the size of my newsletter from twelve pages to twenty, even as I decreased the type size to include a third more material. My subscription base tripled, as did my publishing workload, accordingly. Much of this book, therefore, has been written by experts, people who spend every day doing what they've written about. I could have done some research and come up with my own article on aromatherapy, for example, but instead, I give you the writings of experts in the field — people with different approaches and backgrounds — who are actually practicing the art in their daily lives or businesses. As a consequence, their articles are more enlightening and broadening than any an observer could pen. So it is with most of the major subjects of this book — they are contributions from those who know first-hand what they're writing about. I am deeply indebted to all who so generously shared their know-how and their expertise.*

Lastly, a mention of the wonderful appendix to the book. You can learn about each contributing author and his or her business offerings in the Author's Directory, an alphabetical listing. You can find out how to order the books, publications, products, and materials mentioned in the book in the Resource Directory.

I hope each of you finds as much inspiration and pleasure from Herbal Treasures *as I have had in preparing it for you.*

— PHYLLIS V. SHAUDYS
WASHINGTON CROSSING, PENNSYLVANIA
AUGUST 1990

Please note that the authors' addresses listed with their articles are not *complete addresses. Complete addresses and ordering information are given in the directories in the Appendix.*
We want to stress this so you will not waste postage, or be disappointed when incompletely addressed mail is returned to you!

JANUARY

JANUARY IS THE MONTH for taking a breather, for new beginnings, and for planning the year ahead. What better ways to relax and enjoy a little self-indulgence than by soaking in aromatic, healthful bath waters, creating one's own personal perfume, and developing fragrances for the home that not only dispel germs, but make it pleasant to be cooped up inside? What better time to dwell a little on the many benefits of herbs and essential oils for health and beauty?

Aromatherapy, herbal baths and cosmetics, and perfumery are all interrelated, so you will find aspects of each sprinkled throughout this chapter on personal and home fragrances. This is an extra-long chapter because so much of the information on essential oils is pertinent to the rest of the book, and also because January is the month most of us have a little spare time to read and ponder new experiences.

Many of us in the herb world were practicing some form of aromatherapy long before we ever heard of the word! "Aromatherapy is the use of pure essential oils, extracted from flowers, trees, herbs and spices, to heal both mind and body," according to the internationally recognized authority on the subject, Robert Tisserand from England. One of the fastest growing therapies in the world today, aromatherapy is rooted in herbal medicine, which dates back to prehistoric times. No wonder I found peace and tranquility 33 years ago from "playing" with fragrant herbs, oils, and potpourri! I never considered my toils work, but only spirit-lifting and relaxing relief from the stress of being housebound in the country with two preschoolers; my hobby was aromatic therapy!

Leading cosmetic firms as well as major universities worldwide are researching the beneficial aspects of fragrances to find measurable evidence that backs up the empirical folklore of age-old herbal medicine. According to an article by Gustav Carsch in

Smell is a potent wizard that transplants us across thousands of miles and all the years we have lived.
—HELEN KELLER

a trade journal, Soap/Cosmetics/Chemical Specialties, Avon is a leader in the field of aromatherapy in the United States. And, Judith Jackson's Bath and Body Essences and Facial Treatments were in leading department stores only a year after her book Scentual Touch: A Personal Guide to Aromatherapy *was published in 1986. Just to add a little historical perspective to all of this, it was announced in major newspapers in February of 1989 that an Israeli archaeological team had found in a cave near the Dead Sea, a 2000-year-old jug of once-fragrant persimmon oil (known to the Greeks of that time as balsam oil), which*

was used to anoint the ancient kings of Judah as they ascended the throne.

Scent is certainly a subjective thing — all in the nose of the beholder! In the following articles on bathing with herbs, you will notice that some authors consider lavender to be stimulating and invigorating, while others say it is relaxing and soothing. But there's an explanation for these varied responses. Not only lavender, but also rose geranium, have been documented as having both relaxing and stimulating properties.

When using pure, undiluted essential oils, do not use your

own tuition as to the effects of them on your psyche; please follow the advice of the experts as you experiment for yourself! I urge you to read at least one of the major books on aromatherapy (see Appendix) before you dabble with pure essential oils at home. Have a lovely time pampering yourself and your family. And while you're savoring the benefits of the bottled essences of summer, peek ahead through the next two chapters for dream material as you relax: new and unusual garden designs and herb plants to try this year!

Aromatherapy

AN INTRODUCTION TO AROMATHERAPY

by Colleen K. Dodt

I first met COLLEEN DODT in 1987 at an herb conference sponsored by the Herb Associates of Michigan at Michigan State University, where I was concentrating on becoming better acquainted with a large number of my newsletter subscribers who were in attendance. She talked to me about her radio program on herbs, as well as about a European form of therapy with oils that she was very much involved with. Being quite conservative regarding the healing herbs, I did not pursue the subject further with her. But

Aromatherapy enhances the quality of life through the use of pure, high-quality essential oils from herbs, flowers, roots, barks, and resins. It is hardly a new therapy: Ancient Egyptians used aromatic oils for religious and medicinal purposes; and for centuries, nosegays and tussie mussies were carried through the unsanitary streets of Europe to help mask the stench. As a matter of fact, the essential oils in those flowers actually *were* antibacterial and antiseptic, and thus helped prevent the spread of certain germs and viruses. Rosemary and lavender were burned in French hospital wards to fumigate them — thus the origin of the word *parfume,* which translates as "through smoke." And, of course, flowers continue to be traditional gifts to hospital patients. In spite of its long history of use in Europe, however, aromatherapy is a relatively new phenomenon in America, but it is rapidly becoming an important part of the fragrance and cosmetic industry here (though not all commercial products contain quality essential oils).

There are several forms of aromatherapy. Cosmeticians and

beauticians use *aesthetic aromatherapy* for skin care and as a form of relaxation; *holistic aromatherapy* uses essential oils for body care through massage and inhalation; doctors (in France, primarily) use *medicinal aromatherapy*, in which essential oils in capsule form are prescribed for oral treatment of patients; and *psycho-aromatherapy* is used in the psychiatric field to stimulate patients through scents as an aid toward getting in touch with feelings. This last therapy is based on the fact that we all have an odor memory stored deep in our brains. The olfactory nerve is directly linked to the brain's limbic system, where memory and emotions are stored. We can respond to the sense of smell much more quickly than to something we see, hear, or feel — and smell is the only sense we cannot block out.

Pure essential oils may be used by the beginner in the form of massage oils, bath oils, or inhalations. This simple, self-help therapy will leave you uplifted, relaxed, stimulated, or beguiled, depending on the oil used. It is important *always* to use only a small amount of essential oil in a carrier base such as vegetable oil when using it for massage; for an aromatic bath, use only 4 or 5 drops of essential oil in the bathwater. Essential oils may also be used as room fresheners, either for their antiseptic value or simply to create a subtle mood or atmosphere. A few drops in a bowl of hot water is sufficient, or one can use a burner or an aromatic diffuser designed for the purpose.

In the eighth century, Wang Wei said, "Look in the perfumes of flowers and of nature for peace of mind and joy of life." Today we say, "Take time to smell the roses," when we want a friend to release tensions, and relax and enjoy life. In the theory behind aromatherapy, certain essential oils have sedative effects. Orange blossoms and herbs such as chamomile, marjoram, and lavender, for instance, cause the brain to release a sedative neurochemical that tends to relax us. The oil of lavender, especially, has been known for centuries to be a calming essence. On the other hand, some essences are considered to be stimulating. Rosemary, for example, affects a different part of the brain, where noradrenalin is released. Since this has the effect of waking us up, rosemary is an excellent essence to use in the morning bath. Other fragrances tend to stimulate the memory and mental capacity. Basil, lemon, peppermint, and rosemary aid in reducing mental fatigue and concentration problems. Essential oils of clary sage *(Salvia sclarea)*, jasmine, patchouli, and ylang-ylang *(Cananga odorata)* — an extremely sweet blossom from South Pacific islands — are aphrodisiacs. They stimulate the pituitary gland, which secretes endorphins, known for their tendency to kill pain and induce euphoria as well as sexual feelings.

In order to initiate our customers to the pleasures and benefits of using pure essential oils at home, we have developed an "Introductory Essential Oil Ensemble" for beginners, which includes six bottles of pure, undiluted essential oils, eyedroppers, an information sheet on how to use them, and Sweet Almond Oil to use as a

two years later, when aromatherapy articles were appearing in all the other herb periodicals, I wrote to Colleen and begged her to become a part of my networking family and contribute information about her favorite subject to my newsletter. To make up for my earlier lack of recognition and respect for her expertise, I have used her writings as the lead article on aromatherapy in this book. Colleen has been a one-woman pioneer in importing knowledge to the American public about aromatherapy — and she has been very gracious to those of us who turned deaf ears to her originally!

base for bath or massage oil. You can make your own collection of the oils we have selected for this ensemble: *Eucalyptus,* for use as a decongestant, antibacterial agent, massage oil to relieve muscular aches, and inhalant, as well as an aid to help keep your home "bug-free" (both creepy-crawly bugs and flu bugs); *rose geranium,* for use as an antiseptic, antidepressant, and hair rinse, and for skin care, female problems, and fragrance; *lavender,* for relaxed bathing and for its antiseptic, analgesic, sedative, and antibiotic properties; *rosemary,* for mental clarity, and for use in the morning bath and as a hair conditioner; *sweet orange,* to eliminate the winter blahs, to lighten one's spirits (only 2 to 4 drops are needed in the bath), and as an antidepressant, antispasmodic, and calming agent; and *ylang-ylang,* known as the flower of flowers, for use as an aphrodisiac and sedative, and for insomnia and sexual difficulties resulting from stress or anxiety. Ylang-ylang is often blended with other oils, like lavender and rose, because its sweetness can be overwhelming on its own. We feel that these six essential oils will inspire the newcomer to this field to want to delve further into the realm of aromatherapy.

It is very important that you read *at least* one of the recommended manuals on aromatherapy before you experiment at home with the pure essential oils.   Because of potential hazards, it is vital that consumers understand the individual oils and their properties before using them.

The world of aromatherapy is truly wondrous for those who wish to investigate further. Become an educated consumer — much joy awaits the willing explorer who remembers to stop and smell the roses. I have experienced remarkable changes in every aspect of my life since working with aromatherapy. I have come to look upon essential oils as my friends and allies, for they contain the precious essence of many sunny days, steady growth, faraway places, healing plants, spiritual awareness, and mind attunement.

*Essential oils are for **external use only**, and they must be kept out of the reach of children! Only minute amounts are needed, because the oils are **highly concentrated. Undiluted, or "neat," pure essential oil must not be used directly on the skin,** as it may cause undesirable reactions if not used along with a carrier base, such as almond oil.*

Colleen K. Dodt, Herbal Endeavors, Rochester Hills, MI 48063

Aromatherapy: Using the Scents of Herbs and Flowers

by Clementina Carlin

Clementina Carlin has been studying, researching, and experimenting with herbs and essential oils for several years. She has owned and operated a health and beauty spa, has assisted a chiropractor/nutritionist, and has taught herb classes and lectured to professional

Human beings have always turned to nature for beauty and serenity, for in the flowers, trees, and herbs we find the loving hand of God. This is, in a sense, the essence of aromatherapy — to heal, comfort, and uplift the heart, mind, and body with the scents of herbs and flowers. What could be more simple or more beautiful? A variety of essential oils is like a garden of scents from which we can pick when we need beauty and refreshment in our lives, just as we pick a single rose or a summer's bouquet.

Usually extracted by distillation, the essential oil is called the "soul," or life force, of the plant. In spite of its name, an essential oil is not oily, like olive oil; rather, it is volatile, meaning that it evaporates easily. Used in bath or massage, essential oils are absorbed through the skin and into the body. In facial blends, essential oils penetrate deep into cell layers to stimulate cellular renewal and rejuvenate the skin. When inhaled, the essences pass through the lungs into the bloodstream to cause physiological changes; they also affect the limbic area of the brain, which is related to emotions and memories. Subtle psychological benefits occur, such as the feelings of safety and contentment and the warm memories of childhood that may be called back through the scent of vanilla.

health groups about aromatherapy. My daughters and I learned a great deal about ourselves and our health from Clementina's wholistic questionnaire and consultations through the mail. The oils that she custom blended for us were based on our needs and preferences, and were simply lovely and so very useful.

What is the best way to add a little aromatherapy to your life? Begin simply by choosing the scents that you like best, and by picking those that meet the needs of your lifestyle. (See the Guide for Using Essential Oils for Health and Beauty, pages 6-7.) For example, if you have trouble falling asleep, you may want to put a few drops of lavender oil on your pillow, or take a soothing lavender bath before bed. Even though lavender oil may not be your favorite scent, you are using it

RELAXING	Lavender, clary sage, chamomile, petitgrain, neroli, ylang-ylang, tangerine, sandalwood, rose
ENERGIZING	Rosemary, rosewood, patchouli, peppermint, rose geranium, juniper, lemon, lime, cypress
UPLIFTING	Bergamot, geranium, orange, patchouli, jasmine, rosemary
ANTISEPTIC	Tea tree, eucalyptus, peppermint, lavender
MUSCLE ACHES	Eucalyptus, lavender, rosemary

in this case for its therapeutic properties. Here are a few ways to begin using essential plant oils for health and beauty:

Aromatic baths. Sprinkle 4 to 5 drops of essential oil into a tub full of water just before getting in. Disperse oil droplets well. A thin veil of essential oil will envelope you in rejuvenating scent. Or, for an aromatic shower soap, use a few drops of oil in unscented liquid castile soap, often available at health stores. (For more suggestions on the use of essential oils in bathing, see pages 12-17.)

Insect repellent oil. For topical use, blend 12 drops of eucalyptus, 6 drops of peppermint, and 6 drops of tea tree oil in 2 fluid ounces of sweet almond oil. Add vitamin E as a preservative.

Facial oil. As a facial moisturizer that will nourish and beautify the skin, add 5 drops of lavender oil, 5 drops of rose geranium oil, 2 drops of patchouli or sandalwood oil, and 3 drops of lemon, chamomile, or frankincense oil to a base of 2 fluid ounces of sweet almond, apricot, or jojoba oil. Include a few drops of natural vitamin E or wheat germ oil to keep the mixture fresh.

Hair rinse. For *dark hair*, mix 3 drops of rosemary oil and 1 drop of geranium oil in 1 quart of water. For *light hair*, mix 2 drops of chamomile oil and 1 drop of lemon oil in 1 quart of water. For conditioning and shine, rinse through hair after shampooing.

Perfume. To design your own perfume, add 20 drops of

PRECAUTIONS

Always use pure plant essence oils, and never fragrance or potpourri oils for aromatherapy purposes. Because essential oils are very concentrated, some precautions are important to take before using them on the skin.

- ❤ *Never use pennyroyal, sage, aniseed, clove, thuja, hyssop, wintergreen, cinnamon bark, bitter almond*
- ❤ *If you are pregnant, avoid basil, clary sage, hyssop, juniper, marjoram, myrrh, sage, fennel, peppermint, rose, rosemary*
- ❤ *If you have high blood pressure, avoid rosemary oil*
- ❤ *When sunbathing, avoid bergamot and citrus oils*

Guide for Using Essential Oils for Health and Beauty

OIL	CHARACTERISTICS	USES
ALLSPICE	Spicy scent	Potpourri, simmer
ANISE	Licorice scent	Potpourri
BASIL	Refreshing; relieves mental fatigue and nervousness	Inhalation
BERGAMOT	Citrusy floral scent; uplifting for anxiety and depression; regulates appetite; effective against acne, shingles, cold sores, chicken pox, boils; effective as an insect repellent; blends well with lavender and rose geranium	Potpourri, perfume, facial compress, floral water, facial oil, massage oil, bath
CHAMOMILE	Calming; effective against depression, insomnia, dry, sensitive skin, eczema, menstrual pain (when used as an abdominal massage)	Floral water, bath, facial oil, compress or mask
CINNAMON	Spicy scent	Potpourri, simmer to freshen air
CLARY SAGE	Warming and relaxing; provides a feeling of well-being; powerful relaxant in stress-related illness; effective against menstrual cramps (when used as an abdominal massage); must not be taken with alcohol	Bath, compress, massage oil
CLOVE	Spicy scent; toothache	Potpourri; simmer
CYPRESS	Woody, pine scent; relaxing and refreshing; relieves nervous tension; acts as a flea repellent	Bath, massage, inhalation
EUCALYPTUS	Disinfects the air; aids nasal congestion caused by colds or sinus problems; effective as an insect repellent	Inhalation, bath, facial mask
FRANKIN-CENSE	Rich scent of incense; soothing and comforting against fears and anxieties; slows down the appearance of wrinkles	Inhalation, bath, massage oil, facial oil
JASMINE	Rich floral scent; strong antidepressant; imparts a feeling of confidence	Perfume, massage oil, bath, potpourri
JUNIPER	Light, stimulating oil; said to relieve fear and apathy; useful as a disinfectant; clears the mind when emotionally drained	Bath, inhalation, massage oil, air freshener
LAVENDER	Cooling, relaxing scent; restorative when mentally or physically exhausted; effective against insomnia, jet lag, sunburn, athlete's foot, neck tension, headache, blemishes	Potpourri, bath, facial oil, massage oil, floral water, compress, perfume, facial steam, inhalation
LEMON	Fresh citrus scent; relieves mental pressure	Bath, inhalation
LEMONGRASS	Sweet, grassy, lemony scent; uplifting	Bath, perfume, potpourri, air freshener
LIME	More refreshing than lemon; used in men's after shave	Massage oil, bath, perfume
ORANGE	Encourages cheerfulness; sunny fragrance	Perfume, massage oil, bath, potpourri, air freshener, simmer
PATCHOULI	Stimulating, musky scent; rejuvenating to the skin; potpourri fixative; moth repellent; deodorant	Bath, facial oils, massage oil, potpourri, perfume

Using Essential Oils (continued)

OIL	CHARACTERISTICS	USES
PALMAROSA	Fresh, rose-like scent; re-establishes the balance of the skin; combats wrinkles	Facial steam, facial mask, facial oil, facial compress, bath, perfume
PEPPERMINT	Cooling, refreshing scent; foot bath; effective against sunburn, motion sickness, indigestion (1 drop in water), headaches, menstrual cramps	Bath, inhalation, sip in water
PINE	Fresh, clean scent; comforting for emotional stress, respiratory system, fatigue	Bath, inhalation
ROSE	Relaxing, antidepressant; balances the female reproductive system; tonic effect on dry, sensitive, or aging skin	Baths, facial oil, massage oil, perfume
ROSE GERANIUM	Fresh, green, rose-like scent; said to balance the emotions; relaxing and refreshing; eases tension, anxiety, depression; rejuvenates the skin; soothes oily or sensitive skin	Bath, floral water, facial compress, facial oil, massage oil, perfume
ROSEWOOD	Rosy spice scent; enlivening; soothes sensitive skin; combats blemishes, scars, wrinkles; cellular stimulant	Bath, facial oil, massage oil, floral water, facial mask, perfume
ROSEMARY	Stimulating, pine-like scent; eases physical and mental fatigue, sadness, poor memory, headaches; promotes hair growth and luster; tightens pores	Bath, facial oil, floral water, massage
SPEARMINT	Cooling, refreshing scent; foot bath; effective against sunburn, motion sickness, indigestion (1 drop in water), headaches, menstrual cramps; repels black ants	Bath, inhalation, sip in water
SANDALWOOD	Sweet, woody scent; quieting, meditative effect; used to heal dehydrated or oily skin	Bath, facial compress, facial oil, floral water, inhalation, perfume
TANGERINE	Soothing citrus scent; wonderful for children	Massage oil, bath, perfume, potpourri, air freshener
YLANG-YLANG	Sweet exotic scent; said to soothe anger ; eases oily skin	Bath, perfume, massage oil, potpourri

essential oils to ¼ ounces jojoba oil.

Air fresheners/inhalations. Place a few drops of essential oil in a pan of boiling water or on a light bulb, or sprinkle a few drops on a facial tissue and breathe the scent.

❤ For mental fatigue (especially effective to use in your work environment): Basil, peppermint, rosemary, spearmint
❤ To lift tired spirits: Bergamot, orange, peppermint, patchouli, jasmine, rosewood, lemongrass, juniper, rose, rose geranium
❤ For relaxation: Chamomile, clary sage, frankincense, lavender, pine, rose, sandalwood, tangerine, ylang-ylang, myrrh, neroli, petitgrain

Massage oil. Add 15 to 30 drops of essential oil to a base of 2 fluid ounces of almond oil; add a few drops of wheat germ oil to preserve freshness.

CLEMENTINA CARLIN, THE GINGER TREE, SCHENECTADY, NY 12301

LEILA RAE SOMMERFELD has been a cosmetologist for over 25 years, has studied aromatherapy in both Europe and America, and has owned a skin and hair salon for 12 years, long before it became fashionable here! Although she has retired from this line of work (she now concentrates on interior designing and on growing herbs and flowers for the floral designs and wreaths she sells), the material offered here is excerpted from a book on cosmetic aromatherapy she hopes to complete someday.

♥ *For hand care, use benzoin, patchouli, or rose essence.*
♥ *For a foot bath, add only 1 or 2 drops of lavender and rosemary oils to 5 pints of water.*

Essential oils should be stored properly. Keep tightly sealed in amber bottles, and avoid exposure to excessive heat and sunlight. Before attempting the use of folk or cosmetic treatments, it is advisable to consult your physician or medical practitioner.

LEILA RAE SOMMERFELD, LEILA RAE ENTERPRISES, BEND, OR 97701

ONE ASPECT OF COSMETIC AROMATHERAPY

by Leila Rae Sommerfeld

WHIP UP A FACIAL MASK AT HOME

Facial masks consist of a base to which essential oils are added according to the characteristics of the individual's skin. Commonly used base ingredients include yogurt for cleansing and toning; honey for moisturizing; wheat germ oil for dry, mature skin; clay powder to draw out impurities; and brewers' yeast as an extractive. *Use only 2 drops of essential oils per mask.* The oils are very concentrated and will burn the skin if not properly used.

✿ Basic Homemade Facial Mask ✿

Suitable for all skin types, this soothing mask leaves the face feeling refreshed. The chamomile oil has a calming effect. You may substitute other essential oils for other effects: lavender, lemon, and rosemary are stimulating; sandalwood and peppermint purify and destroy bacteria; almond, comfrey root, and jasmine calm and soothe.

½ cup plain yogurt   *½ teaspoon honey*
½ teaspoon fuller's earth (available   *2 drops chamomile oil*
* at drugstores)*

Blend all ingredients well. Apply to face and neck. Leave on skin for 10 minutes or longer. Rinse, and moisturize the skin.

✿ Herbal Jelly Mask ✿

To use this mask, apply to face and neck, and leave on for 10 minutes or longer. Rinse, and moisturize the skin. This recipe makes about ten applications and will keep, in the refrigerator, for about one week.

3 ounces glycerine   *3 ounces herbal tea*
½ ounce dry pectin

Stir glycerine while slowly adding the dry pectin. Blend well. Add the herbal tea, and blend thoroughly. (You may use an electric mixer.) Refrigerate overnight to thicken.

✿ Herbal Tea Mask ✿

Use 1 cup herbal tea (chamomile to soothe, calm, and soften the skin; peppermint to cool and soothe, and as an antiseptic). Soak large squares of cotton in the tea and apply this compress to face and neck areas. Be sure to cover the eyelids with tea-soaked pads. Leave in place 10 minutes or longer. Remove the compress, rinse with clear water, and moisturize the skin.

MAKE A GARDEN OF YOUR HOME WITH ESSENTIAL OILS

by Clementina Carlin

Here are a few ideas for including fragrance in your life using the essences of herbs and flowers:

❤ *To disinfect and freshen the air of a sickroom,* place a cotton ball dipped in a few drops of eucalyptus, clove, or lavender oil on a small dish.

❤ *To freshen the air in your kitchen and give it a country scent,* add a drop of cinnamon leaf oil or allspice oil to a pan of boiling water. To remove grease or fish odors, use a drop of lemon oil.

❤ *For a scented breeze on humid, summer days,* dab a drop of lavender oil or ylang-ylang oil on a fan or air-conditioner. To freshen and humidify the house in winter, use sunny oils like bergamot or sweet orange on radiators or in simmer pots.

❤ *To set the mood for a party,* add a few drops of fragrant oil to the melting wax around the wick of unscented candles; use pine at Christmas, sandalwood for evening, rose geranium for luncheons, tangerine for a children's party.

❤ *To encourage growth, condition, and body in your hair,* rub a few drops of rosemary oil into hair and scalp before washing and add a drop to your shampoo; rosemary oil dabbed on your hair brush will prevent static electricity, and used as a hairdressing will relax a too-curly permanent.

❤ *For a fixative in potpourri or perfume blends,* use patchouli oil or sandalwood oil.

❤ *For a good base oil for homemade perfumes,* use jojoba oil. It is a wax that does not turn rancid over time as most base oils do. It is also an excellent emollient for both dry and oily skin, and an effective conditioner for hair and scalp. Use jojoba on a wilted perm to bring back the bounce.

❤ *For an afterbath splash or a body rub for tired muscles,* add a few drops of lavender and rosemary oil to a pint of witch hazel.

❤ *For weary or motion-sick travelers,* keep a few cotton balls saturated with peppermint oil in a plastic bag. Remove a cotton ball from the bag for a few minutes to refresh the air in your vehicle on a long trip.

❤ *To get the natural scent of an essential oil,* dip a small piece of paper into the oil, and sniff. Essential oils smell much stronger in the bottle.

❤ *To scent your laundry,* sprinkle a few drops of essential oil on a washcloth, and toss it into the machine with the washload.

❤ *To repel mice and rats,* use peppermint oil. *To repel black ants,* use spearmint oil.

❤ *To relieve mental fatigue at the office,* sprinkle rosemary, peppermint, or basil oil on a tissue and breathe the scent. Try this also on long trips and when taking exams.

CLEMENTINA CARLIN, THE GINGER TREE, SCHENECTADY, NY 12301

❧ IN CASE YOU WERE WONDERING..... ❧

While working on these pages, I became curious about some of the oils being discussed. My research unearthed the following information:

❤ **Bergamot oil** is from the peel of *Citrus aurantium* sub. sp. *bergamia,* a citrus fruit grown in Italy and Sicily (and *not* from the bergamot we grow in our gardens). As with *all* citrus oils, it should *not be used undiluted* on the skin, especially when exposure to strong sunlight or ultraviolet light is a possibility.

❤ **Cinnamon leaf oil** is from the leaves (rather than the bark) of Ceylon's cinnamon tree, *Cinnamomum zeylanicum.*

❤ **Cypress oil** is a fresh, woodsy

essence from the leaves of the Mediterranean cypress tree, *Cupressus sempervirens,* and is excellent for a relaxing bath.

❤ *Geranium oil* is indeed from the rose-scented geranium, *Pelargonium graveolens,* that we grow. This plant originated on the tropical island of Reunion in the Indian Ocean.

❤ In Italy, *juniper oil* is extracted from the berry of the evergreen juniper tree, *Juniperus communis;* it makes an exceptionally invigorating bath essence.

❤ *Neroli oil* is the sweet citrus extract from the orange blossoms of the *Citrus aurantium* tree. *Orange oil* is usually from the pressed *peel* of oranges from *Citrus sinensis* trees. **(Bitter orange oil,** however, is from the *peel* of oranges from *Citrus aurantium* trees.) *Petitgrain oil* is from the leaves of the *Citrus aurantium* tree.

❤ *Rosewood oil,* from a tree *Aniba rosaeodora,* which grows along the Amazon River, has a unique, woodsy aroma with tones of rose and spice. This has a wonderfully enlivening effect when used as a bath oil.

❤ *Tea tree oil,* from the *Melaleuca alternifolia* tree, is a powerful germicide with a scent similar to eucalyptus. It is known in Australia as "the medicine chest in a bottle," because of its usefulness in liniments, insect repellents, and decongestant aids.

❤ *Ylang-ylang,* meaning flower of flowers, is an oil with an exotic fragrance similar to the tuberose and the gardenia. It comes from a beautiful yellow flower *(Cananga odorata)* that grows in the Philippines. This captivating essence is known for its aphrodisiac and antidepressant properties.

JEN AND MIKE MESCHER offer botanicals, oils, potpourris, and bath products through their catalog, as well as very helpful Information Sheets regarding the use of their products. This material is excerpted from their instructions on using essential oils and fragrances.

SOME PRACTICAL HOUSEHOLD USES OF ESSENTIAL OILS

by Jen and Mike Mescher

❤ *To bring fragrance to dresser drawers, furniture cushions, closed luggage, and closets,* scent cotton balls with a few drops of essential oil. (Make sure the product you use is really cotton, and not polyester, which will not hold the scent of the oils.)

❤ *To make a natural insect repellent that is safe to apply to your skin,* combine ⅛ ounces each of citronella, patchouli, and vetiver oils with 3 ounces of sweet almond oil.

❤ *To dispel musty odors in wooden cabinets or closed rooms,* place a few drops of the oils of clove, cinnamon, nutmeg, or allspice on cotton balls left open to the air.

❤ *To use pennyroyal oil as a flea repellent,* do not apply it directly to the animal's fur. Instead, use a few drops in the pet's bathwater or put a few drops on a bandanna or rope collar around the animal's neck for a constantly effective and safe flea retardant. *For a repellent effective against a variety of insects,* mix 10 drops pennyroyal, 10 drops eucalyptus, 30 drops citronella, and 10 drops cedarwood oil with 4 ounces sweet almond oil.

❤ *For a flea repellent for carpets,* combine 3 drops pennyroyal, 3 drops eucalyptus, 9 drops citronella, and 3 drops cedarwood oil

with 1 pound of baking soda. Sprinkle the mixture on the carpet, let it stand one hour, and then vacuum it up.
- ❤ *To keep silverfish or bookworms away,* place patchouli oil near old books.
- ❤ *To make a refill for china or porcelain pomanders,* combine 40 drops of oil with 3 tablespoons of all-clay kitty litter.
- ❤ *To repel moths and scent your linens,* store them with cotton balls scented with oil of lavender, patchouli, sandalwood, or cedar.
- ❤ *To humidify and freshen the house,* add spicy oils to a kettle or simmering water
- ❤ *For a masculine scent in closets or drawers,* mix musk, sandalwood, and cinnamon oils on cotton balls.

Aromatic oils are frequently highly concentrated and sometimes contain ingredients that will react harmfully with other substances. They should not be used on finished wood, plastic, inks, or dyed materials.

FROM "THIRTY-FOUR USES OF ESSENTIAL OILS AND FRAGRANCES" JEN MESCHER, NATURE'S FINEST, BURKE, VA 22015

FRAGRANT FUMIGANTS

by Grace M. Wakefield

The sudden popularity of simmering potpourri is reminiscent of the great hoola-hoop fad. Will it last? Many of the simmering potpourris on the market are simply wood chips made fragrant with synthetic oils tossed about with some petals and other botanic specimens chosen in a seemingly haphazard fashion. Did you know that you can create your own simmering potpourris that are both fragrant and healthful?

In his book *The Practice of Aromatherapy* (Destiny Books, Inner Traditions International Ltd., 1982), Dr. Jean Valnet writes extensively and with supporting scientific evidence of the antibacterial and even antiviral properties of certain herbs and spices. Dr. Valnet concludes that we can kill household germs associated with colds and flu just by simmering in water, singly or in various combinations, the following essential oils and botanicals: cloves, cinnamon, sage, cajeput, eucalyptus, juniper berries, lemon, peppermint, rosemary, pine needles, savory, lavender, and thyme. Dr. Valnet also suggests that essential oils may be used in fine aerosol sprays in sick rooms. He warns, however, that some people are allergic to certain essential oils, thus making their use inappropriate. Dr. Valnet's own special system (which he has used daily for 15 years) is to place several drops of the natural essences of thyme, lavender, pine, and eucalyptus in a crucible over a small heating lamp.

For small craft businesses, this additional use for herbs, spices, and essential oils could open up new marketing ideas. Labels that state that the fragrance of a certain simmering potpourri is not only pleasant, but healthful, should increase customer interest and

GRACE WAKEFIELD has been offering herb and floral craft ideas and related ingredients through her catalog for many years, and you will find several of her delightful projects throughout this book. This article, however, is excerpted from her marvelous newsletter, Herbal Crafts Quarterly. *I include it here for its enlightening tips on aromatherapy.*

MULLING AWAY MICROBES!

From a true case history of a family smitten on the day after Christmas with a fearsome 48-hour virus: Apple cider simmered with cloves, allspice, cinnamon, and lemon peel was the only thing that calmed the fevers, soothed, and brought relief. This simmer is easily done in a crockpot.

GRACE M. WAKEFIELD, TOM THUMB
WORKSHOPS, MAPPSVILLE, VA 23407

purchases. Before venturing into this field, I recommend a thorough study of the subject, using well-documented sources, especially concerning potentially allergy-producing materials.

❦ Simmering Potpourri ❦

Use this simmer for a headache or stuffy feeling — it will make your head clear almost instantly!

½ cup dried peppermint leaves
½ cup cinnamon bark pieces

Mix ingredients together. Place 2 tablespoons in a saucepan of water.

FROM *CRAFTING WITH FRAGRANCE
MAKES SCENTS*
DONNA MADORA MITCHELL, LAVENDER
LANE, CITRUS HEIGHTS,
CA 95621-7265

Bathing With Herbs

EASY-TO-MAKE HERBAL SOAPS

by Linda Fry Kenzle

LINDA FRY KENZLE has been growing herbs for over 20 years, has had an herb business, and is now concentrating on writing about her crafts and experiences. Several of her projects are included throughout these pages. Send her a SASE for details about her current publications.

Making herbal soap is easier than you may think! Rather than going through the process of making soap from lye, you can use store-bought soaps and powders for your base. Aromatic herbs from your garden can be incorporated into the soap base for luscious scents. The following herbal soap recipes call for essential oils to both intensify the scent and make it longer lasting. (Essential oils are distillations of plant material; tinctures are essential oils cut with a high-grade alcohol to a ratio of 1 part oil to 10 parts alcohol. So-called "fragrance" oils are also greatly diluted.)

Chamomile/Sage Facial Scrub. This facial scrub will remove dead skin cells and stimulate circulation. You may store the mixture in a pretty jar, or you may want to make up the little scrub bags in advance and keep them in a closed container. Grate three bars of Dove soap into a bowl. Add 1½ cups of dried chamomile flowers (which have an apple-pineapple scent and are known to relax and soften the skin), ½ cup dried sage leaves (which are a natural cleanser), and 1 cup of oatmeal flakes. Toss all ingredients together until very well blended. To use, place 1 tablespoon of the mixture in the center of a 4-inch square of doubled cheesecloth. Bring the corners up, twist, and tie off with a string. Wet both the cheesecloth bag and your face. Using a circular motion, gently scrub your face with the bag. Rinse thoroughly.

German chamomile (*Matricaria chamomilla*)

Lavender Soap Balls. Lavender flowers are antiseptic and relaxing. Victorian women loved the lingering scent; it's a classic that will never go out of style. Make a "tea" by pouring ⅓ cup of boiling water over 1 tablespoon of dried lavender buds. Steep for 15 minutes. Grate two large bars of castile soap (approximately 3¼ cups). Re-heat the lavender tea, and add 4 drops of lavender oil. Pour this mixture over the grated soap. Knead the soap mixture together, and form it into balls. Place the soap balls on a piece of waxed paper and allow to air-dry for 2 to 5 days. If soap balls have a gritty texture, run them under the tap for a moment, and smooth them with your hands. Let them dry again. Store them unwrapped.

Lemon Verbena Soap Bars. With its clean lemon fragrance, this soap will be refreshing to the skin. For molds, use the top and bottom of a plastic travel case for soap. Spread a thin layer of oil inside the molds so the finished soap can be easily removed. Place 1½ tablespoons of dried, crushed lemon verbena leaves in a doubled, 3½-inch square of cheesecloth. Bring the corners of the cheesecloth together, and wrap with string to form a little bag. Place the bag in ⅓ cup water in a small saucepan, and bring the water to a boil. Turn the heat down, and let it simmer gently for 4 to 5 minutes. This will give you a very subtle, lemon-scented soap. If you desire a stronger scent, add up to 8 drops of lemon fragrance oil. Remove the herb bag. Grate 1⅓ cups of Ivory soap into the decoction, and stir until well-blended. Add 3 drops of lemon oil and 2 drops lime oil. Pour half of the soap mixture into each section of the plastic soap case. Let dry until firm. Pop out each soap bar and age for one week. If you would like to make fancy soap, check the candy-making section of your local variety store for molds in the shapes of seashells, hearts, teddy bears, and so on.

Herbal Foam Bath. This formula is for those who love a bubble bath, but don't want the drying results. Add 4 full droppers of fragrance oil to a bottle of Vaseline Intensive Care Moisturizing Foam Bath. Shake well before use. If you have oily skin, you can add massage oil to any very gentle, hand dishwashing soap. Either formula will give you a tub full of bubbles in which to languish away your worries.

HERBAL BATHS
by Jen Mescher

Luxurious herbal baths have been enjoyed since the time of Cleopatra. They can be relaxing, stimulating, soothing, moisturizing, or simply fragrant — all depending on the herbs or oils used. In addition to the suggested herbs on the lists to follow, you may want to add borax or baking soda, oatmeal, cornmeal, or sweet almond oil for their soothing, softening, or moisturizing properties. Never add loose herbs directly to the bathwater. They will stick to

SOAP-MAKING SUPPLIES
Lorann Oils, Inc. (see Appendix for address) issues a "Food, Apothecary, and Home Crafting" catalog, which features candy-making molds and several other items of interest to the fragrance crafter, such as powdered food coloring for candle- and soap-making, flavoring oils of every possible taste, cocoa butter for skin-care products, turkey red oil, gum arabic powder, beeswax, heliotropin crystals, lanolin, paraffin wax, styrax gum, and bath and massage oils, herbs, and potpourri. Lorann Oils specializes in wholesale distribution of these items, but they do have a retail catalog for home-crafters. They are located in Lansing, Michigan, but do not have a show room or sales department there.

FROM *THE JOY OF HERBS* (THIRD COAST PRESS, 1988) LINDA FRY KENZLE, FOX RIVER GROVE, IL 60021

JEN AND MIKE MESCHER, in their catalog, offer an impressive list of botanicals and oils, both retail and wholesale, plus many interesting items that are sometimes hard to find, such as turkey red oil, natural or flavored apple

pieces, balm-of-Gilead buds, cassia buds, cedar shavings, deer's-tongue, eucalyptus leaf, gum benzoin, citric acid powder, musk crystals, oakmoss, pinhead orrisroot, patchouli, star anise, styrax, uva-ursi leaves, vanilla beans, wood chips in colors, and white willow bark. I notice, too, that they carry many of the unusual fragrance oils that are so often requested, such as peach, raspberry, and neroli. They also carry several of the bath preparations mentioned above, simmer oils, pomander kits, potpourri, and several interesting information sheets. See Appendix for address.

I have seen bath bags made of soft terry cloth toweling and tied with braided rope-type yarn — especially appropriate for gift-giving. PVS

ALL-PURPOSE HERBAL BATH

Combine equal amounts of rosemary, peppermint, lavender, comfrey, lemon thyme, and rose. Prepare as an infusion, decoction, or bath bag.

---

your skin and the side of the tub, and may clog the drain.

THREE METHODS OF PREPARING HERBAL BATHS

- ♥ *Infusion:* Pour 1 quart of boiling water over ¼ cup herbs, and steep for 30 minutes. Strain the herbal water, and add it to your bathwater.
- ♥ *Decoction:* Boil 1 part herb mixture in 4 parts water for 30 minutes. Strain and add to the bath.
- ♥ *Bath Bag:* Place several tablespoons of herbs in a cloth bag, and hang the bag from the tub faucet while the water is running. The bag may also be rubbed on the skin for additional enjoyment. (For a suggestion on how to make bath bags, see pages 16-17.)

Fizzing Bath Salts. Combine ½ cup baking soda, ¼ cup citric acid, ¼ cup cornstarch, 100 drops (¾ teaspoon) fragrance oil(s), and 2 to 3 drops food coloring (optional). Mix well, so that the oil is thoroughly distributed through the dry mixture. Don't overdo the food coloring. Sprinkle 2 tablespoons of the salts over the water just before you get into the tub.

Bath Oil. There are two types of bath oils:
Dispersible bath oil mixes readily with bathwater. It can be made by mixing 3 parts of turkey red oil (treated castor oil) with 1 part essential oil. Use 1 teaspoon of the mixture per bath.
Floating bath oil floats on the top of the bath and coats your skin as you enter and leave the tub. Mix 3 parts of sweet almond, safflower, sunflower, or soy oil with 1 part essential oil. To get full beneficial results from the herbs, always use essential oils rather than fragrance oils, which are highly diluted.

Bath Bags. You can use either oatmeal or cornmeal in these bags, which provide a delightful way to enhance the bath. Oatmeal is softening and soothing to the skin; cornmeal cleans the skin and removes dead skin. Combine 1 part of either meal and 1 part dried herbs of your choice in a bath bag and use it as you bathe.

Bubble Bags. These are fun, and may be used in the shower instead of having to take the time for a soaking bath! Combine 2 parts oatmeal, 2 parts dried herbs, and 1 part grated soap, place in a cloth bag, and use as a washcloth.

Bubbly Bath. Bubble baths are great but, because they can be drying to the skin, limit yourself to one a week. Combine ¼ cup glycerine, 1 cup mild dishwashing liquid (such as Ivory), 1 teaspoon sugar, and 50 drops fragrance oil. Use 2 to 3 tablespoons per bath. The combination of glycerine and sugar helps hold the bubbles.

Bath Jewels. Combine 1 cup of Mescher's unscented and uncolored Bath Jewels (see Appendix for ordering information) with 3 drops of food color and 5 to 10 drops of essential oil. Mix well in a plastic bag until the color and oil are evenly distributed. Use 4 tablespoons per bath. These crystals, which have water-softening properties, are also available ready-to-use in pastel shades, in the following fragrances: April Flowers, Moonbeam, Nosegay, and Spring Bouquet.

HERBS AND OILS FOR THE BATH

Here are some of the herbs you may have in your garden for making your own bath preparations and some of the oils that may be best for your particular needs. The lists are not intended to be complete, but simply to inspire you to further study of this aspect of herbs.

❤ *Herbs for a relaxing bath:* Chamomile, comfrey, lavender, lemon verbena, linden, mugwort, sassafras, and thyme (vanilla is also beneficial)
❤ *Herbs for a stimulating bath*: Bay, elder, hops, jasmine, lemon balm, marjoram, patchouli, peppermint, rosemary, savory, yarrow
❤ *Herbs for a soothing bath:* Aloe vera, birch bark, calendula, catnip, comfrey, elder, hyssop, malva, mugwort, rose, sage, sassafras, tansy, vervain, yarrow, and borax, plus emollients (soothing, protective substances used externally) such as apricot oil, comfrey, glycerine, honey, lecithin, malva, and oatmeal

Because allergic reactions can occur with any herbal or scent ingredient, any bath preparation should be tested on a small area of skin *before* being used in the bath. This simple precaution will enable you to derive the most possible pleasure from your fragrant and healthful bathing experiences.

Enjoy the elegance of your personalized preparations!

FROM AN INFORMATION SHEET ON HERBAL BATHS
JEN AND MIKE MESCHER, NATURE'S FINEST, BURKE, VA 22015

Caraway *(Carum carvi)*

❤ *For dry skin:* Aloe vera, caraway, chamomile, comfrey, elder, orange petals, parsley, rose, yarrow, oatmeal, and almond, castor, olive, or peanut oil
❤ *For oily skin:* Lavender, lemongrass, tangerine peel, vinegar, witch hazel, and apricot, citronella, or soybean oil
❤ *For normal-to-dry skin:* Corn, cottonseed, sesame, or sunflower oil

HERBAL BATH RECIPES

❧ *Bath Salts* ❧

Fill several wide-mouth jars no more than half full with Epsom salts. Add to each a few drops of essential oil and a drop of an appropriate food coloring. Rose, lavender, lemon, hyacinth, and gardenia are good scents to use for bath salts. Stir until the color is well mixed, pressing the salts against the edge of the jar with the back of a spoon. Bath salts look nice packaged in the little apothecary jars designed for spices. I tie a matching ribbon around the neck of the jar with an instructional tag: "Use one teaspoonful sprinkled over the hot water in the bathtub. Hop in and relax!"

BARBARA RADCLIFFE ROGERS, HERBITAGE FARM, RICHMOND, NH 03470

❧ *Randa's Soothing Bath Brew* ❧

To relieve aching muscles and joints

2 cups rosemary (relieves stiff joints)
1 cup bay leaves (relieves aching)
1½ cups sage (helps joints and muscles)
1 cup lavender (for fragrance)
1 cup calendula (soothes; nice color)
1 cup patchouli (for fragrance)

Cover ½ cup mixed herbs with boiling water and steep for 20 minutes. Drain. Place liquid in bathwater and herbs in a bath bag. Rub body with herb bag after soaking in tub for 15 to 20 minutes.

RANDA BLACK, BUTTERPLUM BAGS,
EPHRAIM, UT 84627

❧ *Scented Bath Crystals* ❧

Coarse rock salt (available in supermarkets)
Food coloring (assorted colors to suggest chosen scent)
Essential oil

Place rock salt in a lidded container. For each cup of salt, add 2 or 3 drops of coloring. Mix with a spoon or shake well. Add 2 or 3 more drops of coloring at a time, and continue mixing until desired color is reached. To the colored crystals, add 20 to 25 drops of essential oils, mixing or shaking well until oils are thoroughly absorbed. Display salts in a pretty glass jar. *Keep jar tightly closed* or the oil will quickly evaporate. Use 1 or 2 heaping tablespoons for bathwater or hot tub.

FROM *CRAFTING WITH FRAGRANCE
MAKES SCENTS*
DONNA MADORA MITCHELL, LAVENDER
LANE, CITRUS HEIGHTS,
CA 95621-7265

BATH SCRUBBIE

by Janie Duttweiler

There are many different styles of herb bath bags on the market. I make two bath bags from one purchased washcloth. For a feminine look, I trim them with a double eyelet with beading through which I thread ribbon. Although a little more expense is involved, these bags are quite pretty. If you don't sew (or don't have time to sew), I sell them wholesale by the dozen in assorted colors (see Appendix for ordering information).

A

1 terry cloth washcloth
1 yard double eyelet lace with
*   beading*
1 yard of ¼-inch ribbon

1. Cut the washcloth in half (A). Pin the lace approximately 1 inch (depending on size of washcloth) from long, finished edge of each half.

2. Stitch the lace in place along both sides of beading (B).

3. Fold each piece in half, right sides together, and stitch sides and bottoms, using ¼-inch seam allowance (C). Turn each bag right side out.

4. Using a safety pin, run ribbon through beading. Tie a knot close to end of ribbon (D).

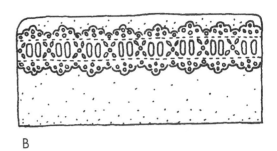

B

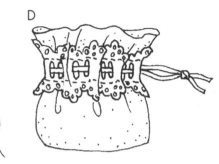

C   D

To use: Place a bar of scented soap or some bath herbs and/or soap flakes inside scrubbie, and pull ribbon tight to close. Use at the sink or in the tub or shower. Rinse out after each use. My favorite filling for the scrubbie is a mixture consisting of equal parts of bath herbs, oatmeal, and grated soap. (Because we have very hard water, I use a hard-water castile soap. Castile soap has a definite fragrance of its own, however, and not everyone likes it.)

JANIE DUTTWEILER, GEORGETOWN, TX 78626

AN HERBAL BASKET FOR THE BATH

by Christine Tarski

I have always kept wreaths of sweet Annie, ambrosia, or eucalyptus hanging in the bathroom. When the steam releases their wonderful herbal scents, I sometimes wish I could spend hours in the bath or shower! Rosebud pomanders are also wonderful hanging or piled in a bowl or basket in the bathroom.

You can also enjoy these herbal scents if you make this basket with herbs wired to the rim. You can use just one favorite herb or a combination. Great herbs to try are thyme, ambrosia, mint, pineapple sage, and all artemisias, including wormwood and sweet Annie. The number of bundles you need will be determined by the diameter of the basket and the length of the bundles. If you are using fresh herbs, tie the bundles very tightly, as they will shrink when they dry. (If you use rubber bands, you will have less trouble with the shrinking problem.) If you are using dry herbs, mist them and let them sit for about 30 minutes before using.

For adornment with everlasting flowers use globe amaranth, marjoram blossoms, Mexican sage blossoms, rosebuds, statice, baby's-breath, bee balm, or any of your favorites. Avoid flowers dried in silica if the basket is to be used in a humid room, such as a bath or kitchen.

CHRISTINE TARSKI sells round and heart-shaped sweet Annie and eucalyptus wreaths and a variety of pomanders through her catalog. See Appendix for address.

Pineapple sage *(Salvia elegans)*

Woven basket

Felt in a coordinating color with basket (optional)

Glue (either Elmer's or a hot-glue gun)

Assorted herbs (preferably fresh)

Fine wire or heavy thread (preferably green)

Velvet or satin ribbon

Assorted everlasting flowers

Sheet moss or Spanish moss

1. If you are using felt, place the basket on the felt, and trace around the bottom. Cut out the felt. Glue the piece of felt to the outside bottom of basket.

2. Arrange small bouquets of herbs in your hand, and tie the stems together with either wire or thread.

3. Cut a length of wire approximately 12 inches long. (You will need several 12-inch pieces in order to complete the wiring, but I find 12 inches a convenient length to work with.) At the rim of the basket, weave one end of the wire in and out to secure it to the rim. Take one bundle of the herbs and twist the wire around it and then weave the wire to the basket. Take the next bundle of herbs, overlap the top of the bundle over the ends of the previous bundle to hide the ends. Again twist the wire around the bundle and then weave the wire to the basket. Continue around until you have covered the entire basket rim.

4. Measure the circumference of the top of the basket and cut a length of ribbon about twice the circumference. Weave the ribbon around the bundles. Tie a pretty bow with the ends or glue them under a few herbs. Ribbon can be wrapped around the handle, too, if you wish.

5. Take either single or small bunches of everlastings, and glue them to the herbs every so often.

6. Glue a small amount of moss to the inside bottom of the basket. If you've used fresh herbs, put the basket in a closet to dry, about a week or two. You've now got a beautiful herbal basket that's naturally fragrant and ready for potpourri, pomanders, scented soaps, or just about anything!

CHRISTINE TARSKI, ROSEMARY LANE, ROCKWELL, TX 75087

Herbal Cosmetics

HERBAL BODY OILS

by Jeanne Rose

I can't think of a better way to introduce a section on herbal cosmetics than to quote a few recipes from the queen of herbal body care, JEANNE ROSE, and to use some of the work from her recently revised Kitchen Cos-

The easiest way to make oils that incorporate the qualities of herbs is to put the herbs in the oil for a few days and then strain them out. In practice, however, it is a bit more difficult than this — though not much more. First, get your herbs together. You can use purchased herbs that are already dried, or pick and dry the plants yourself. Place them and the oil into a wide-mouth gallon bottle, using about 1 pound of herbs to 1 gallon of oil. The more herbs, the stronger the oil. I use various combinations of oils according to my needs. I prefer a mixture of equal parts of soy oil, corn oil, and sunflower oil, however, because this combination provides most, if not all, of the essential fatty acids, and it has a nice, slippery feel. Many old herbals insist on infusing herbs in pure olive oil only, but feel free to use the oil of your choice. A little practice and experience here will teach you a great deal. *The herbs must stay immersed in the oil or mold will occur on whatever floats above the oil.* Infuse the herbs in a warm spot for 5 to 10 days. After this time, put a funnel lined with cheesecloth into a gallon bottle, and strain the oil through it. Let the oil pass through the cheesecloth naturally; *do not* squeeze the cloth. Depending on the ingredients, this oil can be used for rubbing on bodies, as perfume oil (if scented strongly), as bath oil, or as a cosmetic or medicinal oil. Smell the newly strained oil and add an essential oil of your choice that will harmonize with the herbs that you started with.

❧ *Jeanne's Perfection Skin Oil* ❧

I had very dry skin, until I made Jeanne's Perfection Skin Oil. I massage it into my skin once or twice weekly, year-round. In the summer, I add a teaspoon of citronella oil to ward off insects outdoors. My daughters and I use it daily to keep the sun from drying out our skin as we garden, walk, or swim. Although it is true that most citrus oils should not be used undiluted *on the skin when one will be exposed to the sun, the tiny amount in this recipe is greatly diluted.*

1 ounce soy oil	*1 ounce wheat germ oil*
1 ounce corn oil	*1 ounce vitamin E (liquid)*
1 ounce peanut oil	*3 drops orange oil (essential)*
1 ounce safflower oil	*3 drops lemon oil (essential)*

Combine all of the oils, and shake them to mix thoroughly. Store in an 8-ounce bottle. Rub all over your body as often as you like, since this oil blend is an excellent skin food.

metics — *even though most of what we know today about this subject is from either her* Herbs and Things *or her* Herbal Body Book! *Her latest publication is* The Cosmetic Aromatherapy Book. *Certainly, anyone wanting to delve into the subject of herbal cosmetics should own and devour all four of these masterpieces, available through her catalog of New Age Creations, which also includes her Herbal Bodyworks health care products.* Kitchen Cosmetics *includes over 100 recipes for lotions, powders, shampoos, teas, and moisturizers that are easily prepared in the home; many have several different uses and are therefore so practical.*

❧ *Jeanne's Almond Kernel Skin Oil or Perfume* ❧

4 ounces almond oil
A few drops of essential oil of your choice

Mix the two oils together and store in an amber or light-proof 4-ounce bottle. Use directly on the skin as a face or body oil, or as perfume.

FROM *KITCHEN COSMETICS*
JEANNE ROSE, SAN FRANCISCO, CA
94117

❧ FLORAL AND HERBAL WATERS ❧

Rosewater is the best-known floral water and is available at drug and health-food stores. Commercial floral waters have been distilled and will keep indefinitely on a shelf in the bathroom. If you want to make your own, plan to refrigerate and use it within a week or two, unless you have a homemade still on hand. Always use pure, bottled spring water or distilled water, and prepare the blend with nonmetallic containers and utensils. Floral waters may be preserved for slightly longer use with the addition of ⅛ ounce of tincture of benzoin (from the drugstore) to each cup of a prepared mixture. This will turn it to a milky blend. Shake well before use.

A simple recipe for Homemade Rosewater: In an enamel or stainless steel pan, cover several handfuls of fresh, spray-free rose petals with pure spring or distilled water, and bring slowly to a boil. Stir occasionally with a wooden or porcelain spoon. Simmer for 10 minutes, strain through clean cheesecloth and/or a coffee filter, and bottle. Refrigerate and use within a week or two.

According to Gail Duff, in her book Natural Fragrances: Outdoor Scents For Indoor Uses *(Pownal, VT: Storey Communications, 1989), strong decoctions of herbs and flowers make excellent scented waters, to be used without soap as cleansers and refreshers at bedtime or upon arising. Her formula:*

6 tablespoons chopped, fresh herbs (or 3 tablespoons dried) to 1 pint of pure water
or
1 ounce fresh flower petals (or ½ ounce dried) to 1 pint of pure water.

Place the herbs or flowers and water in an enamel pan and bring gently to a boil. Cover and simmer for 30 minutes. Leave the mixture to cool completely, and strain and bottle. It will keep for up to 2 weeks.

Here are some of the herbal combinations recommended by Ms. Duff:

- ❤ Rose and lovage (cleansing and deodorizing)
- ❤ Rosemary and hyssop (refreshing)
- ❤ Lavender and peppermint (refreshing)

- ❤ Rose, lavender, and thyme (refreshing and fragrant)
- ❤ Chamomile and lemon balm (soothing)

Also from Natural Fragrances *are instructions for Scented Waters for the Bath:*
1 pound fresh herbs (or 8 ounces dried) to 1 pint spring water, brought gently to a boil, and then covered and simmered for 10 minutes. Cool completely, then strain, pressing out as much liquid as possible. Add 3 fluid ounces of vodka before bottling. Add ¼ pint to each bath.

Ms. Duff suggests that a mixture of herbs is best, choosing from the following: rosemary, lavender, lemon balm, basil, hyssop, chamomile, elderflower, bergamot, lovage, or peppermint, among others.

❧ Sage and Lavender After-Shave Lotion ❧

Delightfully invigorating

2 cups witch hazel
2 tablespoons apple cider
1 ounce dried lavender flowers
1 ounce dried sage

Combine all ingredients in a large jar with a lid. Close the jar and let the mixture steep for 1 week, shaking it daily. Strain and discard the herbs, and bottle the lotion for use or gifts.

MARYLAND HERB ASSOCIATION NEWSLETTER, ANNAPOLIS, MD 21401

❧ Rosewater ❧

Rosewater may be used in the bath (about 1 cup), hot tub, or as a splash after bathing or showering. Floral waters tone and clear the skin, act as hydrating agents, and help to normalize the acid balance of the skin.

2 cups distilled water
¼ cup vodka
½ cup chemical-free red rose petals (because red looks best!)
15 drops rose oil (optional, if scent from petals isn't strong enough)

Combine water, vodka, and petals in a covered jar, and place it in the sun. In less than a day the sun will extract the color and the fragrant oils from the petals. Strain through a coffee filter, leaving a beautiful and fragrant water. Refrigerate in a covered bottle, and use within two weeks.

FROM *CRAFTING WITH FRAGRANCE MAKES SCENTS*
DONNA MADORA MITCHELL, LAVENDER LANE, CITRUS HEIGHTS, CA 95621-7265

Homemade Cosmetics

by Linda Gannon

❧ Angel Water ❧

A toner and freshener that brings skin back to normal pH after cleansing, this product is very good for your skin, especially if it is oily.

1 cup apple cider vinegar
5 tablespoons rose petals
4 tablespoons sage leaves
3 tablespoons raspberry leaves
2 tablespoons rosemary
¾ cup rosewater

Heat the vinegar, and pour it over the herbs. Place mixture in a quart jar, and cap it. (Do not use a metal lid.) Shake daily for 10 days. Strain. Add rosewater to vinegar. Store, covered, in jars with nonmetallic lids.

❧ Rose/Lavender Dusting Powder ❧

2 cups whole lavender buds
2 cups whole rose petals and rose buds
1 cup whole patchouli
5 drops woodsy rose oil
2 drops patchouli oil
1 pound arrowroot

Blend whole lavender, roses, and patchouli in blender until fairly fine. Blend oils and arrowroot well. Combine the two mixtures and stir to blend well. Store in jars or bags.

❧ Lavender Ointment ❧

Excellent for burns, chapped lips, cold sores, and so on.

4 tablespoons olive or almond oil
3 to 4 tablespoons beeswax
3 teaspoons cocoa butter
2 teaspoons lanolin
10 drops vitamin E oil
15 drops lavender oil
15 drops sandalwood oil

Combine the olive or almond oil, beeswax, cocoa butter, and lanolin, and heat thoroughly in the top of a double boiler. Remove from heat. Add the vitamin E, lavender, and sandalwood oils, and beat well. Pour into little jars or pots, and allow mixture to cool before covering with lids. Keeps 6 to 12 months.

For sources of cosmetic supplies, see Appendix.

Linda Gannon's Magical Celebration Baskets are filled with exquisite handmade herbal treats. Each basket or tin is unique and personalized with a special theme appropriate to the celebration; it contains items based on color and aromatherapy — a veritable feast for the senses! For further information, see Appendix for address.

❧ Floral Water for Normal or Dry Skin ❧

Another wonderful toner and freshener

10 tablespoons rosewater
2 tablespoons orange flower water
2 tablespoons witch hazel

Mix all ingredients together and bottle.

❧ Honey Lip Balm ❧

1 cup almond oil
1 to 2 ounces beeswax
2 tablespoons honey
1 teaspoon essential oil, such as vanilla or rose (for flavor)

Combine almond oil and beeswax, and warm oil to melt beeswax. Stir in honey and essential oil. Pour into small containers. Let cool before covering with lids.

Linda Gannon, The Magick Garden, McFarland, WI 53558

❦ *Basic Body Powder* ❦

8 ounces arrowroot or cornstarch, or
a blend of both
4 ounces baking soda

For scent and deodorizing effect
add one of the following
variations:

Variation I
1 tablespoon ground clove
1 tablespoon ground slippery elm
1 tablespoon ground mace
1 tablespoon ground sandalwood
1 tablespoon ground vetiver root

Variation II
1 tablespoon ground clove
1 tablespoon ground slippery elm
1 tablespoon ground rose petals
1 tablespoon ground lavender

Variation III
1 tablespoon ground clove
1 tablespoon ground slippery elm
1 tablespoon ground orange peel
1 tablespoon ground lemon peel

Blend all ingredients in a glass or ceramic bowl. Store in a large, glass jar, covered, for two weeks, allowing scents to blend. Shake jar well every other day.

For additional scent, add 10 to 15 drops essential oil(s) of your choice. PVS

KATE CARTER FREDERICK, SEVENTH HEAVEN HERB PRODUCTS, ONALASKA, WI 54650

HERBAL BODY POWDER

by Kate Carter Frederick

During the past decade, I have experimented with a variety of body powder recipes. I started making herbal body powders when I learned that talcum powder, which is based on talc, may contain asbestos. The base ingredient in my herbal body powders is starch — arrowroot, cornstarch, or both. Baking soda extends the base and adds to the powder's deodorizing effect. An endless variety of powdered herbs, flowers, and spices can be added for deodorizing, healing, and fragrance. For the simplest powder recipe, blend base ingredients with essential oils.

I make two kinds of body powder — one for women and one for children, including babies. For baby powder, the fewer ingredients, the better. Plain cornstarch is an effective powder for babies with diaper or heat rash. To boost the powder's healing effect, add 1 tablespoon of powdered medicinal herbs, such as slippery elm or myrrh, to each 8 ounces of base. For light fragrance, add 5 to 10 drops of essential oil for each 8 ounces of base. Adding more herbs, spices, or essential oils, however, may further irritate diaper rash or newborns' sensitive skin. Some proven-popular fragrance oils for children's powder are lavender, violet, honeysuckle, heather, apricot, and peach.

You can use a broader range of ingredients when making body powder for women. Follow the accompanying recipes for ratio and quantity guidelines, but be creative and blend a subtle fragrance with ground herbs, flowers, and spices. Do not use larger quantities of herbs and spices, for they may stain light-colored clothes if the powder is used as an underarm deodorant.

For the most fragrant body powder, add essential oils as well as herbs and spices. Use one oil for a simple scent, or combine oils as you would for any fragrance blend. Like any perfume, body powder with a blended fragrance has a slightly different scent on each of those who use it. Each woman's body chemistry blends differently with various scents. Heighten this effect by adding musk oil, which intensifies any fragrance blend, especially floral or spicy blends.

Body powder is a fun and practical way to use some of your favorite herbs and flowers. It makes a delightful gift, too. Package body powder with a powder puff in a decorative box or tin. You can usually find velour powder puffs in the cosmetic department of variety or drug stores. To protect the powder from moisture and maintain a longer-lasting scent, store it in a plastic bag inside its container. You can also make your own unique bandbox with the directions that follow.

MAKING A BANDBOX

by Kate Carter Frederick

I package my homemade herbal body powder in homemade bandboxes. Even before bandboxes became popular along with other Victoriana, I had appreciated the design and utility of old hat boxes, which I use for storing a variety of collections. Bandboxes get their name because of the way they are constructed. The removable lid consists of a narrow band wrapped around the box top. A wider band is wrapped around the box bottom to make the side of the box. Bandboxes can be made in any shape or size, but the box described here will hold 8 ounces of body powder. (These boxes make nice containers for potpourri, too.)

Originally conceived in the eighteenth century, bandboxes were usually made of paperboard covered with decorative paper. They were used to "protect the elaborate and voluminous neckpieces of the gallants." By Victorian times, bandboxes were commonly used by women to store and transport hats, wigs, muffs, and other accessories. These boxes were made by professionals as well as home crafters. Today, two of the most widely known bandboxes are hat boxes and round and oval Shaker boxes, which are considered classics in wooden box design and utility.

1. For a 3½" wide by 3½" high bandbox, measure and cut out cardboard pieces. Use a compass to measure and draw the circles. Make the following pieces:

Lid top: 3 ½ inch diameter circle
Box bottom: 3 ⁷⁄₁₆ inch diameter circle
Lid side: 11½" x ¾" rectangle
Box side: 11½" x 3" rectangle

Label top and bottom circle pieces lightly with pencil. If you plan to make more than one box, it is most helpful to make cardboard patterns of all pieces; put measurements and labels on each one. Save time by cutting out several tops, bottoms, and sides from wrapping paper at one time.

2. Using the cut-out cardboard pieces as patterns, measure and cut out *two* sets of the pieces from wrapping paper, *except* make the side pieces of both box and lid ¼ inch longer and ¼ inch wider than the cardboard side pieces, to allow for overlap. The circles for the top and bottom should be the same size as their cardboard counterparts. One set of wrapping paper pieces will cover the outside of the box; the other set of pieces will line the inside of the box. You may use the same, or contrasting, paper for covering and lining.

3. Make the box lid first. Apply a thin coat of white glue over the entire surface of the *inside* of the lid side (the narrower rectangle).

KATE CARTER FREDERICK has had a home-based business for several years, making and selling very original, high-quality, self-care blends and decorative gift items. About half of her business is through mail order, with the balance on a local scale through home parties, direct sales, and lectures.

Posterboard or lightweight card board (large cereal boxes can be recycled for this project)
Pencil, ruler, compass, scissors (or X-acto knife)
Non-glossy gift-wrapping paper (see Step 2 below)
White glue and tacky glue
Transparent tape

Glue the lining piece to the lid side with the bottom edges aligned, a ¼-inch overlap of lining extending above the top, and a ⅛-inch overlap extending at each end. Smooth all wrinkles out of the lining paper as you glue it in place.

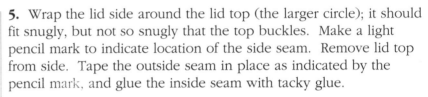

4. Carefully fold the excess lining material at the top down toward the inside of the lid, with right sides of the paper together and with the fold aligned as closely as possible to the top edge of the cardboard lid. The lining need not be completely folded down upon itself; fold it just far enough so that you will be able to put the lid top in place in Step 6 below.

5. Wrap the lid side around the lid top (the larger circle); it should fit snugly, but not so snugly that the top buckles. Make a light pencil mark to indicate location of the side seam. Remove lid top from side. Tape the outside seam in place as indicated by the pencil mark, and glue the inside seam with tacky glue.

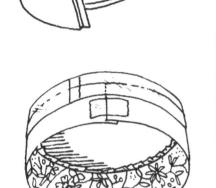

6. Align the lid top with the top edge of the lid side (lining folded to the inside). Run a long piece of tape all the way around the outside top edge of the side piece, allowing half of the width of the tape to extend above the side piece so that it can be folded over to adhere to the top. Tape the top and bottom together, pressing tape until it is as smooth as possible.

7. On the inside of the lid, glue the overlap from the lining side to the inside of the top. It will be pleated, but press until it stays in place.

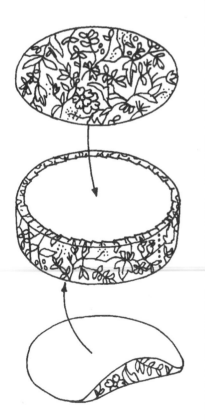

8. Spread a thin, even coat of glue all the way around the outside of the lid side. Lay one end of the cover paper on the glued side, *with equal allowances of paper extending beyond the top and bottom edges.* Place the paper so that its overlapping seam will *not* fall on top of the overlap on the cardboard side. Run the cover paper all the way around the side piece, smoothing out any ripples as you go. Tack down the overlapping end of the paper with a touch of glue. Apply a thin line of glue around both overlapping edges of paper. Bend the bottom edge under to the inside of the lid, smoothing as you go. The cover paper should overlap the lining paper evenly about ⅛ inch. Bend the top edge over to the top of the lid. It will look pleated, but continue pressing down the over-lap until it stays glued down as smoothly and securely as possible.

9. Spread a thin, even layer of glue across the top of the lid and apply the cover paper. Smooth carefully.

10. Spread a thin, even layer of glue across the inside of the lid and apply the lining paper. Smooth carefully.

11. The box is put together following the same steps as you did for the box lid, except that in Step 5 you must check to make sure that the lid will fit the box properly. It should slide on and off easily, with enough allowance for the layers of paper covers and liners. You can adjust the top diameter of the box body by lifting the tape and expanding the side piece if the lid is too loose, or by sliding the top piece ends more closely together if the lid is too tight. When you are certain the lid fits, carefully tape and glue the seam of the side piece.

12. When both lid and box are completely assembled, set the two pieces of the box aside until they are thoroughly dry. Do not leave the lid on the box while the pieces are drying or the box may end up glued shut.

Kate Carter Frederick, Seventh Heaven Herb Products, Onalaska, WI 54650

Natural Deodorants

❧ *Underarm Deodorant Powder* ❧

4 ounces talcum powder
2 ounces cornstarch
1 ounce baking soda
3 drops of your favorite scent (optional)

Combine all ingredients, and mix well.

❧ *Foot Powder Deodorant* ❧

2 ounces cornstarch
4 ounces unscented talcum powder
1 ounce baking soda
1 teaspoon powdered orrisroot
3 drops of your favorite scent (optional)

Combine all ingredients, and mix well.

Reprinted, with permission, from Book #2918 *Making Potpourri, Colognes and Soaps: 102 Natural Recipes,* by David A. Webb. Copyright 1988 by Tab Books Inc., Blue Ridge Summit, PA 17294

Creating Your Personal Essence

by Colleen K. Dodt

I give workshops for people wanting to create their own individual perfumes from essential oils. Traditionally, blending oils has been done by combining a top, a middle, and a base note. I feel a personal essence should reflect its creator, however, and not necessarily adhere to the rules established by perfumers. It is important to consider what types of scents appeal the most to you. Citrus, woodsy, floral, or herbal? Heavy or light? Refreshing or exotic? The scent you wear says a lot about you as an individual. Do you want your aroma to portray an earthy person? Or a professional image? Or an exotic, sensual personality? Remember, your perfume is an extension of you.

In my workshops, I offer my students seven basic types of scents (see chart, page 26), from which the desired predominant fragrance is selected. Smaller amounts of other oils in the same category may be added, as well as complementary essences from the other categories. The participants select the oils they wish to include and then I help them with the amounts and proportions to use. Students are encouraged to give names to their finished essences. Each is also allowed to try again if time permits and the first attempt did not produce the desired result. These workshops are for fun and are meant to encourage further experimentation with the blending of essential oils for a personal "signature" essence.

❤

CITRUS	SPICE	HERBAL	LEAF	GUMS AND BALSAMS	FLORAL
Bergamot	Clove	Rosemary	Lemongrass	Frankincense	Rose absolute
Neroli	Cinnamon	Basil	Palmarosa	Myrrh	Jasmine absolute
Petitgrain	Nutmeg	Thyme	Violet leaf	Benzoin	Lavender
Sweet orange	Allspice	Clary sage	Labdanum	Galbanum	Chamomile
Mandarin	Ginger	Marjoram	Patchouli	Peru balsam	Ylang-ylang
Lime	Vanilla*	Coriander	Rose geranium		
Grapefruit		Angelica	Myrtle	WOOD	
Lemon				Rosewood	
				Sandalwood	

Not really a spice associated with the spice trade.

❤

Basic Blending Advice

BASIC FRAGRANCE	CHARACTERISTICS	BLENDS WELL WITH
SANDALWOOD (*Santalum album*)	One of the most ancient essences used for perfume; acts as a fixative; sweet heavy odor; considered to be aphrodisiac, sedative, antidepressive	Rose, lavender, ylang-ylang, clary sage, jasmine
LAVENDER (*Lavandula officinalis*)	One of the best-known essences; considered the one essence every household should have; clean, fresh scent makes it eminently suitable for a freshener; considered relaxing, calming, balancing	Rose, bergamot, ylang-ylang, clary sage, jasmine
YLANG-YLANG (*Cananga odorata*)	Very sweet (too much so for some tastes); use with caution, for it can overpower a blend; a little goes a long way; considered sedative, soothing, aphrodisiac	Lavender, sandalwood, jasmine, patchouli
BERGAMOT (*Citrus aurantium* var. *bergamia*)	A pleasant essence expressed from a fruit (not to be confused with the herb bergamot, which inherited its name); a citrus, almost floral scent; flavors Earl Gray tea; never use before exposure to sun: it increases the skin's photosensitivity and may cause uneven pigmentation; considered an antidepressant, uplifting, and generally very pleasant; highly valued in perfumery	Almost everything! — lavender, geranium, rosewood, neroli
ROSE GERANIUM (*Pelargonium graveolens*)	A great substitute for the more expensive Rose Absolute; sweet, herbal scent; nice additive to bath and beauty products; considered an antidepressant, uplifting, sedative	Almost any essence — lavender, ylang-ylang, bergamot

OTHER BLENDING SUGGESTIONS

Jasmine or *rose absolute* is always a marvelous addition to any blend; a little of either goes a long way. *Vanilla absolute, clary sage, lime, rosemary, neroli, rosewood,* and a tiny bit of *cinnamon* can turn a little bottle of essences into an olfactory delight. The key to blending is *experiment, experiment, experiment!* Obtain one of the excellent publications on aromatherapy, and begin to use your nose more. Sniff out information on essential oils and the rewards will be many.

One of the best places to wear your personal essence is in your hair; the scent will last much longer because of the protein in your hair. Although you can extend your essence by diluting it with a carrier oil, this may make it go rancid sooner. The essence will improve with age, but it is best to use it within three months. Dark glass bottles are the best for storage. Essential oils are an herb garden in a bottle. They can go with you anywhere, and leave memories that can last a lifetime.

COLLEEN DODT, HERBAL ENDEAVORS, LTD., ROCHESTER HILLS, MI 48063

THE ART OF PARFUMERIE

by Ronda Schooley Bretz

When creating your own fragrance blends, whether for a perfume or for scenting a potpourri, it is important, as much as possible, to use *essential* oils — pure, undiluted extractions from botanicals. *Fragrance* oils are chemically created, but the synthetics do have value in fragrance blending. Reputable dealers clearly mark which oils are undiluted and which are synthetic. Because oils are costly, it is common practice to dilute them to increase the liquid volume for marketing profits.

Good perfume blends, in any form, whether dry or liquid, should have four main elements: *main scent, or key; secondary scent, or blender; contrasting note;* and *fixative.* The main scent is the one overall aroma that you wish to create. The blender is an enhancement and may be a bit of spice, citrus, wood, or any such oil. A contrasting note should be used in minute quantity, for its role is to add an illusive quality that livens the scent. A fixative, such as gum benzoin, patchouli, balsam Peru, ambergris, or civet, needs to blend with the overall aroma, for its primary purpose is to give the blend a long-lasting quality and to release its fragrance gradually.

In order to evaluate perfume blends, they must be sniffed, while keeping in mind the three-phase life cycle of an odor. The first phase, or initial impression, is the *top note.* The second phase is the *body,* which may be identified from 5 to 20 minutes after exposure to air. This is the total fragrance in the life of an aroma, and it lasts 2 to 4 hours. The third phase of a fragrance evaluation

RONDA SCHOOLEY BRETZ has been in the fragrance business for many years. She is noted for her expertise on fragrance-crafting and her potpourri workshops at the early International Herb Growers and Marketers Association conferences. She is currently concentrating on further research and on writing about herbs and fragrances.

is called *dry out*; it is the residual note of the fragrance and the one that will be apparent for the remainder of the scent's life cycle. When you begin your own perfumery craft, consider the endless possibilities. Make sample tests on small squares of blotter paper or thick paper toweling, using an eyedropper for a single drop measure. Enjoy making your own perfume blends to scent many items that find enhancement through the olfactory senses — soaps, potpourri, bath products, massage oil, and on and on. Here are several tried and true perfume blends for your experimentation.

Traditional Eau de Cologne

Parts	Oils or Fragrances
1	Rose
5	Rosemary
20	Lavender
20	Geranium
60	Petitgrain
60	Orange blossom
120	Bergamot

Other Perfume Blends

Parts	Oils or Fragrances	Parts	Oils or Fragrances
1	Honeysuckle	1	Rose
1	Violet	1	Violet
1	Jasmine	1	Patchouli
1	Carnation	1	Jasmine
7	Bergamot	5	Rose
7	Sandalwood	1	Lavender
3	Jasmine	1	Patchouli
3	Rose		
		1	Anise
		1	Cinnamon
		1	Clove

RONDA SCHOOLEY BRETZ, SILVER SPRING, PA 17575

FEBRUARY

FEBRUARY IS THE MONTH in which we celebrate romantic, everlasting love — often with roses, which are symbolic of true love. So it seems a most appropriate time to include the current resurgence of Victorian crafts, heart-shaped projects, and the growing of everlasting flowers.

The recent interest in a return to the charm, graciousness, and romance of the Victorian Age is expressed by the old-fashioned delights of yesteryear, many of which involve herbs and flowers, fresh and dried. Victorian crafts, designs, and arrangements are fast becoming a threat to the "country" look in decorating and gift-giving on the American scene. Several slick new magazines extol the virtues of that bygone era of excess, frills, leisurely afternoon teas, parasols, lavender, and lace. Gardens, potpourris, and gift baskets are being created to express the "language of herbs and flowers," a pastime of the wealthy Victorians, who sent messages usually of love, but also of concern or heartbreak via a single flower or a tussie mussie, with no written explanations. The women of the leisurely class of this period spent much time making both delicate and bold decorations and gifts with the dried flowers and herbs from their gardens.

After you read all about how to express everlasting love through hearts and flowers, start planning your own garden of everlastings for use in crafts, wreaths, and arrangements. Many of them will need an early start under lights or in the greenhouse — the perennials, to develop strong root systems the first year; and the annuals, to insure the most possible blooms before frost. Everlastings are those plants that retain their form and color when dried; they can therefore be considered herbs for their usefulness as decoratives. So many herb wreaths and arrangements include everlasting flowers for color, and thus an everlasting garden is a fitting addition to any herb-lover's environment.

We've been growing our own everlastings in recent years and have found it easy and fun to do. I describe some of my experiences and include several of my findings or tips in the last section of this chapter. You will find complete resource sections on Victoriana and on everlastings in the Appendix.

May every month be February for you, when it comes to everlasting love and eternal joy from your herbs and flowers.

Victorian Gardens and Crafts

MARY DUNN has been growing herbs for several years and has given lectures and workshops to the public along the way. She at one time operated a mail-order business, offering her decorative products, but she has recently moved to a farm (Mountainview Herb Farm) in Thorndike, Maine, where she is now concentrating on growing herbs and everlastings to sell at the farm; on herbal weddings, lectures or workshops; and on writing about herbs for several publications. Visitors are welcome at the farm by appointment, from April to October.

VICTORIANA

by Mary Dunn

The Victorian era (which coincides with Queen Victoria's reign, 1837-1901) was, for the wealthy, a time of carefree fun and exploration — of gardens and garden parties, afternoon teas, croquet games, and extravagant fashions and hair styles. It was also a period when the middle class and "suburbia" were born. And on the dark side, it was a time when the poor were very poor, and the living and working conditions of factory laborers were bleak and full of filth and disease. Although we tend to think of the age as one of romance, pastel colors, lacy ornaments, and flowers, it was actually an era of the bold, colorful, exotic, gaudy, busy, and ornate.

Nature as something to be cherished and enjoyed was of special importance during this time, and crafting with flowers was very popular among the Victorian ladies. They enjoyed drying flowers for winter arrangements as well as making flowers of paper, wax, and even hair. Lavender sticks, potpourris, rosewater, and candy all represented the popularity of both lavender and roses. Other favorite crafts included sachets, pressed flower stationery, wreaths, and herbal vinegars for bathing, skin care, and culinary use. The language of flowers was communicated through tussie mussies. Before Victorian times, these fresh, tightly made, hand-held nosegays of flowers were used for scent and for protection against disease. But by adding a very old idea to these useful items — the symbolism associated with herbs and flowers — the Victorians conveyed meanings through their contents. Not only was the creation of tussie mussies a great way to pass the time, but flowers could as well be used to send hidden messages to special people — mostly messages of love.

Suggested Plant List for Victorian Gardens

The following plants were known to be grown during the Victorian era. The list is not all-inclusive. For further study see sources listed on page 296.

Alyssum
Angelica
Anise
Armeria
*Aster
Baby's-breath
+Bachelor's-button
Balm-of-Gilead
*Balsam
Basil (sweet)
Bay
+Bergamot
Betony
+Bleeding-heart
Bluestar
Borage
Burnet
Butterfly weed
*Calendula
+Campanula
+Candytuft
+Canterbury-bells
Caraway
*Carnation
Catmint
Celandine
+Celosia (Cockscomb)
Chamomile
Chervil
*Chrysanthemum
Cinquefoil
Clary
+Cleome
*Coleus
+Columbine
+Coreopsis
Coriander
+Costmary

Cupid's-dart
+Daffodil
Dahlia
+Delphinium
+Dianthus pink (Gilly-flower)
Dill
Dyer's madder
Elecampane
+English daisy
+Evening primrose
False indigo
Fennel
Fenugreek
+Feverfew
+Flax
+Forget-me-not
Four-o'clock
+Foxglove
+Gaillardia
Gas plant
*Geranium
+Gomphrena (Globe amaranth)
+Heliotrope
Hibiscus
+Hollyhock
+Honesty
+Honeysuckle
+Hops
Horehound
Horsemint
Hyssop
*Immortelle
+Iris
Jacob's-ladder
+Jasmine
+Job's-tears

+Lady's-mantle
+Lamb's-ears
*Larkspur
+Lavender
Liatris
Lily
+Lily-of-the-valley
Lobelia
Lovage
+Love-lies-bleeding
Lungwort
+Lupine
Mallows (marsh, musk, rose)
+Marigold (African)
Marjoram (sweet)
Mugwort
+Mullein pink
*/+Nasturtium
+Nicotiana (white)
+Nigella
Oregano
+Peony
Pennyroyal
Peppermint
+Petunia
+Phlox
Pimpernel
Poppy
Pyrethrum
Quaking grass
+Rosemary
+Rose
Rudbeckia
Rue
Sabatia
Sage
*Salvia

Savory (summer and winter)
*Snapdragon
+Snowdrop
Soapwort
+Southernwood
Spearmint
Spider plant
Spiderwort
Spirea
*/+Stock
+Sweet cicely
+Sweet pea
+Sweet rocket
*/+Sweet William
+Sweet woodruff
Tansy
Tarragon
Thyme (common and lemon)
+Tulip
Valerian
*Veronica
+Verbena
Vinca
+Viola
+Wallflower
Windflower
+Woad
Wormwood
Yarrow
*Zinnia

* *Most popular flowers used in Victorian bedding out gardens*
+ *Other favorites, commonly used in cottage gardens*

MARY DUNN, MOUNTAINVIEW HERB FARM, THORNDIKE, ME 04986

EDEN REVISITED: ENGLISH COTTAGE GARDENS

by Linda Fry Kenzle

After my mother died, I found a print of an idyllic English cottage garden folded up and tucked into one of her favorite books. She must have looked at that print often; its edges were shredded from being opened, looked at, then refolded again and again. My mother had left her touch on every piece of property my family owned. In each place Mother's garden — her sanctuary away from a maddening, stress-filled world — was always a riot of color, undulating from softly quiet areas to brilliant shocking pinks and reds that enlivened the spirit.

Today, many homeowners plop a few evergreen shrubs around the foundation, plant a tree or two, and consider the property landscaped. There are no areas of contrast in color, shape, or texture. The English cottage garden, on the other hand, breathes life into the land and fuses the rectilinear buildings into the flowing forms of the botanicals. Climbers like sweet peas, clematis, wisteria, hops, roses, and morning-glory, supported by lattices or simple strings, are left to ramble willy-nilly, hugging the building. The back of the border shoots skyward with single-flowered hollyhocks and delphiniums. (As children we used to fashion "dolls" out of hollyhock flowers; now I use them as an excellent addition to my signature potpourris.)

One of the secrets of creating a successful English cottage garden is to plant in clumps or masses. A clump of ten to twenty plants makes a gloriously full, lush effect, while a single stem here and there loses impact and fragments the garden design. Secondary plantings include the herbs feverfew, sage, rue, bee balm, lemon balm, valerian, and lavender, as well as cottage garden flowers like sweet William, statice, salvia, Chinese-lanterns, nigella, coralbells, stock, Jacob's-ladder, and phlox. Heartsease, salad burnet, betony, pearly everlasting, and sweet violets are positioned at

---

VICTORIAN COTTAGE GARDENS

When Queen Victoria began her long reign in England, social changes were beginning to alter forever the way of life in that country, and the world. The seeds of the Industrial Revolution were planted, and the influences of Victorian England were felt in America and all over Europe. As the wealth shifted from the land barons and into the cities, the people moved along with the economy. As the factories appeared, so did more cities and suburbs. The people moved from countryside to city and built homes and planted gardens. The Victorian cottage garden thus evolved. Like the home it accompanied, the cottage garden was small, usually filling all available land in front of the house; it was usually fenced in. Through the gate and under the arbor a profusion of color and fragrance flourished. Gardens such as this still abound in England today, and people the world over imitate the charming informal style.

FROM *A VICTORIAN HERBAL*
JAN POWERS, STONE-WELL HERBS,
PEORIA, IL 61604

❧ English Cottage Garden Potpourri ❧

13 drops rose oil
8 drops apple oil
5 drops musk oil
3 drops peach oil
½ cup orrisroot
3 cups rosebuds and petals
2 cups cottage garden herbs and flowers
(try for a variety of colors, textures, and scents)
6-inch cinnamon stick, crushed
1 teaspoon cloves, lightly crushed
10 whole star anise, of which 3 are crushed and 7 left whole

Mix the oils with the orrisroot. Add all other ingredients, and mix together gently but thoroughly. Seal in a container, and age 3 weeks (before using) to allow scents to mingle and blend into a long-lasting, aromatic potpourri.

the front of the border to weave the garden into the solid grassy areas. Some of the fragrant herbs, like thyme, chamomile, and mint, are allowed to creep into the walkways so clothing will brush the herbs and release their special aromas.

Shady areas can be planted with a variety of ferns, forget-me-nots, sweet woodruff, and lily-of-the-valley. Plant tender perennials like rosemary and lemon verbena in tubs around a garden bench where one can linger for refreshment. Many of the cottage garden plants can be used for cut flowers, the herbs can be used in cooking, and both the flowers and herbs are useful for creating fine decorations.

FROM *THE JOY OF HERBS*
LINDA FRY KENZLE, FOX RIVER
GROVE, IL 60021

TUSSIE MUSSIES: GIFTS FROM THE GARDEN

by Mary Dunn

When summer still seems far away, what better time to learn about the antique art of tussie-mussie making and giving. Tussie mussies — bouquets of flowers, herbs, and leaves, all with sentimental meanings — make perfect gifts from the herb garden, for these wonderful treasures incorporate the language of flowers, herb gardening, and bouquet-making all into one.

It is said that in the early 1600s, John Parkinson, a French gardener, herbalist, and physician, was the first to give meanings to tiny, tightly made nosegays of fragrant flowers and leaves, although herbal symbolism can be traced back much earlier in Egyptian, Turkish, Chinese, Greek, and Roman history. *Tussie mussie* is a medieval word meaning *sweet posie*. Back when sanitation was poor and a walk down the street was a far cry from "getting some fresh air," both men and women held these tiny, fresh nosegays up close to their noses to sniff the fragrant leaves and mask the odors of the streets. Men also wore small posies on their lapels or placed them atop their walking sticks. Women held them in their hands, wore them on their arms, or placed them in tiny vials of water attached to their lacy bodices — these "bosom bottles" were most favored by men!

In the early 1700s, the language of flowers was introduced to England in the form of *floriography* — the art of sending messages by flower. At the height of its popularity, in the Victorian era, antique floral dictionaries were readily available, and mothers taught their daughters this very important, and prestigious, means of communication. Many English gardeners devoted a whole bed to herbs for tussie mussies.

Today, tussie mussies are wonderful gifts, particularly for Valentine's Day, but also for Mother's Day, Easter, birthdays, or anniversaries, or for a bride-to-be, someone who is ill or in a nursing home, or just to say, "I love you"! Let your own imagination create special times to exchange these meaningful gifts. Ex-

Peppermint *(Mentha piperita)*, signifying warmth of feeling

Sage *(Salvia officinalis)*, signifying domestic virtue and good health

periment with meanings by including herbs such as rosemary for remembrance, thyme for happiness and courage, lavender for devotion, and sage for good health. You might wish to make a tussie mussie rich in color or with a predominant scent. If you don't have fresh material on hand, dried plants work up just as well — once you begin, you'll never want to stop. Tussie mussies are as much fun to make and to give as to receive.

The Language of Herbs and Flowers

FLOWER OR HERB	SYMBOLISM	FLOWER OR HERB	SYMBOLISM
ALLSPICE	Compassion	HIBISCUS	Delicate beauty
ANGELICA	Inspiration	HOREHOUND	Health
BASIL	Love; good wishes (also hate!)	HYSSOP	Cleanliness
BAY	Glory	LADY'S-MANTLE	Comfort
BEE BALM	Compassion	LAMB'S-EARS	Surprise
BETONY	Surprise	LAVENDER	Devotion
BORAGE	Courage	LEMON BALM	Sympathy
BURNET	Mirth	LEMON VERBENA	Enchantment
CALENDULA	Joy	MARIGOLD	Grief
CARAWAY	Faithfulness	MARJORAM	Happiness
CHAMOMILE	Humility	MINTS	Wisdom/virtue/warmth
CHERVIL	Sincerity	MYRRH	Gladness
CLOVES	Dignity	PARSLEY	Festivity
CORIANDER	Hidden worth	PEPPERMINT	Warmth of feeling
DILL	To lull	ROSE	Love
FENNEL	Strength; worthy of praise	ROSE GERANIUM	Preference
DIANTHUS	Bonds of affection	ROSEMARY	Remembrance
GOLDENROD	Encouragement	SAGE	Domestic virtue; good health
HEARTSEASE	Happy thoughts	SWEET CICELY	Gladness
HELIOTROPE	Devotion	YARROW	Health

FROM CHARTS ASSEMBLED BY PAT AND JON BOURDO, WOODLAND HERB FARM, NORTHPORT, MI 49670 AND MARY DUNN, MOUNTAINVIEW HERB FARM, THORNDIKE, ME 04986

For a special occasion, JAN POWERS suggests creating a tussie mussie that echos the words of the Prayer of St. Francis in the language of flowers.

JAN POWERS, STONE-WELL HERBS, PEORIA, IL 61604

PRAYER OF ST. FRANCIS

Lord, make me an instrument of your PEACE	Lily-of-the-valley
Where there is hatred, let me sow LOVE	Rose
Where there is injury, PARDON	Hyssop
Where there is doubt, FAITH	Violet
Where there is despair, HOPE	Daisy
Where there is darkness, LIGHT	Rue
Where there is sadness, JOY	Marjoram

HOW TO MAKE A TUSSIE MUSSIE OF DRIED FLOWERS

Dried herbs and flowers
Floral tape
Paper doily with an × cut out of the center, or a tussie-mussie holder
    (available in florist supply or craft shops)
Rubber band
Ribbon
Scissors
Paper, pen, gold thread (symbolizing love), and a pin

1. Try to keep the tussie mussie simple. Place the flower or herb representing the most important message in the center, and surround it with your other herbs, working in threes to give it symmetry. Because of the delicate nature of the dried materials, you may find it easier to make many (fifteen or so) tiny bunches of flowers and herbs, each wrapped with floral tape, which can then be combined into a larger tussie mussie. Make an encircling frame with fragrant leaves or ferns. I usually work holding the flowers in my nondominant hand, while adding and rearranging with my dominant hand. Some people prefer using a glass as a holder while they work.

2. When complete, secure the stems with a rubber band, and slip the bouquet into your posy holder.

3. Wrap the stems with floral tape and then ribbon. You may also add a small bow.

4. Using a pin and gold thread, attach the card, with the message and meanings.

❤

If the dried materials should ever droop, just hang the whole thing upside down to re-dry.

❤

Mary Dunn, Mountainview Herb Farm, Thorndike, ME 04986

A MINIATURE TUSSIE-MUSSIE BED

You can create a much-enlarged version of a traditional, hand-held tussie mussie by designing an entire flower bed in this style. Bob Clark's *version features a colorful, aromatic center of miniature rose bushes and lavender plants, outlined by dainty, white sweet alyssum to form a lacy border reminiscent of the doily that traditionally frames the nosegay. You can enhance this effect by bordering the entire bed with pieces of broken white stone. For further accents of color, plant dianthus (symbolizing bonds of affection) between the roses and lavender, and golden marjoram (for happiness and beauty) and lamb's-ears (symbolizing softness and gentleness) among the alyssum. Keep the lamb's-ears small by pinching them back regularly. You will have to replant the marjoram and alyssum each spring from seed.*

Bob Clark, Lancaster, OH

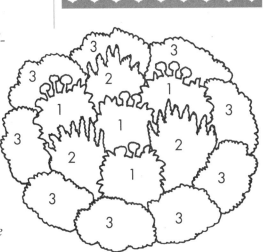

1 - Miniature pink rose, for true love
2 - Lavender, for devotion
3 - White alyssum, for worth beyond beauty

A POTPOURRI GARDEN WITH A TUSSIE-MUSSIE CENTERPIECE

BEVERLY ANDERSON has created a more elaborate arrangement, with the tussie-mussie bed in the center of four symmetrically placed beds containing the various herbs that speak the language of flowers.

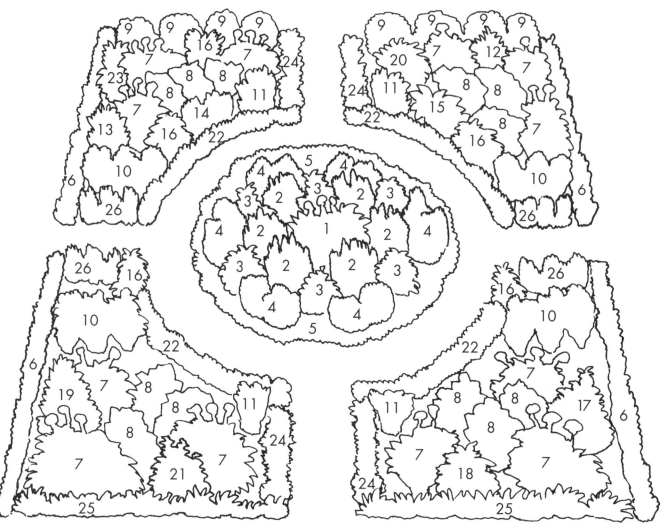

The lamb's-ears in the potpourri gardens are used as an edging to divide those beds from the adjoining ones. Beverly has extensive herb and rose gardens, and an herb shop. She also conducts workshops, gives lectures, and writes for periodicals about herbs. This busy lady is employed by Michigan State University, where I was delighted to meet her during my travels to herb conferences.

BEVERLY S. ANDERSON, ILLUSIONS IN THYME, WILLIAMSTON, MI 48895

THE TUSSIE MUSSIE GARDEN

1 - Fairy rose for love
2 - Lavender for devotion
3 - Thyme for courage
4 - Dianthus (for bonds of affection)
5 - A lacy ruffle border of Silver Lace dusty miller

THE POTPOURRI GARDEN

6 - Dianthus
7 - Hybrid tea, floribunda, and grandiflora roses
8 - Scented geraniums (rose, lemon rose, lemon, ginger)
9 - Ambrosia
10 - Miniature roses
11 - Clove pinks
12 - Peppermint (emerald and gold)
13 - Winter savory
14 - Mignonette
15 - Alpine strawberries
16 - Thymes (lemon, nutmeg, caraway, woolly, silver)
17 - Korean mint
18 - Anise hyssop
19 - Lemon balm
20 - Bergamot (lemon)
21 - Horsemint
22 - Gray santolina
23 - Menthol mint
24 - Lacy dusty miller (temporary)
25 - Lamb's-ears
26 - Germander

Hearts, Hearts, Hearts

VICTORIAN POTPOURRI HEART ORNAMENT, OR WALL HANGING

by Jean Whitley

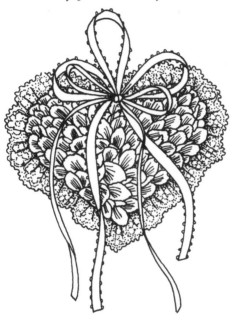

Every once in a while I receive surprise gifts from newsletter readers who just want to share their favorite crafts. One Christmas season, JEAN WHITLEY sent me this luscious heart ornament. It is so fragrant, and now one of the prize tree ornaments in my collection. Jean has also made these as keepsakes for brides, using the wedding rice and flowers, ribbons in the wedding colors, and white lace. She was happy to share the directions, although it took some doing, as she had never written them down before — she had "just made them"!

For the lace, use such colors as Williamsburg blue, colonial rose, or off-white. Home-Sew in Bethlehem, PA (see Appendix for complete address) has a wonderful selection of colors in ¾-inch wide lace, and in prices that can't be matched! Use cardboard from the back of notepads for small hearts and from boxes or cartons for larger sizes. Choose any scent you wish for your potpourri; roses or lavender are most in keeping with a Victorian theme. I prefer Quik glue, as it sets best. If you are using craft glue, apply it to the cardboard, wait until it starts to set, and then put the lace in place with a toothpick.

Patterns are given on page 50 for three different-sized hearts. The smallest size (A) is best for tree ornaments; size B may also be used for tree ornaments or small wall hangings; size C (or make one even larger) makes a nice wall hanging. For the larger hearts, I make large, floppy bows with a couple of different shades and strands of ribbons, and then twist the streamers to make loops, which I glue to the front of the heart on top of the potpourri. Avoid potpourri that contains large chunks of material. Other shapes, such as wreaths, can be made following similar techniques, but I like these romantic hearts best.

Cardboard
Ruffled lace (not eyelet):
   Sizes A and B, ¾-inch
   Size C (and larger), 1½- to 2-inch
Craft glue, hot glue gun (optional), scissors, toothpicks, paper towel
Spanish moss
Potpourri
Plain or picot ribbon:
   Sizes A and B, ⅛- or ¼-inch
   Size C (and larger), ½-inch
Greeting card or gift-wrapping paper for the back of the heart
Essential oil

1. Trace heart shape onto cardboard and cut out.

2. Glue lace as close to the edge of the cardboard as possible. Set aside to dry. (You can use a glue gun for larger sizes, but it will not work on the small hearts, because the lace will not lie flat enough.)

3. Drizzle craft glue over the entire face of the cardboard and on the edge of the lace that is glued to the cardboard. Use a toothpick to spread the glue evenly.

4. Pat a small amount of Spanish moss on top of the glue. Let it set for a few minutes, and then shake the excess off onto a paper towel.

5. Drizzle more craft glue on top of the Spanish moss. Sprinkle potpourri on and pat it down. Set the heart aside to dry overnight (or for 10 to 12 hours). I do these hearts production-style, so I can work on some while others are drying.

6. When heart is thoroughly dry, shake excess potpourri off onto a paper towel. Use this excess (and more if needed) to fill any indentations and/or bare spots. Again let heart dry thoroughly. If the heart has warped because you have used too much glue, carefully bend it back into shape.

7. To make a hanger for the heart, fold a 6- to 8-inch piece of ribbon in half, and glue the ends to the back side of the heart. Allow the glue to dry.

8. Glue a small picture from a greeting card or wrapping paper to the back of the heart to cover the ends of the hanger ribbon.

9. Make a small bow with streamers, and glue it to the top of the heart, on the lace. Allow the streamers to hang over the front of the heart. Add a few drops of fragrant oil to the top of the potpourri, as the natural scent will dissipate over time.

Jean Whitley, Endwell, NY 13760

CRAZY-QUILT HEART SACHETS

by Sally Booth-Brezina

SALLY BOOTH-BREZINA has been sewing items for sale since she was 12 years old. After obtaining a degree in Home Economics, she pursued a teaching career, which included a job as the national teaching director for a chain of craft stores. She then began a home business of designing and selling fragrant products. While living in Hawaii for a number of years, she served as president of the Pacific Handcrafters Guild and as an officer of the Kalani-anole Art League. As this book is going to print, Sally and her husband are moving back to the mainland, and she is undecided about the continuation of her business. Meanwhile, you will find many wonderful craft projects from her throughout the book, and should you want to know how to reach her to learn about her current offerings, send a SASE to me.

I love the look of the old crazy quilts, replete with ribbons, buttons, and decorative stitches. Wanting to share this Victorian "fancy" with others, I designed a Crazy-Quilt Heart Sachet. These are fun to make, and they use up scads of old fabric scraps. Although I make most of them of calico, I have recently started using more elegant fabrics, such as velvet and satin. Brocade fabrics become natural focal points, and moire taffeta adds visual texture, yet is easy to handle in the sewing machine. Although I charge much more for the velvet and satin ones, they sell as fast as I can make them. I point out that the lapped back seam makes it easy to re-scent the potpourri. Bits of lace may be inserted in the seams as you sew on the fabric scraps.

5½-inch square of light-colored muslin or sheeting fabric
Coordinating fabric scraps, thoroughly pressed
Lace scraps, beads, ribbons, or other embellishments

1. Cut a 5½-inch wide heart shape from the muslin.

2. Cut a triangle from a fabric scrap, and place it on the heart as shown in A. (Trim scraps as you work, to make them fit.)

3. Select a scrap large enough to cover the upper right of the heart, and place a straight edge against the upper right edge of the triangle, right sides together and edges even. If you would like some lace trim, sandwich it between the two scrap layers, with the raw edges of the lace lined up with the raw edges of the scraps. Machine stitch about ¼ inch away from raw edges (illustrated by dotted line in B).

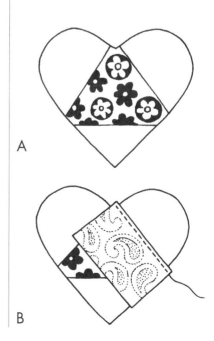

A

B

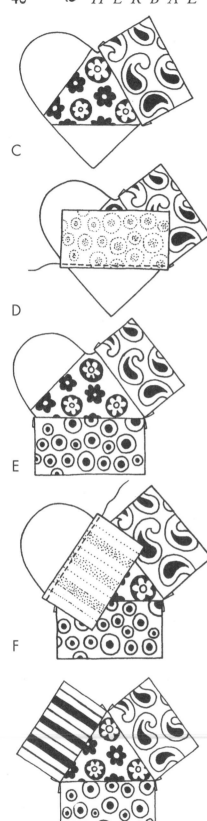

C

D

E

F

G

4. Fold over the scrap applied in Step 3 so that it is right side up (C). (The right sides of both fabric scraps are now exposed.) Press.

5. Select a scrap large enough to cover the lower point of the heart. Place a straight edge of this scrap against the lower edge of the triangle, and proceed as in Step 3. Fold the newly sewn scrap back, and press (D and E).

6. Select a scrap large enough to cover the upper left of the heart. Place a straight edge of this scrap against the upper left edge of the triangle, and proceed as in Step 3. Fold the newly sewn scrap back, and press (F and G). Trim the excess scraps so that their edges are even with the muslin backing.

7. Apply decorative hand and machine stitching, beads, ribbons, or other embellishments.

8. Select a fabric scrap for the backing of the heart. I often use a piece from the same fabric as one of the scraps on the front of the sachet. You will need one piece measuring 5½" x 6" and one piece 5½" x 7". Fold each piece in half with right sides out, so that you have one piece measuring 5½" x 3" and one piece 5½" x 3½".

9. Pin these two pieces together with folded edges overlapping 1 inch. Place the piece on your work surface with the wider piece on top of the narrower one, and the overlap running vertically. Place the crazy-quilt heart face down on top of the backing. Pin in place. Stitch all the way around the heart, ¼ inch from the edge.

10. Trim the excess backing so that the edges are even with the heart. Trim both edges to ⅛ inch at the point and at the V at the top of the heart. Clip the seam to the stitching at the V; do not cut the stitching.

11. Turn *only* one half of the heart right side out. Being careful not to push too hard, use a knitting needle (or something similar) to push out the point. Lightly fill this half of the heart with lavender, sachet base, or potpourri.

12. Turn the remaining fold over to expose the entire right side of the crazy-quilt heart. All seam edges are now enclosed. You may wish to hand stitch the straight back lap seam to keep the contents inside, as the overlap is minimal.

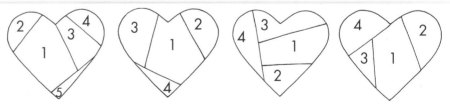

The diagrams above show other ways of attaching the fabric scraps. The numbers indicate the order in which the pieces are applied. Have fun experimenting with your own arrangements!

Heart Sachet with Easy Closure

by Sally Booth-Brezina

For those of you who try to hand-sew openings on the curved seams of hearts, circles, and oval sachets, this construction technique will be quite a change for the better. The closure is a lap seam on the back of the sachet, which results in perfect curves on the outside edge.

5" x 18" piece of fabric
Quilt batting (optional)
Pencil, chalk, or water-soluble pen
Lavender, sachet base, or potpourri

1. Place fabric on work surface with the length running top to bottom and the right side of the fabric up. Fold the top down, 6 inches from the top (A and B).

2. Fold half of the top flap back up, so that its edge is even with the first fold (C). Finger press.

3. Fold the bottom up, 7 inches from the bottom edge (D and E). Fold half of the bottom flap back, so that its edge is even with the fold on the bottom (F). Finger press.

4. If you are using batting, pin it to the wrong side of the unfolded portion of the fabric. I find that batting gives a smoother finish to the heart after it is stuffed.

5. Draw a 5-inch heart on the fabric.

6. Stitch entire outer edge (G). Trim the seam to ¼ inch. Trim the seam at the point and at the V to ⅛ inch. Clip seam at the V, being careful not to clip stitching.

7. Turn only the bottom half of the heart right side out. Use a knitting needle (or something similar) to push out the point. Be careful not to push too hard! Lightly fill this portion with lavender, sachet base, or potpourri.

8. Turn the remaining fold over to expose the entire right side of the heart, with all seam edges enclosed. If your potpourri mixture consists of small pieces, you may wish to hand stitch closed the straight, back lap seam. With normal use, large-sized potpourri will not come out of the heart.

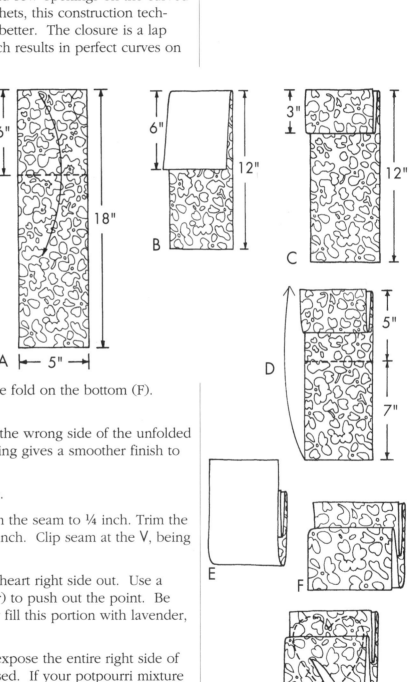

Sally Booth-Brezina

HERB AND FLOWER HEART WREATHS

by Cheryl Willson

I've always been inspired by hearts and flowers, so I came up with this design for my wreaths — and now herb and flower hearts are my trademark. Some of my favorite combinations for my wreaths are golden yarrow, ammobium, and rose hips with cream or rust ribbon; and pink acroclinium, white ammobium, and purple statice with pink or cream ribbon. Combining two ribbons of different colors on the larger wreaths is pretty, too.

Wire, in both a heavy (14-gauge) and a light weight (26- or 30-gauge)
White florist tape
Silver King artemisia or wormwood
Small dried flowers or seed heads, such as yarrow, ammobium, globe amaranth, rosehips, strawflowers, or statice
Narrow picot ribbon
Tacky glue

1. Form a heart from a piece of heavy wire. Make a hanger by fastening a piece of fine wire at the top of the heart, to make a little bridge across the cleft. This wire will later be concealed by flowers.

2. Wrap white florist tape all around the heart to make it less slippery.

3. Attach the Silver King artemisia or wormwood to the wire base by wrapping it spirally with fine wire.

4. Attach dainty seed heads, beginning at the center top and working down both sides. I prefer adding increasingly bushy pieces as I work down the sides to make the heart fuller at the bottom.

5. Wrap the heart with the narrow picot ribbon. End with a bow at the base. On the larger heart wreaths, I like to let long ends of ribbons hang free. Tuck in sprigs of Silver King to fill any sparse spots.

6. Add dried flowers for color and accent. Again, I like to use tiny ones at the top and larger ones toward the base; I also use more flowers at the bottom. Tacky glue makes this step easy.

This design makes charming smaller (5- or 8-inch) heart wreaths for wedding or shower decorations, centerpieces, or candle rings. (If you use dried flowers with candles, protect the flowers from flame with hurricane lamps, or do not light the candles.) For these small wreaths, I use preserved, double baby's-breath. Although these small, baby's-breath wreaths are rather tedious to make, they are very popular. Snip off baby's-breath blossoms with about 1 to 1¼ inches of stem — it takes *a lot* — and fasten these together in tiny bunches. Starting at the center top, wire these bunches to the heart base (I use 30-gauge wire for this), overlapping and covering the previous stems as you go. I add a bow at the base for a finishing touch. For wedding reception centerpieces, you could add ribbons, perhaps entwined around the wreaths, and a few dried flowers in colors to match the wedding color scheme.

One of my best sellers at craft fairs is a eucalyptus wreath — it is so easy to do, and it does not need any decoration. I weave the eucalyptus into a 3-D wire ring base until the wreath is nice and full. I also do smaller versions for candle rings in the same way. You can purchase eucalyptus dyed in several colors. For wedding decorations, choose ribbons and eucalyptus dyed to match the wedding color scheme — they will not only look wonderful, but they will fill the room with fragrance.

Artemisia *(Artemisia ludoviciana 'Silver King')*

Cheryl Willson, Blossoms 'N Spice, Shell Rock, IA 50670

LANGUAGE OF FLOWERS POTPOURRIS

❧ Get-Well Potpourri ❧

A thoughtful gift that sends to a hospitalized friend a message of compassion and good wishes through the language of flowers

⅓ cup cedar chips
1 tablespoon cellulose granules
½ teaspoon ambergris or light musk oil
¼ teaspoon lavender oil
¼ teaspoon lemon oil
2 droppers ambergris or light musk oil
2 cups feverfew flowers (for healing)
1½ cups lavender flowers (for protection)
1 cup calendula flowers (for renewed good health)
⅔ cup eucalyptus leaves (a get well wish)
½ cup chamomile flowers (for patience)
½ cup pine needles (for hope in adversity)
3 tablespoons allspice berries, crushed (for compassion)
½ cup lemon peel (for renewed zest)

Mix together the cedar chips, cellulose granules, and the ambergris or musk, lavender, and lemon oils. Allow these fixatives and oils to blend for a few days before adding them to the rest of the ingredients.

BOB CLARK gives the following helpful advice for potpourri making: Always blend oils and fixatives in a separate, covered container at least 2 days before adding the rest of the dried materials; this waiting period gives the oils a good chance to be absorbed and blended, thus assuring a longer-lasting aroma. If a potpourri that contains a good deal of lavender also calls for citrus peel, orange peel may make the blend too sweet, whereas lemon will tone it down. Feel free to experiment with the following recipes, trying out your own combinations of essential oils. You can make up mixtures of different oils combined with the orrisroot and then divide your dried materials into three or four batches; add a different oil mixture to each of the batches.

❧ Sweetheart Potpourri ❧

½ cup orrisroot, cut and sifted (meaning angelic)
Rose and/or other essential oils of herbs, woods, flowers, and/or citrus
4 cups red and/or pink rosebuds and petals (for love)
1½ cups lemon verbena leaves (for delicacy of feeling)
1 cup orange petals (for purity and loveliness)
1 cup jasmine flowers (for grace)
1 cup rose geranium leaves (for preference)
2 tablespoons allspice berries, crushed (meaning precious)
2 or 3 whole nutmegs, crushed (for intoxicating love)
½ cup myrrh gum, cut and sifted (for adoration)

For more Victoriana, see June, with its ideas for herbal weddings and herbal tea parties. PVS

BOB CLARK, LANCASTER, OH 43130

Mix together the orrisroot and the essential oils, and allow them to blend for about 2 days. Mix in the rest of the ingredients.

The entire HARTMAN family is involved in their herb business. They were the first to publish an annual herb calendar, featuring monthly recipes, crafts, and gardening tips — and beautiful artwork. They sell herb plants and products by mail and at the farm.

FROM *HARTMAN'S 1985 HERBAL CALENDAR*
LYNN HARTMAN, HARTMAN'S HERB FARM, BARRE, MA 01005

❧ Cranberry-Raspberry Valentine Punch ❧

This punch is delicious warm or cold. If you prefer a cool drink, chill it in the refrigerator and serve it with an ice ring or ice cubes.

5 cinnamon sticks
1 teaspoon whole cloves
1 tablespoon dried (or 4 tablespoons fresh) peppermint or orange mint

½ gallon cranberry-raspberry juice
1 quart ginger ale
1 orange, thinly sliced

Wrap the cinnamon sticks, cloves, and mint in cheesecloth. Simmer this bundle in the cranberry-raspberry juice for 20 minutes. Remove the spices and pour the warm juice in a punch bowl. Add the ginger ale, orange slices, and a few fresh mint leaves.

❧ *Everlastings for Romantic Crafts* ❧

I had so enjoyed preserving and using many of my herbs (such as lavender, the silver artemisias, lunaria, lamb's-ears, and yarrow) that I wanted to grow other plants to add color and texture to my wreaths and arrangements. Five years ago, before I was aware of the profusion of books and material on the subject, I used the Park's Seed Catalog as my reference, and the visual material and thorough growing instructions on their seed packages guided me through the start. I then learned of Jim and Dottie Becker's book on everlastings (see page 49), and this was all I needed to round out my knowledge and help me through the harvest procedures. Since then, many other fine books on the subject have come out, some with full-color photographs or sketches. Since growing procedures, harvesting times, and drying methods vary for the different varieties of everlastings, I recommend that you invest in a couple of these guides to familiarize yourself both with the large variety of everlastings available and with each plant's unique growing and harvesting requirements.

My first year, starting in

February or March, depending on the instructions for the individual plants, I sowed everlasting seeds under lights and ended up with more plants than the cold frame could hold for the hardening-off process in late spring. (The overflow ended up under the picnic table, which was covered with tarps each night.) Of the perennials (which require a great deal of patience because they do not bloom the first year), I started out with about a dozen each of German statice, sea lavender, and gypsophila (baby's-breath). I still have at least eight of each to enjoy and harvest every year. The German statice did not bloom at all the third year, which I understand was due to an unusually warm preceding winter; a long cold spell is required to insure blooms. And, last summer, when we had a cool, wet August, the plants seemed to stop blooming at the halfway point. In my experience, perennial statice is the most temperamental, yet worth the space given to it.

We created two separate beds (5' x 20' each) for the everlastings, one for the gypsophila alone. (I had planted several varieties of baby's-breath, and all survived the first winter except the one kind I wanted the most, the double variety. This was before I had read the Beckers' book, which warns that this variety does not do well from seed. But the pink variety and the star-shaped gypsophilas are lovely in the garden.) It was a lot easier to be patient about the nonblooming perennials the first year, because we interplanted the two beds with several annual everlastings, which provided color and excitement throughout the summer. Since the annuals had been provided a head start indoors in the spring, there was something blooming constantly in the new beds, and except for the annual statice, the more flowers we picked, the more that grew. Annual statice is available in lovely pastel colors and the plumed and crested celosias come in gorgeous jewel-like hues. All of these can be quickly and easily harvested and dried. We hung most of them in bunches from our clothes-drying racks. The larger-crested (or cockscomb) celosias dry well when hung individually, with either heavy wire or inverted large paper clips strung through them. Strawflowers and globe amaranth are easy annuals to grow, but I haven't repeated these each year simply because of the lack of time to watch them carefully for the right moment to harvest and then to pre-wire the stems of those that need reinforcement, before drying.

I have found that having all the everlastings together in their own beds has made it easier to keep track of the correct blooming and harvesting times, as most need to be picked just before they open in full bloom. Last year, when we were ordering seeds for flowers to match my daughter's wedding color scheme, I learned of an exciting new development. One can now get the seeds of some everlastings in just one color, rather than in mixed packages. For instance, we were able to grow very gold-crested celosia, thanks to Catnip Acres Herb Farm. Exciting new colors, such as orange and bright red globe amaranths, and apricot and peach shades of annual statice and celosias, are being developed by several of the firms mentioned in the resource section on everlastings in the Appendix.

One is rewarded over and over with everlasting flowers, first in the garden and then in decorative creations for years to come. A favorite from my original harvest is in a low, open basket mounded almost to the basket handle in the center with Sahara (the special material Oasis developed for dried materials). Brilliant red, orange, and gold cockscomb celosias cover the mound of Sahara with insertions of matching-colored bergamot flowers, roses, strawflowers, and tansy buds between the crested celosias. This basket shouts of fall harvest and color, and becomes the first centerpiece to come out of storage each autumn to celebrate the harvest and to signal the beginning of the Thanksgiving season.

Everlastings can be stored for years and will maintain their colors. I was able to use 5-year-old strawflowers and plumed celosia in decorations for my daughter's wedding! (Details about Kim's "everlasting" wedding are in the June chapter.) Each year I still use Christmas wreaths made from my first everlasting harvest several years ago. These are simply stored in boxes at the end of the holiday season. If kept out of sunlight, everlasting creations are just that. They are, however, a little worse for wear, and so I will celebrate completing this book by growing a whole new batch of these useful plants and designing brand new decorations for our home for the next few years!

BARBARA RADCLIFFE ROGERS *has been a prolific contributor to my newsletter for several years, so you will find a great deal of interesting material from her throughout these chapters. It was such a delight to meet this talented crafter and writer at the Canterbury Shaker Fair in New Hampshire. She has authored many books on herbs and related subjects, most recently* The Encyclopaedia of Everlastings *and* Fresh Herbs. *Autographed copies of both are available directly from her.*

In their book A Concise Guide to Growing Everlastings, JIM AND DOTTI BECKER *advise that the only variety of baby's-breath that is an excellent everlasting is* Gypsophila paniculata, *of which the most popular cultivars are Bristol Fairy and Perfecta, and that the best flowers are obtained from root grafting or tissue culture, rather than from seeds. It is best, therefore, to purchase plants of these varieties.*

DRIED FLOWERS AND HERBS AT HERBITAGE FARM

by Barbara Radcliffe Rogers

Nowadays, everyone wants casual little bunches of dried flowers lying in baskets, standing in crocks, or hanging from the rafters. Whether you need long-stemmed flowers for arrangements or medium-length stems for small basket arrangements, nearly all flowers grown to be dried are harvested just short of full bloom. Annual statice is an exception, and needs to be picked at full flower. The best way to dry most flowers is by hanging them in a shady, airy place. Statice that has been dried in bundles, however, often has intertwining stems that are hard to separate without breakage when dry. Laying the stems out flat prevents this, but it takes a lot of space.

The following plants that dry well are grouped generally by color. Your garden and roadsides can probably already supply you with an abundance of material for your own arrangements or for gifts or sale.

WHITE

Pearly everlasting. These are common wayside plants of the *Gnaphalium* genus. They should be picked while blossoms are still quite compact, since they will open out and go to seed as they dry if bloom is too far along. Be sure to leave a few clumps of flowers to go to seed in each location when you pick, since these are annuals or biennials, depending on the variety. It is worthwhile trying to cultivate these, as they are very popular.

Baby's-breath. There are several varieties of *Gypsophila*, and you should plant those with the largest flowers — the so-called "double" varieties — which are perennials. They become rather large bushes when in bloom, so leave space. Don't crowd baby's-breath when you dry it. Also comes in pink.

German statice. This is the perennial variety with very stiff, widely-branched stems. It is well worth cultivating, *but will not bloom the first year.* Instead of hanging this very branchy plant to dry, I simply lay it on the floor for a few days and then pack it in boxes until I need it.

Lunaria (Honesty). Biennials such as this should be planted each year to assure a steady crop. This will be one of your most popular plants, so be prepared!

PINK AND PURPLE

Sea lavender. Many confuse this with German statice, but sea lavender is actually quite different, with fine stems and tiny lavender blossoms. It thrives in tidal areas where the seawater covers it at high tide.

Pot marjoram. This variety is worthless as a flavoring, but it produces beautiful clusters of pink to magenta flowers, which dry very well. You don't even have to hang them — just stand them in vases and enjoy!

Delphinium. The dark blue varieties of this tall perennial dry best. You can dry the whole spike by laying it on its side, or you can pick individual blossoms and dry them face down on a screen. Each blossom has a good stem and can be wired later. The latter system allows you to take full advantage of every flower, since the bottom ones usually fade and fall before those at the top have bloomed. Also, by picking the June blossoms before any can go to seed, you might get a second blooming in early fall.

Scotch thistle. The hardest part of drying this popular perennial is catching it at the right time. The flower heads must have turned blue, but not be overbloomed, or they will fall apart as they dry.

YELLOW AND ORANGE

Marguerite (Dyer's marguerite). A pleasant perennial to grow. Dry it in bunches by hanging; then simply pull the dried petals off to leave the large, yellow buttons.

Goldenrod. This common field flower dries beautifully if picked before full bloom. Its tall spikes are perfect in arrangements, and its individual sprigs work well in wreaths.

Costmary. I grew this for years before it flowered. What a pleasant surprise, as its tall stems produce clusters of tiny, yellow buttons that dry to a creamy yellow.

Tansy **(Tanacetum vulgare).** This is a plant well worth growing, both for its beautiful clusters of yellow buttons and for its foliage, which is a moth preventative. Look for it growing wild in coastal areas, where it grows in great clumps.

Yarrow. Although this is also available in pink, it is more prolific in yellow, which also keeps its color better. Allow it room, and the clumps will expand each year. Cut when just short of full bloom.

Chinese lantern. Be careful where you plant these or they will take over your garden! The scraggly stems are hard to dry, because the lanterns stand at an unusual angle if dried upside down. I sell these mostly to wreathmakers, who clip off the lanterns anyway, so perhaps the easiest way to dry them is individually. Bright orange in full bloom, these can be harvested in the green stage.

GREEN AND GRAY

Silver King and Silver Queen artemisia. I have planted this around the edges of our garden, where it helps hide the wire fence and also helps stop grass invasion. But no matter how much of it I plant, I can't harvest enough of it. I suggest you plant all of this you can, since it is the best base for herbal wreaths, and wreathmakers need a lot of it. Although it is invasive, it spreads

The Park Seed Catalog sheds some light on the difference between German statice and sea lavender. It groups all statice as sea lavender or Limonium, *described as "showy perennials in the garden, excellent for fresh or dried bouquets." Under it are listed* latifolia, *2-foot lavender plants;* tatarica *(German statice) 20-inch silvery white plants with extremely large flower heads; and* perezii, *long stems branching at the top with large flower heads of lavender to bright blue.* JIM AND DOTTI BECKER *explain that German statice is closely allied to members of the* Limonium *genus, and was once classified in that genus. But the botanists have changed their minds, and it is now officially* Goniolimon tataricum, *even though still referred to as* Limonium ataricum *in most books and catalogs Hope this helps clarify the problem. PVS*

❤

Tansy is toxic to cattle; do not plant where cattle graze. Also, Tanacetum vulgare *is not the same as ragwort, which is very toxic to animals. In the Northwest states, ragwort is called tansy because of the physical resemblances, and landowners are fined if this tansy is growing on their property! PVS*

Germander *(Teucrium chamaedrys)*

Wish I had known this trick about wiring strawflowers earlier! I spent much of one summer pushing the wire all the way through the flower, forming a hook at the top, and carefully pulling it all back to lock it into place. These flower heads should be picked before they are fully open, or they will fall apart when dry. PVS

only in the early spring, when it can be easily stopped by pulling up the shoots. When you pull them, try to get some root, and transplant it elsewhere. Since this is often used fresh, have your customers lined up ahead and call them when it is ready — when the flower buds are their whitest. Dry any remainder by hanging in bunches.

Other herbs. Bay, sage, thyme, boxwood, and germander all dry well, but are easier to use fresh while stems are still supple. All are dried by hanging upside down in bunches. *(Flowering basils, mints, oregano, too. PVS)*

Lamb's-ears (Woolly betony). Fresh or dried, these pleasingly furry leaves give a wonderful dimension to wreaths. Somewhat hard to hang, lamb's-ears can be picked separately and laid on screens to dry.

MIXED COLORS

Strawflowers. By far the brightest and most varied of the dried flowers, these are easy to grow from seed or nursery plants. Each annual plant will produce dozens of flowers, which are clipped off their stems right at the base of the flower to allow other buds to develop. Wire them immediately to provide stems. Simply push the floral wire into the cut end of the stem where it will stick tight as the blossom dries.

Annual statice. Because of its bright colors and long, strong stems, this is a big seller. Purple and pink move fast, as will white if it develops full blossoms. You can sell it right from the garden, since it can be used immediately, or you can hang it to dry. Bunches of these are probably the most beautiful of all the drying flowers, so people will often want them to hang them on the kitchen rafters. *(A very easy way to dry a cluster of these stems is to loop them over the rungs of a clothes-drying rack. PVS)*

Globe amaranth. These look like clover and come in a range of colors from cream to deep magenta. They are annuals and need to be picked all summer. The stems are fairly short but can be wired to florist picks or longer stem wires.

Plume celosia. This is one of the few plants that will give you a true red, along with a variety of oranges, yellows, and pinks. If you pick the center plume, side plumes will form. Blossoms are easy to wire.

BROWNS

Teasel. It is sometimes hard to get this annual going, but it is worth the trouble. Let the flower heads dry on the stem before picking them.

Bee balm. Let the seed heads form after the blossoms drop, and cut, keeping a long stem.

Field and garden. There are a number of grasses and grains you will find by the roadside in the fall, along with dock, shepherd's purse, and others. Check your perennial flower garden for the seeds of wild iris, Oriental poppy, delphinium (unless you picked the blossoms), and others. These browns give wonderful contrast to your mixed bouquets, as well as helping to stretch your more precious flowers.

BARBARA RADCLIFFE ROGERS, HERBITAGE FARM, RICHMOND, NH 03470

A Year in Our Garden

by Jim and Dottie Becker

There is no beginning or end in a garden. It is a continuous cycle of the seasons, and there is something to do in every month of the year. It is the balance of growth and dormancy, hectic activity and relaxation, that sustains both the garden and the gardener. Our quiet time is the dark month of December. It is then that we sort and catalog our seeds and order any others that will be needed. The excitement and anticipation of the new season begins as the old one has scarcely ended.

When nice weather appears in January, we begin to tidy up the garden. Leaves are raked into the compost pile, and branches that were blown down by winter storms are removed. In February, the perennial plants are cut back and the task of spring weeding is begun. All perennial flower beds are weeded and fertilized during February and March, just as they are beginning to emerge from the ground. We start many of our perennial plant seeds in the greenhouse in late January and the earliest of our annuals in March. By mid-April, all of our flower seeds have been planted indoors.

We begin to prepare our annual flower beds as early as the weather permits, generally in late March, and this task is often not completed until the first of May. The seeds of love-in-a-mist and safflower are sown directly outdoors in late April. Perennials and hardy annuals that have been started in the greenhouse are also set outdoors in late April, followed by the half-hardy annuals in mid-May and the tender annuals in late May or early June.

June is the month for watering, weeding, and waiting. We begin to harvest our perennials in late June, and most are finished blooming by the end of July. The hardy annuals begin to flower lightly just as the perennials are ending, and this is one of the most beautiful times for the garden. By mid-July all of the annuals have swung us into hectic activity that is non-stop harvesting. Watering, weeding, and harvesting continue right up until October.

We begin to make our handcrafted items as soon as a wide variety of flowers becomes available, and we continue this activity throughout the rest of the year. Meanwhile, as each plant species ends its flowering cycle, it is cut back (if a perennial) or tilled under (if an annual), and a winter cover crop is planted in each fallow bed. Then, as the rains of autumn begin and the frost nips the plants, we settle in for another winter and begin again our longing for spring.

FROM *A CONCISE GUIDE TO GROWING EVERLASTINGS*
JIM AND DOTTIE BECKER, GOODWIN CREEK GARDENS, WILLIAMS, OR 97544

PATTERN FOR VICTORIAN POTPOURRI HEART ORNAMENT (PAGES 37-38).
This heart may also be useful for other projects in the book.

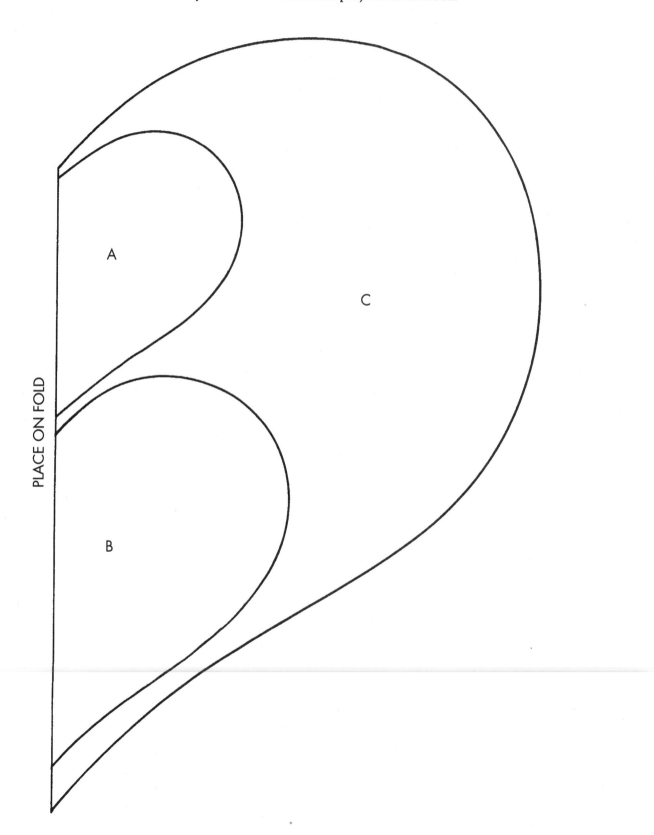

MARCH

NOW THAT OUR HEADS are full of exciting new projects relating to herbal health and beauty, everlasting romance, and the charm of yesteryear, it's high time to get back to earth and down to the basics — the herbs in our gardens, the plants we live, work, and play with on a daily basis. Spirits are raised at the earliest hints of spring, and on the first pleasant days we will be outside again, cleaning up the beds and plotting out new gardens or, at least, spaces for new herbs. It is also the zero hour to order the seeds or plants of the new or different herbs we want to try this year (if we didn't do it on January 2nd).

If you live in the snowbelt and did your hoe-work last fall, any new beds will have been dug up then, the soil will have been tested and corrected for pH level, and the necessary lime and loam, compost and ashes will have been hoed or rototilled in, to benefit from the winter snows. And, now, after one or two more tillings or hoeings as soon as the soil can be "worked," and the addition of any needed fertilization, there is nothing left to do but the fun part — planting the herbs. However, if you're like most of us, you did not spend last November preparing new beds, so you will start digging them up as soon as the soil is not too heavy, and then keep working up the soil and adding nutrients and fillers for the next two months.

In this chapter, you may contemplate simple to sublime garden designs. In addition, the February chapter contains some Victorian garden plans, and the June chapter, some wedding gardens. I offered several more basic garden plans in my first book, The Pleasure of Herbs. Many excellent sources of herb plants and seeds are listed in the Appendix. You should have catalogs from each source in your herb library, for most offer hundreds of varieties of herbs and exciting new plants, and many are informative reference guides. In the pages that follow, you will find a summary of the

new and different herbs that we have recently grown and enjoyed, followed by several in-depth articles from experts about some "new" herbs (to Americans), some newly developed varieties, and some old, but forgotten herbs that have been rediscovered. Hundreds of varieties of herbs are out there awaiting your acquaintance and delight.

Landscaping your property with herbs depends upon your climate, terrain, space, exposure to sun, and soil consistency, as well as your own needs and interests. When planning your herb garden(s), as with any garden, learn about the heights and widths of the individual plants at maturity (the best seed/ plant catalogs will give this information) and plot your garden on paper accordingly, leaving enough space for each plant and keeping the taller plants in the background so they won't shield the lower ones from the sun. *Intersperse varying colors, textures, and accent plants for visual interest. Plant at least three of each plant, so that you will achieve a concentrated rather than a haphazard effect. Consider the needs of the plants. One certainly wouldn't put sweet woodruff, which requires a pH soil acidity of between 4.5 and 5.5 and will thrive in a shady spot, in the same bed with lavender, which must have an alkaline soil (pH level of 7.0 to 7.5) and full sun for optimum growth. The great majority of herbs will live happily in the sun in a slightly acid-to-neutral soil, between pH 6.0 and 7.0, and many will tolerate a 5.0 to 6.0 pH (except for anise, fennel, lavender, and winter savory). On the other end of the spectrum, cassia, henna, horehound, sage, sweet basil, watercress, wintergreen, and yarrow will tolerate soils as acidic as pH 4.5. (See pages 248-49 for information about adding* limestone to correct your soil.)

If you are going to start from scratch and need thorough information about individual herbs and their requirements, I urge you to purchase at least one of the excellent landscaping books listed on page 296. Even if you are not planning new gardens, these books are invaluable for their cross-reference guides, which list both botanical and common names for just about every herb and variety of herb available. In this chapter, to get you started, I have listed groups of herbs that may suit your special needs or interests for specific beds or locations on your property. The lists are not all-inclusive, but should at least give you some food for thought.

Lastly, in this chapter you will find some marvelous gardening and propagating advice and guidance from those-in-the-know. Now that the prodigal sun has returned, rejoice and start digging!

LANDSCAPING AND DESIGNING WITH HERBS

The following lists are not all-inclusive, but I hope they are meaningful enough to inspire your own research and creativity. See the Appendix for suggested further reading, as well as sources of herb seeds and plants.

Specific Herbs For Special Locations and Individual Interests

HERBS FOR PARTIAL SHADE

Aconite
Angelica
Bee balm
Borage
Carpet bugleweed
Chervil
Chives
Comfrey
Common (or sweet) violet
Coneflower
Costmary
English pennyroyal
Fennel
French tarragon
Good-King-Henry
Lady's-mantle
Lemon balm
Liatris
Lily-of-the-valley
Lovage
Lungwort
Mints (not Catnip)
Mother-of-thyme
Parsley
Roman chamomile
Running myrtle
St.-John's-wort
Snakeroot
Sweet cicely
Sweet flag
Sweet woodruff
Valerian
Wild ginger
Wintergreen
Wormwood
Yarrow

HERBS FOR ROCK GARDENS

Artemisia (Silver Mound)
Basils
Bedstraw
Burnet
Calendula
Catmint
Chamomiles
Chives
Clove pink
Costmary
Curry plant
Dittany
Garlic chives
Germander
Golden oregano
Golden, red, or silver sage
Horehound
Hyssop
Lady's-mantle
Lavender
Lavender cotton
Mints
Pansy
Parsley
Pennyroyal
Rosemary
Saffron
Santolina
Southernwood
Scented geraniums
Sweet marjoram
Thymes
Violet
Wild ginger

GROUND COVER HERBS

Bedstraw (sun)
Carpet bugleweed (sun or partial shade)
Catmint (part shade)
Catnip (sun)
Chamomile, Roman (sun)
Coltsfoot (sun, in waste places)
Common violet (part shade)
Creeping thymes (sun)
Dead nettle (sun)
Ground ivy (sun or part shade, in waste areas)
Lady's-mantle (shade)
Lavender cotton (sun)
Lily-of-the-valley (shade)
Mints (sun or shade)
Oregano (sun)
Pennyroyal (part shade)
Running myrtle (shade)
Sweet woodruff (part shade)
Wild ginger (part shade)
Wintergreen (shade)
Woolly betony (sun)
Wormwood (part shade)

HERBS FOR BONSAI

Dwarf lavender
Hyssop
Rosemary
Rue

HERBS FOR CONTAINERS

Alliums
Artemisia (Silver Mound)
Basils
Bay
Calendula
Chamomiles
Chives
Clove pink
Curry plant
Dill
Dittany
Garlic
Garlic chives
Hyssop
Lavender
Lavender cotton
Lemon balm
Lemon catnip
Lemon verbena
Lime balm
Marjoram
Marigold
Mignonette
Mints
Oregano
Pansy
Parsley
Pennyroyal
Rosemary
Rue
Saffron
Sage
Savory
Scented geraniums
Thymes
Violet
Wormwood

Specific Herbs For Special Locations (continued)

HERBS FOR HEDGES OR HIGH EDGINGS

Bay (in hot climates)
English lavender
Fernleaf tansy
Feverfew
Germander
Hyssop
Lemon balm
Lemon verbena
Lovage
Roman wormwood
Rosemary (in hot
    climates)
Rue
Scented basils (holy,
    anise, licorice,
    cinnamon)
Southernwood
Sweet Annie

HERBS FOR LOW EDGINGS

Beach wormwood
Carpet bugleweed
Catmint
Chives
Clove pink
Dead nettle
Dwarf basils
Germander
Parsley
Pennyroyal
Sweet woodruff
Upright thyme
Winter savory

HERBS TO SCREEN AN UNSIGHTLY AREA

Bee balm
Comfrey
Fennel
Valerian
White mugwort
Yarrow

A FRAGRANCE GARDEN

Catmint
Chamomile
Clove pink
Coriander
Costmary
Creeping santolina
Curry plant
Dill
Fennel
Hyssop
Lady's-mantle
Lavender
Lemon balm
Lemon verbena
Lime balm
Mignonette
Mints
Oregano
Patchouli
Pennyroyal
Rosemary
Sages
Savory
Scented basils
Scented geraniums
Southernwood
Sweet cicely
Sweet flag
Sweet marjoram
Tansy
Thymes
Valerian
Violets

HERBS FOR A POND GARDEN

Angelica
Chives
Japanese parsley
Lemon balm
Lovage
Sweet flag
Valerian
Watercress

A POTPOURRI GARDEN

Ambrosia
Anise hyssop
Bay
Bergamot
Chamomile
Clary sage (fixative)
Clevelandii sage (fixa-
    tive)
Clove pink
Fennel
Florentine iris
    (orrisroot)(fixative)
Lavender
Lemon balm
Lemongrass
Lemon thyme
Lemon verbena
Lime balm
Orange bergamot mint
Patchouli
Peppermint
Pineapple sage
Roses
Scented basils
Scented geraniums
Southernwood
Spearmint
Sweet flag (calamus)
    (fixative)
Sweet marjoram
Sweet violet
Sweet woodruff
Vetiver root
    (khus-khus)

A SHAKESPEARE GARDEN

Bay
Calendula
Garlic
Lemon balm
Pansy
Poppy
Rosemary

A BEE GARDEN

Anise hyssop
Bee balm
Borage
Comfrey
Creeping santolina
Fenugreek
German chamomile
Horehound
Hyssop
Lemon balm
Mints
Oregano
Pennyroyal
Sage
Sweet basil
Thymes
Winter savory
Woolly betony

SILVER-GRAY HERBS

Artemisias (Silver
    Beacon, Silver King,
    Silver Queen)
Catmint
Clove pink
Curry plant
Dittany
Everlasting
Fringed and Roman
    wormwood
Horehound
Lamb's-ears
Lamium (Silver Beacon)
Lavender
Lavender cotton
Sages
Sea holly
Silver sage
Silver thyme
Woolly betony
Woolly lavender

Specific Herbs For Special Locations (continued)

HERBS FOR A SALAD GARDEN

Anise (leaves)
Basil (leaves)
Borage (leaves)
Burnet (leaves)
Calendula (petals)
Chervil (leaves)
Chicory, or witloof (leaves)
Chive (leaves, blossoms)
Dill (leaves, umbrels)
Fennel (leaves, umbrels)
Garlic chives
Good-King-Henry (leaves)
Lamb's-quarters (leaves)
Leek (leaves)
Lemon balm (leaves)
Lemon catnip
Lime balm (leaves)
Lovage (leaves)
Marjoram (leaves)
Mints (leaves)
Mustard (white, young seedlings)
Nasturtium (leaves, petals)
Oregano (leaves)
Parsley (leaves)
Rose (petals)
Savory (leaves)
Shallot
Sorrel (leaves)
Sweet violet (petals)
Tarragon (leaves)
Thyme (leaves)
Watercress

HERBS & PLANTS FOR A DYER'S GARDEN*

Agrimony
Bay
Bedstraw
Bloodroot
Blue iris
Blueberry
Brown-eyed-Susan
Butterfly weed
Catnip
Chrysanthemum
Clematis
Coreopsis
Cornflower
Elderberry
Golden marguerite
Goldenrod
Indian paintbrush
Lady's-mantle
Lily-of-the-valley
Marigold
Mullein
Parsley
Pearly everlasting
Queen-Anne's-lace
Red clover
Rhubarb
Rue
Safflower
St. John's-wort
Scotch broom
Sunflower
Tansy
Teasel
Weld
Wild oregano (Pot marjoram)
Woad
Zinnia

See also "Planting a Dyer's Garden," pages 59-64

HERBS FOR A TEA GARDEN

Agrimony
Angelica
Anise (seeds)
Anise hyssop
Basils
Bergamot
Calendula (petals)
Caraway (seeds)
Catmint
Catnip
Chamomile
Costmary
Dill (seeds)
Fennel (seeds)
Garden sage
Horehound
Lemon balm
Lemon-scented marigold
Lemon verbena
Lime balm
Lovage
Mints
Pennyroyal (do not use if you are pregnant)
Rosehips
Rosemary
Saffron
Scented geraniums (rose and lemon)
Sweet marjoram
Thymes
Wintergreen
Yarrow

BIBLICAL HERBS*

Aloe
Anise
Coriander
Costmary
Cumin
Garlic
Hyssop
Lady's bedstraw
Mandrake
Mint
Mustard
Nigella
Pasqueflower
Rose
Rosemary
Rue
Saffron
Sesame
Wormwood

See "A Biblical Harvest" in the September chapter for a more complete list of herbs from the Bible.

Herb Flowers for Color-Coordinated Gardens

PINK	Fenugreek • Dittany-of-Crete • Hollyhock • Hyssop • Clove pink • Cat thyme • Damask rose • Foxglove • English pennyroyal • Dwarf monarda • Basils (dark opal, thrysiflora, purple, holy, cinnamon)
ROSE	Giant allium • Cardoon • Betony • Sesame
ROSE-LAVENDER	Heliotrope • Chives • Purple coneflower • Pasqueflower • Saffron
RED	Bergamot • Cardinal flower • Hollyhock • Scarlet pimpernel • Roses • Pineapple sage • Crimson thyme • Nasturtium
ORANGE	Butterfly weed • Calendula • Coltsfoot • Nasturtium • Elecampane
YELLOW	Nasturtium • Goldenrod • Santolina • Tansy • Primrose • Mignonette • St.-John's-wort • Yellow flag • Silver germander • Witch hazel • Rue • Bedstraw • Yarrow • Lady's-mantle • Evening primrose • Calendula • Curry plant • Dill
WHITE	Garlic chives • Angelica • Chamomiles • Camphor plant • Boneset • Feverfew • Lily-of-the-valley • White mugwort • White yarrow • Dropwort • White flag • Roses • Basils (sweet, lemon, bush) • Florentine iris (orrisroot) • German statice • Pineapple mint • Sweet cicely
BLUE	Sage • Clevelandii sage • Anise hyssop • Dwarf catnip • Rosemary • Cornflower • Chicory • Love-in-a-mist • Borage • Lungwort • Dwarf Russian comfrey • Hyssop • Blue flag • False indigo • Larkspur • Pansy
PURPLE	Lavenders • Violets • Ajuga • Catmint • Oregano • Wild bergamot • Oregano thyme • Saffron • Pansy • Spearmint • Peppermint • Black peppermint • Orange mint
PURPLE-ROSE	Germander • Annual clary sage • Annual statice • Joe-Pye weed • Pyrethrum • Rosey yarrow • Valerian

EXTERIOR DESIGN IN A RE-"MARK"-ABLE HERB GARDEN

by Jan Powers

My love of decorating has expanded to include my yard, and especially my herb gardens. Designing and creating a garden is a real challenge and a wonderful chance to be creative in a whole new way. The gardens that surround the outside of my home are an important part of my environment, and since I spend a lot of time in them doing all the "dirty work" that gardens require, I like to have fun with the landscape, too.

I have an affinity for old garden statuary, especially statues of baby animals, and I also like to incorporate primitive wood pieces into my gardens. The focal point of my "Old-Fashioned Herb Garden" is an old stone well, with catmint and oregano around the base and nasturtiums in the center. Above the nasturtiums hangs an old oaken bucket, deep purple pansies cascading over its sides. Climbing up the sides of the well is an ancient trumpet vine that invites hummingbirds to visit all summer long. Near the well is a 60-year-old espaliered pear tree. Stone statuary, including bunnies, a toad, and a meditating cherub, nestle among the herbs, and an old washtub beneath the downspout catches the rainwater in one corner. In the background are a potting shed (once an outhouse) and a scarecrow by the fence. The garden plants themselves are a collection of medicinal and dye plants, as well as of other herbs associated with folklore and legend. One bed consists of "witches' herbs," another of different thymes. Among the herbs are mallow, vervain, yarrow, woundwort, lady's-mantle, wormwood, mugwort, woodruff, mints, calendula, violets, spiderwort, wood germander, mullein, horehound, evening primrose, rose campion, pennyroyal, bedstraw, and soapwort. Garden ornaments among these herbs are very primitive. A tree trunk holding a birdbath is central to one bed and a wooden sundial graces another.

My "Sampler Bed" is always changing. Ornamented by a crabapple espalier, beehive, and urns, the herbs include scented geraniums, rue, lemon thyme, garlic chives, hyssop, catmint, digitalis, winter savory, chamomile, lavender, valerian, southernwood, sweet marjoram, pearl yarrow, *Rosa rugosa*, and several basils. Visitors to my herb shop are always welcome to pinch off small pieces of these herbs and sniff their distinctive fragrances.

In the front of the house, a perennial border sports a horse hitching post and a very old, dark green lamppost, which we brought from our old neighborhood as a souvenir. Rounded mounds of Autumn Joy sedum (sometimes called Live Forever) share this border with hollyhocks, Russian sage, garden sage, blue salvia, baby's-breath, globe thistle, mums, fairy roses, coreopsis, Silver King artemisia, lamb's-ears, shasta daisy, black-eyed-Susan, Roman wormwood, and feverfew.

Since my gardens are intended to inspire and educate others, I take care to label the herbs and flowers. To make these labels aesthetically pleasing, I use pieces of old, black roofing slate, carefully broken into the desired size and cleaned with soap and water. On the black slate, I like the look of white or gray lettering, done in acrylic paints or permanent paint markers. For a particular theme garden, you could use a whole slate, with a stenciled design in addition to the title of the garden. A stenciled tussie mussie, for instance, is a charming marker for a "Fragrant Garden," and a teacup and saucer is appropriate for a "Tea Garden." (See page 58 for instructions on making your own markers.)

BEE SKEP IN CHAMOMILE

I love the look of bee skeps in an herb garden. When people see the primitive, graying basket nestled among the lush, green herbs, they often ask, "Are there any bees in there?" I explain that the bee skep is a traditional accent for an herb garden,

JAN POWER'S booklet Decorating with Herb Stencils *contains full-size patterns, related herbal facts and fantasy, and creative ideas on how to use them. Available from the author (see Appendix for address). Send a SASE for a price list, which includes prices for her book and pre-cut Mylar designer stencils of herb medleys, beam bundles, and flowering herbs.*

Vervain *(Verbena officinalis)*

Bee: Black and yellow

Bee skep: Antique gold or gray-brown

Chamomile blossoms: White with yellow center

Leaves and stems: Olive green

Platform: Black or dark brown

Herbal Honey

Place a fresh, washed leaf of rose geranium in a small, sterilized, glass jar. Warm the honey, and pour it over the herb leaf. Cap the jar tightly, and allow about 24 hours for the flavor of the herb to permeate the honey. Serve as a sweetener for tea. Don't forget to stencil the bee skep on the lid or front of the jar!

FROM DECORATING WITH HERB STENCILS
JAN POWERS, STONE-WELL HERBS, PEORIA, IL 61604

comparable to a sundial. Just as the sundial is no longer needed to tell us the time, the bee skep is no longer used to keep bees, but the skep's connection to herbs and gardening makes it a pleasant reminder of the past and an enduring addition to gardens today.

Colonial housewives knew that the fragrant herb blossoms in their kitchen gardens were irresistible to the honey bees, and the honey that the bees produced was delicious. To provide a home for a swarm of bees, the beekeeper cut a small opening in the bottom of a handwoven skep, placed a strong branch inside, and positioned the skep in the garden. When the bees had set up housekeeping in the skep and the comb was rich with honey, the beekeeper carefully lifted the skep by its handle and collected the honey for the table.

Although a bee skep is at home anywhere in your herb garden, you may enjoy making a special bee garden, devoted to some of the herbs that particularly attract honey bees, such as bergamot, borage, chamomile, chive, anise hyssop, hyssop, lavender, mignonette, sage, and thyme. Blue seems to be a favorite color of the bees, but pink and white blossoms are enticing also. To keep the skep from rotting, place it on a flat rock or platform off the ground. If you store it inside during the winter months, it will last for many years, its golden yellow changing to a soft gray patina as it ages.

If you like bee skeps, you may wish to stencil my design on a tea cozy, breakfast cloth, or wooden or tin tray, and use it when you serve a comforting herb tea. I have stenciled this design on the front of a denim work apron that I wear in the greenhouse and the garden, and I think it would look great on a T-shirt or a tote bag. If you reduce the design, you can stencil it on a glass jar or metal canister for storage of chamomile tea, bath herbs, or little balls of chamomile soap.

You can also use the stencil for a garden marker, by decorating an old piece of roofing slate with it, adding the words "Bee Garden," and placing it among your garden herbs. Be sure to use permanent enamels, and allow enough room at the bottom to insert the slate into the ground. Spray the finished design with a clear sealer to make it even more durable. It is a good idea to bring these markers inside during the winter months.

PLANTING A DYER'S GARDEN

by Barbara Radcliffe Rogers

No form of herb growing is so woven into the fabric of American history as the planting of herbs for the dye pot. Seeds and "starts" of the most precious plants were in the scant luggage of the early settlers, and old letters, diaries, and inventories are full of references to dyes and plants. The warm, natural shades of wool, cotton, and linen are admired today in our colorful modern setting, but the world of the colonists had very little else to offer than the colors that they could create. Their precious dye plants turned the off-white and buff natural fibers into blues, greens, roses, and yellows that gave spirit and variety to woven, knitted, and embroidered clothing and furnishings. The settlers soon learned to use native plants to supplement and replace familiar European counterparts. Today, we still try to duplicate those warm, muted tones — especially for crewel embroidery and hooked rugs, where color gradations are important. Although analine dyes have given us a wider variety and more intense, brilliant shades, their colors are hard pressed to match the soft warmth of natural dyes. Examples of centuries-old fabrics still have true colors. They may have become lighter or muted, but the color itself has not changed with time. Because of the unique quality of their colors, the wool craftsperson will eventually turn to these natural dyes.

Safflower *(Carthamus tinctorius)*

Many of the dye plants grow wild, available for the gathering. Some of the finest yellows and browns come from the fields and the roadsides, but the rarer and more elusive greens, blues, roses, violets, and oranges require plants not native here. And so the dyer's garden is born. Try not to be discouraged by books on dyes that give recipes for dried or fresh plant material by the pound. Herb gardeners, especially, know how hard it is to grow plants by the pound! Although for large projects, a great deal of dye may be needed, for the crewel embroiderer or rugmaker, one plant can often provide ample color.

You can plant your own dye garden to grow specimen plants for your own experiments, and for propagation of the ones you decide to use in greater quantity. Happily, most of the dye plants have attractive blossoms. In fact, you probably already have a good start in your herb, flower, and even vegetable gardens right now, for many dye plants are familiar ones grown for other purposes. Pearly everlasting, pot marjoram, marigold, coreopsis, rhubarb, rue, safflower, zinnia, marguerite, sassafras, yarrow, and Queen-Anne's-lace all produce dyes, as do artichoke, red cabbage, parsley, carrot tops, blackberries, and onion skins from the vegetable garden. Non-herb gardeners might raise an eyebrow and class many of our dye plants, such as sorrel, as weeds. Fortunately, herb gardeners know that one man's (or woman's) weed may be another's dinner!

Rue *(Ruta graveolens)*

Lady's-mantle *(Alchemilla vulgaris)*

Most of the dye herbs require the same growing conditions as other herbs: a sunny spot, well-drained soil, good cultivation, and freedom from weeds. In the plant descriptions that follow, any special requirements will be noted; both the colors that the dyes produce and the required mordants (mineral salts used to make colors penetrate the fibers) are given. The colors will vary enormously due to soil, season, weather, and dye process, although the range usually stays the same. At times, however, the flowers you grow will give an entirely different result than from the same plant grown elsewhere. This is why growing your own herbs, instead of buying them dried, gives so much more dimension to the art!

It may take two or three years to grow established clumps of some of these plants, but a dyer's garden can be full and attractive even in its first season if you plant annual marigolds *(Tagetes)* between the small, new plants. In addition to those listed, the serious dyer will want to add teasel, mullein, sunflower, blue iris, elderberry, blueberry, butterfly weed, St.-John's-wort, chrysanthemum, cornflower, lady's-mantle, and safflower, to name only a few.

Plants For the Dyer's Garden

PLANT	DYEING INFORMATION	CHARACTERISTICS
AGRIMONY	Leaves and stems with chrome for yellow	Low growing foliage and dainty flowers make it perfect for the front of the garden. A non-spreading perennial, propagated by root division.
BAY	Leaves with alum for pale green and yellow	Easily grown, but must be wintered indoors in northern zones. A fairly slow-growing shrub that adapts well to pot culture. Propagated by cuttings.
BEDSTRAW	Roots with alum for red Flowers with alum for yellow	Grows as a feathery ground cover from which tall, lacy flower stalks spring. A spreading plant, good for foreground of a garden or on a stone wall.
BLOODROOT	Roots with tin for reds Roots with no mordant for orange	Best started as a transplant. A low-growing plant with large leaves and delicate spring blossoms. **Caution**: Bloodroot contains toxic material. Wear gloves, and chop bloodroot outdoors. Extract dye only when you can leave the windows open.
BROWN-EYED-SUSAN	Entire plant with alum and copper for gray-green	Grows wild over vast areas, but its cheery blossom and attractive growth suit it well to garden cultivation. As it is tall, it looks good in showy clumps.
CATNIP	Whole plant with alum for yellow	Easily grown from seed. Pruning back for the dye pot benefits established plants. Cats can't tear up a mature plant, but they may roll in it.
CLEMATIS	Leaves and twigs with alum for yellow	Climbs gracefully on fences, arbors, and lampposts. Its purple blossoms are replaced by fluffy, white seed heads in fall. Trained along a fence or wall, will form a good backdrop for a dyer's garden.
COREOPSIS	Flowers with chrome for orange	Both coreopsis and its annual variety, calliopsis, are common ornamental flowers with clumps of yellow blossoms in midsummer. Its height and showy color make it a good background plant, especially along fences.

Plants for the Dyer's Garden (continued)

PLANT	DYEING INFORMATION	CHARACTERISTICS
GOLDEN MARGUERITE; DYER'S CHAMOMILE	Flowers with alum for yellow Flowers with chrome for gold	The blossom is larger than that of German Chamomile and the petals are yellow. As it is tall, it is nice for fence borders. German chamomile may also be used for dye; it gives a more delicate shade.
GOLDENROD	Flowers with alum or chrome for creamy yellow	Can be domesticated. A clump makes a showy garden background, or it may be left to run wild along a fence, wall, or roadside.
INDIAN PAINTBRUSH	Flower petals with alum for light green	A wildflower that can be transplanted quite easily. Its tall, narrow growth makes it a good filler plant for small places.
LILY-OF-THE-VALLEY	Leaves with alum for green	A fragrant, spring-blossoming perennial that will spread. One of the few dye plants that can survive in shade. Makes nice plantings along a woodland border.
MARIGOLD	Flowers with alum for yellow	All varieties bloom abundantly and make good borders. Pick blossoms as they begin to fade and dry them.
PARSLEY	Leaves and stems for light green	A well-known biennial. Grow yearly from seed.
PEARLY EVERLASTING	Whole plant with alum for yellows and oranges	Grows well in sandy soil. May be allowed to grow wild in meadows or roadside areas. Its pale foliage is sparse, so it is not a showy plant.
QUEEN-ANNE'S-LACE	Whole plant with alum for delicate, pale green	Abounds in fields and is easily transplanted for a feathery garden background.
RED CLOVER	Flowers with chrome for yellow ochre	A somewhat rangey wildflower that grows lush and full with cultivation. A row of plants makes a handsome border, or it may be allowed to spread elsewhere.
RHUBARB	Leaves with tin for yellows and golds	Usually grown for its tasty stalk, but the leaves contain dangerous amounts of oxalic acid, so don't try them as a spring salad green! One plant provides a great deal of dye.
RUE	Roots with alum for rose	Grows to medium height. Its beautiful, blue-gray foliage makes it a lovely garden accent plant. Since the root is used and the plant does not spread, several will be needed.
SCOTCH BROOM	Flowers and leaves with alum for yellow	A perfect plant for difficult slopes. Likes sandy soil. Can grow to 7 feet, making it inappropriate for ordinary beds.
TANSY	Leaves with alum for green	A tall, spreading perennial; give it a lot of room in the garden.
WELD	Leaves and seeds with chrome for gold	Self-sows readily into a nice clump; so give it room. Grows to 2 to 3 feet in height, so it is a good background plant.
WILD OREGANO; POT MARJORAM	Flowers with alum for violet	The blossom of wild oregano is deeper colored than its aromatic cousin, culinary oregano. Its attractive flowers grow a foot tall from compact and slowly spreading clump of foliage.
WOAD	Leaves with any mordant for different shades of blue	An attractive, 2-foot plant with yellow blossoms. The process of extracting color is somewhat complicated, but since it is the only true blue, it belongs in the dyer's garden.
ZINNIA	Flowers with chrome for gold to pink (related to flower color)	A showy annual that grows tall enough to be used as a background plant. Miniatures work just as well, but it takes more plants to yield enough blossoms.

Not all natural craft materials will take dye, even chemical dye. Straw, for example, is very difficult to dye; its shiny surface repels most colors. But half the fun of dyeing is the experimenting, so try different plants on different materials until you find the colors you like.

THE DYE PROCESS

Dyeing wools with herbs and other plant material is really very simple, despite the fuss that is sometimes made over it. Dyeing is certainly easier than making soap, and unlike during soap-making, you can test the product at any point in the process. There are only four basic ingredients — wool, water, mordant, and dye plant — which all go into a pot (or pots) and simmer.

WOOL

Directions are often given for dyeing wool by the pound. You may prefer to dye only small quantities, however, if you are experimenting with colors, if your object is to dye wool for crewel or needlepoint, or if you need only one small strip for a hooked rug. One ounce of crewel-weight wool yields about thirty 10-yard skeins. Ten yards is a generous skein, yet it can be dyed with a mere handful of blossoms, leaves, or roots. With natural dyes you can dye just exactly the amount you need for each project.

It is best to use undyed, unbleached wool, since bleaching sometimes leaves chemical residues that change dye tones. But if natural wool in the size and variety you need is not available, use white. Skein the wool, tie the skeins loosely, and wash them in lukewarm water and Ivory soap adding a teaspoon of Calgon water softener. Squeeze the suds into the wool, and then leave them undisturbed until the water cools. Rinse the skeins thoroughly in cold water. One of the most important rules in handling wool is not to change temperature suddenly. If the wool is warm, don't rinse it in ice water; nor should you plunge room-temperature wool into a boiling dye bath. It is the sudden change in temperature that mats and shrinks the fibers. You can boil wool without damaging it if you let it come to a boil very slowly.

MORDANTS

The only potentially dangerous part of the natural dye process is mordanting, since most of the metallic salts used as mordants are toxic and/or irritating to the skin or lungs. Mordants are substances that are combined with plant material to produce a fixed color. Since you must simmer these solutions, it is important to do this where you can open windows and provide ventilation. Do *not* use chrome, tin, or copper mordants without ventilation, and keep an enamel or stainless steel pan and an extra set of measuring spoons *just for these mordants.* This is an inexpensive precaution that will avoid any possible contamination of your food. Of course, you should never put your face over the steaming kettle.

Different mordants react differently with a specific dye plant to produce various colors. The process is similar for all mordants. Dissolve the measured mordant in ½ cup boiling water, and add it to 1 gallon of lukewarm, soft water. Add wet, lukewarm wool, and stir gently. Bring to a simmer very slowly (it should take 30 min-

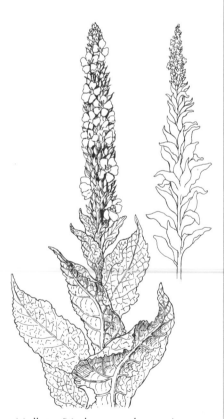

Mullein *(Verbascum thapsus)*

utes), and then simmer, without boiling, for 45 minutes for fine yarns and up to 75 minutes for heavier ones. Remove the wool, drain it over the pot, wrap it in a towel, and squeeze gently. It may then be added to a warm dye bath, or left to cool in the towel and dried for later use.

Iron may also be used as a mordant, but it is best used at the end of the dyeing process. Give the wool a quick rinse in ammonia after dyeing. I find alum, chrome, and tin to be the most useful mordants. I seldom use copper. Tin makes wool very coarse, so I use it only when I must in order to get a special color. As you experiment with dyes and mordants, it is *very important* that you tag the wool, recording both the dye and the mordant you used, since you may later want to know how you made that beautiful shade! Amounts given in the recipes are only guidelines, so make notes on *how much* plant material you used, as well as what kind.

❤

Determining Mordant Quantity

Mordant	Amount per Gallon of Water
Alum	1¾ teaspoons with 1½ teaspoons cream of tartar
Chrome (potassium dichromate)	½ teaspoon
Tin (stannous chloride)	1 teaspoon with 1½ teaspoons cream of tartar
Copper (cupric sulfate)	2 teaspoons

THE DYE PLANTS

The different plant parts should be treated in different ways to produce their characteristic colors. Delicate blossoms, especially reds, blues, and purples, should be *steeped*, like tea, in boiling water for about 30 minutes. Yellow and orange flowers of tougher plants (such as marigolds and zinnias) should be *simmered* 30 minutes. Leaves should also be simmered, usually about 1 hour. Wood, bark, nuts, twigs, and roots are *soaked* overnight and then *simmered and boiled* for 1 hour. Berries are *crushed* and then *simmered* 30 minutes; allowing them to ferment overnight before simmering often improves their color.

Strain all of these mixtures to clean out plant bits that would cling to the wool, cool the liquid to lukewarm, and add the wetted wool. Most recipes call for simmering the wool 30 minutes for a medium shade. If shading is important, as with crewel or rug wool, it is best to put in several skeins, remove one after 15 minutes, and rinse it in *very hot* water. Check the color. If it is too light, return the skein to the dye bath before the wool cools, and check it again in 5 minutes. When the color is right for your lightest value, set it aside to dry. Continue removing and checking other skeins at 5- or 10-minute intervals. The shorter the intervals, the closer the shades will be.

Wool takes on a specific amount of color from a solution regardless of the amount of water that is used. A cup of plant material simmered for a certain period of time will dye an ounce of wool to exactly the same shade in 1 quart of water as it will in 2 quarts. *Time* is more important than the *dilution*. For fresh or

Woad *(Isatis tinctoria)*

KITCHEN DYES

Overripe berries and the outer leaves and other extraneous portions of common fruits and vegetables often make excellent dyes. Use yellow onion skins with an alum mordant for beautiful pale yellows or with tin for brighter shades. Used tea leaves, boiled 15 minutes, give a rosy tan. Try carrot tops with alum or tin for yellows; rhubarb leaves with alum or tin for yellows and orange; red cabbage with tin for purples; cranberries with alum for rose-tan; blackberries with tin for purples; blueberries with alum for rose, tin for blues. Prickly pear (slightly fermented), grapes, turmeric, nutshells, coffee grounds, tangerine peel, and artichoke are all worth experimenting with.

BARBARA RADCLIFFE ROGERS, HERBITAGE FARM, RICHMOND, NH 03470

dried leaves, use about 1 cup to 1 quart of water. For blossoms, use 2 cups; for berries, use 1½ to 2 cups. Nuts, barks, hulls, and woods can be soaked overnight in water equal to their volume, then boiled for an hour to release dye. Dilute this solution with more water to make up for evaporation. For increasingly lighter shades, use the dye bath several times. Each time you dye a batch of fiber, the wool will extract some of the dye from the bath and each subsequent batch will be lighter.

WILD DYES

The woods, fields, and deserts yield plants that were used for dyes by Native American populations long before the Europeans arrived. Black walnuts and butternuts produce rich browns, without mordant; milkweed flowers with alum give yellow-green, and with tin a rich mustard. Milkweed leaves and stems with tin produce bright orange. Try different parts of each plant. Use mullein leaves with alum for green; blackberry or chokeberry bark with alum for lavender; cardinal flower with alum for rose; pokeberry with vinegar (boil berries in vinegar *and* mordant the wool in vinegar) for reds; sorrel roots with alum for pink; tulip tree leaves with chrome for yellow; wheatstraw with alum for yellow; sassafras root, twigs, and leaves with alum for brown; sumac berries with alum for brown; ragweed (whole plant) with alum for green.

Before long, you will want to try your luck with every plant you see! This could use up a lot of wool, but if you test strands of wool treated in different mordants with just a few leaves or twigs in a cup of water, you can determine if there is dye worth pursuing before you waste a lot of time, wool, and energy. If you get a color that interests you, however faint, it is worth gathering additional plant material and doing a more thorough test. But don't ever expect the same shade twice!

You may become interested in dyeing basketry materials, or other craft materials, as well as wool. The Hopi and other Native Americans created beautiful baskets from native plants that they dyed with other plants. Appalachian cornhusk dolls are often dressed in husks of lovely shades of lavender and rose. Traditional Scandinavian and Pennsylvania-German, scratch-dyed Easter eggs are colored with natural dyes, too. Basket splints and reed are easily dyed in black walnut or butternut hulls for varying shades of brown. Because the basket fibers take color more easily than wool does, no mordants, or boiling, are needed. Simple soaking and rinsing are enough. Onion skins, grape juice, red cabbage, Indian corn, sage, and rabbitbrush will all color basket splints. You can dye cornhusks in grape juice. Or, simply soak them overnight in a solution of water and the grape skins strained out during jelly-making; rinse well the next day. To make an onion-skin dye for cornhusks, boil and strain off the dye, but the husks themselves don't have to be cooked in the solution. Red cabbage, with or without vinegar, will dye eggs, as will onion skins, carrot tops, beets with vinegar, and black walnuts.

THREE HERB GARDEN DESIGNS

(Numbers in parentheses refer to number of plants required.)

Knot Garden. This remarkable knot garden, dating to the sixteenth century, appeals to lovers of formal elegance.

This material has been adapted from the Sandy Mush Herb Nursery Handbook, *an indispensable guide — in fact, a veritable herb encyclopedia! — for your herb library. The* JAYNES *have a flawless reputation among my readership for their quality herb plants and service to their mail-order customers.*

1 - Lavender (68)
2 - Green santolina (32)
3 - Gray santolina (36)
4 - Germander (84)
5 - Sage (4)
6 - Lemon thyme (3)
7 - English thyme (3)
8 - Hyssop (5)
9 - Basil, purple and green (1 package of each)
10 - Violet (3)
11 - Tangerine southernwood (1)
12 - Lady's-mantle (2)
13 - Winter savory (2)
14 - Tarragon (2)
15 - Spearmint (3)
16 - Chives (5)

A Little Kitchen Border. Plant this one near your kitchen door.

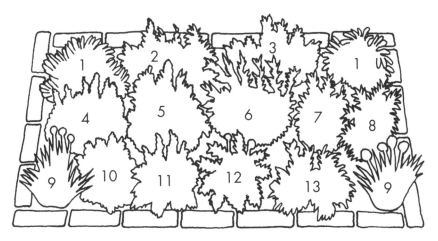

1 - Sage (2)
2 - Peppermint (1 — will spread)
3 - Spearmint (1 — will spread)
4 - Oregano (1)
5 - Marjoram (1)
6 - Tarragon (1)
7 - Lemon balm (1)
8 - Rosemary (1)
9 - Chives (2)
10 - Dot Wells upright thyme (1)
11 - Lemon thyme (1)
12 - Burnet (1)
13 - French thyme (1)

A Fragrant Garden. A group of plants to delight the senses of both sight and smell.

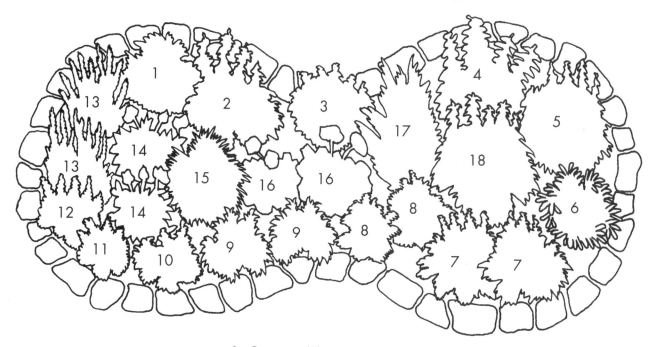

1 - Costmary (1)
2 - Wormwood (1)
3 - var. Pineapple mint (1)
4 - Catnip (1)
5 - Anise hyssop (1)
6 - Pineapple sage (1)
7 - Lemon thyme (2)
8 - Pennsylvania-Dutch tea thyme (2)
9 - Golden lemon thyme (2)

10 - Caraway thyme (1)
11 - Oregano thyme (1)
12 - Corsican mint (1)
13 - Lavender (2)
14 - Rock rose (2)
15 - Lemon verbena (1)
16 - Scented geranium (2)
17 - Tangerine southernwood (1)
18 - Peppermint (1)

FROM THE *SANDY MUSH HERB NURSERY HANDBOOK*
KATE AND FAIRMAN JAYNE, SANDY MUSH HERB NURSERY, LEICESTER, NC 28748

♥ ♥ ♥ ♥ ♥ ♥ ♥ ♥ ♥ ♥

My husband Hugh and I stopped to visit PEG MASTEY *at Heritage Herbs one spring and so enjoyed seeing this vivacious woman who never intended to convert her summer home into a business. The charming shop in the farmhouse is a delight to explore, and the garden designs are so practical and unusual! I was particularly impressed by her use of bales of salt hay as cold frames. She arranges four bales around her plants in a square, and at night, or on cold days, covers the bales with recycled storm doors*

HERITAGE HERBS

When Peg and Tony Mastey purchased a summer home on the banks of the Merrimac River in Canterbury, New Hampshire in 1973, they never planned to farm, much less own a business. But Tony kept looking at the empty fields, saying, "Peg, we can't just stand here like Lord and Lady Barren — it's too wasteful." Then Peg began researching herbs, and 8 years later, Heritage Herbs became a reality. Peg explains, "From the beginning, the beauty of herbs fascinated me, and then, as I studied their history I became even more captivated. Whenever I work among my herbs, I become a part of another world — particularly a woman's world, for the history of herbs very much relates to women. For centuries, they used herbs to cure their sick, season their food, dye their clothes, and sweeten their hearths and their hearts."

Besides teaching about and selling herb plants and flowers, Peg is a recognized authority on herbs and fulfills many speaking engagements throughout New England. She shares on page 129 two popular recipes from luncheons held at the farm.

The garden design included here represents only about half of Peg's garden. In addition, she has a Mother Garden, a Stock Garden, and thyme and honey bee beds, all in interesting shapes.

or windows. One bale is easily moved aside when customers want to examine the potted plants in each enclosure.

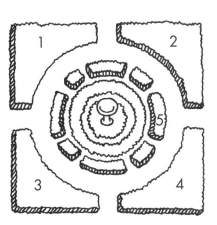
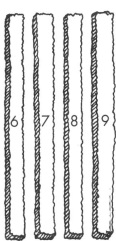
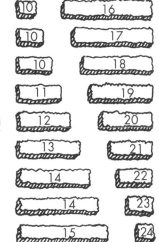
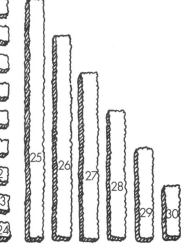

FORMAL GARDEN

1 - White garden
2 - Blue and purple garden
3 - Orange and yellow garden
4 - Red and pink garden
5 - Silver garden
6 - Silver Mound artemisia
7 - Lavender
8 - Lamb's-ears
9 - Flax

PATH GARDENS

10 - Hyssop
11 - Fringed wormwood
12 - Santolina
13 - Feverfew
14 - Yellow yarrow
15 - Pink hyssop
16 - Russian sage
17 - Clove pink
18 - Pink yarrow
19 - Lady's-mantle
20 - Green santolina
21 - Lavender
22 - Woolly yarrow
23 - Catmint
24 - Rue

CULINARY GARDEN

25 - Sage
26 - True oregano
27 - Thyme
28 - Garlic chives
29 - French tarragon
30 - Greek oregano

Peg Mastey, Heritage Herbs, Canterbury, NH 03224

STARTING A TEA GARDEN

by Jim Long

Tea gardens are an interesting and quickly rewarding way to begin using herbs. People who are timid about putting unfamiliar herbs in favorite cooking recipes, may enjoy incorporating herb flavors into beverages. The tea herbs include the various mints, chamomile, lemon balm, bergamot, anise hyssop, lavender, lemon verbena, and lemongrass. Many more herbs are used for teas, but these are the most common. Each of these has a distinctive flavor and can be blended with one or more of the others to make an interesting brew.

It takes very little space to grow enough herbs to provide a

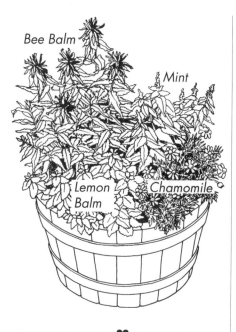

Bee Balm

Mint

Lemon
Balm

Chamomile

Keep the soil in your planter evenly moist, watering more in the heat of the summer. Even in a barrel without drainage holes, it would be hard to overwater such a planting, assuming you have provided the proper soil. Make iced herb teas with the freshly picked leaves and flowers, and remember to dry any excess prunings for winter tea!

FROM *THE OZARKS HERBALIST* (A UNIQUE QUARTERLY JOURNAL) JIM LONG, OZARKS HERBALIST, OAK GROVE, AR 72660

variety of teas for your own use for a season, and if facing a blank stretch of soil intimidates you (or if you have limited gardening space), tea herbs can be nicely grown in a large container. A half-barrel, available at hardware stores, lumber suppliers, and discount stores, is ideal for this purpose. The wooden barrel insulates the soil from summer heat better than large plastic pots, and isn't as expensive or as easily broken as large clay pots.

If possible, drill four holes in the bottom of the barrel for good drainage during heavy rains, and line the bottom 2 inches or so with gravel. Next, obtain some good soil. Soil straight from the garden compacts too much, but garden soil is fine to use if you mix it with 1 part sphagnum peat and 1 part sand (unless your soil is already very sandy) to 8 parts soil. Next, add some good compost or dried cow manure to the mixture. Do not use composted peat, but pay the extra money for sphagnum peat, so you'll have a loose, friable soil. Mix all these together well, and then fill your barrel nearly to the top. The soil will settle over time.

Now you're ready to put in your plants. It's best to choose herbs that are easy to grow, and hardy enough to leave in place during the winter. For a beginning tea garden, we recommend bergamot, lemon balm, mint, and chamomile, all of which will fit nicely in the half-barrel for the first year, and can be thinned out or moved to a garden location the following year. Some of these plants (such as the bergamot and mint) may seem too tall for container growing, but you can pinch out the tops when they reach 2 feet or so, causing them to branch out and provide more of a tea harvest for you.

Use this attractive display on your patio or by your porch (to gaze upon as your guests sip the delicious harvest!) Be sure to place the taller plants in the back, the medium growers in the middle, and the shortest plants in the front. All will grow quickly, allowing for teas during much of the season. Bergamot and mint are perennials and will spread by runners; lemon balm, which remains more in a clump, is also a perennial, although you should keep the seed stalks picked off, as it self-sows freely and will act as an annual. Chamomile is the only annual in this plan, but it will reseed itself for transplants the following year.

A SHOP AND GARDEN FOR REMEMBRANCE

by Ronda Schooley Bretz

I recently transplanted myself from Iowa to Pennsylvania, reluctantly leaving my shop and garden behind. I would like to share with you my early experiences in establishing my garden, with the hope that they will be helpful to you.

My Remembrance Garden was located directly in front of my shop. In a formal Colonial style, it was a 30' x 30' treasure of fragrances and garden ornaments, each with a story to tell. A picket fence in true pointed style proudly enveloped the garden. Cut from barn boards we removed from a collapsing pole barn, this fence made a fine barrier against sharp winter winds and created a blanket effect for the herbs when snow covered them. Paths were bordered with 100-year-old lumber milled for the purpose. The stone on which to walk was scooped from the Mississippi River bottom near our valley. A four-piece planter of cast cement, decorated with collected stones and shells, was made by my great-uncle over 75 years ago and became the focal point for the garden and home for the rosemary. Assorted bricks with town names pressed into them, cobblestones from Philadelphia, slate markers from Cape Cod roof tops, garden statues found in antique shops, and a cement bench from the local Salvation Army — all found their place amidst the herbal fragrances, past and present. The herb plants, as well, had been gathered from across the United States and Canada and lovingly brought to Iowa, the results of my many travel tours. The variety of herbs gave my memory a tease each early spring. Walks through the Remembrance Garden brought to all who visited sentimental thoughts, and a fragrant memory to take home.

RONDA SCHOOLEY BRETZ, SILVER SPRINGS, PA 17575

1 - Pineapple sage
2 - Oregano
3 - Chives
4 - Garlic chives
5 - Dill
6 - Variegated sage
7 - Sage
8 - Burnet
9 - Lavender
10 - Scented geraniums (15 varieties)
11 - Summer savory
12 - Bush basil
13 - Comfrey
14 - Lemon verbena
15 - Thyme
16 - Bergamot
17 - Bee balm
18 - Pennyroyal
19 - Scented strawberries
20 - Baby's-breath
21 - Sweet woodruff
22 - Fragrant roses
23 - Camphor southernwood
24 - Bay tree
25 - Costmary
26 - Butterfly weed
27 - Lamb's-ears
28 - Tansy
29 - Anise
30 - Parsley
31 - Coriander
32 - Lemon balm
33 - Broom straw
34 - German statice
35 - Florence fennel
36 - Cumin caraway
37 - Catnip
38 - Mints (8 varieties)
39 - Silver Mound artemisia
40 - Echinops
41 - Chamomile
42 - Lemon marigolds
43 - Sweet marjoram

Woodland Herb Farm Plant List

1. Thyme (Thymus adamovica)
2. Chives
3. Garlic chives
4. Curly chives
5. English pennyroyal
6. Feverfew
7. Multiplier onion
8. Multiplier garlic
9. Sweet cicely
10. Angelica
11. Calamus
12. Golden feverfew
13. Thyme (Doonevalley)
14. Creeping thyme
15. Red valerian
16. French sorrel
17. French tarragon
18. Lemon balm
19. Golden lemon balm
20. Lovage
21. Orange balsam thyme
22. Lemon thyme
23. Golden lemon thyme
24. Oregano thyme
25. Silver thyme
26. French thyme
27. Golden thyme
28. Wild thyme
29. Mother-of-thyme

(Continued next page)

WOODLAND HERB FARM:
A FORMAL HERB GARDEN THAT ELICITS SERENITY

Pat and Jon Bourdo have created in their formal display garden a special place of beauty and serenity. "I'm drawn to every aspect of art — to architecture, anthropology, and music. Gardening and interior design blend in. Your garden is an extension of your home," says Pat.

In 1975, the Bourdos purchased a 15-acre family farm in Northport, located on Lake Michigan. Their first accomplishment was to convert the dirt-floor garage into an herb shop. Later, they added the formal herb garden, increased their plantings of field herbs, and added several small sheds for potting and drying. Pat's herbal creations and gourmet culinary treats are featured in the shop. They have recently added edible flowering annuals to their garden. Pat explains, "We now tuck in nasturtiums; Lemon Gem marigolds; Spicy Globe, opal and bush basils; and scented geraniums, wherever space allows. Also, we found that the cedar hedge that borders the garden has disadvantages as well as benefits. It creates more shade for some plants than we wanted, and has invasive roots that make the soil hard-packed, robbing the herb plants of moisture. (We had to dig up hundreds of pounds of roots and put down roof flashing and fill in!) On the plus side, the hedge protects from wind, lessens road noises, and keeps the public from wandering into areas we'd rather they didn't!"

PAT AND JON BOURDO, WOODLAND
HERB FARM, NORTHPORT, MI 49670

Woodland Herb Farm Plant List
(continued from previous page)
30. Edelweiss
31. Catnip
32. Catmint (Nepeta mussini)
33. Veronica (green)
34. Veronica (gray)
35. Soapwort
36. Greek oregano
37. Pink yarrow
38. Anise hyssop
39. Clary sage
40. Caraway thyme
41. Winter savory
42. Oregano
43. Roman wormwood
44. Lavender (Hidcote)
45. Woolly thyme
46. Lavender (rosea)
47. Artemisia (Silver Queen)
48. Lavender (Munstead)
49. Bee balm (Croftway Pink)
50. Lavender (Lavandula vera)
51. Artemisia (stellerana)
52. Artemisia (Silver King)
53. Rue
54. Lemon southernwood
55. Camphor wormwood
56. Wormwood (Artemisia absinthium)
57. Yarrow
58. Southernwood
59. White hyssop
60. Pink hyssop
61. Blue hyssop
62. Santolina (incana)
63. Santolina (Pretty Carrol)
64. Santolina (green)
65. Santolina (neopolitana)
66. Santolina (incana-nana)
67. Lady's-bedstraw
68. Winter marjoram
69. Roman chamomile
70. Lamb's-ears
71. Costmary
72. Golden oregano
73. Horehound
74. Nutmeg thyme
75. Germander
76. Dianthus
77. Bee balm (Cambridge Scarlet)
78. Red yarrow
79. Comfrey
80. English thyme
81. Sage
82. Dwarf sage
83. Woolly yarrow
84. Maryland dittany
85. Pearly yarrow
86. Silver lemon thyme
87. Coconut thyme
88. Creeping winter savory

THE SPINNING WHEEL —
A SYMBOL OF CREATIVE ENDEAVOR

by Grace M. Wakefield

I gave a lot of thought to the design for my new herb garden after we moved to our present location. I drew up many plans, but kept coming back to the spinning wheel for the central focus. For me, it has a special meaning, as it represents the thoughts and ideas of Mahatma Gandhi, who used the spinning wheel as a symbol of the struggle for self-sufficiency through cottage industry. It is thus a symbol of the creative small endeavor, and it is honored in the Far East as a mystical shape. The wheel shape is very practical for a garden, for it can be easily divided into eight, neat sections by wooden landscaping timbers, which represent the spokes of a wheel. We built a brick walk around our wheel, and then created an outer circle of flower beds. A wooden lattice enclosure wraps the entire garden in its own special place.

You can use whatever plants you wish, although you will have best results with plants that stay small and compact. We had to remove yarrow from our wheel when it became too large. We have many perennials in our garden, but also like to save space for a few annuals each year. Some favorites are Johnny-jump-ups (which make especially nice pressed flowers), Silver Mound artemisia, lavender, feverfew, pennyroyal, southernwood, and chives. In the center, we like to grow lamb's-ears, mullein, and variegated thyme, and for a spring treat, we have some daffodils in the very center as well.

FROM *HERBAL CRAFTS QUARTERLY NEWSLETTER*
GRACE M. WAKEFIELD, TOM THUMB WORKSHOPS, MAPPSVILLE, VA 23407

BOOKS ON LANDSCAPE DESIGN AND HERBS

Until 1984, there was no professional book totally devoted to herb garden designs, and then Herb Garden Design, *by Faith H. Swanson and Virginia B. Rady, was published as a labor of love. Sponsored by the Herb Society of America, this outstanding volume took some seven years to complete; upon completion it became the property of the Herb Society of America. In my opinion, every herbalist must have a copy in his or her herb library. Lovely photographs and descriptions of formal herb gardens enhance many other fine books, such as* The Complete Book of Herbs and Spices *by Sarah Garland;* Herbs, Gardens, Decorations and Recipes *by Emelie Tolley and Chris Mead; and* Southern Herb Growing *by Madelene Hill and Gwen Barclay. Adelma Simmons, Gertrude Foster, and James Adams* (Landscaping with Herbs) *also have helpful advice in their books. Many of these can be ordered from the Herb Society of America (for address, see Appendix). Their current book list, which includes both new and classic books, is available for a nominal fee. Among their own publications are the annual* Herbarist, Judging Herbs: A Handbook for Horticultural Judges, The Traveler's Guide to Herb Gardens *(over 500 gardens to visit in the U.S. and Canada),* The Beginner's Herb Garden, A Basket of Herbs: A Book of American Sentiments, *and* Herbs for Use and Delight.

New and Unusual Herbs for Your Garden

SHOPPING FOR NEW OR UNUSUAL HERBS

Order three or four (or all) of the catalogs listed in the Appendix under March, Herb Seed and Plant Catalogs, and you will be amazed at the great feast of new varieties or unusual or hard-to-find herbs now available from these so-reputable sources. I find it hard to contain myself (and my checkbook) when I peruse these catalogs each spring — so many fun herbs to try!

Catnip lovers, did you know there are enough different catnips to fill a garden? I thought I had seen them all when I looked at the "Companion Plants" catalog: catnip (Nepeta cataria), *camphor catnip* (N. camphorata), *Greek catnip* (N. parnassica), *Himalayan catnip* (N. nervosa), *lance-leaved catnip* (N. lanceolata), *lemon catnip* (N. cataria 'Citriodorata'), *and ornamental catnip, or Persian catnip/catmint* (N. mussini). Then I opened the "Sandy Mush Herb Nursery Handbook" to learn that the Jayneses offer several of the above, plus grandiflora catnip (N. grandiflora), nepeta catnip (Reichenbachiana) from China, and Siberian catnip (N. siberica) from Russia. A glance at the Lost Prairie Herb Farm catalog revealed yet others: catmint (Calamintha officinalis), catnip lavender (N. xfaasseni) — which is liked by one of the farm's nine cats — plus cat thyme (Teucrium marum), which is really a form of germander and which looks like a beautiful thyme plant. Cats are attracted to this thyme, as are humans, for its showy, fragrant pink flowers. It is used primarily as a potted plant or as a hedge or border in a rock garden. Some of these varieties bloom all season, many are compact and ornamental, and some are extremely hardy. And some, like the lemon catnip, appeal more to humans than to cats! We love this in tea, yet our two cats ignore it (possibly because they can find N. cataria scattered throughout the gardens, wherever the wind or birds deposited the seeds from the previous year). Imagine, a whole herb bed just for the felines in your family?

I know of several basil-philes who have whole beds of all the basils each year. Many of the varieties are discussed in the August chapter. Are you wild about sage? The New Hope Herb Farm lists thirteen varieties. And Sandy Mush Herb Farm lists eighteen varieties of rosemary. Hartman's Herb Farm sells nineteen different thymes.

Of course, mint plants should not be planted together in one bed, but did you know that there are enough varieties to have a collection spread out all over your property? We have a different mint in each garden on the place! The Lost Prairie Herb Farm lists all the well-known kinds of mint, plus anise mint (Pycanthemum sp.), basil mint (Mentha sp.), Egyptian mint (M. spicata var.), ginger mint (Mentha sp.), grapefruit mint (M. citriodora xavensis), Korean mint (Agastache rugosa), lemon mint (Monarda citriodora), lime mint (M. spicata sp.), mint—The Best (M. spicata var.), Morrocan mint (Mentha sp.), mountain mint (Pycanthemum sp.), and silver mint (Mentha sp.). Lemon mint, which is related to bergamot, has strikingly gorgeous, pinkish flowers, and mint—The Best has an excellent spearmint flavor. Many of these mints are especially recommended for tea or for potpourri.

Would you like a lavender that blooms abundantly twice each season? Tom DeBaggio has developed three varieties that do so! Would you like a rosemary that could live in your garden over the winter, even in more northern zones? Now, the ARP cultivar rosemary is sold by several herb farms and has been proven hardy to 0° F., although it is still being tested in several areas.

Among the other herbs that we have tried in recent years, one that I just love is balm-of-Gilead (Cedronella triphylla), which I searched for because one of my newsletter subscribers sent me some dried leaves and lamented the fact that no one was writing about this very fragrant plant

Balm-of-Gilead (*Cedronella triphylla*)

these days. It is a tender perennial in the north and suitable for pot culture in cold climates. I found it in the Companion Plants catalog, with this description: "This 2-foot, ornamental plant, which needs full sun, is one of the few members of the Labiatae with compound leaves. A botanical oddity that makes good potpourri material, it is a different plant than that referred to in the Bible, a plant whose export from its native country is now forbidden. What is commonly sold as balm-of-Gilead buds is derived from a native American poplar and not from this plant." Of my three plants, two have survived a very wet summer and a winter inside under lights. Quite overgrown by March, the plants were cut back and re-potted. I was

Marigold *(Tagetes tenuifolia 'Lemon Gem')*

rewarded with lush growth and six (out off eight) rooted cuttings after two weeks in water! I now have eight of these lovelies to harvest for potpourri this summer.

The whole family fell in love with the edible, citrus-scented and -flavored Lemon Gem and Tangerine Gem mini-marigolds (Tagetes tenuifolia) *from Lost Prairie Herb Farm. These marigolds spread out to make a lovely ground cover in the garden, and became our favorite edible flowers, adding a tangy goodness, as well as bright orange and yellow highlights to many summer salads and beverages. From the same source, one can also get Mexican marigold* (T. minuta) *for nematode protection in the soil,* and sweet marigold (T. lucida), *which can be used as a tarragon substitute. A very close second in popularity with all of us is lime balm* (Melissa officinalis var.), *which is definitely fragrant of lime. A darker green than lemon balm, with the same growing characteristics, it is very nice in summer beverages and in citrus-type herbal vinegars. Other plants from Lost Prairie, which I did not find from many other sources, were vanilla grass and pearl yarrow. Vanilla grass* (Anthoxanthum odoratum) *is a sweet perennial grass that is a marvelous accent plant in the garden. Used in Native American ceremonies, it is also a source of fragrant dried leaves for potpourri and basketmaking. The pearl yarrow* (Achillea ptarmica) *is a small, white flower that is excellent for cutting or drying.*

Bronze fennel (Foeniculum vulgare *var.* rubra) *makes a spectacular show in the garden, and is a good culinary variety. If I am lucky, this tender perennial will reseed itself in my garden, as we forgot to pot it up and bring it inside for the winter. This is available from several of the sources. We brought our tender perennial lemongrass* (Cymbopogan citratus) *inside for the winter and it thrived in a sunny window. We had enjoyed the fresh leaves in summer "sun tea" with other citrus-flavored herbs, but we were totally unprepared for the constant joy one of our cats exhibited all winter as he climbed into the large pot and chewed away at his leisure every day. The plant is thriving, nevertheless, and may actually have benefited from the feline prunings!*

These are just a few of the herbs — the ones most worthy of mention — we have had the pleasure of adding to our gardens in recent years. One summer was unusually cold and wet, and we lost several new plants to root-rot as a consequence. I plan to re-order the elusive (to me!) ambrosia, mignonette, and several exotic thymes, like the orange balsam, caraway, creeping, and Italian oregano varieties. We did have success with Greek oregano, but I don't agree with many who say that this, or the Mexican oregano sold in the South, are the best varieties for culinary use. I'll stick with my common oregano (Oreganum vulgare), which has survived for almost 30 years and through four moves among our gardens for rejuvenation.

I hope that these examples have convinced you to keep your herb library stocked with catalogs from all the major herb farms. They are wonderful educational tools, and you will find it enlightening to look up one plant at a time in the different catalogs in order to compare the descriptions and information. But, most of all, whenever you hear about an herb that tickles your fancy, you'll be able to find a source of it right away!

UNUSUAL HERBS TO TRY THIS YEAR

by Madeleine H. Siegler

New seed catalogs, big glorious plant catalogs, tiny seeds rattling in little packets — nothing else gets a true gardener through the winter. If it were not for winter, we would never get a rest and neither would our plants. But when winter has been long enough for you, then is the time to read and plan a few new garnitures for your heart's delight — your herb garden. What may make your planning particularly exciting, is to look for some new herbs that you haven't used before.

Culver's root *(Veronicastrum virginicum)*. This is an old Native American healing herb named for a Dr. Culver who lived in the colonies, learned its uses from the Native Americans, and added it to his own pharmacopoeia. It grows to at least 5 feet and has multiple spires of tiny, white flowers. The flowering spike resembles black cohosh *(Cimicifuga racemosa)*, but the foliage is quite different. The narrow, pointed leaves of Culver's root surround the stems in a very artistic pattern, quite rare in form. Culver's root is easily grown from seed, although it has never self-sown for me nor have I tried saving seed — though I plan to. If you would enjoy a new showy perennial in your herb garden, this native American plant may be the answer.

Annual clary sage *(Salvia viridis)*. If you aren't familiar with the delightful herb known as annual clary sage, there is a treat in store for you this summer. Its nomenclature is quite confused. *Hortus Third* lists it as *S. viridis*, but some seed catalogs still call it *S. horminum*. And to further compound the problem, some seed lists call it clary sage, with no distinction between this annual and the very different *biennial* that is the true clary, *S. sclarea*. Annual clary sage is very easy to grow from seed. The fat, pebbly-leafed seedlings look much like garden sage or even the true clary sage. It can be started indoors 6 weeks before planting-out time, or directly sown when the soil has warmed. You need plant it only once; from then on it will take care of itself, for it readily self sows, without being a nuisance. It provides a large mass of color in my garden from July until late September. Although its very tiny, true flowers hug the stems and are attractive only to honeybees, the glorious color of its bracts make up the top 5 or 6 inches on each plant. They look like leaves, but show color when the small, true blossoms appear. A packet of mixed seed will give you pink, blue, and white bracts or flowers. The Thompson & Morgan seed company has perfected the pink strain; they call their new variety *S. claryessa*.

Mace plant *(Achillea decolorans)*. Why not add some spice to your garden with the mace plant? The small, pinnate leaves of this achillea actually do carry the flavor and fragrance of mace. *A. decolorans* is quite unlike any of the achilleas we may have grown

I spend as much time as possible with MADELEINE SIEGLER at herb conferences, as we've become very close friends through the years. She writes regularly for my newsletter, so you will discover some marvelous contributions from her throughout this book. Having written and lectured extensively about herbs for many years, Madeleine has now retired from her herb business in order to concentrate on writing — and mostly to be free to spend more time with her retired husband!

Annual clary sage *(Salvia viridis)*

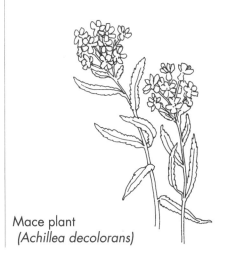

Mace plant
(Achillea decolorans)

If you have trouble starting ambrosia in your garden, try this technique suggested by DEAN PAILLER (Catnip Acres Farm, Oxford, CT). In mid- to late fall, scatter seeds where you want the plants to grow. Because germination is fairly late in spring, don't cultivate the area until seedlings are up. PVS

Ambrosia (*Chenopodium botrys*)

♥

To ease maintenance, contain creepers like costmary and the mints by sinking strips of tin or treated boards around them.

♥

Russian sage
(*Perovskia atriplicifolia*)

for their easily dried, yellow flowers. My herb garden has been graced at various times with yellow varieties, such as Coronation Gold, Parker's Yellow, Moonshine with its gray leaves and lemon-yellow flowers, and the ground-hugging tomentosa known as woolly yarrow. (I have never had any fondness for the pink or red varieties; they spread much too rapidly and the flowers all have a muddy cast when dry.)

Mace plant is a good choice for a small herb garden, as the basal clumps of shiny, green, pinnate leaves are rarely over 5 inches in diameter. My plants provide flower stalks about 1 foot tall, with white flowers similar in form to other achilleas, but only an inch wide. It is a good white for drying, as it does not quickly take on the gray cast of the wild white yarrow. Divisions are easily made from mature plants. I have grown this perennial successfully in both full sun and partly shady locations.

Ambrosia, or feather geranium (Chenopodium botrys). An annual I would wish for every garden is *ambrosia.* Mouth-watering name, isn't it? It is *not* easy to grow from seed. The seed is very small and requires light and heat for germination, which can take 25 days. It can be started indoors if you have a warm greenhouse, or it may be sown directly in the garden after the soil is well warmed. The reddish-brown seedling leaves, which resemble those of an oak, can easily be missed and cultivated out by neat gardeners. Seedlings need to be thinned to about 10 inches apart. The ones you disturb will be so resentful they will dwarf and flower when only 8 inches tall, but leave them alone, for they will cast seed that will guarantee you plenty of seedlings next year. An undisturbed seedling grown in rich soil in full sun will be 2 feet tall and almost as broad by August. Ambrosia has fat, arching trusses of stout stems surrounded by tiny, feathery leaves, which are a delicate green and quite sticky, with scent glands that give off a strong, but not unpleasant fragrance. I harvest the entire plant by cutting at the soil line. To dry it to a soft gold shade, I simply sling it over a nail in a beam in the shed. A fresh plant of this size, secured in a shallow container with water, is a complete and pleasing arrangement that will last for several days.

Russian sage (Perovskia atriplicifolia). Although this herb is relatively unknown, once you have seen it in bloom, you will not rest until you have located a source for the plants and a spot in which to grow them.

Not a sage at all (nor even Russian), this member of the Perovskia genus is easily grown, and hardy to Zone 3. All it requires is full sun, good drainage, and plenty of space. A fully grown plant can reach almost 4 feet in height and nearly that in width. A group of three for the garden should be planted 2 feet apart, and placed in the back of the bed or border. The silver-green leaves are small, serrated, intensely fragrant, and sticky with the scent glands. They form along the entire length of the stalks, which are slightly hoary and silvery in color. The sagelike aroma is rich and warm, and the dried leaves provide a nice base note in potpourri, according to many crafters. By August, the entire plant blooms with multitudes of tiny, lavender-blue flowers. Russian sage, combined with a bit of purple perilla, a splash of silver artemisia, and some pink *Salvia horminum*, makes a prize-winning bouquet. I leave the tall, bare stems on the plants until spring and then cut them back to about 8 inches. New leaves will break out all along the remaining stem by May 10th in my area (Maine). I fertilize the plants at this time and just wait for another August. Stem cuttings taken in midsummer will root quickly in perlite.

Dittany of Crete *(Origanum dictamnus)*. A beautiful romantic herb worth having, not for cooking or even for tea, but for beauty of form, for its long poetic history, and for sheer durability.

Dittany is wonderfully aromatic — rather like pennyroyal, but sweeter. Its long, arching branches cascade from the center, where new growth starts continually. The gray, hairy leaves are nearly round, thick to the touch, and often veined with purple. It is a tender perennial, and so it spends the long Maine winter in our solar greenhouse along with the rosemarys, lemon verbena, bay, and scented geraniums. During the summer, it hangs outside in the sun, and flowers in August. The flower is a 1-inch, pink catkin with darker pink stamens protruding, much like a hop flower. The flowers dry very well, and I have used them to advantage in very special wreaths.

Using very unscientific methods, I have had very good luck rooting 5-inch cuttings in water in a sunny window. The cuttings have rooted in 2 weeks and then been planted in Pro-Mix in small pots. It is best to obtain a dittany plant, for it is not to be started from seed.

Dittany is a durable plant; for me, it permits more neglect than my rosemarys or bay. It survives with little water; in fact, overwatering could be the death of it. I fertilize it with dilute, liquid plant food every other month. Once a year I replant it into fresh Pro-Mix. This is a good time to groom the plant, which usually results in finding small divisions that can be removed and potted separately.

Here are a few mail-order seed and plant suppliers of the herbs mentioned above (for addresses, see the Appendix):

Culver's root *(Veronicastrum virginicum)*: seed, Lost Prairie Herb Farm; plants, Wayside Gardens

Annual clary sage *(Salvia viridis)*: Thompson & Morgan and Nichol's Garden Nursery

Mace plant *(Achillea decolorans)*: Logee's Greenhouses and Well-Sweep Herb Farm

Ambrosia *(Chenopodium botrys)*: Park Seed Co.

Russian sage *(Perovskia atriplicifolia)*: New Hope Herb Farm, Logee's Greenhouses, Wormwood Farm Herbs, Sandy Mush Herb Nursery

Dittany of Crete *(Origanum dictamnus)*: Fox Hill Farm and Lost Prairie Herb Farm

*A branch of healing Dittany
   she brought
Which in the Cretan fields
   with care she sought
Rough is the stem, which
   woolly leaves surround.
The leaves with flowers, the
   flowers with purple
   crowned.
Well known to goats; a sure
   relief
To draw the pointed steel and
   ease the grief.*

—*VIRGIL, THE AENEID, BOOK XII*

If you collect seed from your herbs, store it in an inexpensive Styrofoam cooler in a location where it will remain in a cool, constant temperature until needed. Seed stored longer than a year should be kept in the freezer.

❤

Your herb garden's appearance will be substantially improved by edging it with something permanent, such as brick or stone. If you do this in such a way that it raises the bed somewhat, drainage will be improved.

KATE AND FAIRMAN JAYNE, SANDY MUSH HERB NURSERY, LEICESTER, NC 28748

❤

MADELEINE H. SIEGLER, MONK'S HILL HERBS, WINTHROP, ME 04364

❤

BLENDER BASILS

Basils add not only sweet fragrance to potpourri, but also character, bulk, and, in the case of dark opal or purple ruffles basil, even color! Sweet basil, licorice basil, and Thrysiflora basil (with its unusually shaped and colored, flowering spikes) are other excellent potpourri blenders. And, of course, lemon basil is very appropriate for citrus-scented blends.

❤

Sweet flag *(Acorus calamus)*

MARILYN HAMPSTEAD, FOX HILL FARM, PARMA, MI 49269

GROWING YOUR OWN FIXATIVES

by Marilyn Hampstead

For the ultimate in creating your own garden potpourri, grow your own fixatives and blenders. Here are several we grow on the farm for our customers:

Clary sage (Salvia sclarea). Biennial. This tall, lanky plant sports lovely purple blossoms in its second year and can be a pervasive self-sower. Plant in full sun and clean, well-drained soil. Do not mulch over the winter, as this can cause crown rot. The plant is used to make muscatel oil, used in perfumery for a musky fragrance.

Clevelandii sage (Salvia clevelandii). Tender perennial. This woody, semi-evergreen shrub provides a distinctive fragrance of its own, as well as a fixative function. It will grow to 3 feet in height and 2 feet in diameter if grown in full sun, in a humusy, rich yet well-drained soil. Feed regularly. It is difficult to transplant once established in the garden. For the largest harvests of this and patchouli (following), northern gardeners should purchase plants each spring and grow them in the garden. You can also grow Clevelandii in containers and overwinter them on a sunny windowsill, but harvests will be limited. You will get more if you can overwinter them in a greenhouse.

Patchouli (Pogostemon cablin). Tender perennial. Another semi-woody, semi-evergreen shrub that is a rampant grower, patchouli requires a rich, well-drained, humusy soil in full sun with ample warmth. It will attain 4 feet in height and girth and will endure prunings during the hot season. If grown in a container, it is a heavy feeder and will not tolerate a too-small pot for very long. Patchouli's flowering spike is quite unusual, with hundreds of tiny, green florets clustering in an almost triangular inflorescence. *(Another variety of patchouli,* P. heyneanus, *requires heat to thrive, and is recommended for southern gardeners. It is available from Sandy Mush Nursery (see Appendix for address), which lists it as "Patchouli, smooth." PVS)*

Sweet flag (Acorus calamus). Perennial. A lowlands (swamp or bog) plant, sweet flag normally requires a deep, rich and very humusy and wet environment in full sun or part shade. We have found, however, that sweet flag can also be successfully grown in heavy soils in the shady part of a garden. The rhizome is prized for its sweet fragrance and fixative qualities.

Orrisroot or Florentine iris (Iris germanica). Perennial. This lovely, simple, white-flowering iris holds the haunting scent of violets in its tubers. It requires good soil with ample bone meal and water to produce good tubers. Plant so that the tuber is at the soil level, and allow for good air circulation between the plants. Do not harvest until the plant is 3 years old. Replant active tuber eyes to increase orrisroot production.

GROWING EXOTIC HERBS

by Carolee Bean

Duam kasum, coriander, and kaprow may not be the first words that come to mind when you think of herbs, but they top the list at the New Hope Herb Farm in central Indiana. Foreign students at Indiana University provide a market for exotic herbs that our farm has been filling for many years. We delight in serving their needs and learning how they use these unusual herbs. And we collect recipes, seeds, and plants from our Malaysian customers at the Bloomington (Indiana) Farmers' Market, Saturday mornings from May to October. You may want to grow some of these herbs in your garden, where they will add beauty and fragrance, and offer new dimensions for your cooking.

Kasum (Malasia); also called **Rau Ram** (Vietnam) and **Phak Pheo** (Laos) (may be listed in herb catalogs as perennial, Vietnamese, or lemon coriander). Remarkably similar in appearance to smartweed, but with an aroma unlike any other herb, *Polygonum odoratum* is used as a culinary herb in Malaysia, as well as in Vietnam and in some parts of Thailand.

It is tolerant of a wide range of cultural conditions: full sun to semi-shade, sandy to clay soils, aquatic to fairly dry locations. It prefers full summer heat (90° to 100°), but it will survive a moderate frost and can be maintained at 45° without difficulty. Under full sun and abundant water, it will produce a clump 8 to 12 inches in diameter and as much as 3 feet tall from a single cutting. However, kasum tends to sprawl if not supported. If continued vigorous growth is desired, kasum needs repeated cutting. We harvest it throughout our growing season every 3 weeks, and these repeated cuttings produce branching. Our stock is maintained vegetatively. *P. odoratum* is an excellent plant for hydrophonic and other soilless cultural practices. The influx of Vietnamese to this country may eventually lead to a more widespread use of this interesting plant.

Some herb dealers market it as coriander, but it is *not* a coriander and neither its flavor nor its aroma resembles that of either coriander or lemon!

CAROLEE BEAN's New Hope Herb Farm is fast becoming famous for its spectacular herb festivals each spring and fall. Featuring many herbal craftspeople, demonstrations, herb plants, and products, these fairs are attended by thousands from all over the country. The seeds or plants of the herbs mentioned in this article are available by mail from the farm.

❧ *Laksa* ❧

Often served as a snack in Malaysia.

1 package laksa (rice noodles)	6 cups water
2 teaspoons chili powder	Three 6½-ounce cans tuna,
1 large onion, diced	packed in water, drained
4 tomatoes, diced	1 cucumber, sliced
Two or three 8-inch branches duam	1 tomato, sliced
kasum, chopped	1 small onion, sliced
1 tablespoon sugar	Lettuce
1 pinch asam (tamarind paste)	Lemon wedges

Soak the laksa in cold water until soft. Bring it to a boil, and boil it until it is tender, but do not overcook or you will have mush. Drain. Combine the chili powder, diced onion, diced tomatoes, kasum, sugar, and asam, and blend well. Add the water, and bring the sauce to a boil. Add the tuna, and continue cooking until the tuna is thoroughly heated. Remove from the heat.

Place the noodles in a large bowl, cover with the sliced cucumbers, tomatoes, and onions and pieces of lettuce. Pour the sauce over the top. Serve with fresh lemon wedges.

Coriander *(Coriandrum sativum)*

Coriander *(Coriandrum sativum)*. An annual that self-sows, *Coriandrum sativum* is called cilantro in Spanish, and I expect that it will soon replace sweet basil as the "trendy" herb of our time. Already, New Jersey parsley fields are being converted to coriander production, and coriander from Mexico fills much of the U.S. winter demand. This herb is essential to most of the world's cooking. The Chinese use it extensively (hence it is often marketed as Chinese parsley) as do Southeast Asians, Middle Easterners, and South Americans. Its dry seeds are used in Indian curries and European baked goods. The fresh plant has a flavor that is quite different from that of the familiar dry seeds.

Coriander is not difficult to grow, but it resents transplanting and will bolt if stressed. When young, the plant resembles a light green, flat-leafed parsley. As it matures, whether from stress or age, it produces a flower stalk from the growing center. Its tiny, white flowers rapidly form seed, at which point it is useless for producing fresh-cut vegetation. We plant coriander seed about ¼ inch deep and 3 inches apart in rows spaced 12 inches apart. It is necessary to keep the seeds constantly moist from planting until the plant begins to bolt, as hot, dry weather will send even small seedlings into reproductive behavior. While it does not germinate well at cold temperatures, coriander is quite cold hardy and ideal for fall planting, since it will overwinter. To maintain a season-long supply of the fresh herb, it is necessary to succession plant every 3 weeks. Even then, in the dry, hot part of summer it may be impossible to keep it from going directly to flower.

The leaf and stem are harvested like parsley. Pick the older, larger outside leaves first, leaving the young, central leaves to grow. When the plants are 5 weeks old, it may, depending on germination rates, be necessary to thin them. In Thailand, because coriander *root* is used as a flavoring in soups and with chicken, it usually is harvested by pulling up the whole plant. Dirt can be washed from the roots, but coriander must not be wet when it is stored or it will rapidly rot. Fresh material placed in a plastic bag will keep 2 weeks in the refrigerator, provided the leaves are not damp. It may become a little wilted, but it will taste just fine.

Kaprow *(Ocimum sanctum)*. The sweet basils familiar to Americans are all *Ocimum basilicum* varieties. However, we raise a culinary *O. sanctum* that needs to be given much more attention. Known in Thailand as bi kaprow, this plant is essential to many stir-fried meat dishes. Like all basils, it is very tender and

❧ *Tomato-Yogurt Salad* ❧ *(from India)*

2 cups plain yogurt
½ cup minced onions
1 cup peeled, diced tomatoes
¼ cup minced green peppers
1 teaspoon ground cumin
Salt and pepper to taste
¼ cup chopped fresh coriander
   leaves

Mix all ingredients in a bowl and refrigerate for 1 hour before serving.

❧ *Coriander Fried Chicken* ❧

8 cloves garlic
2 tablespoons peppercorns
2 tablespoons coriander roots
20 pieces frying chicken

Combine the garlic, peppercorns, and coriander root, and grind the mixture to a paste. Rub the paste on *dry* fryer parts (mixture will not stick to moist pieces). Let the pieces stand for at least 30 minutes. Fry the pieces in hot (375°) oil until golden brown.

much disposed to going to seed. However, on rich ground, in semi-shade, with lots of water, it can be kept in vegetative condition for 2 to 3 months. When it does begin to flower, it should be cut back to within 3 inches of the ground. When it is not cut back, kaprow produces a lank bush 3 feet tall and up to 2 feet in diameter. Repeated cutting will result in a shorter, wider plant. We space our plants 15 inches apart in rows 24 inches apart. Germination of fresh seed is excellent, but old seed (6 months or older) is often very disappointing. Growing requirements are similar to other basils.

With its deep purple stems, purple-green leaves, and pink to purple flowers, kaprow is a very decorative plant for the garden. We find that the dark purple branches make an attractive dried swag; they are also very useful as a filler or accent in arrangements, when harvested during flowering. Although the flavor is not well retained when it is dried (like most herbs, fresh is best), its spicy aroma is quite durable. Kaprow combines well with chicken and with fruits. One-fourth teaspoon dried kaprow added to cherry pie filling is a delicious substitute for mace.

Kaprow is one of the strains of *O. sanctum* that many Indian Hindus like to have growing around their homes, not only because in India, the holy basils are sacred to Vishnu, the Lord of Wisdom and Creation, but they are also said to keep away scorpions. It should be noted that the "holy basil" offered by most seed companies is not the variety Hindus want.

❧ *Red Chicken with Kaprow* ❧

2 cups chicken, uncooked, cut into
    bite-size pieces
2 tablespoons sherry
Oil for sauté
½ cup sliced shallots
½ cup sliced garlic
10 (or more) fresh red chiles, grilled

2 tablespoons shrimp paste
2 teaspoons salt
2 cups straw mushrooms, washed
    and halved
½ cup tomato sauce
Sugar, to taste (optional)
Kaprow leaves
Cooked noodles or rice

Marinate the chicken in the sherry. Sauté the shallots until crisp. Set aside. Sauté the garlic until crisp. *(Do not cook the shallots and garlic together.)* Set aside.

Make a red chile paste by pounding together the red chiles, shrimp paste, and salt. "Fry" the paste in a little oil. Add the chicken, stirring well. Add the mushrooms and tomato sauce; stir well. Add salt to taste. You may also add a dash of sugar, if the sauce seems too sour. Add the shallots and garlic. Mix well. Add a generous handful of kaprow leaves. Stir. Serve on a bed of cooked noodles or rice.

For an extra touch of fragrance, top with some kaprow leaves that have been quickly fried in hot oil.

NAMING ORIENTAL HERBS

Much of the confusion about the names of Oriental herbs is most likely due to the different Eastern groups having their own names for each plant, and possibly different varieties of the same plant. In a section on "Oriental Herbs" in her new book, The Herb Garden Cookbook, *Lucinda Hutson lists* Polygonum odoratum *as rau ram, Vietnamese coriander (which Carolee Bean calls kasum). It is often found in Oriental markets in the warm, summer months. A tender perennial that rarely blooms in the U.S., it must be wintered over in a greenhouse. She adds that "Bai grapao, sometimes called bai kaprow, or Thai basil (also called holy basil or tulsi basil in India and sacred to the Hindus), has highly aromatic and slightly downy leaves with reddish-purple markings. Thai cooks use this sweetly perfumed herb with fish, chicken, and beef curries. I find that it makes a delicious ruby-colored herb vinegar when flavored with ginger slices. I also add it to stir-fries and chicken salad, and with it, I flavor a spicy Szechuan sauce that tastes delicious with grilled chicken or fish." (For more about Thai basil, see pages 84-85.) PVS*

Scalloped Potatoes with Chinese Chives
YIELD: SERVES 4

3 cups sliced, cooked potatoes
3 tablespoons chopped Chinese
*   chives*
2 tablespoons margarine
¾ cup warm milk
½ teaspoon salt
Pepper, as desired

Preheat oven to 350° F. Layer the potatoes, with chives sprinkled over each layer, in a buttered casserole. Combine the margarine, milk, salt, and pepper, and pour this mixture over the potatoes. Bake for 35 to 40 minutes. Serve topped with a sprinkle of fresh chives.

Epazote (Chenopodium ambrosioides)

Garlic, or Chinese, chives *(Allium tuberosa).* Garlic chives are a must for any herb gardener. Easily grown in most soils, this hardy perennial will thrive in full sun or part shade. Garlic chives are a delight for the eye and the palate. The dark green, ribbonlike leaves form graceful clumps. In late summer, white flowers on tall, straight stems not only add to the landscape, but also make excellent cut flowers. The blooms can be hung to become pretty dried flowers, too.

We harvest the leaves by cutting them at ground level as soon as they are 10 to 12 inches long. Unlike regular chives, Chinese chives are flat, with a mild, garlic flavor. With adequate water, the plant will quickly grow again for second and third cuttings. If you want flowers, harvest only a few leaves at a time, not the entire clump. We sell them banded together in large bunches (4 inches in diameter) for our foreign customers, who sauté large amounts to serve as a side dish. American customers, however, prefer bunches the size of a half-dollar. The buds, picked closed or when they are just beginning to open, are also considered a great delicacy by the Chinese.

Garlic chives are wonderful in any stir-fry or salad dressing, in herb butter, or added to sour cream or yogurt for a dip. They are a versatile herb that should find widespread acceptance in American cooking and gardens.

Epazote *(Chenopodium ambrosioides).* In our part of the world, epazote has long been regarded as a weed, which we pull from nearly all our fields. It is known in Indiana as wormseed or goosefoot, but I haven't met any Hoosiers who eat it. It is used extensively in Mexican cooking, however, chiefly as an antiflatulent with beans. Only a few leaves (about two per serving) cooked with a pot of frijoles are said to prevent gas. Epazote tea has traditionally been used to worm children, and this use accounts for one of its common names.

Epazote is an annual and a rampant self-seeder. It has a distinctive, rather pleasant aroma. Only the leaves are harvested, to be used fresh or dried. Grow it in sun or partial shade, with lots of moisture. Although its flowers are not particularly attractive, epazote does have interesting, goosefoot-shaped, light green leaves, sometimes showing red spots and tinges. Its height is 1½ to 2 feet. It will also do well in containers. While we do not grow epazote as a cash crop, we keep a few plants around for tour groups, which often include a savvy ex-farmer who declares, "See Mildred, I told you they just grow a bunch of weeds"!

Lemongrass *(Cymbopogon citratus).* Because lemongrass is a tender perennial, we stuff it into pots, trim all the leaves to soil level, and stack the pots in a dark corner of the greenhouse for the winter. We water the pots just enough to keep the roots alive. Our greenhouse is a cool one, 45° at night and on cloudy days, warmer if the sun shines. When March arrives, we divide the clumps, and then repot the plants into 3-inch pots, water them well, and place them on a sunny shelf. They begin to grow immediately and are ready to go into the field by our frost-free date (May 10). We plant most in the field, but I always put a few in the display garden and have a big pot by the back door. It is a coarse grass, but quite attractive. Give it full sun, good drainage, and adequate water.

We harvest lemongrass by cutting it close to the ground. It is bunched for fresh market, or air-dried in small bunches for later sales. Some customers prefer the coarse, outer leaves for the lovely lemon flavor they impart to food; the leaves are cooked with foods, but removed before serving. Other customers, particularly Vietnamese, want only the tender inner stalks. In the tropics, lemongrass reaches over 3 feet in height, but in Indiana we cut it at 25 inches. We get two harvests in the field, plus the small, final cut as we bring the stock in for winter. Lemongrass will perform well as a container-grown plant, and it is an excellent houseplant.

Fresh or dried lemongrass makes a pleasant tea, and it is widely used as an insect repellent. It is a common culinary herb in many lands, and is gaining in popularity in the U.S. It is also reputed to repel snakes and increase sexual desire, but I will not attest to either attribute!

❧ *Lemongrass and Herb Stuffing* ❧
YIELD: SERVES 4

This recipe calls for chicken breasts, but the stuffing is equally good with Cornish hens or veal.

4 tablespoons chopped lemongrass (inner stalks and tender leaves only)
3 cups bread crumbs
½ teaspoon lemon thyme
½ teaspoon marjoram
¾ teaspoon sage
Salt and pepper, to taste
2 eggs
2 tablespoons water
4 chicken breasts, boned and flattened
1 teaspoon lemon juice
1 tablespoon margarine, melted

Preheat oven to 350° F. Combine the lemongrass, bread crumbs, lemon thyme, marjoram, sage, and salt and pepper, and mix lightly. Beat the eggs with the water, and stir this mixture into the bread crumbs. Divide the mixture into 4 equal parts and place 1 part on each of the chicken breasts. Fold the breasts in half and secure each with a toothpick.

Bake for 30 minutes. Mix the lemon juice and margarine, and drizzle it over the chicken. Bake 10 more minutes. Remove the toothpicks before serving.

In our greenhouse, insect pests are minimal and controls are used only if necessary. We use a synthetic pyrethroid product to control whitefly on various plants, as well as to control thrips on alliums and aphids on rosemaries. Improved circulation lessens the tendency of rosemaries and salvias (officinalis especially) to develop mildew. An effective remedy for scale encountered occasionally on sweet bay (Laurus nobilis) *is to rub up a rich lather of Ivory soap suds in your hands, wash this into a gallon container of water, and apply this to the bay. Citrus oil is also an effective control of some scales.*

KATE AND FAIRMAN JAYNE, SANDY MUSH HERB NURSERY, LEICESTER, NC 28748

CAROLEE BEAN, NEW HOPE HERB FARM, SPENCER, IN 47460

Visiting LOUISE AND CYRUS HYDE'S Well-Sweep Herb Farm is a joyful experience, as their beautifully designed and meticulously kept gardens are an inspiration, and the herb plants and dried materials are of such high quality. I've also enjoyed purchasing many of my plants from them at their booth at the Philadelphia Flower Show almost every spring. The Hydes have open houses and workshops at the farm, as well as an extensive mail-order business. All of the herbs listed in their article are available from their catalog, in either seed or plant form. I feel privileged to have their expertise on these pages.

UNUSUAL HERBS FROM WELL-SWEEP HERB FARM

by Louise and Cyrus Hyde

Many "unusual" herbs are new to us because they come from foreign lands and are rarely found wild in temperate North America. Some are new varieties, some are old favorites, long forgotten, and some are unfamiliar to us because so little has been written about them. Keep in mind that what is unusual to one may be commonplace to another. Some of these could be considered spices. In fact, there is no clear-cut distinction between what qualifies as an herb and what qualifies as a spice, and there can be much overlap. Most references define *spice* as part of a tree, woody shrub, or vine, used for flavoring. Some herbs, however, are extremely woody and resemble small shrubs. Used in cooking or for medicinal purposes, many herbs fit the description of a spice. We believe most so-called spices are really herbs and many herbs may correctly be called spices. We hope you find the herbs discussed here to be intriguing. Perhaps you'll be interested enough to try growing a few on your windowsill or in your herb garden.

Silver corkscrew chives (*Allium senescens* var. *glaucum*). Perennial. An attractive, decorative allium, this variety of chives is the perfect border plant. It never needs trimming, and its silver-gray foliage is decorative when used as an edging. Short, curly leaves form upon little bulblets or clumps. Initially, a bulblet will have only two leaves, but as growth continues, a tight clump is formed, which produces a round, showy plant. The leaves grow about 6 inches high, forming a pretty backdrop for the 9-inch-tall flower stalks. Stunning lavender ball flowers bloom in late summer.

Allspice (*Pimenta dioica* or *P. officinalis*). Tender perennial. Native to the West Indies and Latin America, the allspice tree has smooth bark and evergreen leaves. Cultivated primarily in Jamaica, it grows to a height of 40 feet. The green fruit is harvested and dried before it becomes ripe. The plant's aromatic leaves are used for seasonings and as a tea. Oil from the leaves is used to season meats, condiments, gum, and pastries. Both whole berries and the oil squeezed from the berries are used in pickles, meats, gum, ice cream, soft drinks, and pastries. Oils from both leaves and berries are also utilized in the production of cologne. The flavor of the allspice berry can best be described as a combination of cinnamon, nutmeg, and cloves. The allspice tree makes a nice addition to your greenhouse or home, for the fragrant leaves are an instant pick-me-up.

Thai basil (*Ocimum citridorum* 'Thai'). Annual. Native to Thailand and Burma, Thai basil is used extensively in Thai and Indian cooking. Compared to sweet basil, it has a darker leaf and a slight anise flavor. Its seed — which, when soaked in water increases up to eight times its original size and takes on a resemblance to fish eggs — is used as a decoration on desserts or as a topping on ice cream. Used in this manner, it adds an interesting quality and texture to the food.

Tulsi green basil *(Ocimum sanctum* 'Tulsi'*)* and **tulsi purple basil** *(O. sanctum purpureum* 'Tulsi'*)*. Annuals. The tulsi basils are native to India, where they are revered as sacred. Planted at the doorstep of the house, they are thought to have protective powers against evil, as well as to be an inspiration to the inhabitants to lead pure and righteous lives. The Hindus pray to these plants every morning and use them in religious ceremonies. Both purple and green tulsi basils like rich, moist soil and plenty of sun. In mid-summer they bear whitish lavender blossoms. Take care not to confuse tulsi green and tulsi purple basils with sacred basil *(O. sanctum)*, also known as tulsi basil. "Tulsi" is the Indian word for basil, but only tulsi green and tulsi purple are true tulsi basils.

Well-Sweep miniature purple basil *(Ocimum basilicum* var. *minimum* x *purpurascens* 'Well-Sweep'*)*. Annual. Miniature purple basil was developed right here at Well-Sweep Herb Farm about eight years ago when Cy crossed a large-leaved, purple basil with a tiny green-leaved, miniature basil. Over a period of three or four years, crosses were made and seeds kept, and the best offspring of each of these crosses was selected. The end result was a miniature basil with tiny, purple leaves. Growing into a purple mound about 8 inches wide and 6 inches high, this basil is very showy as well as decorative. The distinctive leaves are flavorful for cooking and add a nice color accent to salads and meat dishes.

Golden bay *(Laurus nobilis* 'Aurea'*)*. Tender perennial. One of the most widely known herbs is the sweet bay tree *(L. nobilis)*; the lesser known, but more decorative, variation of the sweet bay is the golden bay *(L. nobilis* 'Aurea'*)*. Golden bay is a tender perennial in northern climates, to be overwintered indoors, just as sweet bay is. It is usually kept in pots in the North. The leaves of the two grow similarly but the new growth of the golden bay has a golden tinge. Showy and pretty as a specimen planting, the golden bay can be used in soups, stews, and sauces, or to make bouquet garni for fish and various meat dishes. The leaves of either bay are used to repel weevils in flour and other grains. The golden bay came to Well-Sweep from England.

Cinnamon tree *(Cinnamomum zeylanicum)*. Tender perennial. Native to Ceylon and Southwest India, the cinnamon tree is an evergreen that can grow to a height of 50 feet; in climates not tropical enough for it to grow outside, it can be grown as a houseplant, for its lush growth makes it quite desirable. When crushed, its green, shiny, leathery leaves release a strong, spicy aroma. The powerful, hot, clovelike oil produced from them is used to flavor chewing gum, candies, beverages, and liqueurs. The oil from the bark is used mainly in the production of soft cola drinks, candy, and ice cream. Cinnamon sticks and powdered cinnamon come from the inner bark, which has been rolled into quills and thoroughly dried. Most of the cinnamon used in the

Consider a low hedge for your herb garden. A bush thyme or germander makes a neat, attractive hedge when kept trimmed; use about one plant per foot. You can also use annuals such as curly parsley, purple basil (dark opal), or marigolds.

KATE AND FAIRMAN JAYNE, SANDY MUSH HERB NURSERY, LEICESTER, NC 28748

Cinnamon *(Cinnamomum zeylanicum)*

Start recycling pint-, quart-, and gallon-size jars, especially those with wide mouths, for making your own herbal vinegars this summer. Mayonnaise jars are great, as are large juice bottles. Save salad dressing containers to use as gift containers for your finished products. Soak the empty bottles in hot, sudsy water to remove the labels before sterilizing in the dishwasher. You'll be glad you stored these up, for once you get started with vinegars it's hard to stop! It's also a good idea to start stocking up on white wine vinegar each time you get groceries. The base of most herb vinegar recipes, white wine vinegar bought in large quantities can be expensive, but you won't notice it so much if you buy an extra bottle now and then. PVS

If you would like to grow herbs that are too tender to survive the winter outdoors in your region, pot them in clay pots, and then plant the entire pot in the ground. These can easily be taken up and moved inside for the winter, and then repotted in spring as needed.

KATE AND FAIRMAN JAYNE, SANDY MUSH HERB NURSERY, LEICESTER, NC 28748

United States today is actually cassia *(C. cassia)*. The cassia bark is heavier and thicker than cinnamon bark, but the taste is not as strong or flavorful. Cassia powder is reddish-brown; cinnamon powder is tan in color.

Cilentro *(Eryngium foetidum)*. Perennial. Native to tropical America and the West Indies, cilentro has 2- to 8-inch long, spiny-toothed leaves, which appear first, followed by flower stalks. Cilentro resembles sea holly in growth and shape. It has a strong coriander fragrance. The leaves are used for making soups and curries, in rice and fish dishes, and in most Mexican cooking. Most of us know coriander as the greens of *Coriandrum sativum*, an annual with a milder coriander flavor and a shorter season of growth. *Eryngium foetidum*, on the other hand, is the true coriander.

Well-Sweep golden lemon crispum geranium *(Pelargonium crispum* 'Variegata Aureum Well-Sweep'*)*. Tender perennial. This geranium was developed at Well-Sweep by Cy after he discovered a variegated branch had developed on one of his lemon crispum geranium topiaries. He rooted and propagated this sport, which has now developed into a beautiful, very showy specimen plant, with green leaves edged with gold. The leaves have a strong lemon fragrance and can be used to make potpourri, tea, cakes, and the like.

Well-Sweep variegated horehound *(Marrubium vulgare* 'Variegata'*)*, perennial; Variegated lemon verbena *(Aloysia triphylla* 'Variegata'*)*, tender perennial; and Well-Sweep variegated germander *(Teucrium chamaedrys* 'Variegata Well-Sweep'*)*, perennial. Some unusual plant developments from Well-Sweep Herb Farm are the variegated-leaved plants of lemon verbena, horehound, and germander. Each has white striping in the leaves; the lemon verbena boasts pale green and white stripes as well. Any of these showy new developments can add a decorative, festive accent to your herb garden. The horehound can be used in tea and cough drops; the verbena, for tea, desserts, cakes, fruit cups, jellies, and salads.

Hardy white jasmine *(Jasminum officinale)* and hardy pink jasmine *(J. x stephanense)*. Perennials. Among our collections of plants is a group of jasmines from all over the world. Each is different, lending its own special aroma to the world of fragrance. Most jasmines are tropical and cannot withstand freezing temperatures, but we have two hardy varieties, given to us by Reverend Douglas Siedel and Dr. Arthur Tucker: hardy white and hardy pink jasmine. Both require well-drained soil and protection from winter winds. The hardy white jasmine boasts green leaves and white flowers that contain the essential oil used in perfumery. Most often mentioned in ancient herbal literature, this jasmine was introduced to North Africa, Sicily, and Spain by Arabs from its native Persia. The hardy pink jasmine has pink flowers that open to white. A vining plant with an intense jasmine fragrance, this plant is a cross between a common jasmine and a pink Himalayan species *(J.*

officinale x *J. beesianum*). These two hardy jasmines are easy to grow. We have several other, nonhardy, but very special, jasmines suitable for greenhouse culture as well.

Tzopelic Xlhuitl *(Lippia dulcis)*. Tender perennial. Pretty *Lippia dulcis's* deep-veined leaves cascade down long leaf-arms, forming a lush, hanging plant. An aggressive spreader, *L. dulcis* is readily grown from seed or cuttings. The intensely sweet leaves of this unusual herb are reputed to be ten times sweeter than sugar. In fact, Aztec Indians were the first to use *L. dulcis* as a sweetener. The active ingredient in its leaves is hernandulcin.

Sweet herb of Paraguay *(Stevia rebaudiana)*. Tender perennial. Another potent sweetener is the sweet herb of Paraguay. The leaves of this herb can be used either fresh or dried. It is reported that the plant's sweetening agent, the glycoside stevioside, is 300 times sweeter than granulated table sugar. Stevioside, however, is far more than a nonfattening sugar substitute: It actually triggers hypoglycemic activity, reducing blood-sugar levels as it sweetens. It has been reported that Paraguayan Indian women use a tea of the sweet herb as a contraceptive, and tests performed on laboratory rats have confirmed that it reduces fertility. Although about 100 various species of *Stevia* grow wild in Paraguay and Brazil, it is not easy to grow. Commercial production has not met with great success because it does not seed readily and is a sparse grower; in addition, production has been reduced as a result of criticism of the clearing of rain forest. Just a taste of the intense sweetness of one leaf, however, makes this interesting plant a worthwhile addition to your herb collection.

Sweet olive *(Osmanthus fragrans)*. Tender perennial. The sweet olive, or tea olive, was so named because of its wonderfully sweet blossoms, which were used in China to add flavor and scent to tea, and also for flavoring desserts much as we use vanilla. The Chinese call it *Kwai*. Although sweet olive can grow to a height of 30 feet, it can be grown in the greenhouse or as a houseplant. Its small, cream-white flowers, which will bloom all winter, smell much like orange blossoms, and their fragrance will scent an entire house.

Pink Queen-Anne's-lace, or wild carrot *(Daucus carota)*. Biennial/Hardy annual. Most of us know Queen-Anne's-lace as it grows in the fields and meadows across the U.S. Here at Well-Sweep Herb Farm, Cy has worked for the past 5 years isolating a pretty pink variety. As on white Queen-Anne's-lace, the flower heads are a flat cluster of flowers composed of approximately 500 separate, small flowers. On this new variety, however, they range in color from pink to maroon to almost red. The flowers bloom from May to October on 24- to 36-inch stems with green, lacy leaves. This plant makes a showy statement in your garden. We sell this only as seed and cannot guarantee results. It will become a hardy annual if planted in the spring and a biennial if planted in the late summer.

Damask 'Bella Donna' rose *(Rosa damascena* 'Bella Donna'*)*.

A strategic part of our farm operation — our compost heap — contains nonwoody vegetation (minus seed heads), sand, black woodland dirt, daily donations from the goats, and wood ash from the cookstove.

PAT AND JON BOURDO, WOODLAND HERB FARM, NORTHPORT, MI 49670

Showy savory *(Calamintha grandiflora)*

❤

We've found that the most efficient mulch for our field herbs is water-soaked newspaper, overlapped in layers on the ground between plants and row, and then covered with mulch hay. The black ink of newsprint is very good for the soil, weeds are minimal, and the plants are clean for harvesting.

PAT AND JON BOURDO, WOODLAND HERB FARM, NORTHPORT, MI 49670

❤

Perennial. The Bella Donna rose is an old-fashioned, moss-type rose that is so beautiful and so heavily scented that everyone should experience one. It blooms from June into July with lovely, pink, ultra-double flowers. The flower petals can be picked for potpourris, teas, and, best of all, for wonderful rose-petal jam. The petals impart their sweet, rose scent to jam that tastes just like the rose smells. Not as invasive as most damask roses, the clumpy, upright Bella Donna needs occasional pruning. Fortunately, it is not threatened by many pests or diseases.

Showy savory (Calamintha grandiflora). Perennial. The tangerine scent of the leaves of showy savory is so sweet and pervasive that it lures you back again and again. About 14 inches high, with pretty, deep-pink to purple-mauve flowers, the plant makes a nice mound shape that is excellent in either the herb garden or the flowering perennial garden. The leaves can be dried for potpourri or tea; used fresh, they add a pretty accent to fruit salads and desserts.

Sweet goldenrod; Blue Mountain tea (Solidago odora). Perennial. Sweet goldenrod is native to the U.S., where it is found in dry, open fields from Massachusetts and New Hampshire to the Blue Ridge Mountains and the South. Its small, yellow flower heads form into clusters that bloom from July through September. It has narrow, green, anise-scented leaves that have a flavor like French tarragon; in fact, when chewed, the leaves even numb the tongue like the true French tarragon does. The leaves can be dried and brewed into a tea, which the Pennsylvania Dutch use as a pleasant after-dinner tea, called Blue Mountain tea. The flowers, leaves, and stems have long been used as a dye. A strong tea from these flowers produces a brown liquid, which, with the addition of a mordant such as powdered alum, changes to a brilliant golden color; the dye is extremely colorfast on woolens and cottons. Goldenrod has long been maligned as the cause of hayfever, due to its appearance in the fields during the heavy pollen time. The real culprit, however, is ragweed *(Ambrosia artemisifolia),* which has inconspicuous, light yellow flowers on a green plume. Ragweed pollen is airborne, while the goldenrod is carried by bees and insects, and thus does not produce the same overwhelming nasal reactions.

Vetiver, or khus-khus (Vetiveria zizanioides). Tender perennial. Vetiver is a tall grass, native to India, Burma, and Ceylon, and much of the tropics. In the United States it is grown in Louisiana as a very clumped perennial grass. In the North, it is planted outside in the spring, then dug in the fall and brought in for the winter. The fibrous, spongy roots are trimmed back, then washed, cleaned, and dried. As they dry, the scent of the vetiver becomes increasingly stronger. The essential oil yielded by the roots is used to flavor fruit drinks in India, can asparagus, and, most importantly, manufacture perfume. Not only does the sweet, woodsy scent of the oil enhance perfumes, colognes, soaps, cosmetics, and flavorings, but it is a good fixative that extends the life of any mixture to which it is added. During the Victorian era, vetiver was a favorite scent for dresser drawers and chests; it was also used in linen closets to protect clothing from insects. In India, mats and window screens woven of the roots are sprinkled with water daily, and their scent pervades the house.

Yerba buena *(Satureja douglasii).* Tender perennial. Yerba buena is a Spanish herb whose name translates as "good herb." Native to the western U.S., this plant has long, trailing stems, which make it very showy for hanging baskets — the full stems cascading from the container remind one of long lace curtains. The white-to purplish-flowers are tubular. The Spanish use yerba buena to steep a stomach-soothing tea, the flavor and scent of which are similar to that first of freshly cracked hickory nuts, then of strong menthol.

The plants mentioned in this article are available through the Well-Sweep Farm catalog. PVS

LOUISE AND CYRUS HYDE, WELL-SWEEP HERB FARM, PORT MURRAY, NJ 07865

Herb Propogation

PROCEDURES FOR PROPAGATING HERBS FOR THE NATIONAL HERB GARDEN

by Catherine Russell
(U.S. National Arboretum Volunteer)
and
Holly H. Shimizu
(Former curator, The National Herb Garden)

Seeds are sown, according to the chart that follows, in flats containing a dampened mix of 1 part milled sphagnum and 1 part Q-Roc, a crushed stone product. The wet mix is tamped and seeds sown evenly, in rows. Most seeds are covered about three times their diameter; fine seeds, such as digitalis, need not be covered. The top is tamped and moistened, with care taken not to wash the seeds. Flats of seeds that need cold stratification are enclosed in plastic bags and refrigerated as necessary. Most seeds do not need to have bottom heat, but they do need to be kept at about 70° to 75° F. The flats are covered with clear plastic or glass. When they have acquired their first set of true leaves (the second set of leaves to appear), seedlings are potted into cell packs or very small pots. They are protected from bright sun for several days, then allowed more sun to promote healthy growth. They are planted out after all danger of frost is past and after seedlings have been hardened-off for several days inside a greenhouse maintained at 40° F. Plants that are cold-hardy are set out earlier, also after

HOLLY SHIMIZU was the original curator of the National Herb Garden, a gift from The Herb Society of America to the nation. For several years she did a remarkable job of overseeing the project and inspiring the public to enjoy the results. She has been a prolific writer and a dynamic speaker about herbs. Currently, she is the Public Programs Specialist for the United States Botanic Garden in Washington. This is a description of the way more plants are obtained to supply The National Herb Garden at the U.S. National Arboretum, rather than an explanation of the many methods that can be used to propagate herbs.

Time Chart for Propagation Using Seeds

SEED	COMMON NAME*	FALL[1] OUTDOORS	FEBRUARY INDOORS	MARCH-APRIL INDOORS	MAY[3] IN PLACE
Agastache	Anise hyssop			x	
Allium tuberosum	Garlic chives			x	
Anethum graveolens	Dill	x		x	x
Angelica archangelica ❧	Angelica		x		x
Anthriscus cerefolium ❧	Chervil		x		x
Artemisia annua	Sweet Annie			x	x
Borago officinalis	Borage			x	x
Calendula officinalis	Calendula; Pot marigold		x	x	
Carum carvi	Caraway	x		x	
Chrysanthemum parthenium	Feverfew; Pyrethrum			x	
Coreopsis tinctoria	Calliopsis; Dye plant			x	
Coriandrum sativum	Coriander	x		x	
Cuminum cyminum	Cumin			x	x
Foeniculum vulgare	Fennel	x		x	x
Ilex paraguariensis ✳	Yerba maté; Paraguay tea			x	
Isatis tinctoria ❧	Woad; Dyer's weed			x	
Levisticum officinale	Lovage		x		
Lippia graveolens	Mexican oregano			x	
Marrubium vulgare	Horehound	x		x	
Matricaria recutita	German chamomile			x	
Myrrhis odorata ❧	Sweet cicely		x	x	x
Nepeta cataria	Catnip	x		x	
Nigella sativa	Bitter fitch; Bible plant			x	
Ocimum	Basil			x	
Origanum majorana	Sweet marjoram			x	
Petroselinum crispum	Curly parsley	x	x		
Poterium sanguisorba	Burnet		x		
Rumex scutatus	French sorrel			x	
Salvia sclarea	Clary sage			x	
Satureja hortensis	Summer savory			x	
Tropaeolum majus [2]	Nasturtium			x	
Verbascum thapsus	Mullein			x	
Viola	Violet family			x	x

CODE:

✳ Cold stratify

❧ Sow as soon as ripe or keep refrigerated

[1] Not always reliable

[2] Soak in warm water 24 hours

[3] These resent transplanting; use extreme care if alternate method is used

* Common names added by PVS for your convenience

Other Propagation Methods

Divisions[3]

PLANT	COMMON NAME*
Alchemilla vulgaris	Lady's-mantle
Allium schoenoprasum	Chives
Allium tuberosum	Garlic chives
Artemisia dracunculus var. *sativa*	French tarragon
Artemisia ludoviciana	Silver King
Asperula odorata	Sweet woodruff
Chamaemelum nobile	Roman chamomile
Glycyrrhiza glabra	Licorice
Hydrocotyle asiatica	Gotu kola
Inula helenium	Elecampane
Levisticum officinale	Lovage
Marrubium vulgare	Horehound
Melissa officinalis	Lemon balm
Mentha x *piperita*	Peppermint
Monarda didyma	Red bee balm
Monarda fistulosa	Lavender bee balm
Nepeta cataria	Catnip
Nepeta x *faassenii*	Catmint
Origanum	Spreading oregano
Symphytum officinale	Comfrey
Thymus	Creeping thyme

CODE:
- ◆ Cuttings in Spring — softwood; cuttings in late July —with heel of old wood
- [1] Cuttings in September-October — with heel of old wood
- [2] Most authorities advise to let sit out a day to harden-off; we find unnecessary and use mildest hormone powder
- [3] Early spring, as new growth appears
- [4] Usually midsummer
- [5] Can also be propagated by layering

* Common names added by PVS for your convenience

Stem Cuttings[4]

PLANT	COMMON NAME*
Aloysia triphylla	Lemon verbena
Artemisia, perennial types	Southernwood; Wormwood; etc.
Helichrysum angustifolium	Curry plant
Hyssopus officinalis	Hyssop
Ilex paraguariensis [1]	Yerba maté
Laurus nobilis [1]	Sweet bay
Lavandula ◆	Lavender
Lippia graveolens	Mexican oregano
Marrubium vulgare	Horehound
Mentha (perennial type)	Mint
Origanum dictamnus [5]	Dittany of Crete
Origanum vulgare	Oregano
Pelargonium, scented [2]	Geraniums
Rosmarinus officinalis ◆	Rosemary
Ruta graveolens ◆	Rue
Salvia (perennial types)	Sage
Santolina ◆	Lavender cotton
Satureja montana	Winter savory
Stevia rebaudiana	Sugar substitute from Paraguay
Tagetes lucida	Sweet-scented marigold
Teucrium chamaedrys	Germander
Thymus	Thyme

Root Cuttings

PLANT	COMMON NAME
Amoracia rusticana	Horseradish
Artemisia dracunculus var. *sativa*	French tarragon
Humulus lupulus	Hops
Symphytum officinale	Comfrey

CAUTIONS

*Both pruners and mixes
should be sterile. To eliminate
errors, all cuttings, seed flats,
and seedlings are clearly labeled. Special clones of flavorful
or fragrant herbs such as Thymus, Lavandula, Mentha,
Origanum, and Rosmarinus are
propagated vegetatively since
they may not germinate true to
type from seed.*

REPRINTED WITH PERMISSION FROM
HOLLY H. SHIMIZU, FORMER CURATOR,
THE NATIONAL HERB GARDEN. FOR A
BROCHURE ABOUT THE NATIONAL
HERB GARDEN, WRITE TO: INFORMA-
TION CENTER, NATIONAL HERB
GARDEN, U.S. NATIONAL ARBORETUM,
WASHINGTON, DC 20016

having been hardened-off. (A cold frame is very good for hardening-off.)

Division is probably the easiest way to increase plants. Clumps of hardy plants are dug in early spring just as the new shoots break through the ground. With a sharp knife or two digging forks, the clumps are cut into sections that are then planted in desired locations. Certain plants, such as *Artemisia dracunculus* var. *sativus* (French tarragon), can be separated in the fall when they are dug for overwintering, and potted separately.

Stem cuttings are best made sometime between mid-July and the end of August. Nonflowering stems are removed from the plant just above the semi-hard wood. When possible, more than one cutting is made from a stem. The bottom of each cut should be made just below a node (the place where a leaf emerges). These bottoms are dipped in water, shaken, then dipped into the mildest possible rooting hormone, and shaken again, leaving a thin film of hormone. The cuttings are stuck 1½ to 2 inches apart, upright, in a bench filled with a mix of 1 part milled sphagnum and 1 part large perlite. A mist system is used to keep them moist. Bottom heat, maintained at 68° to 70° F., helps with root formation. Cuttings are potted in a general-purpose mix when they have acquired roots about 1 inch long, returned to a similar environment for about 1 week, and then moved to a sunny location until time to plant them outside.

Root cuttings are made in late fall or in spring, as soon as the ground is workable. A root is cut into 2-inch pieces, which are placed on a flat filled with a mixture of 1 part sand and 1 part peat, firmly tamped and dampened. They are covered with about ½ inch of the mix, tamped firmly, then moistened and placed under mist, using bottom heat at about 68° to 70° F.

TIPS ON ORGANIC INSECT/DISEASE CONTROL FOR THE HOME GARDENER

For greenhouse pests — or outdoors — yellow strips of plastic smeared with petroleum jelly are effective traps for most small, flying insects. Yellow Stiky Traps are available at home and garden centers, and also from Necessary Trading Co. (see Appendix, March, Natural Gardening Sources). Safer's Insecticidal Soap works safely on herbs to combat aphids, whiteflies, red spider, thrips, and mealy-bugs. Rotenone and pyrethrum are a bit stronger, yet are safe organic materials for insect control on culinary herbs. Ladybugs love aphids, and Encarsia formosa are whitefly parasites that may work for you. For fungal disease try horsetail tea (¼ cup leaves per gallon of water) or liquid sulphur or liquid copper.

CELIA "CRICKETT" HEFNER, EDITOR, NEWSLETTER OF THE NORTH CAROLINA HERB ASSOCIATION

HERBS AND NATURAL GARDENING

by June King

Just as herbs play an important part in the health of our gardens, natural gardening increases the well-being of our herbs. Using only natural, organic products in our soil and on our gardens increases the health of the plants, ourselves, and our environment.

Plants are very much like people — not only do they require food, air, water, and sunshine as do we mortals, but they also have likes and dislikes when it comes to their companions. It is a known fact that plants growing together interact in certain ways. One species may provide special nutrients needed by neighboring plants, or perhaps the root system of a certain plant helps to loosen the soil. Many plants are bug repellents, while others emit fragrances that attract beneficial predators. With proper knowledge of this natural interaction, we can grow our herbs, flowers, and vegetables together. Our ancestors often took advantage of these characteristics, and their gardens thrived without poisonous chemicals. We can do likewise.

Roses like garlic, but dislike boxwood; tomatoes like basil; cabbage likes dill and sage; carrots like lettuce and chives; basil dislikes rue; cucumbers dislike sage; carrots dislike dill; most plants dislike fennel. The alliums are generally good companions as they deter insects, but peas and beans are inhibited by them. Nasturtiums are a good bug repellent and are beneficial to radishes and apple trees. Yarrow benefits surrounding plants, but wormwood inhibits plant neighbors with its toxic root secretions. Petunias and marigolds are generally beneficial throughout the garden. Caraway planted here and there helps loosen the soil.

One of the most important essentials of natural gardening is the proper use of fertilizers. Commercial synthetic fertilizers create many problems for the soil, such as build-ups of ammonia, chlorine, nitrates, acids, and salts that destroy beneficial soil organisms. In addition to compost, many natural fertilizers are available to provide nutrients for healthy plants. Fish emulsion is highly recommended as an excellent source of nitrogen for herb beds. Bone meal and crab meal provide valuable nutrients and help neutralize acid soil. Green sand, made from ocean deposits, is a good source of minerals, as well as an excellent addition to too-heavy or clay soil. Better yet, several natural soil conditioners contain a blend of many natural beneficial soil builders; use these both when you create new herb beds and when you restore established gardens. Because your local garden center may not carry these, I urge you to send for and study the catalogs of those who specialize in natural products.

Several natural, homemade sprays work well for insect and disease control. Soapy water (any nondetergent) may be effective in a solution of 3 tablespoons to a gallon of water. Strong-smelling

---

JUNE KING wrote Natural Gardening *as part of her determination to speak out for the environment. What appears here is drawn from her sections on fertilizers and natural insect and disease control. She also covers soil management, composting, resources, and more. She writes,* "Many herbs grow well in Florida as long as they are protected from the hot, afternoon sun. The few cold days we experience are no problem compared to the summer heat. If a sheltered spot is not available on one's property, herbs should be grown in pots that can be moved to a shady spot on summer afternoons. Some herbs that do well for me are rose geranium, rosemary, winter tarragon, pineapple sage, southernwood, Silver King artemisia, thyme, basil, winter savory, lemon balm, perilla, comfrey, chives (especially garlic chives), oregano, tansy, wormwood, and bay laurel."

❤

To avoid the fungal diseases that herbs for the most part are prone to, cuttings are maintained as dry as possible. Water thyme cuttings by hand; thymes are more difficult to root in flats under mist because they are extra prone to rot (practically overnight). Between waterings, keep them dry, almost to the point of wilting.

KATE AND FAIRMAN JAYNE, SANDY MUSH HERB NURSERY, LEICESTER, NC 28748

❤

FROM *SPEAK OUT FOR THE ENVIRONMENT WITH NATURAL GARDENING* JUNE KING, KEYSTONE HEIGHTS, FL 32656

herb plants (chamomile, chives, garlic, thyme, rosemary, catnip, and so on) are helpful. Blend them with water, plus a little soap or oil to help the solution adhere to the plants. Garlic is particularly popular. To make a garlic solution, bring to a boil a quart of water, add several crushed garlic cloves, cool, and strain. This mixture will deter insects and also help control fungus. Both garlic and chamomile "teas" are known to help prevent powdery mildew and damping off of seedlings. Many effective natural commercial controls are also available, including pyrethrum, rotenone, and diatomacious earth, for emergencies. Follow package instructions carefully and use pyrethrum and rotenone cautiously. Remember, natural poisons can be dangerous, too.

Speak out for the environment by practicing natural gardening with your herbs and in your herb beds!

APRIL

BECAUSE OF THEIR curiosity about fragrances, flavors, and textures, young children are instinctively drawn to the sensual delights of herbs. A child responds eagerly to the sensations of smell, taste, and touch, so it is a rewarding experience to expose a youngster to a garden of herbs! Your own children will come by this fascination naturally, almost by osmosis, if you allow them to help you with your herbal projects — whenever they ask, no matter how young they are. Small ones just love to do whatever their mommy and daddy are doing, so it is easy to make sure that their first experiences with herbs are exciting and joyful. Several good books on children's gardening projects (including a book devoted to herb projects) are listed on page 298. Whether to help you guide your own youngsters or to aid you in teaching herbs to 4-H, scout, or "Y" groups, these references will supplement the projects for children in this book (see Children in the index) and

serve as useful instructional tools. Spring is certainly a good time to start making family or group plans for the herb gardening season ahead.

This is an appropriate time, too, to think about (which is all I sometimes do on this subject!) housecleaning jobs. I remember one fall when I wished I had done heavier spring cleaning — and summer cleaning. It was a year when I was concentrating on my first book (as my family and friends know, housekeeping is nowhere near the top of my list of priorities, any year), and we ended up with a flea infestation from our three pets that took the entire fall to rid ourselves of. This meant constant cleanings of the entire house and the pets, over and over again, to catch all the cycles of the flea population's growth, from egg to adult. I am more attentive to housekeeping needs now, therefore, and I am especially pleased that this chapter includes sound herbal advice on this subject.

The rest of this chapter covers wonderful spring salads and

crafts to honor the season. What better ways to celebrate the defrosting of winter than to embark children on a lifetime

adventure with herbs, use our much-loved plants to help with the housecleaning chores, and savor our first garden-fresh

salads of the year? May this season of resurrection and renewal revitalize your spirits and lives.

Herb Projects for Children

PLEASE DO PICK THE LAVENDER!
(MAKING HERBS A FAMILY AFFAIR)

When our children were young, they eagerly participated in every aspect of growing herbs and flowers and making herbal and floral creations, except the weeding! Because we lived in an isolated country home and I wanted a hobby that allowed me to keep my eye on the youngsters as they played outdoors, I started gardening as an escape from "cabin fever." Little did I know when I started concentrating on herbs that my hobby would engulf the whole family and lead to many outdoor and indoor activities to be shared by all. It wasn't long before our son and two daughters wanted to "play with mommy." Soon they were helping to plant, harvest, dry, and defoliate the herbs, and to make potpourri, sew sachet bags, and package and label the finished products. During their teens, when we started a small herb business from "Mom's hobby," they were paid for their assistance. And I didn't have to train them or supervise their work, as they had shared the pleasures and the fun for years at their own choosing!

Young children are instinctively drawn to the beauty and fragrance of flowers and herbs, so the joys of being creative with our own gardens and preserving the harvests for winter use have been year-round delights for our family. As early as nursery school, each of our children used herbs for "show and tell," plus "see and smell." In later years, we kept a running notebook on herbs, and they enjoyed researching my collection of herb books and making notations in the notebook on the uses and properties of each new herb that we grew. From this they prepared essays and speeches about herbs for school assignments; herb samples were always part of their presentations.

Truly, herbs can and should involve the whole family. It always pleased me to see children accompanying both parents at local evening lectures I gave on herbs. With so many men now helping with or doing the cooking, gourmet dads are very likely to appreciate and share mother's delight with the herb gardens. It is extremely

preferable that both parents are knowledgeable about identifying herbs in the garden, so that careful supervision is in effect from the start if the children are to become involved. Nonedible herbs should be either grown separately, with a strict hands-off policy for younger family members, or not grown at all while there are toddlers in the family. It is vitally important to teach little ones that only certain plants can go in the mouth, especially when they could be watching as you, for example, show your neighbor how fresh spearmint tastes.

Perhaps the most family fun of all was our children's delight with the flavors of herbs. During the summers, we had tea-tasting parties at night as we worked on the day's harvest or started potpourri for the winter. We created a chart for everyone to rate each new taste treat from the garden. (Children love to have their opinions count!) And the girls helped Grandma Shaudys make homemade bread for each family picnic. For each batch, they experimented with different fresh-herb flavors and had great fun deciding which herbs would best complement the main course for the meal. As they became more sophisticated about the culinary herbs, they created home-grown herb tea blends and culinary mixes to give to their teachers and relatives as gifts. It is very necessary to teach children at an early age always to label their trays of drying herbs, so there will be no confusion later, especially regarding the edible herbs. They will look different when dried, and some of the aromas are similar enough to be difficult to identify, if not clearly marked. It is also a good idea for children to learn always to list the ingredients of any culinary or fragrant gift they might give. This teaches them not only the importance of knowing what they are eating (or giving others to ingest), but also the necessity for notifying the recipient of any ingredient, edible or not, that might cause allergic reactions.

How our children loved to make their own sachets or jars of potpourri for Christmas gifts and school fairs! We shared many precious hours together creating gifts from the summer's harvest. Many important decisions were made in July or August as to who would receive which fragrance. And the grandmothers never complained that their bureau drawers were filled with sachets in all possible scents and fabrics, so lovingly fashioned after months of careful planning. Some good projects include sachets, sweet bags, jars of natural room-fresheners, herbal pillows, moth-repellent bags or closet "bouquets," and, espe-

cially, catnip toys for kitty.

Our youngsters also enjoyed defoliating the dried herb stems, saving the leaves for kitchen or potpourri use, and then bunching the fragrant stems to tie together with colorful ribbons and package in plastic food-storage bags. This gift was accompanied by instructions to place stems on burning embers in a woodstove or fireplace, as the bunches emit a brief but delightful herbal scent.

It is pure joy to have a child beg to pick the lavender, or to hear one's children and their friends become exhilarated with the delightful aroma they are creating through the house as they defoliate spearmint or lemon southernwood or bergamot, or to watch one's teenage daughter prepare a pot of hot peppermint tea to serve to her friends for a snack. Our younger daughter, Kim, who began doing much of the family cooking during the summers after she was 16, has created many of her own recipes, always seasoned with herbs from our gardens (some of her recipes are included in later chapters). Karen, our older daughter, gardens as a vocation as well as an avocation. What a thrill for me when she was in charge of the herb, rose, and vegetable gardens for 2 years at the Atlanta Botanical Gardens in Georgia! Son Kirk, too, loves to garden, never refuses a dinner invitation when I'm cooking, and seemed very pleased that his bride wanted an herbal wedding. Kirk and Vickie's little Dannie was strolling the herb beds and smelling the plants as early as 14 months of age, and

when he was 16 months old, would start to sniff as soon as he entered our house. "Gramma, sniff, sniff" was his salutation to me!

The long-range and far-reaching effects of a family adventure with herbs will add much richness to your lives, indefinitely. And, after your children have spent a summer or two with you in the gardens, you will never again have to admonish them with a sharp, "Don't pick the flowers!" The family hobby will have taught them an awesome respect for nature's bounties. In fact, after you are growing plenty of herbs and flowers for your winter projects, you will be saying, "Please do pick the lavender"!

❤

After collecting pine cones (or other cones) in the spring, place them on a cookie sheet and heat them in a very low oven to kill insects (about 1 hour). Store for winter projects (see pages 234-36).

❤

TEACHING CHILDREN ABOUT AND WITH HERBS

by Susan Betz

After I witnessed SUSAN BETZ'S marvelous presentation on "Herbcrafting with Kids" at the Celebration of Herbs conference at Michigan State University, I asked her to share the highlights in writing for us. Susan has an herb shop and enjoys teaching others about herbs.

Herbs and herb gardening can be used as very effective teaching aids when working with children. Always popular as seasonings for food, herbs can also enhance other activities, such as educational studies or leisure-time hobbies. Herbs stimulate not only the five senses, but also the imagination and curiosity of a child. From the first leaf that pops up through the soil to the development of a fragrant smell or interesting texture, they unfailingly attract a child's interest. Whether used in medicines or foods, as decorations or symbols, herbs are an important part of the folklore and history of many cultures. Every plant has a special story to tell, and children enjoy associating these stories and legends with the plants. If a child's interest can be aroused, he or she will want to learn more. If you are a classroom teacher, for instance, why not offer a cup of Oswego tea while studying colonial times, or have a home-economics class wash dishes with the juice of bouncing Bet? They might laugh, but you will get their attention.

It has been said that the hobbies and leisure-time activities people enjoy as adults were first discovered when they were between the ages of 4 and 14. Gardening and herb-crafting can be lifetime adventures and loves. My 80-year-old neighbor's garden still remains one of the great joys in her life, and she started gardening as a child. Because they don't need a lot of room, herbs are an especially nice way to introduce a child to the world of gardens and the art of gardening — you can even make an herb garden in several containers on a windowsill, if space is a problem. Patient and tolerant, herbs are very adaptable to various growing conditions — a necessity with kids.

Just as you always research a plant's preferences before you plant it, you should also study the child or group you will be working with in order to make your presentation suit their frame of reference. All children, and, of course, age groups, differ in their interests, personalities, and aptitudes. If you wish to introduce techniques for garden design, create theme gardens that fit the group's interests. For example, plan an herb and everlastings garden for a group of 4-H crafters, a fairy-tale garden displaying plants mentioned in folklore and fairy tales for outside a library, or a wildlife garden to attract butterflies and insects for collectors. The possibilities are endless. Allow the group to help with suggestions in the creation of its own garden. The communal sharing of a common goal makes group gardening both fun and rewarding.

Visit the gardens during the growing season to offer the children hands-on help as well as verbal advice. Start small and teach good, basic principles; then expand at the child's or group's pace. Raised beds are easier to maintain in the long run. Little

Bergamot *(Monarda didyma)*, for Oswego tea

children enjoy tools that fit their hand size; toddlers and small children love watering cans. What they enjoy the most, however, is the parent's or instructor's interest in the progression of their endeavors. Not everyone enjoys working the earth and creating a garden, yet everyone enjoys the beauty of the harvest.

Herb crafting, too, is fun for both children and adults. Children enjoy creating their own potpourris, wreaths, floral arrangements, jewelry, ornaments, and holiday decorations. All of the plant materials can be grown in your own garden, or purchased at a food co-op, herb, or craft shop. If funds are short, wild gathering is a possibility, yet never abuse Mother Nature's order by taking rare plants or by taking so much that the area won't quickly recover. If you use your imagination, rummage and garage sales yield abundant craft supplies, such as beautiful lace for trim, table scarves for sweet pillows, old linen hankies for sachets, and an endless supply of various containers for floral arrangements. Essential oils can add fun and fragrance to projects such as play dough, clay, and candle- and soap-making.

The learning experience or project time can be delightful and fun — or very boring. Children and young adults enjoy a hands-on learning environment, one in which they personally participate in a group or individual project. It gives them a sense of belonging and success when they realize the fruits of their efforts. As a craft project in our Vacation Bible School, for example, one group made an herbal-spice wreath, with each herb or spice used in the wreath related to a Bible verse. On the table, I placed a variety of herbs and spices in bowls from which the children could make their selections. Next to each bowl was a large copy of the relevant verse. We talked about how the Pharisees paid taxes with mint, and the fact that 200 years ago when children got bored in church — just as children today might — they were given seeds of dill, fennel, and coriander from Mother's pocket just as now they might receive gum and lifesavers from Mom's purse. The session resulted in a decorative wreath, as well as exposure to fragrant herbs and spices and a bit of lively history.

Simplify your recipes and ideas to the skill level of the group you're working with. Hot glue guns are difficult to use with age groups under 10 years, and even older children may get a burn if not well supervised. Employ quality ingredients, for the crafts and projects will be only as nice as the materials used. When herb-crafting with children, make sure that the projects are completed. Don't expect the parents to help finish something; an unfinished craft that goes home will probably stay that way.

No two projects ever look alike. I always get a thrill watching hands and imaginations work together to create wonderful botanical designs and herbal delights.

Plants have a language of the creator intended for our translation.

— *LOUIS AGASSIZ (1807-1873)*

❤

It is vital to relate to your groups that some herbs are poisonous or allergenic!

❤

Heart Wall Pocket

Lightweight cardboard
Wallpaper
Scissors, glue
Lace trim
Ribbon
Dried flowers and herbs

1. Glue a piece of wallpaper to the lightweight cardboard, covering it smoothly and completely. Cut two identical hearts from this piece.

2. Trim the edge of each heart with lace; the edge of the lace should face inward. To make a hanger, glue a piece of ribbon across the cleft of one of the hearts, allowing it to form a moderate loop (see illustration).

3. Glue the two hearts together along their edges, insides facing. Leave the top of the heart open.

4. Attach a small bow to the center front of the heart. Fill the heart with dried flowers and herbs.

Lavender Hearts

Two hearts attached by a satin ribbon — simple, yet fragrant and pretty.

2½-inch, metal cookie cutter heart
3" x 6" sheet of Styrofoam, ¼ to ½ inch thick
Tacky glue
1½ cups dried lavender flowers
Dried flowers and herbs including small, dried rosebuds
2 greening pins (available at crafts stores and florists' suppliers)
1 yard ⅛- to ¼-inch wide satin ribbon
Lavender oil

1. With the cookie cutter, cut a pair of hearts from the Styrofoam.

2. Completely coat the Styrofoam hearts with tacky glue. Cover the glue with dried lavender buds. Let dry.

3. Glue a tiny arrangement of dried flowers and rosebuds (symbolizing love) to the front of each heart.

4. With greening pins, fasten one end of the ribbon to the cleft of each heart. Tie the ribbon into a bow at the center. Add a bit of lavender oil to the hearts.

Susan Betz, The Little Farm Shop, Hillsdale, MI 49242

Herb Gardening with Our Children

by Mary Dunn

Last year our garden was designed with several goals in mind: to produce organic vegetables and herbs for our family, to produce herbs and flowers for drying for my business, and to provide a positive gardening experience for our two children, aged 16 months and 4½ years. We made two separate "kiddie plots" in our main garden, one for the toddler and a very different one for the preschooler.

For the toddler, we dug up a section and then filled it with sand, water, and play garden toys. He loved playing there in the dirt and mud for hours at a time, watching and smelling the herbs blow in the wind, with butterflies and insects buzzing around. The variety of textures around him stimulated all of his senses (even the delicious taste of mud — oh, well), and his first gardening experiences were certainly fun for him!

Our preschooler had her own garden plot — her design, her choice of plants, her labor. The experience stimulated her curiosity, sense of responsibility, and love of nature. She enjoyed herbs that tasted good, felt soft, and looked pretty: lemon thyme, dill, chives, mint, lamb's-ears, yarrow, chamomile, johnny-jump-ups, basil, and catnip (which she learned she could tie in a sock to tantalize her kitty with). Herb gardening with kids should always be fun and stimulating, with no pressures! She watered, weeded, fertilized, and cultivated. But mostly she watched, waited, tasted, and asked endless questions. Her favorite job was carrying the weeds to the compost pile and watching things like cucumber seeds sprout there.

We generally discuss the uses our plants may have, and then carry through by using them in various projects and recipes. Pressing flowers and herb leaves is such fun, as is candying violets, using flowers in salads, weaving with herbs, and starting herb seeds in egg shells and between wet paper towels. Potpourri making is the biggest hit! Harvesting mints and chamomile for tea, rubbing pennyroyal on kitty as a flea preventive, and collecting seed pods are also fun activities for our preschoolers.

One should keep in mind that some herbs and flowers are poisonous and should *not* be grown with kids around. A few common ones are delphinium, larkspur, bittersweet, foxglove, arnica, and blue flag. I would strongly recommend checking a good guidebook and/or an experienced herbalist before beginning the child's garden. Also, your local poison control center may have a list of poisonous plants that grow in your area.

Most seed catalogs offer "kid's" seed packets and/or kits. Gurney has such a kit for 1 cent — a price that's hard to beat! It requires separating the seeds before planting them, but children enjoy and benefit from that. Mellinger's has the widest variety of

Lamb's-ears *(Stachys byzantina)*

Most important, I stress to my kids, "NEVER, NEVER EAT ANYTHING OUTSIDE WITHOUT CHECKING WITH MOM FIRST!" The reasons are discussed in great detail.

Johnny-jump-up or heartsease *(Viola tricolor)*

children's gardening materials, at the least expensive prices. They offer a kiddie-size wheelbarrow, Kinder-Garden Kit, and reasonably priced children's garden tools.

The best activity for our family, by far, is simply being outside together on spring, summer, and autumn days — sunny or rainy — enjoying the herb garden. We always take time to sit on the ground in the middle of it all and let our senses be stimulated. And always, "Please touch the herbs"!

MARY DUNN, MOUNTAINVIEW HERB FARM, THORNDIKE, ME 04986

Housekeeping with Herbs

HERBAL HOUSEKEEPING

by Barbara Radcliffe Rogers

Pennyroyal *(Mentha pulegium)*

Here are some tips to aid your spring housecleaning — and some plants you might want to add to your garden this year to help with housework chores all year long!

Moths aren't the only pests you can use herbs to repel. Fleas and mosquitoes will avoid **pennyroyal.** Rub the fresh leaves on your skin *(but not on your face -PVS)* or package the dried leaves to put in a pet bed. Tansy was often planted around the foundations of old houses because ants do not like to pass through it. Ants don't like catnip either, and a sprinkling of it along an ant path will encourage them to turn around and leave. But just try to keep catnip in the ant path if you own a cat!

When Italian cooks discovered that houseflies don't like **basil,** they placed a sprig of it over the bowl of peeled tomatoes as they worked. (Fortunately, the basil and tomato flavors do like each other!) Clover flowers and sweet bay are also useful in keeping away flies, so a bouquet of green and purple basil, sweet bay and red clover not only looks and smells good in the kitchen, but keeps the flies away as well.

Mint repels mice; long stems of it placed along the eaves in the attic will encourage mice to seek a winter home at your neighbor's house instead of yours. Anise, on the other hand, attracts mice, so a little anise oil or a few anise seeds mixed with peanut butter is far more effective than cheese as bait for a mousetrap. Valerian is also good bait for mice, as well as for rats.

Bay leaves will keep weevils out of stored flour, cornmeal, and other grains. A whole bay leaf laid on the top will not flavor the food at all, but will protect a whole container full. The fungus that infects dried beans and grains can be prevented by placing a small, cheesecloth "sachet" filled with broken cinnamon stick, black peppercorns, coarsely ground black mustard seed, and green garlic into each gallon can or jar.

Although dogs and cats aren't properly classified as pests, they are not welcome in garbage cans; very quickly discourage them by giving the can covers a good sprinkling of **cayenne pepper.**

HOUSECLEANING HELPS

While the number of good soaps available to us means that we don't need to crush the chopped roots of soapwort or yucca to produce cleansing suds as our ancestors did, it is good to know that **soapwort** is still the best cleaner for delicate fabrics. Gather, wash, and pound the root when the plant is in bloom, or crush the fresh leaves. Mix either the root or leaves with water to form suds. Not only does this clean silk safely, but it restores its sheen — which washing in soap cannot do.

Fresh **sorrel** leaves are good for restoring the shine to copper pots; just wet the pot and a handful of leaves, and scrub. Lemon balm leaves are not only an excellent polish for wooden furniture, leaving it clean and shining, but the herb's oil will keep cats off the furniture as well!

If you forget clothes in the washer overnight and they smell a little stale, put them into the drier with a sachet of **lemon verbena or mint** (or both) — they will come out smelling fresh and clean.

MOTH-CHASER POTPOURRI

It is not enough for a "moth-chaser" potpourri to repel or discourage moths — it must do so without repelling and discouraging people as well! Fortunately, this isn't too difficult, since only a few herbs and spices have scents that are less than delightful. Those few, however, all belong in the best moth blends. Let's get them out of the way first.

Santolina, although a pretty plant in all its forms, does not please the nose as it does the eye. Harvest it either by pinching off the tips and drying them on a screen, or by cutting long sprigs to hang in paper bags. Since it is fragile when dry, it shouldn't be left hanging loose unless the spot is well out of the way. **Southernwood** grows taller and is more rangey; it is also best dried in bags to protect it. **Pennyroyal** does not actually have an unpleasant scent, but it is strong and penetrating. Its low growth doesn't make neat bundles, but you can screen dry it or just drop sprigs loosely in a paper bag to dry. Use any or all of these, in addition to some scents we love but moths don't. **Cedar shavings** provide bulk, creating the air spaces that are essential to good potpourri, and a scent most popularly associated with repelling moths; buy this in pet-supply departments, where it's much less expensive than in craft stores. **Lavender** is an excellent moth preventive. While it is hard for me to believe, there are actually people who don't like its scent. Its use in moth potpourri is therefore optional, because it will always predominate unless it is used very sparingly. Any **mint,** but peppermint in particular, is an essential addition not only to

Soapwort *(Saponaria officinalis)*

Any fragrant herb or herb blend sprinkled on the carpet and vacuumed up will scent the room delicately and get rid of that "just-been-vacuumed" smell; the warmth of the motor increases the scent carried into the air by the exhaust.

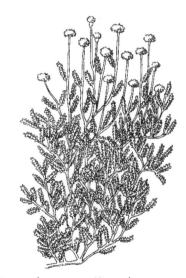

Lavender cotton *(Santolina chamaecyparissus)*

❧ Herbitage Farm's Moth Potpourri ❧

½ cup cedar shavings
¼ cup pennyroyal
¼ cup lavender
¼ cup santolina or southernwood
¼ cup peppermint
¼ cup lemon verbena
¼ cup thyme
¼ cup rosemary
¼ cup orrisroot
⅛ cup whole cloves
⅛ cup lemon peel
⅛ cup black peppercorns
6 drops cedar oil
6 drops lemon oil
6 drops lavender oil

deter moths, but to discourage mice from nibbling around in stored clothing. Whole cloves, lemon peel, lemon verbena, tansy, thyme, rosemary, black peppercorns, and bay leaves are secondary ingredients — all effective and all adding to a pleasant, if pungent, blend. **Orrisroot** (in chipped, not powdered form) is necessary, since moth bags need to last if they are to be useful. The oils should reflect the ingredients, and I blend a special oil just for the moth potpourri. It is 2 parts each cedar, lemon, and lavender (optional) and 1 part each pennyroyal, peppermint, and bayberry. Because the blend needs to project if it is to be useful, use about 50 percent more oil than you would for normal potpourri.

It is not necessary to use all the moth-chasing ingredients or even all the oils in the same potpourri. Just be sure you have at least two (if possible, four) of the primary ingredients and one of the three major oils listed.

Packaging moth potpourri can be as simple as tying it into squares of old sheet fabric, or as fancy as you wish. But bear in mind that these are no-nonsense household necessities to be hidden away, so frilly little lace or organdy sachets would look a bit silly. I have always packaged mine in wool flannel, which my customers find very amusing if not downright arrogant! So far, none has been found with a moth hole. Use 6-inch squares, and stitch to form a 3" x 6" bag. Turn and fill with potpourri and tie to close.

The one thing to remember here is to be generous with the potpourri. Use at least ½ cup in each bag. A bow or loop of some type is handy if the bags are to be put on clothes hangers.

Padded hangers may be filled with the blend, too. Use a wooden coat hanger without a pants bar. Measure the wooden part from the center to one end and make a satin tube 1 inch longer and about 1½ inches wide. (You can double 1½ -inch-wide satin ribbon and stitch along each selvedge.) Stitch across one end and leave the other end open. Turn the stitched tube right side out, and slip it over one end of the hanger. Repeat for the other end. Fill each side tightly with potpourri, and blind stitch the ends together at the center. Wrap the hook with narrow ribbon, holding it in place over the end with white glue. Wrap the other end once around the hanger to hide the seam, and stitch it in place. Cover the end with a bow tied around the handle.

If it is nicely made, your moth potpourri can have two bonus uses. It will keep trunks and seldom-used closets and chests from developing a musty smell, and it will keep luggage fresh-smelling both when traveling and when in storage.

BARBARA RADCLIFFE ROGERS,
HERBITAGE FARM, RICHMOND,
NH 03470

🍃 *DO HERBAL MOTH REPELLENTS REALLY WORK?* 🍃

Many of us have been using, giving, and/or selling herbal moth bags over the years, assuming and hoping that the colonists knew what they were doing! Having read that insects detest spicy odors, I had concluded that the cinnamon, mace, and cloves in my own preparations had as much of a repellent nature as the herbs themselves. A recent study of this subject was done by Rita Buchanan, the recipient of The Herb Society of America's 1985 Scholarship Grant for this purpose. The following summary is drawn from her article on the subject in the 1987 Herbalist. *See also her book* The Weaver's Garden *(Loveland, CO: Interweave Press, 1987).*

Ms. Buchanan explains that clothes moths and carpet beetles are drawn instinctively to wool, camel hair, mohair, angora, alpaca, and other animal hair fibers because they can digest the protein keratin from these fibers to develop tough outer coverings. Keratin contains sulphur, which explains the foul odor of burning wool or hair. She adds, "The insects that can digest keratin may have a sensitivity to the scent of sulphur compounds that helps them locate potential sources of food. To supplement the protein in their diet, they seek the salts and oils of sweat, grease, and stains on soiled items. Easily disturbed by light, ventilation, and movement, these insects are most likely to cause damage in neglected or out-of-the-way spots." The author builds a very strong case for practicing the housekeeping habits of our mothers and grandmothers. Remember beating the carpets on the clothesline and airing all the woolens in sunlight and moving all the furniture during every spring and fall housecleaning? Maybe I wouldn't have complained so much about coming right home after school to help with these projects, had I known then that these rituals would actually prevent moth infestations! Ms. Buchanan stresses the necessity for regular inspections, cleanliness, and proper storage of woolens; she explains, "Use herbal products as a supplement to, not a substitute for good preventive care."

Plant products containing volatile compounds that are used for natural moth control in airtight storage include red cedar wood, tobacco leaves (nicotine), pennyroyal leaves and stems (pulgeone), and pyrethrum daisy flowers (pyre-thrins). Ms. Buchanan suggests further deterring insects by using essential oils to coat fibers with natural "anti-feedant" compounds. She adds a few drops of oil of cedar, eucalyptus, or pennyroyal to the final rinse water of sweaters she washes by hand, and lets them soak for a while to provide some protection. After all her research, she is not convinced that wool moths are repelled by pungent odors. Rather, she states:

"I believe that the most likely mode of action for an herbal moth repellent is to confuse and disorient the egg-bearing adult female, so that she cannot locate a potential food supply and instead lays her eggs in an inappropriate place. Given the limited motility of the very young larvae, particularly clothes moth larvae, if the female does not target in on a food supply, the offspring are unlikely to locate one. Recalling that the sulphur content of keratin protein may be an olfactory clue to a female moth or beetle searching for animal fibers, any strongly fragrant herb product that masks the wool odor may have potential as a repellent. These herbs may have no effect on eggs or larvae that are already present, neither killing the insects nor reducing their appetite. I think they are best used along with good housekeeping measures, to prevent new infestations, but not to control existing problems."

The author suggests that herbal repellents should emit their fragrances generously, so only the most aromatic herbs should be used, with no fixatives. She recommends placing cloth or paper packages of herbal mixtures in each bureau drawer, in the knitting basket, and in quantity in closets and chests, and replacing them yearly.

Ms. Buchanan lists the following herbs as insecticidal and useful for moth control. I have included only a portion of the informative material she includes about each herb.

♥ ♥ ♥ ♥ ♥ ♥ ♥ ♥ ♥ ♥

I feel that, because of the HSA's concern and Ms. Buchanan's research, we can now say with confidence that herbal moth repellents using the plants at the right do work to drive away clothing moths, providing expert housekeeping methods are practiced for prevention. These findings are all the more vital, because recent reports indicate that some moth balls (those containing p-dichlorobenzene) may be cancer-producing.

HERBS USEFUL FOR MOTH CONTROL

Camphor basil, Mint Family *(Ocimum kilimand-scharimum).* Tender perennial in frost-free areas; annual elsewhere. Easily grown from seed; early start inside helpful. Becomes a 3- to 5-foot shrub. Makes nice hedges or back borders. Harvest the leaves during the growing season, or the whole plant before frost. Place in a brown paper bag and hang to dry. Leaves will shake free from dried stems, which are aromatic for use in the fireplace.

Eucalyptus, Myrtle Family. Although there are hundreds of species, most are not hardy below 20° F., but some can be treated as annual bedding plants or will respond well to pot culture. Silver-dollar tree *(Eucalyptus cinerea)* and blue gum *(E. globulus)* will grow up to 6 feet a year and tolerate hard prunings. Lemon-scented gum *(E. citriodora)* does well as a houseplant in a sunny window.

Pennyroyal, Mint Family. Either the European *(Mentha pulegium),* which is a spreading perennial to 10° F. if mulched and which requires fertile soil in sun or shade, or the American variety *(Hedeoma pulegioides),* which is a self-sowing annual that should be grown in dry, sandy soil, may be used as insecticides. Harvest upright stems when in full bloom; hang in bunches to dry.

Pyrethrum, Composite Family. Painted daisy *(Chrysanthemum coccineum)* has red, pink, or white flowers, and Dalmatian insect flower *(C. cinerariifolium)* has white flowers. Both are hardy perennials requiring a sunny spot with coarse, well-drained soil. Raise from seed for second-year bloom or propagate established plants. The pyrethrins are produced only in the yellow disk flowers in the center of the daisy inflorescences. No other parts of the plants contain the active insecticidal ingredients. For maximum concentration of pyrethrins, harvest the flowers on the day they open from the bud, dry them quickly on screens, and store them in tightly sealed jars in a dark place. Grind the dried flowers into a fine powder to add to herbal moth-repellent mixtures. The odorless vapor dissipates rapidly, so discard and replace pyrethrum sachets at least twice a year.

Red cedar. Cedar chests should be renewed periodically by sanding the interior surface or by treating the wood with fresh cedar oil, as the oils near the surface of the wood evaporate.

Southernwood, Composite Family *(Artemisia abrotanum).*

Pyrethrum *(Chrysanthemum cinerariifolium)*

Because of its use as a wool-moth repellent, southernwood is called *garde-robe* in French. Harvest southernwood in early to midsummer. It is effective for 6 to 12 months.

Tansy, Composite Family (Tanacetum vulgare). Tansy contains the insecticidal compound, thujone. Harvest the leaves any time during the summer or fall, and hang in bunches to dry.

RITA BUCHANAN'S SUGGESTED HERBAL MOTH-REPELLENT MIXTURES

❤ For a single distinctive scent, use camphor basil, pennyroyal, eucalyptus, southernwood, or rosemary leaves. Combine equal parts of the dried fragrant plant with finely ground pyrethrum flowers, which are unscented, to increase the effectiveness of the repellent without altering the aroma.
❤ Mix equal parts of southernwood, wormwood, and tansy for a sweet mix.
❤ Mix equal parts of camphor basil, lavender, and rosemary for a tangy, penetrating aroma. Add purchased camphor or cinnamon if you choose.
❤ Mix 2 parts lavender, 2 parts southernwood, 1 part rosemary, 1 part pennyroyal, and 1 part wormwood. Add a tablespoon of powdered cloves to each 2 cups of herbs and mix well.

EXCERPTS FROM MS. BUCHANAN'S ARTICLE ARE REPRINTED WITH PERMISSION OF *THE HERBARIST*, THE ANNUAL PUBLICATION OF THE HERB SOCIETY OF AMERICA. ANNUAL ISSUES OF *THE HERBARIST* ARE AVAILABLE TO THE PUBLIC FOR A FEE (SEE MAY, HERB GROUPS AND ORGANIZATIONS IN THE APPENDIX FOR ADDRESS).

NATURAL FRAGRANCES

by Gail Duff

❧ *Gail's No-Buff Furniture Polish* ❧

4 ounces linseed oil
4 ounces malt vinegar
40 sweet cicely seeds, chopped and crushed,
or 1 teaspoon each lemon oil and lime oil,
or 1½ teaspoons lavender oil and 4 drops peppermint oil

Pour the oil and vinegar into a jar, and seal it tightly. Shake well to mix, rather like a salad dressing. Add the sweet cicely or essential oils, and shake again. If you use the sweet cicely mixture, leave it for 2 weeks in a warm place and shake it daily; if you use essential oils, you may polish with it immediately.

To use, impregnate a duster with the mixture, and rub it hard on your furniture or paneling. It will polish and dust at the same time, with no need to buff afterwards.

❧ *Dried citrus peel* ❧

To prepare dried citrus peel for potpourri and sachet mixtures, thinly pare the outer rind from the fruits. Rub them in a little powdered orrisroot (2 tablespoons for 6 large oranges; 1½ tablespoons for 6 large lemons; and 1 tablespoon for 6 limes). Place the coated peels onto nonstick baking sheets, and put them into the oven, preheated to 300° F. The orange and lemon rinds will take 2½ to 3 hours to dry and the lime rinds 2¼ to 2½ hours. They should be hard but not too brittle. Cool completely and then store in airtight containers. Just before use, coarsely crush or bruise them with a pestle and mortar.

❧ Old Colonial Sweet-Bag Mixture ❧

2 ounces rose petals
1 ounce lavender
1 ounce hyssop
2 tablespoons lime peel, crushed
2 tablespoons blade mace, crushed
2 drops patchouli oil
2 drops vetiver oil

Put the dried rose petals, lavender, and hyssop in a large mixing bowl. Add the lime peel and mace, and mix with your fingers. Add the oils, 1 drop at a time, and mix after each drop. Put the mixture in a closed container and allow to age for 6 weeks, shaking every other day.

FROM *NATURAL FRAGRANCES* BY GAIL DUFF (POWNAL, VT: GARDEN WAY PUBLISHING, 1989)

❧ Scented drawer liners ❧

You will need some wallpaper with an attractive pattern and not too shiny a surface. The cheaper wallpapers that are not "wipe-clean" or "steam-resistant" tend to absorb the most scent, but you can also use wallpaper to match your bedroom decor. Then, if there is curtain material to match, you can make sweet bags from the same pattern for placing among your clothes. Begin by cutting the wallpaper to the size of the drawers that it is to line.

Make up your favorite sweet-bag mixture. Put a few drops of a matching essential oil on a cotton ball. Rub the cotton ball on the underside of the wallpaper. Sprinkle the sweet-bag mixture quite thickly over the pattern side of one piece of liner. Lay another on top and sprinkle that with the mixture. Continue until all the liners are used. Roll them up and seal them in a plastic bag. Leave them for 6 weeks.

Brush away all the sweet-bag mixture from the paper before lining your drawers. Reserve the mixture to use as a filling for sachets. You can also rub the insides of cupboards and drawers with the predominate sweet oil used on the liners and in the sweet-bag mixture.

For more housekeeping products and tips, see January

KATE JAYNE and CLAUDETTE MAUTOR, both of Sandy Mush Herb Nursery, have written a delightful primer on the art of potpourri. Living with Potpourri *(White Plains, NY: Peter Pauper Press), traces the course of scents from earliest recorded history to present times, and includes recipes for holiday potpourri and mixes for the bath, bedroom, and linen closet, as well as for the teapot and soup kettle. It is the first account I have seen of the symbolism of color in potpourri.*

FROM *LIVING WITH POTPOURRI* (WHITE PLAINS, NY: PETER PAUPER PRESS), BY KATE JAYNE AND CLAUDETTE MAUTOR

LIVING WITH POTPOURRI: A CHARMING PRIMER

❧ Herbal Potpourri to Freshen and Protect Linens ❧

To put the freshness of a clear, summer day into your linens, use this potpourri of dried herbs in the closet. Together, these herbs provide a gentle and welcoming scent, and each is known to have properties that repel insects, making this a fine potpourri to use when packing away off-season clothing.

½ cup anise hyssop
1 cup sweet bay
1 cup eucalyptus
½ cup lemon verbena
¼ cup santolina
¼ cup southernwood

Combine all ingredients, and place the mixture in a cloth bag or a box with small perforations in the sides. Place the container between the linens or on the shelf beside them, or tuck a bag of the mix into the pockets of suitcases and handbags, near shoe racks, or in closet corners.

Safe, Natural Flea Control

by Diane Downs

It doesn't take much searching through my mail to discover that people really dislike using chemical pesticides, especially on beloved pets. And with good reason! Most flea collars contain chemical ingredients that can affect the nervous system, cause hair loss or skin irritation, or even attack your pet's natural defense system, making it vulnerable to other toxins. Some pet owners have even reported severe illness and death as a result of their pet's chewing on one of the new, long-lasting flea collars. And, if fleas have driven you to the point of having your whole house fumigated, your pet isn't the only one receiving a dose of these chemicals. A safe solution to this problem exists — and one that will not harm you, your pets, or the environment.

Before you can solve your flea problem, you need to understand the flea's life cycle. When an adult flea lays an egg, the small whitish form drops into the carpet, a crack in a wood floor, the upholstery, or a dusty corner. After a period of time, the egg develops into a larva quite able to exist by feeding on dust, debris, or any organic matter. Outdoors, these larvae take up residence in lawns, where they feed primarily on vegetable or animal matter in shady locations. The larva then spins a cocoon and eventually emerges as an adult, ready to jump on the nearest warm body for a meal of blood. One of the reasons fleas are so hard to eradicate is that they can exist, almost suspending animation, until a suitable meal arrives — you may have heard of a vacant house suddenly alive with fleas when someone moves in.

Because the egg, larva, and cocoon stages are of different lengths in various species, your initial attack should consist of a conscientious 3- to 5-week program. In this way, you will gradually get ahead of the massive number of fleas and eggs now sharing your home. If only your pet seems a victim, or you have only outdoor pets, follow the instructions concerning lawns and the animals themselves.

Vacuum not just the rugs, but *under* the rugs as well; include floors, corners, upholstery, pillows, sofa cushions, under couches and mattresses — the works! — and don't forget the basement. Then, either burn the vacuum bag or seal it and its contents securely inside a plastic bag and dispose of it. If you neglect this step, the newly vacuumed-up larvae will feed on the dust and lint, and happily leave the vacuum bag to set up housekeeping in your rug, your pet's fur, or on you! After patting yourself on the back for already cleaning up hundreds (probably thousands) of fleas, eggs, and larvae, wash all throw rugs, pet's bedding, and your bedspreads in water as warm as the fabric allows.

At this point you've made encouraging progress, but you will soon lose ground again unless the next steps are taken. To kill the

Diane Downs's expertise is well researched and documented, as she was knowledgeable enough for The Mother Earth News *magazine to publish her writings on natural pest control as early as 1980. She has been in business for over 10 years, and her enlightening catalog offers hundreds of herb plants, plus natural insect repellents of all kinds — even aids for mole/gopher/grasshopper control.*

❤

*The first step — and one you will repeat often initially — is to vacuum your home **thoroughly**.*

❤

Remember, natural products like pennyroyal are not residual, so they must be replenished.

fleas, eggs, and larvae still hiding in your carpets and furniture, sprinkle dried pennyroyal *(Mentha pulegium)* or pyrethrum powder (made from the dried flowers of *Chrysanthemum cinerariifolium)* into rugs, under sofa cushions, under mattresses, and in Wolf and Blackie's bedding. In rare instances, pennyroyal oil has caused abortion in pets, but the much less-concentrated dried pennyroyal should pose no danger. While enduring pennyroyal's pleasant aroma, you can rest assured you are not harming your pets or family, but are suffocating fleas. After 3 or 4 days, repeat the vacuum and wash cycle again (don't forget to destroy or seal the vacuum bag), and reapply fresh pennyroyal.

While all this activity is taking place, your canine or feline friend needs some immediate attention, too. Whether cat or dog, a bath is in order, followed by a rinse water of strong pennyroyal tea (made simply by steeping some pennyroyal in hot water), cooled to lukewarm. Or, add a few drops of a combination herbal oil to the bathwater. When the pet is dry, a thorough brushing, combing (using a fine-toothed flea comb), or even vacuuming (if not too terrifying) is in order. To reinforce this attack at the source, sew a cloth tube, stuff it with pennyroyal, and fasten it around your pet's neck. If your furry friend is an outdoor animal, fasten the collar with elastic for safety's sake. Replenish the pennyroyal inside the collar every 3 or 4 days, or if it gets wet. If your problem is especially severe, you may wish to use a few drops of a combination herbal oil (not pennyroyal oil) on your pet's hind legs, feet, neck and tail, or use a pyrethrum flea powder.

While all your in-house efforts are taking effect, consider the lawn. Because fleas have undoubtedly taken up residence there (in fact, it is most probably where they came from in the first place), all your indoor achievements will be short-lived if something is not done to eradicate the breeding grounds outside your door. For an attack co-ordinated with your house and animal de-fleaing, sprinkle garden-grade diatomaceous earth over the lawn, under bushes, and in shady places. This powdery substance, made from the shells of microscopic sea creatures called diatoms, is so safe it can even be fed to pets and livestock to aid in parasite control, as well as used in vegetable gardens as an insect dust, but it contains minute, sharp particles that lacerate the exoskeleton of fleas, causing them to die of dehydration. After applying to your lawn, avoid watering for a day or two, and then water if necessary and reapply.

The long-term solution is to plant pennyroyal plants this spring or summer in your lawn flea-breeding grounds. There's no need to destroy the entire lawn or landscape, but using pennyroyal plants as an attractive, fragrant, low-growing ground cover in various corners, beside pet paths or kennels, and around bushes, can be a landscaping plus, as well as an effective, safe pesticide. In very cold regions (like Montana), pennyroyal is not always reliably hardy, although I have had it survive 40° below zero when mulched. It will, however, often self-seed following the purple flower cluster's demise.

As this initial 3- to 5-week program progresses, you should begin to notice a marked reduction in the number of fleas. As long as there are fleas, continue the above steps weekly, and consider a spring or summer planting of pennyroyal. (Pennyroyal can also be rubbed on your own arms and legs as a mosquito repellent; and in England, it is planted around cottage doors to keep flies away and worn as wreaths when walking through the woods.) Use your harvest of leaves to keep your fuzzy follower's flea collar and bedding regularly replenished with pennyroyal.

After this mega-assault, maintain vigilance and take action immediately if fleas appear to be getting out of hand again. Normally, once fleas are conquered, an herbal flea collar, herbal baths, pennyroyal in the pet's bedding and in the yard are all that are needed to keep fleas under control.

❤

Pennyroyal does work! A pet owner from New York wrote to me, "I planted pennyroyal 3 years ago and it has spread rapidly. This is the second year I have had very happy dogs. Not one flea is evident and this has been a very bad flea year."

❤

DIANE DOWNS, LOST PRAIRIE HERB FARM, KALISPELL, MT 59901

Celebrating Spring with Herbs

THE MAGIC OF HERBS: SPRING DANDIES!

by Bertha Reppert

Both Jews and Christians greet spring with important Holy Day celebrations. Certain very lowly herbs link these occasions, for the Last Supper undoubtedly included the "bitter herbs" that have been served in the traditional Passover celebration since the time of Moses.

Biblical botanists do not always agree on which were the bitter herbs, but most will list lettuce, endive, chicory, dandelion, sorrel, and watercress — all weedy plants common to the Holy Land at the time of the Passover. Many add the horseradish that some scholars say could not have been known in the Holy Land at the time of Moses. Other writers assume the bitter herbs to be mints, which are the herbs most frequently mentioned in the Bible.

The bitter herbs were eaten as a raw salad and in combination with every mouthful of unleavened bread or meat (the paschal lamb). Since these same herbs perform their magic and reappear every spring, today as in the time of Moses, they are a fitting inclusion in Lenten menus. In their wisdom, ancient Jews recognized the need for fresh, new greens in the diet and as an aid to digestion. We, too, should not overlook these wild foods, gifts of fields and roadside.

The *Williamsburg Art of Cookery* by Helen Bullock (Williamsburg, VA: 1938) gives us this interesting Lenten recipe, dated 1753, which uses the bitter herbs of spring: "Get Chervil, Beets, Chards, Spinach, Sellery, Leeks, and such like Herbs, with two or three large Crusts of Bread, some Butter, a bunch of Sweet-herbs, and a little Salt; put these with a moderate Quantity of Water, into a Kettle, and boil them for an Hour and a half, and strain out the Liquor through a Sieve, and it will be a good Stock for Soups, either of asparagus buds, lettuce, or any other kind fit for Lent or Fast-Days."

I look forward to gathering tender, young dandelion greens for our Easter dinner each year, as my mother did before me. Served with great quantities of hard-cooked eggs, and wilted down with delicious hot bacon dressing, this bitter herb has become an Easter tradition in our house. It was my secret pleasure to note that the children, as they grew older, were eating it more and teasing me less about my annual urge to gather dandelions.

BERTHA REPPERT, THE ROSEMARY HOUSE, MECHANICSBURG, PA 17055

❧ *Rosemary's Sorrel Soup* ❧

YIELD: 6 TO 8 SERVINGS

Favorite, first spring soup from the garden.

2 cups sorrel (mid-ribs removed)	*1 teaspoon thyme*
6 leeks or Egyptian onions	*5-ounce can evaporated milk*
4 tablespoons garlic chives, or 2 cloves garlic	*10¾-ounce can cream of chicken soup*
¼ pound butter	*10¾-ounce can cream of mushroom soup*
6 chicken bouillon cubes	
8 cups water	*Salt to taste*
6 potatoes, cubed	*Chives, parsley, chervil, or paprika*
¼ teaspoon rosemary	

Place in a blender the sorrel, leeks or onions, and garlic, and blend until almost puréed. Cook this mixture in the butter until limp, but not brown. Add the bouillon, water, and potatoes. Cover and cook 30 minutes. Add the rosemary and thyme the last 5 minutes. Add the milk and the soups. Heat to simmer, but do not boil. Add salt to taste. Serve garnished with chives, parsley, chervil, or paprika.

FROM *A BOUNTIFUL COLLECTION* (PENN-CUMBERLAND GARDEN CLUB; AVAILABLE FROM THE ROSEMARY HOUSE, MECHANICSBURG, PA 17055)

THE JOY OF SPRING SALADS

by Madeleine H. Siegler

Early spring is early April here at Monk's Hill in Maine. Although the snow is nearly gone, the air is still cold, and the lawns, gardens, and all the dirt roads are still soggy. Not very promising weather for a trip to the herb garden, but that is where the best part of our salad is waiting. I put on my winter parka and my rubber boots and walk out to the herb garden. The crushed rock paths are bare of snow and so is the patio, but since I usually venture further afield once I am out, I will go well prepared. A colander will hold all I plan to pick.

First, a handful of crisp, green salad burnet. This perennial herb with the faint flavor of cucumber will look bare and brown after a winter with no snow cover. This year it has been well protected by snow and the leaves have remained green and tender all winter. I pick only six. An old clump of Good-King-Henry is already putting forth new, arrow-shaped leaves. This chenopod (member of the Goosefoot Family) was first brought to America by the colonists, who knew it as one of the earliest greens they could find in the spring. The flavor is mild, but it is a good source of vitamins and minerals, and it has a nice, "green" taste. One large clump would supply several meals of cooked greens if picked throughout the spring, but for our first herb garden salad of the year, just six leaves will suffice.

Salad burnet *(Poterium sanguisorba)*

The many varieties of thyme have come through the winter looking as green as they did in the fall. I cut just one sprig of English thyme and one of lemon. In my enthusiasm, I snap off an arching spray of caraway thyme. We will have a bit of each. Dark green shoots of chives are just emerging. The clump nearest the rock wall is tall enough to allow me to snap off a modest handful of 5-inch stalks. The best is last. French sorrel, that wonderful, perennial herb with the sharp, acid flavor, is emerging with vigor. The much-wrinkled leaves will be larger later, but now I pick just four, each no more than finger length. Taking a few leaves of luscious, green lemon balm, I go back to the kitchen to warm my hands, and build the salad (see at right).

Another early spring day, when the upper end of the vegetable garden has dried out a bit, I walk up there and gather another favorite salad. A pail and a stout spade for this job. The Jerusalem artichokes are there, but last year's dead stalks are the only evidence. I dig into the muddy, icy soil and pull out a clump of crisp, dripping tubers. Next to them is a row of top-multiplier onions, lusty with new growth. I break off several dark green, 6-inch shoots.

Back in the kitchen, the artichokes are well scrubbed and scraped, then thinly sliced into the salad bowl with the same basic vinaigrette dressing I used for the first salad. The onion shoots are briefly rinsed under water, and thin rounds are snipped into the bowl. The white slices of artichoke and the green of the onion are now left for a few hours "to get acquainted" with the dressing. Should there by any left over from supper, it will be refrigerated and taste even better tomorrow.

As spring pushes along and the days get warmer, we start talking about fiddleheads. The black flies have to arrive before ever a fiddlehead fern emerges. We watch our small patch near the house carefully to time our foray afield for a major picking of this lovely ostrich fern. We garner only the short-stemmed, tightly furled "fiddleheads" — the ones that weren't there yesterday. I always cook more than we could possibly eat for our first meal.

❤

FRESH SPRING SALAD

Into the ancient, maple salad bowl goes half a clove of garlic via the garlic press. (Marvelous tool, this.) Then one tablespoon of salad oil and one teaspoon of vinegar. We use a variety of herb vinegars in our salads: tarragon, chives, basil, salad burnet. This time it is salad burnet vinegar to heighten the cucumber illusion. A faint pass over the bowl with salt and pepper, then this is all well blended with the wooden spoon. Now I add all the herb bounty from the garden (see at left). The green leaves and the chives are snipped with scissors. The tiny thyme leaves are stripped from the tough, wiry stems and dropped in. All this is stirred into the dressing, and then, finally, iceberg lettuce is torn into bits and added. The entire operation takes less than five minutes. Salad for two is ready.

❤

Two-thirds of them are well buttered and served at the table. The rest are drained of their juices and marinated in the vinaigrette dressing, along with lots of fresh chives. Served on a bed of lettuce, they are almost better than as a hot vegetable. Frozen fiddleheads, too, taste much better to us marinated for a salad than served hot.

By now, spring has advanced to pea-planting time in Maine, and soon there will be a glut of new lettuce for salads. But we have had a fine head start on fresh salad flavor with our perennial herbs and vegetables.

MADELEINE H. SIEGLER, MONK'S HILL HERBS, WINTHROP, ME 04364

COLORING EASTER EGGS WITH NATURAL DYES

by Bob Clark

Throughout this book, you will find many recipes and crafts that BOB CLARK was excited to share with you, and which are printed here in loving memory of him with permission from his parents. Bob died in December 1989 at the age of 37 from complications resulting from serious illness in his youth. We rejoice for the life he lived and shared, for the joy he found in creating beautiful mementoes of nature, for the satisfaction he found in his love of herbs and flowers, and for the brave battle he fought and won to live an enriched and meaning-ful life in spite of his painful and crippling afflictions. He will be sorely missed, but not forgotten.

When you use natural materials for dyeing Easter eggs, you will get pastel hues, rather than bright colors. To get deeper tones, allow the eggs to sit in the dyes longer. The general rule for dye preparation is to boil cut-up plants or fruits and whole seeds or hulls in water to cover in a stainless steel or enamel pan for a minute or two, and then simmer for 20 to 30 minutes. Strain the contents. Carefully drop dry, hard-boiled eggs into the hot dye. A teaspoon of vinegar added to each dye bath (except when using onion skins) will help the dye adhere to the eggs. Stronger colors can sometimes be obtained by boiling the eggs right in the dye.

BLUES AND PURPLES	Red cabbage Blueberry juice Cranberry juice and purple grapes Blackberry juice
REDS	Cooked beets, steeped for several hours Raspberries, cranberries, and blackberries
GREENS	Spinach or carrot tops
YELLOWS	Calendula flowers Yellow or brown onion skins Turmeric Annatto seeds
BROWNS	Coffee grounds Walnut hulls or bark Cayenne powder Alkanet root or maple bark

❧ *Woodland Violets Potpourri* ❧

A heavenly blend for Easter, and all year long.

3 cups pink rosebuds and petals
1 cup hibiscus flowers
2 cups blue malva flowers
1 cup lemon balm or lemon verbena leaves
2 tablespoons allspice berries, broken pressed violets,
or viola flowers (optional)
20 drops violet oil
10 drops spring floral oil
¼ cup calamus root
¼ cup peeled orrisroot (Florentine orris)

Add the essential oils to the calamus root and orrisroot. Add all other ingredients.

❧ *Sweet Meadow Potpourri* ❧

20 drops clover oil
10 drops new-mown hay oil
¼ cup orrisroot
¾ cup oakmoss
2 cups chamomile flowers
1½ cups pink rosebuds and petals
1½ cups lemon verbena leaves
1½ cups heather flowers
1 cup sweet woodruff
¾ cup blue malva flowers
¾ cup life-everlasting flowers
⅓ cup thyme
⅓ cup gingerroot, cut

Add the clover and new-mown hay oils to the orrisroot and oakmoss. Add all remaining ingredients and mix well.

BOB CLARK, LANCASTER, OH 43130

CREATIVE TWIST PAPER SACHETS FOR SPRING

by Grace Wakefield

These paper ribbon sachets are nice for banquet favors (or, at Christmas, for tree ornaments).

Sack sachet. Unravel Creative Twist paper, and cut a 12-inch piece. Fold the paper in half. Fold over a ¼-inch edge on both of the 6-inch sides, and sew with a hand running stitch or a machine stitch. Fill the sack three-fourths full with potpourri. Close the top with a ribbon bow. Decorate the sack with such dried herbs and flowers as globe amaranth or tiny strawflowers. Fold the top raw edge to the inside. Flatten and flare out the top of the sack.

The easiest and fastest way to untwist paper ribbon is to use a drill with reversible speed.

CLARA BERGER, HARVEST THYME, CINCINNATI, OH 45230

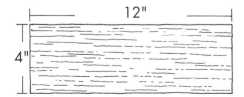

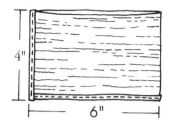

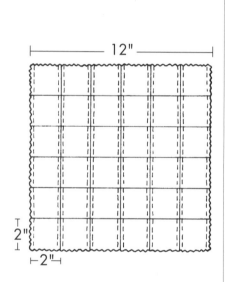

GRACE WAKEFIELD, TOM THUMB
WORKSHOPS, MAPPSVILLE, VA 23407

Pouch sachet. Cut a 12-inch piece of unraveled Creative Twist paper, and fold it in half. Turn over ¼ inch on the 4-inch edge and on one 6-inch edge. Stitch, and turn the pouch right side out. Fill the pouch with potpourri. Gather the pouch at the neck and tie with a ribbon bow. Flare out the top to form a little vase, and insert a cluster of flowers. Push in the two bottom points to form a rounded pouch that will stand upright.

SMALL SACHET SQUARES

by Sally Booth-Brezina

From time to time, we all need an inexpensive sachet to sell or to give away. Herb businesses can often use them as a promotional item or a donation to a charity or organization needing favors for a banquet or party. I have devised these small squares for scenting purses, stationery, sewing boxes, shallow desk or bureau drawers, and even for tucking into a letter or gift card. One piece of fabric 12" x 24" will result in 36 tiny sachets!

1. Cut a piece of fabric into 12-inch squares with pinking shears. Place two squares together, right sides out, and press.

2. Using an air- or water-soluble marking pen, chalk, or light-colored pencil, mark off 2-inch squares.

3. Machine stitch ¼ inch away from all vertical lines, on both sides of the drawn lines, and along both vertical edges.

4. Machine stitch ¼ inch away from the horizontal lines above the lines only, and above bottom edge.

5. Cut strips across fabric on horizontal lines, using pinking shears. You now have six, 2" x 12" strips with thirty-six little pockets.

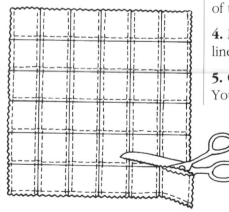

6. Fill pockets lightly with lavender or sachet base. Pin, to hold filling in pockets.

7. Stitch top of pockets ¼ inch away from top edge. Remove pins. Cut apart on vertical lines, using pinking shears. You now have thirty-six, completed, small sachets!

SALLY BOOTH-BREZINA

MAY

MAY IS THE BIGGEST month of the year for herbal festivities, judging by my newsletter's "Herbfest" column, in which herb organizations and businesses list their special events. Herb farms, shops, and groups use fairs, exhibits, symposiums, and open houses to launch the spring season when herbs are ready for purchasing and planting. (November is the second most active month, when crafts from the harvest are ready for holiday sales.) The recipes in this chapter are from such spring occasions and utilize the herbs and foods available at this time of year.

I am amazed at the large number of herb clubs and study groups that have developed around the country in the past 10 years. Small, large, and in-between-sized groups, in cities, towns, and rural areas, are meeting regularly to learn about herbs. In most cases, after they become established, these clubs maintain a public herb garden, offer public tours of members'

gardens, hold fairs or exhibits, and do whatever they can to educate the general citizenry about the benefits and joys of growing herbs. The many comments I receive about how "herb people just love to share their knowledge," lead me to think that these clubs are an expression of that truism. In a populated locale, a little newspaper publicity, perhaps a radio interview, and some notices in public places around town can help a nucleus of two or three turn quickly into a group of twenty to sixty interested folks. Groups meeting at night report enormous interest from men. The response ranges from those who know nothing yet about herbs to owners of related businesses, such as food, gardening, medical industries, and so on. It is a good idea to let the make-up of the group determine when and where to meet and what kind of program to offer.

Some established groups limit their size because they meet in private homes or because they feel the level of their herbal study is too advanced for beginners. Others limit membership to those who will work hard and devote much time and energy to the group's projects. These self-starter organizations are as varied as the people who comprise them. Some begin as subcommittees of garden clubs. Many are formed by herbophiles who move to a new locality and want to find friends who share their love of herbs. Such folks tell me that they quickly meet the "nicest people" and become acclimated in their new environments much more quickly because they have involved themselves in their new communities this way.

Another phenomenon of the past decade is the onset of state herb organizations. Formed by herb businesses, these groups have as one of their purposes a mission to educate the public about herbs. Membership and the group's newsletter are therefore usually available to any and all who are interested in herbs, whether they are residents of the state or not. Many such groups, along with some smaller and some larger groups with open membership, are listed in the Appendix under May, Herb

Groups and Organizations. The largest new herb group is the International Herb Growers and Marketers Association (IGHMA), which sponsors a marvelous herb conference and trade show in a different region of the country each year. Nonmembers may learn much from these conferences, either by attending them or by ordering their "Proceedings," a collection of the inspiring lectures of experts from around the world. So, even if you live out in the middle of nowhere and cannot find another living soul with whom to share your herb interest, you can become a member of a number of herb groups, by mail, and learn much from them.

Newsletters can provide another means of introduction. Many folks, for instance, have found herb pals through the networking section of my newsletter over the years. You might be surprised to learn of interested folks just a hop, skip, and jump away from you. For some folks, it is easier to find a pal through an herb publication than by advertising locally of an interest in starting a group. Thirty years ago I knew of no one, besides Adelma Simmons,

who loved herbs. Nowadays, anyone interested in finding herb friends will find tremendous opportunities for doing so!

Although, for me, May is a favorite month to stay home, work in the gardens, and start enjoying the warmer weather, in recent years I've attended two open houses at herbal shops in May, and I wouldn't have missed either for the world. Since I was the featured guest at both events, and thus received royal treatment, I thought you'd like to read about how two of the experts — Bertha Reppert and Betsy Williams — treat not only their guests of honor, but every visitor for such an occasion. Since both were autograph-signing sessions, the hostesses served many recipes from my first book (including punches, cookies, tea breads, and dips) in order to promote sales. New recipes from both Bertha's and Betsy's open houses, however, are included here.

I hope your May is filled with shining moments in your garden and herbfests of your own making all month long as you celebrate the new growing season.

Herb Societies and Fairs

FORMING AN HERB GROUP

by Donna L. Strudwick

An herb society can start with the interest of just two people. After working with herbs for several years, I became acquainted with a local woman who had an English herb garden. Our mutual enthusiasm motivated us to form a small study group, which had its first meeting in her garden in June 1983. For two years, our group met almost monthly to study different facets of herbs. Sometimes we selected individual herbs to report on; sometimes we made herbal vinegars, potpourri, wreaths, and other gifts from our gardens. We had an herbal tea-tasting party and visited nearby herb gardens. Our meetings were informal and very enjoyable. During the summer of 1985 I attended the Great Lakes Herb Symposium at Hiram College in Hiram, Ohio, and that exciting experience made me determined that our group should grow and become more organized.

In the fall of 1985, we held an open meeting in November, which we entitled "An Herbal Thanksgiving." The energetic efforts of our publicity chairman and others resulted in two articles in local newspapers. Earlier attempts to encourage new members had been disappointing, but because of this good publicity, and perhaps also because we switched to an evening time, our Thanksgiving meeting was well attended. With the help of a member of the Herb Society of America, we developed a statement of purpose and formed a nucleus of officers.

In our second year, with forty-five members, we felt that we had a very solid beginning and exciting future possibilities. Our community projects included assisting the local historical museum to set up an exhibit on winter weeds, presenting a panel on health with herbs, planting herbs at a retardation center, and promoting herbs through demonstrations at our local co-op health food store. Our monthly programs have included basic information on selecting, planting, harvesting, and preserving herbs; a slide program of herb gardens around the United States; workshops on making herbal wreaths and vinegars; and an August evening tour of local herb gardens. We have a "cooking with herbs" sub-group and hope to start one on medicinal herbs. We are very proud of our outstanding newsletter and have high hopes of continuing one of our major goals in the future, "to help others realize that 'growing with herbs' can be an exciting and fulfilling way of life."

How pleased I am that DONNA STRUDWICK is willing to share with us her experiences with starting an herb club! I relish such contributions from "lay folks" who love herbs so much that they just want to spread the word.

DONNA STRUDWICK (PRESIDENT, WESTERN MICHIGAN HERB SOCIETY), MUSKEGON, MI 49441

❧ *Rosemary Fruit Punch* ❧

46-ounce can pineapple juice
½ cup sugar
5 teaspoons fresh rosemary (2½
   teaspoons dried)
1½ cups lemon juice
2 cups water
Fresh lemon slices and fresh sprigs of
   rosemary
1-liter bottle pale-dry ginger ale

Make a concentrate by bringing to a boil 1 cup of the pineapple juice, the sugar, and rosemary. Decrease heat and simmer for 5 minutes. Strain and cool.

To serve, add the concentrate to the remaining pineapple juice, the lemon juice, and water. Pour into a punch bowl over ice and add the ginger ale. Float fresh lemon slices and rosemary sprigs on top.

❧ *Sage Cream Cheese* ❧

A nice spread for crackers or gourmet breads.

Two 8-ounce packages cream
   cheese, softened
½ cup butter or margarine, softened
1 tablespoon lemon juice
3 or 4 teaspoons minced fresh sage
   (1½ teaspoons dried)
1 clove garlic, minced

Blend all ingredients well. Serve at room temperature.

HAVE YOURSELF AN HERBFEST!

by Ronda Schooley Bretz

Fairs, fetes, and festivals are the classic means for presenting herbs and herbal crafts. When I hear of such an event, even hundreds of miles away, my spirit tingles to be there. Whether you envision an informal affair with tea, cookies, and crafts to sell on the patio, or a gala occasion on spacious meadows complete with herb gardens for touring and tents filled with herbal goodies, it is wise to plan ahead on paper first, at least a year in advance. If your fair becomes an annual event, you will learn and grow through each year's experience. Let me suggest how to plan for a big fair, and you can cut corners to fit a personal scheme.

Nothing is as effective a profitmaker as a fair, provided it is unique, well done, and well advertised. From a publicity stand-point, an herb fair should be held at the same time each year — if possible, the same weekend each year. Customers remember and look forward to it. To entice folks to attend a fair at all, offer them some inducement beyond the mere suggestion that their presence and money will be appreciated. Your aim should be amusement, entertainment, and profit. If you succeed in the first two goals, you will find that pocketbooks will open.

You cannot get something for nothing. Expenses will return with interest added to principle. Consider a budget for advertising, refreshments, and an attractive decor, with herbs and everlastings in every detail. Advertising need not be costly. Remember the four W's of news writing — who, what, when, and where — and create two half-page flyers on 8½" x 11" paper (a printer can cut your paper if you don't have a paper-cutter). Leave a stack of them wherever you have a contact person, such as in gift and craft shops, natural food stores, antique shops, and decorators. Some shops will keep them on a counter by the cash register. Make large, colorful posters, simple but well done, announcing that on a certain day something quite novel and delightful is to happen, and place them on public bulletin boards and in store windows. If your fair is offered as a free civic event with craft demonstrations and the like, you'll qualify for the social activities section of the local news-paper. Some radio stations offer public service announcements for such events. Establish a local mailing list by taking a notebook with you everywhere you go. Ask any new acquaintances who are interested in herbs to write their addresses and phone numbers in the notebook so you can notify them of herb festivities. If you have a business, increase your mailing list by having sign-up sheets in your shop or at any festivity. You can mail your flyer without an envelope, simply by folding it in half and securing the long edge. (Check with your post office to be sure it satisfies postal requirements.)

If your fair will be large, it may be necessary to secure extra liability insurance and, if a meal is to be served, a health permit just for that day. Give careful consideration to parking. In the country, you will probably have adequate space away from highways, but in the city, with street-side parking, you may have trouble. Inform your neighbors of the upcoming event and solicit their support of your need for additional space on the street.

When my business was located in Iowa, our Flower Valley turned into an impressive expanse with several fly tents (canopies), benches, and picnic tables set about the grounds the day before our herb festival each year. Provided at no cost by the local Boy Scout camp, each tent was designated for a special purpose. Posterboard signs guided guests and customers nicely through the day. One tent housed a potpourri demonstration, with fresh batches of handmade blends on sale. The wreath craft instructor's tent was always full. Here, both pre-made and in-process wreaths could be purchased; often buyers would wait hours to have their own wreaths custom-crafted. A basket weaver demonstrated and sold her wares in another area. Herb-dyed yarns spun on an antique wheel created great interest; the dyeing procedure was explained or demonstrated. A tent for displaying, making, and selling herb vinegars always caught a cook's eye (and nose!). Other craft demonstration possibilities are numerous, so locate talented folks in your area to help you make the event a success. And, of course, sell fresh herb plants! I haven't met an herbie yet who could resist purchasing one more herb for the garden or windowsill. Consider introducing an herb food contest. Those with discerning palates could judge the best dish. Publicize the specific time of this event, so that those participating will know when to have their food in place. Announce a prize, such as a special herb apron or cookbook.

For each festival, we filled our retail shop from loft to floor with every herb gift that we could think of to sell. A clerk was available in the shop at all times during the fair. To speed cashier work and keep congestion at a minimum, customers took their selections to a special sales counter outside the shop. Point-of-purchase signs throughout the area are a must to help answer customer questions and to encourage purchases.

In your largest tent, offer your guests wonderful, free herbal refreshments. Hostesses need to be on hand to answer questions about the foods and to replenish dwindling treats. Supply recipes for the food you serve. Food seasonings will sell well if taste samples are available. Use paper cups and napkins, and locate plastic-lined waste containers in strategic locations about the fair. Provide plenty of seating, especially in the food area. Pine benches and bales of straw are great. If you sprinkle the bales with lavender buds and spikes, they will smell heavenly when sat upon. This is a good location for a classy touch of music. A friend who makes and plays dulcimers entertained the folks at our big events — and the music was particularly suited to an herbal scene.

You, the crafters, and the workers should be dressed to

❧ *Lavender Cookies* ❧

2 eggs
½ cup margarine
1 cup sugar
1 teaspoon lavender leaves
1½ cups flour
2 teaspoons baking powder
½ teaspoon salt
Confectioner's sugar
Rosewater

Preheat oven to 375° F. Put eggs, margarine, sugar, and lavender (in that order) into blender, and run on low until well mixed. Sift flour, baking powder, and salt into a mixing bowl. Add other ingredients, and stir until well blended. Drop dough, a teaspoonful at a time, onto ungreased cookie sheets. Bake until lightly browned. Place cookies on racks to cool.

Blend enough rosewater into the confectioner's sugar to make a smooth frosting. Ice the cookies and let them set until the frosting is firm.

❧ *Herb Broth* ❧

2 parts beef bouillon
1 part cranberry juice
Fresh thyme, to season
Fresh herbs such as mint, chives, dill, or parsley

Heat the bouillon, cranberry juice, and thyme. Serve hot, garnished with a choice of fresh snipped herbs, such as mint, chives, dill, or parsley.

Curry Cookies

These are delicious!

*1 cup butter or margarine
2 cups brown sugar
2 teaspoons vanilla
2 eggs
1½ cups chopped walnuts
1½ cups whole wheat pastry flour
1½ cups unbleached flour
½ teaspoon baking soda
1 teaspoon baking powder
2 teaspoons curry powder
½ teaspoon salt*

Preheat oven to 325° F. Cream butter and sugar. Add the vanilla and eggs, and continue to cream the mixture. Mix together the walnuts, flours, baking soda, baking powder, curry powder, and salt. Stir these dry ingredients into the creamed mixture. Refrigerate until dough is chilled.

Bake in preheated oven until golden.

RONDA SCHOOLEY BRETZ,
SILVER SPRING, PA 17575

If you have fresh berries or chive blossoms in May or June, peek ahead to the July chapter, where fruit, floral, and herbal vinegars are featured. You'll find easy instructions for wonderful raspberry and blueberry vinegars and chive blossom vinegar, along with delicious recipes for use. PVS

complement the occasion — in colonial clothes and spice jewelry, herb-garnished bonnets, and festive garlands for the hair, for instance. This both adds charm and helps guests and customers identify participants. Name tags add an extra friendliness — you are special, so show it.

Depending on the scope of your fair, plan for good helpers before, during, and after the big day. As the hostess of these events, I had to be free to see that all was running smoothly, and to take groups through the garden for tours. Pay your helpers for their time by giving them some of your products or by throwing an "afterglow" party in the evening.

Depending on your space limitations, you might also hold a late fall open house, with displays in your house or herb shop (of course, you wouldn't have garden tours and demonstrations in inclement weather). With taped dulcimer music and the added flavor of Christmas approaching, such an affair could be both cozy and gala. An herbfest or fair in all its glory should be a joy for everyone!

Mint Nut Bread

*2½ cups flour
1 cup firmly packed brown sugar
3½ teaspoons baking powder
3 tablespoons oil
1½ cups milk or ¾ cup apple juice
    and ¾ cup milk
1 egg
1 cup chopped walnuts
1 cup chopped fresh mint (⅓ scant
    cup, dried)*

Preheat oven to 350° F. Mix the flour, sugar, and baking powder in a large mixing bowl. Whisk together the oil, milk, and egg. Blend the mixtures together. Add the walnuts and mint.

Bake in greased bread pans in the preheated oven for 50 to 60 minutes. Cool and slice. Ages and freezes well.

FRIENDSHIP POTPOURRI: A COLLECTIVE LEARNING EXPERIENCE

by Bob Clark

I always take pleasure in finding new ways to inspire others to explore the wonders of nature all around us. Most successful of these has been a sharing experience I call making a "Friendship Potpourri." Perfect for herb clubs and garden groups, this program is equally as rewarding with scout troops, women's organizations, or as a senior citizen project.

A two-meeting program is ideal, as the first can be spent on gathering and drying potpourri materials, such as flowers, herbs, citrus peel, berries, and so on. I suggest people without gardens check with friends or look in fields or vacant lots, sniffing as well as looking. A prepared hand-out sheet should be distributed in advance if two meetings are not possible. Be certain to stress that all plant material must be totally crisp and dry. Each person should bring at least one container full of herbs, flowers, citrus peel, fixative, spice, or essential oil. I bring some of the last three, plus extra in case anyone forgets; I also bring a large garbage bag or tub for mixing. Each person tells what he or she brought and adds it to the blend. When complete, each person takes home as much potpourri as he or she contributed — for example, one cup for one cup. The last time my herb club made Friendship Potpourri, we had about 50 quarts!

BOB CLARK, LANCASTER, OH 43130

Herbal Recipes for Open Houses

As we have seen, when large herb farms have open houses or other seasonal festivities, there may be acres of gardens to tour, many guest craft exhibitors, ongoing demonstrations or talks about herb projects, lots of food, and maybe even music and entertainment, and many herb organizations offer similar happenings at their annual festivals. When an herb shop has an open house, however, there is not likely to be the room to handle large crowds or to provide so many different activities. It was fun, therefore, for me to learn how Bertha Reppert (The Rosemary House) and Betsy Williams (The Proper Season) held their open houses in their shops and handled the steady flow of customers.

It was an honor to be the featured guest at The Rosemary House's 20th Anniversary celebration in 1988. Daughter Kim accompanied me, and the sense of festivity greeted our arrival the night before with a gorgeous fresh bouquet of red roses, mint, and lamb's-ears awaiting us in our room. (Of course, we brought Bertha's creation home and dried the materials for potpourri.) We were then treated to a lovely dinner with the Reppert family in a restaurant overlooking the Susquehanna River. When we arrived at The Rosemary House the next day, Bertha greeted us with beautiful fresh tussie mussies with accompanying scrolls, which gave the meanings of our custom-made bouquets. The shop is quaint and charming and filled with wall-to-wall-to-ceiling herbal goodies. I autographed copies of my first book on a delightful, long side porch, amidst potted herbs, hanging baskets of herbs, a refreshment table, and herb plants for sale.

Bunches of pastel balloons heralded the event both inside and outside the shop, and herb favors, herb seeds, door prizes, and many free handouts were a part of the festivities. Visitors could enjoy the lush herb and rose garden behind the shop and see an herb videotape in the workshop behind the garden. The Reppert family, plus some assistants, were on hand to greet guests, visit with them, and take care of sales. The Rosemary House is now a booming family venture — Father takes care of the books, and daughters Suzanne and Nancy run the shop and the new adjoining tea room, respectively, while Mother keeps churning out wonderful books and lectures. The ample refreshments were catered by Nancy, and included Mai Bowl Punch (from The Pleasure of Herbs*), cookies, Lemon Cake, and quantities of fresh strawberries served with Vanilla Sugar. It was a day full of happy reunions and the makings of new friendships. Some people came great distances, not only to meet me, but to meet the famous and well-loved Bertha. It was a very special occasion for me, as Bertha has, from the beginning of my own writing endeavors, given me generous encouragement and support, even when the chips were down. Now, I had finally met this soul sister and her wonderful family.*

Mint Sugar

Put four to six mint leaves and a cup of sugar in the blender. Add a few drops of green food coloring. Blend on high until well mixed. Dry the sugar overnight on a cookie sheet before storing for later use on cookies and grapefruit and in tea. Or, for an attractive, delicious garnish, roll little green grapes in this sugar.

From *Herbs with Confidence*
Bertha Reppert, The Rosemary House, Mechanicsburg, PA 17055

Vanilla Sugar

Place one or two vanilla beans into a canister full of sugar, and allow the vanilla flavor to permeate the contents for about two weeks. Stir occasionally. You will get faster results if the bean is cut into pieces and then sifted out. You can use the same technique with confectioners' sugar. The sugar will seem much sweeter than usual, so use less in recipes for puddings, chocolate sauces, and so on. The same beans can be re-used to flavor many pounds of sugar.

Lemon Cake

1 package yellow cake mix
3¾-ounce package lemon instant pudding
1 cup water
4 eggs, unbeaten
3 tablespoons dried lemon verbena, crushed
1 teaspoon powdered rosemary

Preheat oven to 350° F. Blend all ingredients, and beat 8 minutes. Pour into 13" x 9" x 2" pan, lined with brown paper. Bake for 45 to 50 minutes.

Nancy Reppert, The Herb Tea House, The Rosemary House, Mechanicsburg, PA 17055

TWO OPEN HOUSES IN ANDOVER

When deciding which book-signing invitations to accept, one of my criteria has been to go to areas where I have a lot of newsletter subscribers, as these folks were responsible for my books, and I like to meet as many members of "The Pot-pourri Family" as possible. When Betsy Williams generously offered to host two events to give me a chance to meet my subscribers — a daytime open house in her shop, The Proper Season, and an evening reception in Hardwaye Cottage, the renovated barn by her home that serves as her workshop — I was ready to go. Distance was another factor, of course, but knowing and revering the hostess were factored into the decision. I had been in awe of Betsy Williams long before she became one of my subscribers, so

I couldn't resist an opportunity to meet her and to see first-hand her beautiful floral and herbal creations.

As if these two events weren't enough, Hugh and I were treated to an elegant dinner, whipped up by Betsy, upon our arrival the night before. (For her recipes on this occasion see "Dinner on Chestnut Street," page 125.) Between the dinner and the activities for the next day, this human dynamo prepared and delivered the fresh flowers for an herbal wedding!

Betsy's enchanting shop provided a festive atmosphere for an autographing party. It was so full of exquisite creations that whenever there was a lull in the crowd I kept adding to my pile of treasures to take home. My favorite purchase, which I wore all day and for several summers

thereafter, was one of her beautiful pink rosebud necklaces, interwoven with tiny pearls and tied with pink satin ribbon. This fragrant jewelry is a keepsake I shall treasure always. The custom-made "May Basket Cake" seemed too lovely to cut. It consisted of four lemon seed cakes with a basketweave frosting on the sides, purple and pink flowers and ribbons on top, four basket handles decorated with streamers, and fresh bleeding-heart flowers and sage branches emanating from the middle and sides. Along with the cake, Betsy served herbal teas and coffee, plus a large bowl of Herbed Cheese Dip (from The Pleasure of Herbs) and crackers. Herb plants were available at the entrance and handouts were free for the taking. That extra little touch that Betsy is known for came in the shape of a fresh flower given to each visitor as a memento.

The reception at Hardwaye Cottage in the evening was filled to capacity, mostly with students from Betsy's classes and subscribers to my newsletter. The room was gorgeous, filled with dried floral wreaths on the walls, fresh flowers on the refreshment tables, and dried bunches of flowers and herbs hanging from the rafters, literally covering the ceiling! Betsy and her aides served two kinds of punch, cookies, and tea breads (from The Pleasure of Herbs), plus eggs and dips (see page 126). For those wanting "one for the road," there was Swiss almond coffee with cardamom. Recipes for all the foods served, as well as my herb-growing chart, were given to attendees.

I had taken a large bouquet of my pink lilies-of-the-valley to Betsy. She at first used it as a centerpiece, then added a few to the bridal party's bouquets on Saturday, and shared the rest with the guests that night, suggesting they press their mementos in their copies of my book. This caring and sharing typified our every experience with Betsy and Ned Williams. Our weekend in Andover was lovely in all ways!

BETSY WILLIAMS'S DINNER ON CHESTNUT STREET

❧ *Betsy Williams's Melt-in-Your-Mouth Mustard Chicken* ❧

YIELD: 6 SERVINGS

Betsy makes her own horseradish, homemade mayonnaise, and homemade mustard for this recipe. If you use purchased ingredients, be sure to choose high-quality ones.

6 tablespoons Hardwaye Herb Mustard	6 teaspoons horseradish
6 tablespoons mayonnaise	6 boneless, skinless chicken breasts

Preheat the oven to 450° F. Mix the mustard and mayonnaise with a spoon. Place 1 tablespoon sauce and 1 teaspoon horseradish down the middle of each chicken breast, and roll the breast up with the filling in the center. Tuck the breasts close together in a lightly greased pan, spoon the rest of the sauce over the top, and cover the pan. Bake for 15 to 20 minutes. You may brown this dish under a broiler, if desired.

❧ *Hardwaye Herb Mustard* ❧

This mustard thickens better if you use whole wheat flour. You may substitute white wine for part of the vinegar. If you have fresh herbs, use double the amount. The mustard will keep in the refrigerator for several months.

4 cups vinegar	1 clove garlic, crushed or pressed
2 cups dry mustard	¼ cup mixed dried herbs (such as
2 cups unbleached or whole wheat flour	basil, thyme, parsley, marjoram, and rosemary)
1¼ cups sugar	

Add the vinegar to the mustard, flour, and sugar, stirring well until lump-free. Stir in the garlic and herbs. Let the mixture stand overnight, then stir again. If the mustard is too thin, add more flour. Pour into covered crocks or jars.

❤ ❤ ❤ ❤ ❤ ❤ ❤ ❤ ❤

This luscious menu consisted of Melt-In-Your-Mouth Mustard Chicken, buttered artichoke noodles (Betsy suggests spinach fettucini would be a good alternative), fresh asparagus, herbed tossed salad, and Andover Rhubarb-Strawberry Sauce with Angelica. PVS

❧ *Andover Rhubarb-Strawberry Sauce with Angelica* ❧

Stew tender, young, cut-up rhubarb stalks in a small amount of water and sugar to taste (Betsy says to use "a lot" of sugar). Stir occasionally, until of sauce consistency. Remove from the heat, and stir in several sliced, fresh strawberries (about a pint) and ½ teaspoon tender, young, chopped angelica stems. The heat of the sauce will soften the strawberries. Serve warm, with cream (and cookies, if desired).

Make plenty ... this is unbelievably good! PVS

Yogurt Cheese

Place 1 quart yogurt on a piece of cheesecloth or other loosely woven material. Draw the four corners of the material up and tie securely to form a bag. Hang this overnight from the kitchen faucet or anywhere it can drip; place a container underneath to catch the whey. The thick mass left in the bag is the yogurt cheese, which can be used in any way that cream cheese is used. You can save the whey to enrich soups and stews.

BETSY WILLIAMS, THE PROPER SEASON, ANDOVER, MA 01810

THE RECEPTION AT HARDWAYE COTTAGE

❧ Mary Lou's Sage Cheese ❧

This cheese may also be made with other herbs of your choice.

1 quart yogurt cheese
8-ounce package cream cheese

¼ cup chopped fresh sage (or ⅛ cup dried)
1 large clove garlic, peeled

Place all ingredients in a food processor and blend for 1 minute. This can be used as a dip or spread.

❧ Herbed Eggs ❧

6 hard-cooked eggs
2 tablespoons plain yogurt
2 tablespoons mayonnaise
½ tablespoon mustard
2 tablespoons chopped chives

1 tablespoon chopped dill
1 tablespoon chopped tarragon
1 tablespoon chopped chervil
Salt and pepper, to taste
Fresh dill sprigs

Shell the boiled eggs, and cut them in half lengthwise, removing yolks carefully. Mash the yolks, moistening them with the yogurt, mayonnaise, and mustard. Season them with the herbs. Add salt and pepper to taste. Pile the mixture back into the egg whites, arrange the eggs on a platter, and garnish with feathery sprigs of dill.

HERBAL "FAST FOOD"

by Jim Long

JIM LONG is an accomplished culinary expert, besides being very knowledgeable about herbs, an excellent writer (he publishes the Ozarks Herbalist, *a quarterly herb journal), and the owner of Long Creek Herbs. He is the master architect of the Heritage Herb Garden at the Ozark Folk Center in Mountain View, Arkansas, where herbal events take place all year long. At his own Long Creek Herbs, he hosts an annual Herb Day in May, which features demonstra-*

❧ Frozen Fruit Salad ❧

Any fruit in season can be used in this recipe.

16-ounce can fruit cocktail
3 cups fresh or frozen blueberries
2 cups strawberry pieces
2 pears, peeled and diced
2 apples, peeled and diced

2 cups watermelon pulp
1 cup white seedless grapes
1 tablespoon chopped, fresh lemon verbena
¼ teaspoon ground cardamom

Combine all ingredients, mixing well. Spoon into fruit cups and place in freezer. Remove 30 minutes before serving.

❧ *Jim's Stuffed Bread* ❧

YIELD: 12 SANDWICHES

This bread is easy because you use frozen, whole-wheat bread dough. After the breads are stuffed and baked, they can be wrapped and again frozen. They're an easy sandwich substitute for the patio or picnic. Simply pop in the microwave, or wrap in foil and heat in a slow oven before serving.

Two 1-pound loaves frozen whole-
   wheat bread dough
2 pounds round beef, ground
2 tablespoons vegetable oil
1 medium onion, chopped
1 tablespoon chile powder
2 tablespoons garlic tops (the
   leaves), chopped
15-ounce can tomato sauce

2 teaspoons fresh marjoram leaves
   (1 teaspoon dried)
¼ cup slivered almonds
3½ ounces black olives, chopped
¼ cup raisins
½ cup grated Monterey Jack cheese
Cornmeal
1 egg
1 tablespoon water

Thaw the bread dough overnight in the refrigerator. In the morning, set the loaves out, and let them come to room temperature.

Brown the beef in the oil in a large skillet. When the beef is nearly browned, add the chopped onion. Add the chili powder, and simmer, stirring, until onions are cooked. Add the garlic, tomato sauce, marjoram, almonds, olives, and raisins, and mix well. Add the cheese and set aside.

When the bread has started to rise, cut each loaf into six pieces. On a floured bread board, roll out each piece to about the size of your hand. Lay a piece of rolled bread dough in your hand, coat the *edges* of half of the dough with water, then put about ¼ cup of the ground beef mixture in the center. Fold the bread dough over, pinching the edges together to seal. Fold all seams under, and place on a cookie sheet that has been dusted with cornmeal. Don't place pieces so close together that they will touch when they bake, as this will cause the insides to come out while cooking. Continue making the little pocket sandwiches until you've used up all the material. Set aside to rise, about 30 minutes.

While the bread is rising, preheat the oven to 350° F. Brush the sandwich tops with the egg beaten with the water. Bake about 25 minutes, or until golden brown. Cool on a rack.

❧ *Long Creek Herbed Cheese* ❧

2 pounds mozzarella cheese, cut in
   1-inch cubes
3 tablespoons sunflower oil
1 tablespoon fresh marjoram

4 tablespoons fresh parsley
A few sprigs of chives or onion
1 or 2 celery leaves (optional)

Combine herbs in food processor, and chop until fine. Put cheese, oil, and herbs in a bowl and mix well. Refrigerate overnight. Drain off oil, and serve cubes on crackers.

tions and talks by leading experts, herbal tastings and samples, crafts, plants, books, an herbal luncheon, and walks through the garden and nature trail.

These recipes, which Jim developed for the 1988 Herb Day in May, were devised to be make-ahead, easy-to-serve, picnic-style foods. This particular meal was served in individual baskets to the guests.

❧ *Creamy Marinated Vegetables* ❧

This dish can be made ahead and is better if left in the sauce for a day or two in the refrigerator.

64-ounce jar artichoke hearts,
   including juice
8 to 10 ripe avocados, peeled and cut
   up in large pieces
8 to 12 large carrots, chunked
1 bunch celery, cut up
2 cups chopped onions or pearl
   onions
3 tablespoons chopped chives
2 tablespoons chopped garlic chives
2 tablespoons chopped fresh tarragon
1 teaspoon chopped thyme leaves

Combine all ingredients, mixing lightly. Refrigerate. Drain before serving.

❧ *Minted Chocolates* ❧

1 pound chocolate almond bark
1 pound vanilla almond bark
2 cups fresh mint, finely chopped, in
*   a food processor, if possible*

Melt almond barks separately over hot water. Combine chopped mint with chocolate bark, and mix well. Taste. If not minty enough, add more chopped mint. You should have a thick mixture, consisting mostly of chopped mint. Keep the chocolate over hot water as you drop small amounts from a buttered spoon into candy papers or onto a buttered cookie sheet. As soon as candies are firm, top each of them with a spoonful of vanilla almond bark. Cool. Store candies in a container with an airtight lid, at room temperature. They will keep for weeks (if you can stay out of them).

♥

Always be sure you use only unsprayed rose petals for culinary purposes.

♥

FROM *THE OZARKS HERBALIST*, A QUARTERLY HERBAL JOURNAL
JIM LONG, OAK GROVE, AR 72660

❧ *Lemon Balm-Blueberry Cake* ❧

¾ cup milk
1 to 2 tablespoons fresh lemon balm
1 tablespoon lemongrass (fresh or
*   dry)*
1 teaspoon lemon thyme
2 cups flour
1½ teaspoons baking powder

¼ teaspoon salt
2 eggs
1 cup sugar
6 tablespoons soft butter
1 tablespoon grated lemon zest
2 cups fresh or frozen blueberries

Preheat oven to 350° F. Scald milk. Put milk, lemon balm, lemongrass, and lemon thyme in a food processor or blender. Process until well chopped. Set aside to let steep. Combine flour, baking powder, and salt. Place milk mixture and flour mixture in a food processor. Add eggs, sugar, butter, and lemon zest. Blend well until dough is mixed. Combine the blueberries into the dough by hand.

    Pour mixture into a greased, 9" x 5" bread pan. Bake in the preheated oven about 50 minutes. Test with a straw (I use the stiff, more unusable part of a lemongrass leaf for testing cakes). If tester comes out with batter on it, continue baking for a few more minutes. Serve with Rose-Petal Topping. Baked in 4" x 6" bread pans, this makes a fine gift. It also freezes very well.

❧ *Rose-Petal Topping* ❧

2 cups rose petals
2 cups sugar

1½ cups hot water

Combine water and rose petals, and bring to a boil. Reduce heat, and simmer until the color is gone from the petals — about 5 minutes. Strain. Return to heat and add sugar. Simmer, stirring until sugar is dissolved. Continue to simmer until the water volume is reduced some. Remove from heat and allow to cool. You may refrigerate the syrup overnight, or preserve it. To preserve, pour the hot syrup into washed and sterilized canning jars, screw on new lids, and place the jars in a hot-water bath for 5 minutes to seal. To serve, add fresh rose petals and pour a small amount over slices of Lemon Balm-Blueberry Cake.

❧ Peg's Opulent Chicken ❧
YIELD: SERVES 6 TO 8

6 whole chicken breasts, boned and
　split
Paprika, salt, and pepper
½ pound butter
Two 15-ounce cans artichoke hearts

1 pound fresh mushrooms, sliced
¼ teaspoon tarragon
6 tablespoons flour
1 cup sherry (dry or sweet)
3 cups chicken bouillon

Preheat oven to 350°. Coat the chicken breasts with paprika, salt, and pepper. Sauté chicken in one stick of the butter until brown. Place chicken in a casserole dish, and add artichoke hearts. Sauté the mushrooms and tarragon in the remaining stick of butter for 5 minutes. Sprinkle with the flour, and add the sherry and chicken bouillon. Simmer for 5 minutes, stirring to blend. Pour the sauce over the chicken and artichokes. Cover the casserole and bake 45 minutes.

❧ Minted Cucumber Salad ❧
YIELD: SERVES 6 TO 8

4 cucumbers, peeled, halved, seeded,
　and sliced
½ cup chopped fresh mint
¼ cup chopped fresh parsley

1 orange rind, grated
½ cup olive oil
1 cup red wine vinegar
¼ cup granulated sugar

Toss the cucumbers in a bowl with the mint, parsley, and orange rind. Whisk the oil, vinegar, and sugar together in a small bowl, and pour over the cucumber mixture. Cover and refrigerate for at least 4 hours. Toss again before serving on a very cold bed of lettuce.

PEG MASTEY has found these two recipes popular, and easy-to-make, for spring herbal lunceons.

Tarragon (Artemisia dracunculus)

PEG MASTEY, HERITAGE HERBS, CANTERBURY, NH 03224

❧ Curried Rice Salad Diane ❧

3 cups long-grain rice, cooked
　(about ⅔ cup uncooked)
3 tablespoons minced green onions
½ apple, cut into ½-inch pieces
⅓ cup raisins, plumped in hot water
　and drained
1 stalk of celery, cut in ¼-inch slices
3 radishes, thinly sliced

While the rice is cooking, prepare the remaining ingredients and the dressing. Combine rice, vegetables, fruits, and dressing. Chill overnight.

Dressing

2 teaspoons Dijon-style mustard
1½ teaspoons white wine vinegar
1 teaspoon curry powder
1 teaspoon honey
¼ teaspoon salt (optional)
3 tablespoons sour cream
2 tablespoons mayonnaise
¼ cup vegetable oil

Mix ingredients together in order given.

DIANE LEA MATHEWS, SALISBURY CENTER, NY 13454

These variations on boursin are a nice way to offer herb-tasting experiences to the public.

BOURSIN WITH FRESH HERBS

by Lucinda Hutson

I like to divide a batch of this homemade cheese spread into four parts, and flavor each with different herbs. The cheeses may be served with crudités, crackers, thin slices of baguette, as a sandwich spread, or stuffed under chicken breasts. You can create an attractive party platter of open-faced sandwiches by using the following variations and placing different fresh herb sprigs on each variation.

Serve each variation directly from a 1-cup ramekin, or you may line the ramekin with plastic wrap, fill with the mixture, and then chill overnight. At serving time, turn the cheese out on a platter lined with ornamental greens, and garnish with complementary herbs. Adorn the platter with chive blossoms, if available. If basic boursin is not divided into four parts, add approximately ½ cup chopped fresh herbs and additional freshly ground pepper to the basic recipe.

❧ Basic Boursin ❧

1 pound farmer's cheese or ½ pound cottage cheese and ½ pound ricotta cheese
8 ounces cream cheese, softened
1 stick butter, softened
4 large cloves garlic, minced
2 medium shallots, minced

½ cup finely minced parsley, tightly packed
3 tablespoons minced chives
1 teaspoon freshly ground pepper
¼ teaspoon cayenne
Salt (optional)

In a medium-sized bowl, blend the cheeses and butter. Add the other ingredients. Divide the cheese mixture into four small bowls or ramekins, and make the accompanying variations.

Boursin au Poivre
(Pepper Boursin)

½ to 1 teaspoon freshly cracked pepper (white and black)
¼ teaspoon crushed, dried red chile pepper (optional)

Mix peppers with one-fourth of the basic boursin. Serve with cold cuts and/or roast beef. Meat may be rolled around cheese.

Danish Boursin

3 tablespoons chopped fresh dill
2 teaspoons chopped fresh chives

Mix both herbs with one-fourth of the basic boursin. Serve on dark bread with cucumber slices, caviar, or smoked salmon and fresh dill sprigs.

French Boursin

2 tablespoons chopped fresh thyme (part lemon thyme preferable)
2 teaspoons chopped fresh chives

Mix herbs with one-fourth of the basic boursin. Serve with crudités, or stuffed under the skin of chicken breasts.

Italian Boursin

3 tablespoons chopped fresh basil
¼ to ½ teaspoon crushed red chili pepper
2 teaspoons chopped garlic chives (or onion chives)
2 tablespoons freshly grated Parmesan cheese

Mix ingredients with one-fourth of the basic boursin. Serve with crudités, in stuffed, broiled mushroom caps, or on garlic baguette croutons with roasted, red bell pepper strips.

FROM *THE HERB GARDEN COOKBOOK* BY LUCINDA HUTSON (TEXAS MONTHLY PRESS)

❧ *Shrimp (or Crawfish) Dill Salad* ❧

YIELD: SERVES 8

2 tablespoons chopped shallots
1 tablespoon chopped garlic
1 tablespoon Dijon mustard
1 tablespoon honey
1 tablespoon raspberry vinegar
1 tablespoon red-wine vinegar
½ cup chopped fresh dill
1 tablespoon chopped parsley

⅔ cup peanut oil
1 pound peeled shrimp (or crawfish tails), cooked
1 head Boston lettuce, clean and torn
2 avocados, thinly sliced
2 tomatoes, thinly sliced

Mix the shallots, garlic, mustard, honey, vinegars, dill, parsley, and oil for dressing. Beat until well blended. Pour this dressing over the seafood, and allow to marinate several hours.

Arrange marinated seafood on lettuce. Garnish with tomatoes and avocado.

DAVID UTLEY
BRONZE MEDAL, "SALADS"
FROM *THE CHEF'S HERB FESTIVAL COOKBOOK* (HERBS '88, INTERNATIONAL HERB GROWERS AND MARKETERS ASSOCIATION)

A May Gardening Project

FRESH HERBAL TOPIARY

by Linda Fry Kenzle

Topiary is back! Since early Roman times, skilled gardeners have been snipping privet, taxus, and buxus into shaped forms. Today, as the trend in gardening shifts from informal, massed plantings to more formal, rigid shapes, we can update the types of plants used for topiary to include our beloved herbs.

The idea behind basic topiary is to create a *standard* — a single-stemmed plant with a pom-pom top. Look at your plant collection now and select as candidates those with as straight a stem as possible. I have worked successfully with rosemary, lavender, curry plant, and scented geraniums. The latter, particularly lemon-scented Frensham and rose-scented Dr. Livingston, are my personal favorites. Many of the smaller-leafed geraniums that attain a medium to tall height will also work.

My approach to herbal topiary is rather simple. A trip to my local hardware store provides the two items I need — a spool of heavy-gauge wire, to support the stems, and fine-gauge wire for a wrap. Working with a 12-inch specimen of Frensham geranium, I clip all of the leaves from the base of the soil up, leaving the top 3

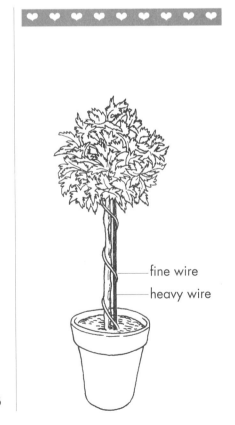
fine wire
heavy wire

inches intact. Next, I cut a piece of heavy-gauge wire approximately 17 inches long, and insert it into the soil parallel to the plant stem. The top end of the wire is concealed in the leafy pom-pom. I then insert a length of fine wire into the soil, and *gently* wrap the fine wire around both stem and wire support. It is important *not* to wrap the stem too tightly, or the plant may be weakened or possibly severed. When the stem is completely fastened to the heavy-gauge wire, I snip off the end of the fine wire and tuck it into the foliage.

Once the plant has attained the desired height, I pinch back the main stem to force growth at the pom-pom. Any stray leaves that appear along the stem are immediately snipped off with manicure scissors. As the plant grows, it sometimes needs to be removed from its pot to have its roots trimmed back, and then re-potted using fresh soil. Ideally, the pot should equal one-third the length of the entire topiary.

For continuing care, I treat the plant with the usual amount of sun, water, and nutrients. I use a time-release fertilizer for my topiaries. Since the plant now has less leaf surface, a daily misting is recommended.

LINDA FRY KENZLE, FOX RIVER GROVE, IL 60021

JUNE

BECAUSE OF THE fragrance and the meaningful symbolism of herbs, an herbal wedding is very unique any time of year — whether fresh or dried herbs are used, and whether the wedding is held outdoors or in. Herbs and flowers, either fresh or dried, can be used for the bridal party bouquets and boutonnieres, church arrangements, pew sprays, church and reception doors, table centerpieces at the reception, and wedding favors. Using the symbolism of the language of herbs and flowers adds a delightfully appropriate touch when the meanings are explained in some way to the guests. You will find the symbolic wedding herbs listed in the pages to come, as well as suggestions for sharing the symbolism with those in attendance. Because we spent the entire summer preceding my daughter's winter wedding growing, harvesting, and drying most of the herbs and flowers we used for the event, I felt that this chapter was the appropriate place to include a description of our preparations.

June is a good month for summertime, outdoor tea parties. Victorian teas were held in the gardens after a game of croquet; nowadays, many garden or herb clubs have outdoor teas or picnics for the final program of the year. Warm and sunny June is usually a perfect time for such activities, before the onslaught of high heat, humidity, and the whole insect population! We enjoy making our own Herbal Sun Teas all summer long, as you will see in this chapter.

Lastly, what is more perfect than a day in June, if not a rose? Roses are synonymous with beauty — and with June — when they are in all their glory. Many rose recipes and projects are included in this chapter, as well as a few for lavender, which is a close second in loveliness and is probably also blossoming for you now.

Herbal Showers and Weddings

A VICTORIAN HERBAL SHOWER

When daughter Kim was married, our older daughter, Karen, was her maid-of-honor. Home to help with the wedding preparations, Karen wanted the shower, planned by her and the other attendants, to be elegant and Victorian in theme, and, of course, herbal. It was therefore held at Grandma Shaudys's home, where there is more china, silver, lace, and space than here. I was pleased to be free of any responsibility for this, as I was busy finishing up the church decorations and trying to work on this book at the same time. During the last week before the event, however, Karen was having a hard time finding recipes for "Victorian" desserts and beverages, until I suggested she look in The Pleasure of Herbs. *As a result, she rounded out the buffet with Sage Cheese Wafers, Herbed Tea Sandwiches, and Rose Geranium Cake, as well as Lavender Cookies (which you will find in this book). I created a Rose Geranium Glaze for the cake, as she wanted it cut in small, finger-food-sized pieces, without frosting, and I garnished the cake plate with fresh leaves from the rose geraniums in our window garden. Others provided scones and a lemon cake.*

The color scheme for the shower was to be burgundy and silver, so I was asked to decorate my artemisia tree accordingly.

This would be used as a large centerpiece for Grandma's long, extended dining-room table, and the gray of the artemisia would blend in so well with the other colors. It didn't take long to remove all the lavender and pink ornaments that had adorned it, and I had to spend only one evening turning it into an appropriate decoration. Because the tree was 3 years old, it needed some brightening up, which I did by sprinkling it with little white net fans made of Lacelon ribbon. The Lacelon stays stiff when you press it out with your fingers, so I made five narrow folds in each piece to create the fans, wound satin ribbon twice around the center, folded out the ends, and pressed them into fan shape. I also placed in amongst the branches some muted (grayish) red eucalyptus, which proved to be the perfect burgundy shade, along with some leftover maroon button flowers, tied together to make lovely accents. I used dried, very silvery, lamb's-ear leaves at the top of the tree. Bleached (very white!) baby's-breath completed my efforts at lightening up the old tree; maroon and white satin bows made the finishing touch.

The refreshments and the centerpiece brought raves from the guests, but I think the hit of the party was the Forever Yours tea, a rosy-red, spiced tea from

❦ Rose Geranium Glaze ❦

Place 3 rose geranium leaves in ⅛ cup water in a microwave-safe container, and microwave this rose geranium "tea" on high for 3 minutes. Steep for 3 minutes and drain. Mix with ¾ cup confectioner's sugar and 1 teaspoon vanilla.

The Rosemary House, which we used for both the punch and the favors for our guests. Karen had planned to make our own herbal tea, but discovered rather late that when we made the wedding potpourri we used up the particular herbs she had intended to use for tea. A quick call to Bertha Reppert solved the problem. I inquired about her Love Tea, but she laughingly replied that we might not want to give our guests aphrodisiac favors! Instead, she recommended her new Forever Yours tea, which is packaged beautifully and includes recipes for tea and punch. It is just delicious, hot or cold.

Antique fans were placed around the living room, and silver and white balloons graced the entrance hall. For Kim, there was a fresh rose arrangement and a corsage. Large satin bows with streamers were placed on the front door and on the mailbox by the road. Big Sis did us all proud with her entertaining skills, and Kim was delighted with her every effort and thoughtful gesture.

AN HERBAL KITCHEN SHOWER

by Bertha Reppert

Theme. Use herbs — in abundance — and a pretty color scheme, too. Include some of your own favorite things, such as baskets, a doll collection, butterflies, or an assortment of hearts to set the stage.

Invitations. Glue pressed herbs or dried spices onto recipe cards, and request that guests bring favorite recipes, as well as the main seasoning ingredients to go with them. Supply the bride-to-be with a recipe file and a spice cupboard or a pretty basket to receive these personalized, herbal goodies.

Centerpiece. In the center of the table or buffet, group many "things herbal," such as pots or bunches of herbs, dried herbs in apothecary jars, a cookbook, glass jars or bowls of potpourri, scented candles, a mortar and pestle, whole spices, an herbal kitchen towel, and so on. With any combination of these, you can make a charming grouping — just as on the cover of your favorite herbal — especially if you place them on a cutting board or in a flat basket. These can be your own things or additional gifts to bestow upon the honored guest.

Gift suggestions. Kitchen gadgets, herbal things, or whatever the bride needs for the kitchen.

Favors. Herb charts rolled into a scroll with a bag of parsley, sage, rosemary, or thyme tied on with a bow to match your color scheme. A recipe served at the party, written on a card, with a tablespoon of the main seasoning ingredient attached in a small envelope. Spice posies made by gluing spices and dried flowers in a white doily decorated with ribbons — charming and fragrant, these can be made well in advance. A nosegay of fresh herbs with symbolism attached — marjoram for joy, thyme for courage, rosemary for remembrance, and so forth — all tied with ribbons and laces. A small bottle of your favorite seasoned salt, herb jelly, or

BERTHA REPPERT'S Rosemary House offers a collection of twenty herb tea parties, each with a theme presented in recipe booklets that suggest dips, sandwiches, cakes, cookies, and herb teas to serve. Bertha also carries herb napkins, spice charts, fresh herbs in summer, and all things herbal. For her herbal weddings, which she manages in the Mechanicsburg (PA) area, Bertha presents each bride with a suggestion sheet for incorporating herbs into all the wedding festivities. These include such ideas as giving sprigs of myrtle (the emblem of love) or rosemary (the wedding herb) to each wedding guest, or topping the wedding cake with an herbal tussie mussie with ribbons and laces, to be used for the throw-away bouquet.

A Bride's Bouquet

*Here's Thyme to give you
    courage
Rosemary for the past
Sweet Lavender, a loyal heart
Yarrow, a love to last —
Sage for a life that is long and
    brave
Mint to quicken the brain
Violets to ward off evil ones
Basil to cure the pain and
    then for fun and fragrance,
Southernwood will do. Rose
    and Lemon and Ginger
    mean a Sixpence in your
    shoe.*

—FROM A POSTER AVAILABLE
FROM THE ROSEMARY HOUSE

homemade tarragon vinegar. A packet of herb seeds (if the seeds are from your own garden, they will make a special gift to your guests). Little pots of labeled herbs, placed in the center of a table for decoration, and then given to departing guests. An old-fashioned nutmeg grater and a nutmeg tied with ribbons in the party colors. A whole, long cinnamon stick with the recipe for mulled cider attached. Small sacks of wedding rice with rosemary for remembrance and roses for love.

Menu. Advance planning is the secret. Have herbal sandwiches, an herbal dip, spicy cake or cookies, and edible flowers, too. Along with the many delicious things to serve that include herbs and spices, be sure to serve a good herbal tea, such as peppermint, rosehip, Red Zinger or Bigelow's Constant Comment — hot or cold, iced or spiced. It's fun, too, to put an attractive basket of assorted herb tea bags on the party tea tray. Some guests will enjoy trying more than one kind.

Extras. Do use napkins with herbs pictured on them. Be sure to garnish foods with colorful, *unsprayed*, edible flowers. Bouquets of fragrant herbs throughout the house, especially in the powder room, and a dried herbal wreath on the door add charming ambience. Greet the guest of honor with a tussie mussie.

BERTHA REPPERT, THE ROSEMARY HOUSE, MECHANICSBURG, PA 17055

An Everlasting Wedding

Some of the decorative herbs can be dried using the same methods used for floral preservation, such as microwaving in silica gel, glycerin, and borax/cornmeal "sand." The many useful books that give thorough coverage of these methods and others are listed in the Appendix under February, Books on Everlastings. In particular, I would highly recommend Betty E. M. Jacob's Flowers that Last Forever: Growing, Harvesting, and Preserving (Pownal, VT: Garden Way Publishing, 1988).

We were fortunate to have had over a year to plan and prepare for our daughter's February wedding. Kim wanted it to be simple, yet elegant — meaningful and memorable for everyone involved. And, best of all, from my point of view, she wanted to use dried flowers and herbs for the church and reception decorations.

Not exactly sure how or where we would use them, or what colors we would need, we started harvesting and preserving just about every flower and herb on the place the preceding spring. Kim dreamed of making bookmark mementoes for the guests,

and employing the language of herbs and flowers with her own calligraphy, so hundreds of violets and sweet woodruff clusters were pressed between white tissues in our old encyclopedia set. Later, we added to this collection tiny flowering herbs as they blossomed. By late spring, the wedding colors had been selected, so we planted everlastings and even some new roses in some of these shades — ivory for the bride's gown, burgundy and teal for the attendants, and gold for accents. Kim wanted the church bouquets to be basically white or ivory, with touches of red and gold to blend in with the stained-glass windows, altar, and carpet. So, by midsummer, we were drying everything we could grow in these colors.

A real romantic, the bride-to-be wanted to use mostly plant material she had grown up with on our place, including favorite shrubs, herbs, and perennial flowers. By August, we were preserving all kinds of blossoms and foliage in silica gel, in a cornmeal/borax blend (see box below at right), in bunches hanging upside down from our three clothes-drying racks, pressed in books, and in glycerin. Almost every sunny day, one of us would go around the property and pick and preserve whatever we could find that would fit in with the plans.

For greenery, I preserved in a large plastic washtub of glycerin and green food coloring the ivy that graces a stone pillar at our driveway. The circular shape of the tub kept the ivy in its natural curved state. I was thrilled to see that fern-leaf tansy, my favorite greens for fresh bouquets, was preserved very well in the glycerin bath. The tansy ended up soft and pliable, almost alive-looking, even though some branches were a darker green than their original hues. More of the tansy, plus rose-scented geranium branches, dried very well in the cornmeal/borax "sand." These were more brittle, of course.

We had hoped to use Grandma Annie's hydrangea flowers for the church bouquets, but it rained the entire week the bush was coming out in bloom, which made it impossible to preserve the blossoms in their whitest and most fulsome stage.

We had some luck drying small clusters in silica sand, however, and the large branches that we had preserved in cornmeal/ borax mixture dried to a light beige and could be used in the back of the church bouquets. I used fabric softener to preserve some of my fillers (see box at right). Although this new method is still in the experimental stage, it is cheaper than glycerin and thus appealing to many. It does not work with evergreens, leafy plants, woody stems, or hydrangeas.

Although I've had no trouble air-drying fillers, such as my own baby's-breath, statice, and sea lavender, the ones I preserved in fabric softener needed special attention. We were having such a humid spell when these had to be harvested, that even the air-conditioners weren't keeping the house really comfortable. In addition, I must have left them in the solution too long, as the stems rotted up to the level of the liquid. Nevertheless, I was able to use what was above the solution level, and they did not shatter at all.

Kim had felt all along that our large annual supply of lunaria would be an adequate backdrop for the church bouquets, and as it turned out, she was right. Fortunately, we had air-dried dozens of branches from our smoke bush (Cotinus) when the hazy blossoms were a burgundy hue, and using this wispy background behind the shiny lunaria pods left no gaping holes in the arrangements. The hundreds of Queen-Anne's-lace flowers that Kim had harvested and successfully preserved in either silica or

---

FABRIC SOFTENER

A high-quality, concentrated fabric softener may be used to preserve filler materials such as baby's-breath, German statice, sea lavender, and artemisia; fillers are less apt to shatter than when air-dried. Use full strength, or dilute using 1 part glycerin to 3 parts softener. Remove the leaves from the bottom 4 inches of the just-cut stems, and place the stems in 3 or 4 inches of fabric softener for 2 to 4 weeks, or until the material feels supple and bounces back when squeezed; the stems should bend without breaking.

❤

CORNMEAL/BORAX "SAND"

For centuries, flowers have been dried in very fine, clean, dry, sand. The sand does not absorb the moisture, but holds the petals or leaves in shape while they dry naturally in an open container (3 to 5 weeks). Gently drizzle sand over the petals, which rest in a layer of sand. I use a "sand" consisting of 3 parts cornmeal to 1 part borax (1 to 1 is also adequate). Cornmeal is lighter in weight than beach sand. I prefer white cornmeal, as the yellow variety may leave tiny yellow specks on the flowers. This medium may be used over and over. This method is useful for flowers with stems or false stems (which can be left sticking up out of the container).

cornmeal/borax solutions completed the basic white/ivory look she wanted for the church bouquets.

By early fall, we had harvested and air-dried an abundance of golden and burgundy celosias, both the plumed and the crested varieties, as well as golden yarrow. Many ivory- and burgundy-hued roses had been dried to perfection in silica "sand." Before the first frost, we picked and dried everything in flower, just in case we might need it. Fortunately, we could store all of our dried treasures in large boxes in the warm, dry environment of Grandma's second floor.

As the wedding date neared, I became nervous about whether or not we'd have enough material for eight large church bouquets, fourteen church pew arrangements, thirteen table centerpieces, and two wreaths for the church and/or reception doors, and so I made a trip to a wholesale florist outlet and bought several dozen dried, long-stem red roses, teal-colored statice for accents (as nothing we grew dried in that shade), some extra baby's-breath, and tiny blossoms that looked like yarrow and were really golden. As it turned out, my fears were well founded. With the hydrangea blossoms a wash-out, I needed almost everything else we had preserved, just for the church decorations. Fortunately, I made these up early enough to allow us time to make alternative plans for the reception.

By late fall, too, we had given up the bookmark idea for mementoes, as none of us was finding the time to make 140 of these. With the holidays upon us, we sent an SOS to Mary and John Spencer, of From the Countree (for address, see Appendix, February, Dried Flowers), who agreed to make up for us a quantity of their elegant tasseled sachets, which Kim and I consider the most beautiful we have ever seen. Her staff made these up in ivory lace and satin and filled them with our own wedding potpourri, which we had made in the fall from our flowers and herbs. We also ordered from Mary gorgeous dried bouquets in cloth doilies, which resembled tussie mussies. We used two on each table at the reception and placed them back-to-back in large, juice-size glasses, using crystal marbles from the florist for weights in the bottoms of the glasses. They gave

the large dining room a most elegant look for the candlelit evening dinner. The guests raved about them, especially those folks who were designated to take one home after the party — the members of the bridal party and the family members of the bride and groom. The beautiful memento sachets were left at each place setting. They perfumed the whole room before they quickly disappeared into purses and pockets, "so they wouldn't get lost."

I enjoyed making two 15-inch, baby's-breath wreaths for the church doors during some leisure moments. I found that taping the little bunches together before slipping them into the florist's satin that was wound around the straw wreath bases was a very relaxing activity amidst the hustle and bustle of the wedding month. These were adorned with ivory satin, lace ribbons and streamers, and our glycerin- preserved ivy. Although we learned at a late date that there were not nail holes for hanging wreaths on the doors of the church or the reception dining hall, these festive wreaths became the perfect decoration for the two main columns in the dining room, leaving no doubt about what kind of party we were having!

Although we still have hundreds of unused pressed flowers, and a garage full of more plastic containers filled with cornmeal/borax sand than I'll ever need again, and although I had fantasized about a fresh herb wedding, I wouldn't trade our year of joyful anticipation and shared preparation for all the summer weddings in any given year! It was very nice seeing and knowing how the church and reception room would look — well in advance. It was extremely joyful to use plant material from our property and gardens. And, it was wonderful to have permanent keepsakes from this so-happy occasion.

I'm sure we broke a rule or two when we combined dried and fresh flowers for the occasion. Kim was certain, however, about wanting fresh roses for the bridal party's bouquets and drieds for all other decorations, and I wanted our so-special daughter to have her heart's desires for this celebration of a union that seems to have been golden-edged and blessed from the start.

After all was said and done, and Mom and Dad had arrived home at midnight to an empty house, both exhilarated and exhausted, what did they do? Dad collapsed on the couch within minutes. Mom exchanged her satin dress and slippers for comfy clothes and got out the silica sand and the glycerin and started unwinding the floral tape from the fresh bridal bouquets to preserve them. It was just the unwinding I needed after the Big Event! By the time I had put all the roses and the flowers from the top of the wedding cake in silica sand, and all the greens from the bouquets in the glycerin bath, and frozen the top layer of the cake, it was 5:00 a.m. and I was sufficiently "unwound." My adrenalin still at a high level, and a short snooze was all I needed before the out-of-town

family members and friends arrived for coffee and Danish buns before their trips back home. Sometime before their first anniversary, I will re-wire and re-tape the preserved materials and try to duplicate the bridal bouquets from the photos as best I can, and present Kim and Tom with the final permanent mementoes of their big day and their everlasting wedding.

We shared with the wedding guests the language of flower designations of the flowers we used in the church bouquets and the sachet mementoes. On a small tag attached to the sachets was the following message:

❤ *WEDDING POTPOURRI* ❤

In the Victorian Tradition of the Language of Flowers:

Rosebuds symbolize Undying Love, Lavender/Devotion, Rosemary/Remembrance, Orange Blossoms/Bridal Festivities, Marjoram/Joy, Vanilla Beans/Good Luck, Sage/Domestic Virtue, Oakmoss/Ardent Love, Bergamot/Compassion, and Frankincense/A Faithful Heart.

Tom and Kim February 24, 1990

On the wedding program we added :

CHURCH PEW DECORATIONS

Special containers for this purpose from a florist supply house made it easy to place the dried materials into the Sahara and decorate with lace and ribbon streamers; we stored the completed arrangements on the clothes-drying racks we dry herbs on. The pew decorations were placed on alternating pews down the main aisle. We used:

Fern-leafed tansy and smoke tree blooms for the background

Queen-Anne's-lace (which, with short stems, stuck to the background material), roses, cockscomb celosia, lavender and tiny yarrow implanted in the Sahara in the center

Rose geranium leaves, baby's-breath, and teal statice as fillers or accents

A NOTE ABOUT THE FLOWERS:

The dried flower arrangements for the church were grown, preserved, and arranged by Karen, Kim, and Phyllis Shaudys. The flowers chosen have special meanings, not only in The Language of Flowers, but because they represent to the bride and her family many happy hours of preparation for this joyful event.

*Red Roses symbolize Undying Love
Lavender represents Devotion
Honesty means Sincerity
Baby's-Breath symbolizes Gentleness
Yarrow represents Health
Statice and Celosia are Everlastings,
which symbolize Eternity.
The Smoke Tree blossoms represent
Grace to the bride's family, and
The Queen-Anne's-Lace flowers are
naturally Bridal in design.*

Thank you for sharing our special day with us.

CHURCH BOUQUETS

Smoke tree blossoms and leaves for background

Honesty to frame the arrangement

Queen-Anne's-Lace (wired to florist "stems" with white-covered florist wire), red roses and leaves, deep red- and gold-plumed celosia, and gold yarrow for main color accents

Small amounts of lavender and teal statice for accents

Baby's-breath for filler

Containers and Sahara from floral supply house

See June, Herbal Weddings in the Appendix for the addresses of several experts who can help you plan your own special occasion. Among them are Betsy Williams, who offers her booklet Planning a Fresh Herbal Wedding, *as well as wedding herbs in both a small favor size and in a large plastic bag tied with lace and ribbon, and Jean Cope, who specializes in everlasting creations for weddings — by mail. Many herb farms also now provide herbal decorations for weddings. To find out if there are any near you, order the catalogs from herb farms in your area.*

An Herbal Wedding Garden

by Diane Downs

With the current enthusiasm for herbs what it is, almost anything herbal can be profitable. If you love to grow herbs, have some unused ground, like dealing with people — even those who are under pressure — and relish the thought of having some extra money, consider creating an herbal wedding garden. Before you decide to turn some idle ground into an area where breath-taking, symbolic, herbal weddings can take place, however, certain things must be considered. As with any business venture, first consider your qualifications. Are you an experienced gardener who is meticulous about weeding and general maintenance around your gardens? Are you organized about your use of time and are you *on time, all* the time? Are you diplomatic and calm when those around you are flustered and tense? If you feel you fulfill these qualifications, the next step is to determine whether your city or county zoning will allow such a venture in your area, what kinds of licenses will be required (if any), how much parking room is required, and what kind of insurance will protect you if someone is injured while on your property. Consider, too, your neighbors. Will anyone living nearby object to ten, twenty, or fifty cars coming up your road on Saturdays during the fine-weather months?

The garden I have designed was created with dimensions of 22' x 12' in mind, but you can expand or shrink it to suit your location by adding or deleting herbs. I recommend using Kate

1 - Fern
2 - Peppermint
3 - Marjoram
4 - Spicy globe basil
5 - Monkshood
6 - Veronica
7 - Feverfew
8 - Maiden pinks
9 - Larkspur
10 - Chervil
11 - Lavender
12 - Ivy
13 - Creeping thyme
14 - Ambrosia
15 - Rosemary
16 - Bronze fennel
17 - Sage
18 - Angelica
19 - Chamomile
20 - Daisies
21 - Violets
22 - Cedar
23 - Sweet woodruff
24 - White rose
25 - Red rose
26 - Arborvitae

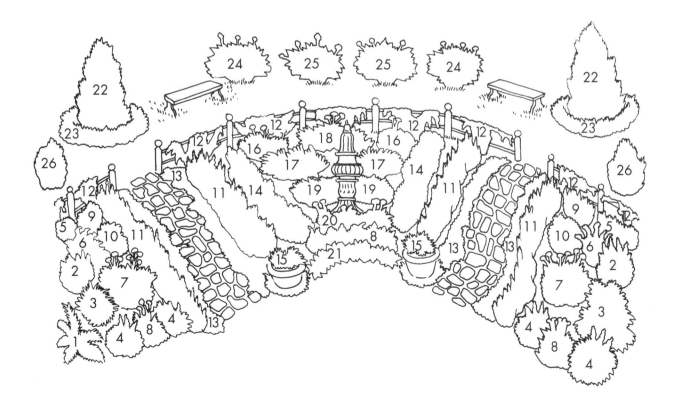

❦

When your garden is thriving and lacking only a bride and groom, place brochures listing your service in bridal boutiques, clothing stores, and with the Chamber of Commerce. Consider having an open house at your garden to familiarize the public with the opportunity you are providing. And don't forget to acquaint local church officials with the site you have available, as churches are often booked up during the busiest wedding months.

❦

Greenaway's *The Language of Flowers* or Kathleen Gips' *The Language of Flowers* as definitive guides toward choosing symbolic herbs. Pathways should be at least 4 feet wide to allow two people to walk side by side comfortably. The trees I have listed are suitable for a northern garden, but in warmer regions many others would thrive and could be substituted. The diagram of the garden shown requires at least two or three of each herb, planted 1½ to 2 feet apart to form a large clump. This makes for more harmonious color in the garden and avoids the spotty effect that results when only one plant is located here and there. After a couple of years of growing, many of the herbs will need to be divided or thinned. You could then grow extras in order to provide the bridal couples with wedding-related potpourri or wreaths. Before you put that first herb in the ground, however, remember to prepare the soil carefully. It will save you thousands of hours of work later if you first get rid of weeds, enrich the soil with compost, and lay the pathway stones perfectly.

To extend the peak season of the garden, underplant the entire bed in bulbs, all around the herbs. In spring, when most of the perennials are just breaking out of their dormancy, the bulbs will be at the height of their glory. As the bulb foliage fades, the herbs will grow up to cover the withering leaves. If you can't underplant the entire garden of herbs, remember that bulbs look best planted in groups. For tulips or daffodils, use at least a dozen, 6 to 8 inches apart, in each group. For smaller bulbs, twenty or so to a clump will do. Crocus symbolize *youthful gladness*, while red tulip is a *declaration of love*. Daffodils mean *respect*, and the star of Bethlehem stands for *purity*.

For the open area of the garden where the bridal participants will stand, you will want to cover the ground with an easy-to-walk-on, mud-free substance, such as bark chips, that won't wreck shoes; small, sharp gravel, for example, is great for pathways, but scrapes the leather right off heels. You might wish to create a white, wooden arbor for the bride and groom to stand under.

Diane Downs, Lost Prairie Herb Farm, Kalispell, MT 59901

❦

Plant List

(SYMBOLISM FROM KATE GREENAWAY AND KATHLEEN GIPS)

AMBROSIA	Love returned
ANGELICA	Inspiration
ARBORVITAE	Unchanging friendship • Live for me
BASIL	Spice of life (my definition) • Good wishes
CEDAR	I live for thee • Strength
CHAMOMILE	May all your wishes come true
CHERVIL	Sincerity
DAISY	Innocence
FENNEL	Strength
FERN	Fascination
FORGET-ME-NOT	True love
IVY	Marriage
LARKSPUR	Lightness • Levity
LAVENDER	Devotion
MARJORAM	Blushes
MONKSHOOD	Chivalry
PEPPERMINT	Warmth of feeling
PINKS	Pure and ardent love
RED ROSES	Love and unity
ROSEMARY	Remembrance
SAGE	Domestic virtue • Long life • Good health
SWEET WOODRUFF	Be cheerful and rejoice in life
THYME	Strength and courage
VERONICA	Fidelity
VIOLET	Faithfulness
WHITE ROSES	Unity • I am worthy of you

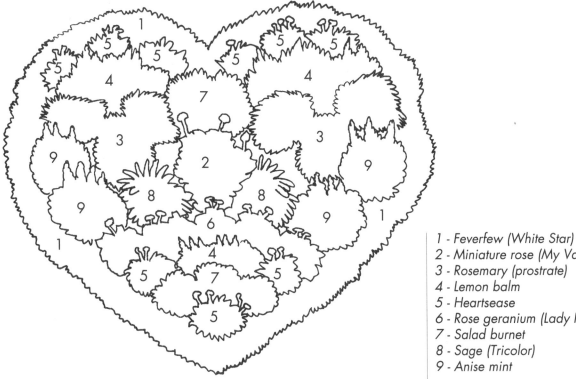

1 - *Feverfew (White Star)*
2 - *Miniature rose (My Valentine)*
3 - *Rosemary (prostrate)*
4 - *Lemon balm*
5 - *Heartsease*
6 - *Rose geranium (Lady Plymouth)*
7 - *Salad burnet*
8 - *Sage (Tricolor)*
9 - *Anise mint*

A HEART-SHAPED GARDEN FOR THE BRIDE

by Linda Fry Kenzle

Here's a very special wedding garden designed for the bride, based on the language of flowers. Even the shape of the garden — a heart — speaks boldly of love. Of course, the garden would need to be planted in the early spring to be lush and blooming for a summer wedding. To present the best view of the distinctive heart shape, position the garden on a slope, with thyme or chamomile surrounding the garden to set off the design. The garden can be planted on level ground, of course, but it will be a little more difficult to distinguish its shape. To accommodate all of the plants shown in the sketch, the garden should measure 6 feet across the shoulders and 6½ to 7 feet from top to bottom.

To dramatize and unify the wedding garden, dwarf feverfew is planted all around the outside edge. White Star feverfew (seed available from Burpee) grows only 8 inches tall, with deep green leaves; it is dimpled profusely with white, ball-shaped flowers that bloom nonstop. The centerpiece of the heart is a delightful miniature rose called My Valentine. Sprays of deep red blossoms (symbolizing true love) cascade from this plant, which grows 12 to 15 inches tall. On either side of the Valentine rose, you can plant

❧ *Wedding Garden Potpourri* ❧

½ cup of cellulose fiber
15 drops rose geranium oil
5 drops musk oil (an aphrodisiac)
4 drops coconut oil
2 cups rose petals
2 cups feverfew flowers
1 cup rose geranium leaves
½ cup anise mint
¼ cup lemon balm
Heartsease flowers

Scent the cellulose fiber with the essential oils. Blend together the remaining ingredients, except for the heartsease flowers. Seal, and age for 3 weeks. Meanwhile, dry a handful of heartsease flowers to sprinkle atop the finished product.

three prostrate rosemaries to add a contrasting texture, scent, and color. Rosemary (for remembrance) can weave its way through the neighboring lemon balm and anise mint (virtue) to prevent them from invading the rest of the garden.

Two variegated herbs — tricolor sage with its droopy white-, pink-, and green-stained leaves (signifying domestic virtue) and the lovely, white-splashed leaves of Lady Plymouth rose geranium (denoting preference) — add a lively note of contrast to the solid green leaves of the rose, feverfew, mint, and lemon balm. Salad burnet (for a merry heart) nestles at the peak of the heart and below in a spread of lemon balm (fidelity in love). And that most romantic of herbs, heartsease (you are ever in my thoughts), is tucked in openings throughout the garden, sprinkling tiny, purple, white, and yellow flowers into the tapestry.

This romantic herb garden is not only lovely to look at, but will supply all of the ingredients to make a delightful cup of tea (lemon balm, anise mint, and rose geranium) or to enliven a salad (all except feverfew) — or to create the very special keepsake, Wedding Garden Potpourri (at the left).

LINDA FRY KENZLE, FOX RIVER GROVE, IL 60021

TWO MARITAL TRIBUTES

by Madeleine Siegler

Herbal wedding wreath. For many years I made these special wreaths for brides. Each was a basic, full artemisia wreath (14-inch diameter), containing small bunches of sweet marjoram, lavender, rosemary, sage, and chamomile worked in while the wreath was being constructed. The wreaths were trimmed with a variety of small flowers, usually a number of small, white helichrysums, and always many rosebuds. Each was accompanied by a card of herbal design on which I typed or hand-printed the message at the left.

Anniversary potpourri. When we celebrated our fortieth wedding anniversary in 1984, it turned into quite a party. For one thing, it marked the first time our six children had all been together around one table in twenty years. With two living in Arizona and one in Germany, a family reunion was no easy task. They organized the party and invited many of our close friends. I felt that the day should be marked herbally in some way, and so we did it with potpourri. I had a large number of miniature hat boxes, which were used for potpourri during Christmas sales at craft fairs. A rush job at my printer's got us some cards small enough to fit in the

MESSAGE FOR WREATH

Your Herbal Wedding Wreath contains lavender for devotion, rosemary for remembrance, marjoram for joy, sage for wisdom, rosebuds for undying love, and chamomile for patience in adversity. The circle, symbol of unending life, is wound with artemisia, which was named for the goddess of fertility.

boxes, and each guest at the party had one to take home. The outside of the card was printed with our names and the date we were celebrating. Inside we explained the symbolism.

❤

MESSAGE FOR POTPOURRI

Our Recipe for a Happy Potpourri — rosebuds for love, lavender for devotion, marjoram for joy, rosemary for remembrance, and chamomile for patience. Blend with wisdom, age with constant attention, share generously.

MADELEINE H. SIEGLER, MONK'S HILL HERBS, WINTHROP, ME 04364

QUICK TOUCHES FOR AN HERBAL WEDDING

by Barbara Radcliffe Rogers

Beautiful, handmade herbal remembrances for your wedding don't have to take weeks of your time. With a few minutes here and there, and a few scraps of lace, fabric, and ribbon (even those left over from your dress and accessories), you can make sachets to scent your honeymoon luggage. Or give them as favors and gifts to wedding guests, attendants, and those people who have helped make your wedding day the most memorable day of your life.

✿ Hand-Sewn French Sachets ✿

8 inches of double-edged insertion lace
8 inches of 3-inch white satin ribbon
16 inches of narrow, white lace
16 inches of ⅜-inch white grosgrain ribbon
White sewing thread and needle
8 inches of ⅜-inch white satin ribbon
½ cup fragrant, dried rose petals

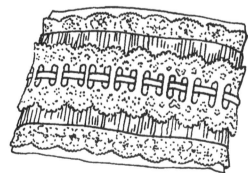

Lay the insertion lace along the center of the 3-inch ribbon. Cut the narrow lace and the grosgrain ribbon each into two 8-inch lengths, and lay these on each edge of the wide ribbon, so that the ribbon is just under the edge of the eyelet, and the straight edge of the lace is covered by the other edge of the grosgrain. The effect will be a series of stripes. Hand stitch through all layers at both edges of the grosgrain ribbon to secure everything to the wide ribbon base. Run the ⅜-inch satin ribbon through the insertion eyelet. Fold the piece in half, wrong sides together, and slipstitch the side edges to form a pocket. Fill the pocket with the rose petals, and slipstitch closed by turning the raw edges inside to form a neat end. Each sachet takes about 20 minutes to make.

❦ *Something Blue Sachet* ❦

8 inches of 3-inch white lace
8 inches of 3-inch pale blue satin ribbon
White thread and needle
½ cup floral potpourri
12 inches of very narrow, white satin ribbon

Fold the lace in half to form a 4-inch length. Fold the 3-inch ribbon over it, smooth side in, so it encloses the lace. Stitch all sides, leaving half of one selvedge side open. Turn right side out, and fill with potpourri. Turn the edges under and blind stitch the opening. Tie the narrow ribbon into a neat bow with long tails, and stitch it to the sachet. Each sachet takes less than 10 minutes.

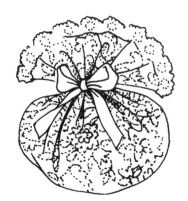

❦ *Lace Lavender Bags* ❦

24 inches of narrow, flat, white or ecru lace
7-inch circle of matching lace fabric
Needle and thread to match
4-inch circle of thin, plain white fabric
⅛ cup lavender flowers
15 inches of narrow, satin or picot, blue or lavender ribbon

Stitch the flat lace around the edge of the lace circle, using a basting stitch. (Don't bother to turn under an edge.) Place the plain fabric circle in the center of the lace, on the wrong side. Form into a cup shape in your palm, and fill with lavender. Gather the edges, and tie with ribbon right at the edge of the inner fabric circle. Adjust the bow, and pull the lace edges to form a tight bundle with a fan-shaped ruffle. If you are making a lot of these, push the circles into the indentations in an egg carton when you are filling them. Each sachet takes less than 10 minutes if you cut several circles together.

❦ *Lace Heart Sachet* ❦

4" x 8" piece of white lace or lace fabric
4" x 8" piece of plain white fabric
Needle and white thread
½ cup rose potpourri
½ yard of narrow, white, gathered lace
6 inches of narrow, white satin ribbon

Cut two 4-inch hearts from the lace and two from the plain fabric. Stack hearts with edges matching, so that the two lace pieces are in the middle with one plain fabric heart on top and one on bottom. Stitch around the edge, leaving one straight side open for stuffing. Turn so that both lace hearts are on the outside, fill with potpourri, and blind stitch to close. Using long stitches, tack the gathered lace around the outside edge. Tie the ribbon into a bow, and stitch it at the cleft of the heart. Each sachet takes about 15 minutes, or less if you stitch the hearts together on the sewing machine.

BARBARA RADCLIFFE ROGERS,
HERBITAGE FARM, RICHMOND,
NH 03470

THE BRIDE'S HERBAL

by Bertha Reppert

PEW BOWS

Pew bows take kindly to herbs. Use them to mark seating for VIP's, or if you'd like to be lavish, place one at every other pew all along the main aisle for a truly dramatic setting. In spring or summer, hang the herb bunches upside down, as if to dry, so they can wilt gracefully. In the fall, when weather has conditioned them, arrange casual handfuls of herbs upright in each bow. The Oasis company has come out with a nifty gadget designed especially for pew bows. A framework supports a round piece of foam that can be used wet or dry. The bows, herbs, and flowers are quickly poked into place, and then the entire arrangement is simply hung over the edge of the pew by an attached hook. No fuss or bother! (These pew holders are available from The Rosemary House.)

Herbal Chaplets

With or without veiling, a crown of precious herbs and small flowers is an enchanting hair ornament. As they have since ancient Roman times, the bride (or her bridesmaids) will be blessed with the wearing. Big and little girls alike look pretty wearing fragrant herbs and flowers in their hair or on a wide-brimmed hat.

Making such a charming circlet is not difficult. A day or two before the wedding, gather rosebuds, clove pinks, lily-of-the-valley, violets, daisies, small zinnias, lilacs, mums, and many others. Condition them well in warm water for several hours, but do not submerge the flowers. When the plant material is filled with as much moisture as possible, you can start working. Several willing friends would be a great help if there are many halos to be made.

Even if you don't have a wedding coming up in your family, you certainly have friends who will ask you about herbal weddings. And, even if you aren't into herbal anniversary parties or showers, you never know when you might want to entertain in herbal style! I can't tell you how thrilled I was with Bertha Reppert's The Bride's Herbal: Weddings and Other Parties! *It's "A Handbook Helpful for The Bride, Her Family and Friends .... proffering Joy and Beauty for Weddings, Receptions, Showers, Anniversaries...including 100 Herbal recipes, Favors, Decorations and Crafts...augmented by the Timeless Symbolism of Herbs." The recipes alone make this book worth buying — for anyone who loves herbs. From the many party cakes and punches, entrées and salads, snacks and dips, here are just a few samples from Bertha's book.*

A thin, wire coat hanger
White florist tape
Many small flowers
3 yards (or more) narrow, satin ribbon
White nylon tulle (optional)
Baby's-breath (optional)

1. Well in advance of the wedding day, form a wire ring from the coat hanger. Adjust it to fit the head. Cover the ring with white florist tape, stretching and pulling the tape to smooth it around the wire.

2. Cut all the herbs and flowers into 2- to 3-inch pieces. Cut a few 3-inch pieces of the satin ribbon and a few 4-inch squares of the tulle.

Spray Queen-Anne's-lace with hair spray before picking it, and place stems in water as you harvest it, then it will not wilt before you are able to place it in a drying medium. PVS

3. Place an herb or two against the wire, and wrap it in place with florist tape. Without cutting the tape, lay another snippet or two of herbs and flowers overlapping the first one, and tape securely. Continue in this manner, always overlapping the herbs and using a continuous piece of tape. Include a loop of the ribbon and a tuft of the tulle occasionally until the crown is well covered, balanced, and complete. Tuck in baby's-breath, too, if desired.

4. Complete your chaplet by attaching little bows here and there or one bow with streamers at the back. Attach hair combs in several places.

5. Spray very lightly with water, then keep the herbal chaplet in a plastic bag under refrigeration until needed. It will keep for a day or two.

INSTANT HERBAL WREATH FOR AROUND THE PUNCH BOWL

Assorted sprigs of well-conditioned, fresh herbs around the punch bowl make an effective decoration for a party buffet, surpassed only by two punch bowls (perhaps one alcoholic and one nonalcoholic) with instant herbal wreaths. Carry out an herb and spice theme by stirring your punch with a very long cinnamon stick.

To assemble your instant, fresh herb wreath, cut 4- to 6-inch pieces of bright green curled parsley, grayed oregano, soft lamb's-ears, both green and gray santolina, pale marjoram, aromatic sweet Annie, all kinds of basils, ferny southernwood, chartreuse lemon balm, mints of all kinds, rosemary in abundance, and scented geraniums. Clip a goodly assortment, toss them in warm water in your sink to freshen them, condition them in a dishpan full of water to which a floral preservative has been added, drain them, pop the whole shebang into a large, plastic bag, and keep it under refrigeration until needed. Shortly before serving, scatter the herbs around the punch bowls or cake plate. Thus prepared, your fresh herbs will last through a long party without water.

Herbs treated with floral preservative will be inedible. PVS

DO-AHEAD PREPARATIONS

To make good use of time and scheduling, cut pieces of attractive, small-patterned evergreens, such as boxwood, juniper, Korean holly, azalea, and so forth, to use as a basis for many last-minute, fresh herb bouquets and decorations. Secure the heavy-stemmed evergreens in wet Oasis, covered and reinforced with chicken wire (if necessary). Keep the bases cool and misted for up to 2 weeks before the party or wedding. At the last minute, well-conditioned sage, rosemary, lavender, rue, and southernwood may be quickly and easily added, along with any colorful flowers you have. Bows, also finished weeks ahead, complete the project.

❧ *Stuffed Nasturtiums* ❧

8-ounce package cream cheese
3 tablespoons mayonnaise
¼ cup chopped nuts
¼ cup grated carrots
1 tablespoon finely minced green
   pepper

2 teaspoons fresh herbs such as basil,
   parsley, or dill or 2 tablespoons
   chives, cucumber, and/or
   green onion, minced
1½ dozen brilliant nasturtium
   blossoms, washed
Chopped chives or edible blossoms

Soften the cream cheese with the mayonnaise. Add the remaining ingredients, except the nasturtiums and chopped chives or edible blossoms. Roll this mixture into balls and fit the balls into the nasturtium flowers. Top with a bit of chopped chives or any edible blossom. Ring a platter with round, bright green nasturtium leaves, or serve as individual salad garnishes, each on a leaf or two.

❧ *Lavender Sticks* ❧
YIELD: 12 NIBBLES

12 stalks fresh lavender flowers
1 egg white, beaten until frothy
½ cup granulated sugar

Dip the lavender sprigs (flowers only) into the egg white. Roll the flowers in sugar, or dust on the sugar.

FROM *THE BRIDE'S HERBAL*
BERTHA REPPERT, THE ROSEMARY
HOUSE, MECHANICSBURG, PA 17055

A FANCIFUL FLORAL WEDDING "RING"

by Grace Wakefield

This dainty, pixie wreath can be used around a candle, as a center-piece, or as a wall hanging.

Plastic margarine tub cover
Green florist tape
Glue
Green moss
Dried flower heads
Stardust gypsophila

1. With scissors, puncture a hole in the center of the margarine tub cover. Cut from the center to the rim in several places. Cut out all of the center, leaving only the rim intact.

2. Wind the florist tape around the rim to cover the plastic completely.

3. Glue on the green moss to cover the front and sides of the rim.

4. Arrange the flower heads over the entire front and sides of the ring, creating a pretty color scheme and pattern. Glue the flowers in place. Add Stardust gypsophila as a lovely finishing touch.

GRACE WAKEFIELD, TOM THUMB
WORKSHOPS, MAPPSVILLE, VA 23407

PINE CREEK WEDDING HERBS

by Kathleen M. Gips

Those of you who are familiar with The Pleasure of Herbs *will remember Kathleen for her articles on tussie mussies, herbal vinegars, and jellies. Since then, she has written the very comprehensive (over 600 entries) dictionary of floral lore* The Language of Flowers, *which explains the meanings of herbs, flowers, trees, shrubs, and even weeds common*

For centuries, herbs have been used as part of the wedding ceremony. Because of their fragrance and their symbolism they are perfect to shower on the bride and groom to wish them happiness together. The herbs and flowers included in this aromatic wedding herb mixture are those traditionally associated with weddings. Each guest may be given a small handful of the wedding herbs to throw on the bride and groom as they leave the celebration. The following traditional herbs and flowers are especially appropriate, because through them, wishes for the bridal couple and their future together can be expressed in the romantic language of herbs and flowers:

ROSE	Love	Use small miniature roses, especially The Fairy
ROSEMARY	Remembrance, fidelity, and loyalty	
MARJORAM	Joy and happiness	
MINT	Warmth of feeling	Especially silver mint
RUE	Vision and virtue	Use sparingly, and only for symbolism, as many are allergic to this plant
PANSY	Happy thoughts	
VIOLETS	Loyalty	Best dried by pressing
MYRTLE	Love and passion, as well as peace and home restfulness	If myrtle is not available, boxwood leaves or uva-ursi leaves look similar
LAVENDER	Devotion	
SAGE	Long life and good health	Especially *Clevelandii*; use sparingly, so the scent will not overpower the blend
THYME	Strength and courage	
SWEET WOODRUFF	Be cheerful and rejoice in life	Cut it into ½-inch pieces after dried
CHAMOMILE	May all your wishes come true	
CORIANDER	Hidden worth; your closeness is welcome	
AMBROSIA	Love returned	Separate the small, fluffy, green sprigs and use whole
GILLYFLOWER OR CLOVE PINK	Bonds of affection	The favorite pink is *Dianthus caryophyllus* Hudson Pink; most attractive when dried in silica gel
FEVERFEW FLOWERS	You light up my life	Use the whole flowers that have been air-dried by hanging (silica gel makes them brittle)

to Victorian gardens. She has done a superb job of editing The Herb Journal, *a publication of The Western Reserve Unit of The Herb Society of America in Cleveland, Ohio.*

Mix wedding herbs in any pleasing combination. My recipe changes according to availability and gardening seasons. Try to leave the herb leaves whole, if possible. For each quart of the herb and flower mixture, use 1 cup of oakmoss and ½ dram of rose oil for fixative and fragrance. Place the required amount of oakmoss in a pile on top of the herb mixture. Drop the oil onto the oakmoss, covering as much of it as possible. Allow the oil to soak in for a day, and then mix thoroughly. Store in a glass jar with enough head space to allow the mixture to be shaken thoroughly each day for 2 weeks. Given this time to age, all the ingredients will mellow and blend with the rose fragrance.

To supply 100 guests with a small handful (one tablespoon) each, package 2 quarts of the wedding herbs in a gallon plastic bag. This can be enclosed in a pink gingham cloth bag or just tied with lace and ribbons. Be sure to include the meanings of the herbs and flowers on a notecard tied to the ribbons. A small vial of additional rose oil may also be included.

Additional suggestions. To insure maximum fragrance on the day of use, keep the potpourri in a closed container in a cool, dry, dim location to prevent evaporation of the essential oil. Table-spoonfuls of the wedding herbs may be placed into small net or tulle squares and tied with ribbon, and then distributed to guests from a silver bowl next to the exit door or by a bridesmaid or flower girl carrying a basket. Wedding herbs may be used in sachets as shower favors. A sachet may also be placed with the wedding gown in storage. (Caution: Do not allow the potpourri to come into direct contact with the gown.)

KATHLEEN GIPS, PINE CREEK HERBS, CHAGRIN FALLS, OH 44022

POTPOURRI FROM TREASURED BOUQUETS

by Barbara Radcliffe Rogers

Your daughter's wedding was lovely, and you have all those flowers — your corsage, the carnation from her father's lapel, the arrangement from the bridal table. The latter will be fresh for a few days in your home, but it, too, will soon fade away. You can preserve these indefinitely in the form of a potpourri your daughter and her family will treasure for generations. Take the blossoms (and the foliage) from the corsage and boutonnieres first. Cut the stems short and lay the flowers in a single layer on a screen or in an airy basket to dry. If there are roses, put them in silica gel immediately, since they will provide the highlights for a jar of finished potpourri.

Keep the long-stemmed flowers in a vase until they are barely past their peak — do enjoy every last minute of them fresh! Remove them before the blossoms droop and fade, cut them from the stems, and lay them out to dry. Include the foliage and the ferns, since these retain a nice, green color. When there is nothing left except statice and baby's-breath, put these in a bud vase with no water, so you can enjoy them as they dry. If possible, dry some garden flowers that were blooming on the wedding day. Almost any cut flower will do, but white flowers may turn brown (you can later discard these). Don't worry about shriveling, since you can break flowers up.

When all the flowers are dry, sort them out. Pull the petals off the carnations and any other large flowers, except the roses. Keep whole any flower that is perfect. Snap the statice and clusters of baby's-breath from the long stems. Mix together all except the roses you've put in silica gel. Now use your artistic eye. Are the colors all drab or pale? If so, add a little lemon verbena, or flowers that complement the colors you have. Add a little rosemary (for remembrance) or other herbs or blossoms for scent, but don't add too much. If you have a lot of roses or carnations, add whole cloves. Concentrate on appearance.

Put your mixture in a glass jar at least twice the volume of the blend. Add 1 tablespoon of chipped orrisroot for each pint of potpourri. If the flowers suggest certain oils, use those oils in your blend. If you have carnations and roses, these oils alone are all you need. Use 6 to 8 drops per quart (you can add more later to refresh it). If you are in doubt about oils, use rose oil alone, as it always gives a nice floral scent and is the perfect blender. Close the jar and let the Wedding Remembrance Potpourri age for at least 2 weeks; shake the jar each day. When you put it in a jar to present or use, place the perfect roses and flowers on top.

Perhaps the flowers you treasure are from another special event — bouquets from the garden of your first home or flowers thrown to you from the balconies of La Scala or the bouquet from your husband on your anniversary. Whatever the occasion, its memories and the flowers that marked it can be yours forever!

I recommend adding the oils to the fixative a few days before placing all the ingredients together. Calamus root, oakmoss, or some other fixative can be used instead of orrisroot. PVS

BARBARA RADCLIFFE ROGERS,
HERBITAGE FARM, RICHMOND, NH

Summer Herbal Teas

AN *HERBAL* TEA FOR A SUMMER AFTERNOON

by Linda Fry Kenzle

These recipes serve 6 and should be accompanied by an array of wonderful herb teas. Edible flowers that may be used for garnish include anise hyssop, mint blossoms, violets, and roses *(all unsprayed)*.

* Lemon Balm Canapés *

1 cup albacore, salmon, shrimp, or chicken (flaked)	*¼ cup diced celery or cucumber*
½ cup mayonnaise	*2 tablespoons minced lemon balm*
	Whole, fresh lemon balm leaves

Mix all ingredients together. Chill until just before party time. Spoon onto toast rounds or crackers. Garnish with a fresh lemon balm leaf.

FRAGRANT FINGER TOWELS

Rinse and wring out colorful, clean washcloths, and wrap several sprigs of scented geraniums, lavender, or lemon verbena in each. Fold in half and roll up. Snuggle together on a plate, place in the microwave, and heat for 1½ minutes on high. After dinner, or a finger-food tea, pass a tray of these around and let your guests pick a towel and empty the herbs onto the tray. Serve with tongs, if the towels are very hot. PVS

❧ *Baked Apples with Fennel* ❧

6 apples
2 tablespoons raisins
2 tablespoons walnuts
¾ teaspoon fennel

Cinnamon
Honey
Butter
½ cup water

Preheat oven to 300° F. Core the apples, and place them in baking dish. Combine the raisins, walnuts, and fennel, and divide the mixture into six even portions. Stuff the mixture into the apples. Top each apple with a dusting of cinnamon, a drizzle of honey, and a pat of butter. Pour water into the pan around the apples. Bake for 1 hour, or until apples offer no resistance when poked with a fork.

❧ *Rose Geranium Cream* ❧

YIELD: SIX ½-CUP SERVINGS

1 egg, separated
6 tablespoons sugar
2¼ cups milk
3 tablespoons tapioca

2 or 3 rose geranium leaves
1 teaspoon vanilla extract
Crystallized flowers

Make a meringue by beating the egg white with 3 tablespoons of the sugar until soft peaks are formed. In a heavy saucepan mix the egg yolk, milk, tapioca, and rose geranium leaves. Allow ingredients to come to room temperature. Cook over medium heat, stirring constantly, until a full boil is reached. Remove rose geranium leaves. Pour egg-yolk mixture into egg-white meringue. Add the vanilla extract, and stir until just mixed.

Cool in the refrigerator for about 1 hour. Serve in dessert dishes and decorate with crystallized flowers.

❧ *Mint Bombe* ❧

Here's an opportunity to use your favorite mold. The amount of ice cream and sherbet required will be determined by the size of your mold.

Vanilla ice cream
Mint leaves
Orange sherbet
Crystallized fresh mint leaves (or you may use more fresh mint leaves)

Pack vanilla ice cream into a mold to form a 1-inch layer over sides and bottom. Press a layer of mint leaves against the ice cream to cover it completely. Fill the center with the orange sherbet to within 1 inch of the top. Cover with another layer of mint leaves. Fill the mold with a final layer of vanilla ice cream. Place the mold in the freezer. Just before serving, unmold and decorate with additional mint leaves.

❧ *Lemon-Glazed Pound Cake* ❧

2 tablespoons warm water
½ teaspoon vanilla
Fresh lemon verbena leaves
1 cup confectioners' sugar
¼ teaspoon grated lemon zest
A pound cake
Lemon twists

The night before your party, combine the water and vanilla, and place a few of the lemon verbena leaves in the mixture. Allow to soak overnight.

The next day, remove the lemon verbena leaves. Stir the confectioners' sugar and lemon zest into the flavored water to form a glaze. Pour the glaze over your favorite pound cake, letting the glaze drip down the sides. Garnish with lemon twists and more lemon verbena leaves.

FROM *THE JOY OF HERBS*
LINDA FRY KENZLE, FOX RIVER GROVE, IL 60021

HERBAL SUN TEAS

We place herbs and flowers in a gallon jug of water and set this in the sun early in the day. By late afternoon, the sun has brewed for us all the tea we will need, to ice for the evening cookout or picnic and for refreshing drinks afterward. Here are some of our favorite combinations. We sometimes add honey or a few packets of low-calorie sugar substitute to the water when we fill the jar. In this case, the tea must be shaken or stirred after it is warm and ready, and before it is strained. So that it is out of the way of the lawn mower, little children, and bugs in the grass, we place our lidded jug on top of the picnic table. This is located close to the hose, making it easy to fill the jug outdoors and to wash off the herbs and flowers before adding them to the water. Herbed sun teas offer such an opportunity to be creative! Let the children help you pick the herbs and flowers for this project; it can be an educational experience regarding what's edible, and they will not only love to watch the tea changing color as it warms up, but will be anxious to taste the results!

I.

A handful each of lemon catnip, lemon balm, lemon verbena, lemon basil, and some lemon- and tangerine-scented marigolds, plus 1 cup of honey, if desired. Place all in a gallon jug of water. Citrus peel, optional.

II.

A handful each of spearmint, lemon balm, and chamomile flowers, 3 or 4 regular tea bags, and 3 packets of low-calorie sugar substitute.

III.

A handful each of applemint, peppermint, lemon balm, and bee balm leaves and flowers. Honey, if desired.

IV.

(Shaudys favorite)
4 Celestial Seasonings Lemon Zinger tea bags, 2 or 3 handfuls of lime balm, a few lemon- and tangerine-scented marigolds, and 1 cup of honey.

In her charming booklet A Victorian Herbal, *JAN POWERS* lists plant choices for Victorian gardens, "Floral Fashions & Fancies," a Tussie-Mussie Bouquet and Garden Design, Victorian Potpourri Recipes, and a very informative section on teatime traditions, which includes the menu and these two, as well as other, recipes for a Lavender and Lace Tea Party.

Iced Lavender-Mint Tea Punch
YIELD: SERVES 6

If fresh herbs are available, use twice as many as you would of the dried. In the summer, you may prefer to make Sun Tea, as described above, instead of boiling the water. Add the lavender to the jar when you bring it in from the sun to cool.

6 teaspoons dried mint
6 cups water, boiling
1 tablespoon dried lavender blos
*   soms*

1-litre bottle ginger ale
1 cup purple grape juice
Ice cubes, with a fresh mint leaf
frozen in each

Brew the mint in the water in a teapot for 10 minutes. Add the lavender blossoms to the pot. Allow tea to cool. Strain the tea, and add the ginger ale, grape juice, and ice cubes. If serving in a punch bowl, float lavender buds and mint sprigs on top.

❧ *Lavender Drop Cookies* ❧

¼ cup butter or margarine	1 cup flour
½ cup sugar	1 teaspoon baking soda
1 egg	¼ teaspoon salt
1 tablespoon lavender buds, crushed fine	1 teaspoon lemon zest
	1 teaspoon finely chopped mint

Preheat oven to 375° F. Cream together the butter or margarine and the sugar. Add the egg and the lavender buds, and mix well. Sift together the flour, baking soda, and salt. Add the dried ingredients to the creamed mixture, and mix well. Fold in the lemon zest and mint.

Drop by teaspoonfuls onto an ungreased cookie sheet. Bake in the preheated oven for about 10 minutes. Watch carefully so cookies don't over-brown.

FROM *A VICTORIAN HERBAL: A COLLECTION OF TEAS, TRADITIONS, AND HEIRLOOM GARDENING*
JAN POWERS, STONE-WELL HERBS, PEORIA, IL 61604

❧ *Anna's Minted Iced Tea* ❧

Although spearmint is usually intended, almost any mint — including apple mint, orange mint, lemon balm, and peppermint — will do. You can keep some of this minted tea on hand in the refrigerator, along with a simple syrup to sweeten it. To make the syrup, heat 1 cup of sugar in 2 cups water, stirring to dissolve, and bring just to the boiling point. Store in a recycled syrup bottle.

6 to 8 sprigs of fresh mint, 12 inches long
4 cups water

Wash the mint, and then liquefy it in the blender with the water. Let set 30 minutes; strain. Sweeten and enjoy.

ANNA LEE TERRY, FAIRMONT, WV 26554-9806

❧ *Chamomile Jelly* ❧

This is my favorite herb jelly; its honey-like flavor is wonderful on biscuits or toast.

1 cup chamomile flowers, packed	1 box Sure-Jell
3½ cups water	4 cups sugar

Place chamomile blossoms in a medium-sized saucepan, add water, and bring to a boil. Remove from heat, cover, and let stand 10 minutes. Strain through two layers of cheesecloth. Measure 3 cups. Mix chamomile infusion and Sure-Jell in a large saucepan. Bring to a hard boil, and add sugar. Again bring to a hard boil and continue to boil for 1 minute, stirring constantly. Remove from heat and skim off foam. Pour at once into hot, sterilized jars and seal.

PATRICIA BOAZ, INDIANAPOLIS, IN 46205

❧ *Rose Petal Cubes* ❧

Rose petals embedded in ice cubes will add a festive note to any punch bowl. Fill an ice-cube tray halfway with water and freeze. Place a rose petal on each cube, anchor with a teaspoon of water and freeze again. Then fill completely with water, and freeze until needed.

❧ *Herb Sugar* ❧

Add a few leaves of any sweetly flavored herb — such as lemon balm, mint, or rose geranium — to ½ cup granulated sugar. Blend on high in blender until herb and sugar are one. A drop or two of suitable food coloring may be added. Very nice for teas.

FROM *AN HERBAL CELEBRATION*
THE HERB GUILD

Roses for Everyone

EUELL GIBBONS'S Stalking the Healthful Herbs, first published in 1966, is back in print (Putney, VT: Alan C. Hood). Stressing both the nutritional and the medicinal properties of wild herbs, the author shares wonderful recipes created to utilize these beneficial plants. In an attempt to make bearberry fruit (Arctostaphylos uva-ursi) palatable, for instance, he created Bearberry Marmalade with orange and lemon juice. Gibbons thought it was excellent — his wife and critic also enjoyed it, but felt it would have tasted better without the bearberry! (The leaves of this wild, ground-hugging shrub, found in sandy northern regions around the world, are often used in potpourri these days.) In the chapter "Beating the Cats to the Catnip," Mr. Gibbons extols the nutritional benefits of catnip tea. He enjoyed lemon juice with catnip tea so much that he devised Candied Catnip Leaves to blend the flavors. My favorite chapter is called "How To Eat A Rose," from which Rose Petal Jam and Rose Omelet are garnered. For a cooked rose-petal jam recipe, see page 172.

"HOW TO EAT A ROSE"

UNCOOKED ROSE-PETAL JAM

This jam is astonishingly easy to make. I was amazed to find that 15 minutes after I had gathered the roses, I was pouring the jam into the jars, and I hadn't hurried at all. I would like to think it was sheer genius that caused me to get all the proportions right in my first attempt to make this fragrant ambrosia, but I know it was just blind luck.

Gather freshly opened roses before the sun has distilled too much of their ethereal flavor and fragrance away. Wild roses are best, but any fragrant rose will do, provided it has not been sprayed with poisonous insecticides. The deep red roses give the color I like best, but by using a different color for each batch, you can soon make your jam cupboard resemble a well-planned rose garden. The white base of the rose petal contains a bitter substance, and should be snipped away. This is not nearly the tedious job that it sounds. Grasp as many petals as you can hold between your finger and thumb, pull them from the rose and snip the white bases from all of them at once with a pair of shears.

Prepare 1 cup of petals in this manner, and put them into a blender along with ¾ cup of water and the juice of 1 lemon. Blend until smooth, then gradually add 2½ cups sugar with the blender still running, and let it run until you are sure all the sugar has dissolved. Leave this mixture in the blender container.

Stir 1 package of powdered pectin (such as Sure-Jell) into ¾ cup water, bring to a boil and boil hard for 1 minute, stirring constantly. Pour the pectin into the rose-sugar mixture and run the blender on slow until you are sure the pectin has been thoroughly incorporated with the other ingredients.

Pour immediately into small, sterilized jars with screw caps (baby-food jars are ideal). Allow the jars to stand at room temperature for about 6 hours, and the jam will be nicely jelled. It will keep for a month in the refrigerator. If you want some for next winter, store it in the freezer, so that when the wind is howling about the eaves and the sleet is pelting against the storm windows, you can bring a bright June day right into your kitchen by opening a jar of this rosy jam. I have tried many other recipes for Rose Petal Jam, but this one is easily the best of them all. Because the roses are uncooked, all the flavor, color, and fragrance of the freshly blown rose is captured.

ROSE OMELET

I make this omelet when I want to impress an overnight guest with an unusual breakfast. Break 8 eggs into the blender, season with 1 level teaspoon celery salt and a pinch of marjoram, then add ½ cup of clean petals from freshly plucked roses. Blend at medium speed until the eggs are fluffy and the petals practically liquified. Every good cook knows that in order to achieve a perfect omelet, the process of cooking is as important as the ingredients. Even a slightly scorched omelet isn't fit to eat. Pour the mixture into a greased pan over medium heat. If you have the heat just right, the bottom will be lightly browned when the top is just set. Make a crease across the top with a spatula, fold the omelet over and, in order to keep it from breaking apart, slide it onto a plate without trying to lift it. Decorate the omelet with a bright trail of paprika, and garnish the dish with dewy rosebuds. The rose petals in this omelet not only give it a spectacular color, but are actually good, and will be appreciated by anyone whose sense of taste is not overpowered by prejudices. With a dish of Canadian bacon, this is a breakfast that can be set with no apologies before the most discriminating gourmet.

FROM STALKING THE HEALTHFUL HERBS BY EUELL GIBBONS (PUTNEY, VT: ALAN C. HOOD PUBLISHER)

❤

CANDIED CATNIP LEAVES

Select medium-sized catnip leaves that are free from insect damage. Thin the white of 1 egg with the juice of 1 lemon; do not beat them together, but gently stir until the egg and lemon are thoroughly mixed. Dip each catnip leaf in this mixture, then sprinkle both sides with granulated sugar. Allow to dry at least 1 day before use. If the candied leaves are well dried and kept in a tight container in the refrigerator, they will stay perfectly fresh and tasty for weeks.

❤

ROSE BEADS

by Barbara Radcliffe Rogers

It is difficult to believe that the natural and elusive fragrance of flowers can be preserved for a century without fading — but rose-petal beads do exactly that. Strings of rose beads generations old will still effuse the delicate and unmistakable scent of fresh roses when they are worn against the warmth of our skin. The materials are free and the equipment simple.

You will need about a half bushel of rose petals. The best kind for fragrance, and also the most available, are the old "wild" roses — the kind that grow along stone walls and fences and around old cellar holes. Pick the petals only, or pick up those fresh ones that have fallen to the ground. The petals may be faded, but they must be fresh, not dried or brown. Gather about a shopping bag full. This may sound impossible, but if you find an old rose bush, you will be amazed at how fast the picking goes. By picking only the petals, you avoid later sorting and don't interfere with the development of rose hips if the bush is a hip-bearing kind.

You can do as our grandmothers did and grind the petals to a paste in a mortar and pestle, but it is easier to put them through a

❧ *Quick Rose Beads* ❧

In a cast-iron pot, simmer together the following for 1 hour: 4 cups fresh rose petals, finely snipped; 1 cup water; and 4 large, or 12 small, rusty nails (to blacken the solution). Remove from heat, stir with wooden spoon, and leave overnight. Repeat this procedure for a day or two until mixture darkens, adding water when necessary. Set aside for a few days until dry enough to handle; the consistency should be that of wet clay. Roll into marble-sized balls; they will shrink. Lay on several layers of paper toweling until partly dry (24 to 48 hours). Thread a large needle with dental floss, and string beads so they don't touch. Hang to dry, rotating beads to keep the holes open, for about a week. It's tedious to roll the balls, but they turn out so nicely, it's worth it!

FROM *A BEGINNER'S GUIDE TO POTPOURRI*
DONNA METCALFE, GOOD SCENTS, RIALTO, CA 02387

hand food grinder. (As soon as Grandmother got a grinder, she did hers that way, too.) The result will be a mass that resembles modeling clay, and your kitchen will smell of roses. Put the ground petals in a cast-iron skillet or pot (be sure there's not rust in the pot), and regrind daily for 2 weeks. You will see the paste become thicker each day until it reaches a consistency where it can be formed into smooth, hard beads. To do this, roll little lumps (smaller than marbles) between your hands with a circular motion until they are smooth and well-rounded. Put a large common pin through the center of each and stick the pin into a soft board. Continue rolling, piercing, and attaching to the soft board (at least ½ inch apart) until you have as many beads as you need. Keep in mind that the finished bead will be half the size of the freshly made one. It will take about 60 for an adult-sized necklace.

Let the beads dry for at least two weeks — longer if the weather is humid. Remove the pins and polish each bead with flannel or other soft cloth. String them on button thread, using a dark color so it will blend with the mahogany tones of the beads. Polish the entire string of beads (which highlights them and is easier than doing each bead). If the strand is long enough to slip over your head, you will not need a clasp. Otherwise you will need a very plain clasp either from an old necklace or a craft-supply store.

As you wear the beads, they will continue to darken and polish, and release their rosy fragrance. One note for the future: If you store them away, be sure to put a note with them so anyone finding them will know their age and what they are. You may very well be making your great-granddaughter's wedding necklace, and you'll want her to know its history!

BARBARA RADCLIFFE ROGERS, HERBITAGE FARM, RICHMOND, NH 03470

SUMMER POTPOURRIS

Making Potpourri, Colognes and Soaps, *by DAVID W. WEBB, is a marvelous new book that intrigues me, in particular, because the author uses some innovative ingredients for potpourri and room fresheners. Included are recipes for making your own Tincture of Chlorophyll from grass clippings (for use in homemade spray deodorants), your own Tincture of Peony for Peony Potpourri, and 100 other ways to use nature's bounty for fragrant and useful products. Besides a section on Southern botanicals and recipes, and information about fruit-flavored blends, there are chapters on making potpourri, sachets, soap/candles/bubble baths/shampoos, perfumes/colognes/toilet waters/aftershaves, deodorants and room fresheners; selling your creations; and finding supplies. The book is available from Tab Books, Inc. The author's dissection of a rose potpourri provides insight into his unique teaching style.*

❧ A Rose Potpourri Dissected ❧

1 pint dried rose petals, packed tightly into a Mason jar (these add fragrance, color, and bulk to the mix)
2 tablespoons table, rock, or pickling salt (this absorbs excess moisture and acts as a preservative)
3 tablespoons brown sugar (not white sugar)(this sweetens the mix and acts as a preservative)
1 ounce powdered orrisroot (this acts as a fixing agent to control the volatility of essential oils and adds a violetlike scent of its own, which complements the bouquet)
1 ounce powdered benzoin gum (this stimulates the perfume of the mix and acts as a fixing agent)
1 teaspoon each of cinnamon and cloves and 2 teaspoons allspice (the spices enhance the fragrance)
1 ounce cognac or fruit brandy (the alcohol acts as a solvent; cognac adds alcohol esters and oenanthic ether, which stimulate the perfume and give it an extra-potent "zest")

Mix all ingredients well. Cover and let set for a few days. Shake again to disperse ingredients. It is now ready to put into other containers. For a more intense rose fragrance, add 1 drop rose oil or 1 or 2 drops homemade rose perfume.

MOIST POTPOURRI

by Margaret Thorson

Our best seller and my favorite potpourri is our Old-Fashioned Moist Rose Potpourri. To make this, I collect rose petals from our local wild roses, *Rosa nootkana*, which have a wonderful, strong, spicy fragrance, and from my own collection of old garden roses, which includes *Rosa gallica officianalis*, Madame Hardy, and *Rosa centifolia*. The blend of scents from the spicy, wild roses and the perfumelike garden roses makes an especially lovely aroma.

To make moist potpourri, the petals must be partially dried until they feel leathery. (If they begin to get crisp, continue drying them and use them in a dried-petal potpourri instead.) In a large, ceramic, plastic, or stainless steel crock or bucket, layer 3 cups of partially dried rose petals and 1 tablespoon of coarse or kosher salt. Mix thoroughly, and then weight the mixture down with a plate topped with a rock or a quart jar of water. (If you use a jar of water, make sure the lid is tight. You don't want to ruin a batch of potpourri by spilling water into it!) Continue to add rose petals and salt as long as petals are available. Each time you add petals, add salt in the correct proportion and mix the new petals thoroughly with the old ones. As they begin to turn brown, they will smell quite strong, but as they age, the scent will mellow. Soon you will

❧ Summer Room Freshener ❧

4 ounces cedarwood chips
2 ounces sandalwood chips
2 ounces balsam fir needles
2 ounces sweet woodruff
1 ounce orrisroot powder

Mix all ingredients well, and place in open dish where it will not be disturbed.

❧ Thousand Flower Farm Old-Fashioned Moist Rose Potpourri ❧

1½ gallons cured rose petals
6 ounces dried orange peel
1 ounce powdered orrisroot (optional)
1 ounce powdered cinnamon
1 ounce powdered allspice
1½ ounces powdered cloves

Return this mixture to the crock, put the weight back on, and let cure for a month. Because this potpourri is moist, salty, and granular — and not especially pretty — it doesn't work in cloth sachets. We sell it in little wicker sachets that can be hung on the Christmas tree or in a closet. It is also nice in ceramic or pewter potpourri jars.

have a crockful of caked, brown rose petals. Let them sit for a month or so; continue to stir them around every few days and then weight them as before.

After aging, the potpourri can be used as is, or you can add spices and a fixative to the mixture. After experimenting for several seasons I have come up with the combination on page 159, which I just love.

MARGARET THORSON, THOUSAND FLOWER FARM, WALDRON ISLAND, WA 98297

LAVENDER BIRD CAGE

by Kathy and Steve Mathews

Our specialty is creating unique dried arrangements in natural colors. Here is one of them.

Pick lavender when the blossoms first start to flower, and plan to work on the project immediately, while the plant material is still fresh and pliable. You will need to make two wreaths. For each, pick three handfuls of lavender stems approximately 8 inches long. Lay the stems in a line, overlapping each by 1 inch. Beginning at one end, tightly wrap nylon fishing cord around the lavender. When you come to the end, form the piece into a circle by overlapping the beginning and the end by 2 inches. Continue wrapping the cord to fasten the ends securely together. Make another wreath the same size (approximately 6 inches in diameter). They never turn out exactly the same and the wreaths are pliable, so you don't have to worry about making one smaller than the other in order to fit them together. You can make them in any size, depending on the amount of lavender you use.

Next, put one wreath inside the other, and wire them together at top and bottom. Attach loops of narrow, satin picot ribbon at the bottom, and attach a bow and a hanger fashioned from wider, satin picot ribbon at the top. Make a nest out of German statice, and place it within the "cage." Add a hummingbird and flowers for decoration. The fragrance is wonderful, especially when a breeze drifts through!

KATHY AND STEVE MATHEWS, HEAVENLY SCENT HERB FARM, FENTON, MI 48430

JULY

I N MANY AREAS OF THE U.S., July is the first month when lush herb growth may be harvested. It is the time, therefore, to begin concentrating on preservation of the bounty for use all winter long — whether for culinary, decorative, or fragrant use, and whether for the year's cooking or for crafts and decorations for fall bazaars or holiday gifts. The Pleasure of Herbs *covers the most basic methods of preservation, such as air-drying on screens or hanging in bunches, silica gel, freezing culinary herbs in ice-cube trays or plastic bags, or drying tiny herbs in the crockpot. In this chapter and the next, we add some new information about preserving the flavors of herbs in vinegars and pestos.*

Whichever methods you choose to preserve your herbal harvests, the important thing is that you do *preserve them, as you will be rewarded many times over from now until next summer by your stored treasures. Next to making potpourri (an-*other way to save your herbs — see September), I think that mixing flavorful blends of herbs and vinegar is second in line of delightful things to do with herbs. There is no limit to the possibilities for creativity in making herbal vinegars. Each result, whether a golden lemon herb brew, a ruby purple basil blend, or a spicy and tawny sage-apple cider vinegar, will look, and taste, like a new jewel in your collection of herbal treasures.*

Flavored Vinegars

STOCKING THE VINEGAR CUPBOARD

Herbed, floral, or fruited vinegars are easy to make, very low in calories (2 calories per tablespoon), and wonderful seasoners to enhance our foods or even to use for cosmetic or medicinal purposes. The creative cook will always have a well-stocked cupboard full of flavored vinegars to accompany different foods. Herb vinegars are most often used for making salad dressings and for marinating or basting complementary meats, poultry, and fish (besides adding flavor, vinegar is also a tenderizer). They also add a gourmet zip to raw or cooked fruits and vegetables and to soups, stews, and sauces. Special herb vinegars are very handy to have on hand to help combat illnesses, insects, or heat problems. You will find marvelous recipes and tips ahead, but first, here are the fundamentals of making flavored vinegars.

To make these vinegars at home, use as the base a commercial vinegar from the grocery store; any such vinegar has at least 5 percent acidity. Vinegar (which, in French, means sour wine*) is obtained mainly by the fermentation of wine, malt beer, or cider, or by the distillation of grains. Wine vinegar (white or red) is the primary vinegar of France and much of Europe, and it is considered by most food writers to be the best base for flavored vinegars. Regular*

distilled white vinegar, which is used for pickling, is thought too strong for delicate and mellow flavoring. Apple-cider vinegar, most common in the United States, is regarded as a tonic because it is rich in potassium and other nutrients. Made from hard cider, this golden vinegar has the aroma of ripe apples and is especially enhanced by the addition of apple-scented mints or by fruits. In general, both white-wine and apple-cider vinegars blend well with fruits, as they themselves are fruity in nature. Rice vinegar from the Orient can be used for flavoring,

as can sherry or champagne vinegars. Malt vinegar, considered the vinegar of England, is amber in color and rather bitter. Balsamic vinegar, an Italian vinegar that has been aged in an oak cask for 10 years or more, has too fine a taste of its own to need embellishment!

Before you make herb vinegar, decide how you want to use it. If you make a lot of oriental stir-fried entrées, use rice-wine vinegar as a base and flavor it with fresh gingerroot, garlic, and lemongrass. If Italian dishes are your forté, start with a red-wine vinegar

General rule for making herb vinegar: Use 1 cup of fresh herbs to 2 cups of vinegar. For fruited vinegar, use 1 cup of fruit with 1 cup of vinegar.

and add basil, oregano, garlic, and maybe hot peppers. If you will use your herb vinegar mostly to enhance green salads, add the herbs and spices you enjoy in tossed salads. And, be sure to make a vinegar to enhance any fish meals, whether for marinating, basting, or a complementary sauce; dill, lemon balm, thyme, and lemon peel in a white-wine vinegar base would be excellent for this.

Vinegar is a preservative by itself, and what you buy in the store will be sterile. It is important that any additions to the base vinegar are as clean as possible, so as not to introduce bacteria into the blends. All herbs, flowers, fruits, or spices that are added to the base vinegar must be washed and dried. Moisture must not enter the process, as this will cause the vinegar to cloud up.

The vinegar mixture is blended, or "aged," by one of several methods. Heating the vinegar on the stove before adding the herbs or fruits will hasten the mellowing process. Some cooks even heat the additions together with the vinegar on the stove. Some experts consider it unnecessary to age the blend after stove heating. Care must be taken never to let the vinegar reach the boiling point, as this will destroy some of the acidity and the flavor. The second you see a bubble or two, immediately remove the vinegar from the heat. Some cooks heat the blend in the sun for a few days, but this method is not recommended for those living in the Sun Belt, where the sun is hot enough to cause the product to become cloudy, to fade, or to

lose its flavor. Lastly, some experts believe in using no heat of any kind, but just allowing the mixture to blend for a few weeks — usually three or four. Many of the recipes that follow will give specific methods and times. After you experiment a little on your own, it will be easy to choose the method you prefer and to be creative according to your supply of herbs and your taste preferences.

PREPARATION OF HERBS FOR VINEGARS

The easiest way for me to clean and dry herbs for vinegar making (and also, by the way, for herbal pestos) is to pick a warm, breezy day and place two or three bowls of tepid water (from the sun-soaked hose) on the picnic table in a shady spot. I then harvest the herbs, swish them in the bowls of clear water, and shake as much water off them as possible. I then place the herbs between layers of white paper towels and allow them to air dry outside for 2 or 3 hours, during which time I change the toweling once or twice. Most herbs dry well enough this way to be ready for use. Basil leaves take longer, however, so I de-stem their foliage and frequently pat the individual leaves between the layers of paper towels. (The paper towels may be dried and re-used later.) Thyme dries fastest, so I use whole sprigs of this. If you pick a humid day to make your creations, it will be better to dry the herbs inside, using a fan or air-conditioning to hasten the drying. Again, pat the herbs between layers of paper towels

and change the toweling regularly. Remove any stained or damaged leaves as you wait for the herbs to dry.

Large amounts of flavored vinegars are usually made in wide-mouthed, gallon-sized jars, and then strained into smaller, more practical-sized bottles or into decorative containers for gifts. For home experimentation and use, however, you can start with quart- or even pint-sized jars, if desired. Whatever size the jar, a wide-mouthed container makes it easier to remove the herbs and strain the mixture. Once your flavored vinegar has aged for the proper time (or whenever you like its flavor), it is necessary to strain and rebottle the blend. I prefer to place into a funnel, first, a coffee filter,

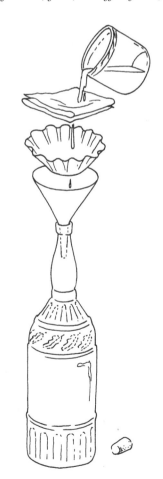

and then, three or four layers of folded cheesecloth, lapped over the sides of the funnel. Although this double layer slows the drainage somewhat, I find the vinegar has to be strained only once. Using a wooden or porcelain spoon, hold the herbs back while slowly pouring the liquid into the funnel. Do not squeeze the herbs, as this could introduce unwanted sediment into the new containers. At this time, you can add clean and dry, fresh herb sprigs to the rebottled vinegars. This enhances the finished product and is also a nice way to identify the kind of vinegar in the bottle. For best flavor, the finished product

❤

Dried herbs, if completely clean , can be used to make herb vinegar. Use 1 cup dried herbs for each 3 or 4 cups vinegar. Heat them together to the boiling point. Cool, strain, bottle, and store in a cool, dark place.

❤

VINEGAR-MAKING SUPPLIES

❤ *Recycled and sterilized, wide-mouthed jars in all sizes, such as mayonnaise, pickle, peanut-butter, baby-food, processed-cheese, large juice, and gallon-sized jars; the smaller sizes are handy for any excess vinegar*
❤ *Plain white paper towels*
❤ *Plastic funnels in several sizes (for example, 3½ inches wide for pint jars; 6 inches wide for quart jars)*
❤ *Coffee filters*
❤ *Cheesecloth*
❤ *Nonmetallic utensils*

should be stored in a cool, dark place and used within 6 or 7 months.

Be certain to use sterilized and dry containers, lids, or corks for your flavored vinegars. This can be done by washing them in your dishwasher on high heat, by boiling them in water for several minutes and then drying them in an oven set at low heat, or by letting boiling water sit in them for 10 minutes and then oven-drying them.

Because metal reacts chemically in vinegar, use only non-metallic utensils, including glass or plastic measuring glasses, enamel or stainless-steel pots, porcelain or wooden spoons for stirring, and plastic funnels or colanders. If you must use metal lids, separate them from the container with waxed paper or plastic wrap.

If you know someone who works in a restaurant or school cafeteria, ask him or her to save the empty, wide-mouthed gallon jars or jugs that institutional foods come in. Vinegar is available by the gallon from specialty food shops, wholesale grocers, or restaurant-supply houses. Decorative containers can be obtained from gourmet specialty shops or wholesale bottling companies, as well as some herb firms. Check the Yellow Pages for the largest city near you to find many of these suppliers, and see the supplier list on page 301. Some cooks save pretty wine bottles or regular salad dressing bottles when they wish to use their flavored vinegars as gifts. It's always helpful to label your vinegars and to give suggested recipes and uses along with the

gift condiments.

If using corks for your containers, you can seal them to prevent air from entering the bottle. Melt paraffin in a double boiler, and add either food coloring or ground spices (or both) to it. Tie some cheesecloth over the cork and the top of the bottle, and dip it into the warm paraffin. As you slowly turn the coated bottle top a few times, allow the excess paraffin to drip off into the pot. Let it cool completely before storing it. This not only gives the vinegar a good seal, but also adds a most decorative touch to your product.

If you want to sell herb vinegars and get into this on a grand scale, you can use equipment sold by beer- or wine-making companies. You would most likely need a license to make and sell food products, and the flavored vinegars should be re-pasteurized, to be certain no living organisms from the herbs, spices, fruits, or sugars that you have added remain in the liquid. This is done by heating the finished brew to 200° for 20 to 25 minutes. Remember, however, never to boil flavored vinegar.

There's one last way to make herb vinegar — the easy way! Whenever I have herbs that are ready, but I am not, I dip into my ever-present supply of Regina red or white wine vinegars from my grocer, and simply place the clean, dry herbs in these attractive green bottles of vinegar. These are placed on my sunny window sill for a week or two and then strained, rebottled, labeled, and relegated to our dark, cool cellar. I don't have a wine cellar, but close to it!

❧ *Floral Vinegars* ❧

Steep 2 cups of petals in 4 cups of white wine or apple cider vinegar for 6 to 8 weeks (or 2 weeks, if vinegar has been pre-heated). Strain and rebottle. Use the blossoms of nasturtium, lavender, rose, violet, carnation, citrus-scented marigolds, chives, or other flowering herbs. Complementary herbs and spices may be used along with the flowers.

❧ *Scented Vinegars for the Bath* ❧

Follow the same proportions and procedures as for Floral Vinegars, and use lavender, rose, carnation, violet, or citrus-scented marigold flowers, and/or lemon verbena, peppermint, scented geranium leaves, or other herbs. After straining, add an equal amount of bottled spring water, and allow the mixture to blend for a few days. Use 1 cup in bath water, pouring it under the tap as you fill the tub. Or, for a relaxing treat, soak a washcloth in some of the scented solution, wring it out, and apply it to forehead.

As the vinegar level in the bottle goes down with use and the decorative herb sprigs you have added to the finished brew are no longer completely covered with vinegar, be sure to remove them. Otherwise, mold may form on the herbs, spices, or rinds when exposed to the air in the jar.

❧ LEMON HERB VINEGARS AND RECIPES FOR THEIR USE ❧

I have made nearly twenty kinds of herb vinegars. Because of their flavor and versatility, my favorites are three variations of lemon-herb combinations. I use these in just about all recipes calling for vinegar (or wine), and they've enhanced every dish I've tried so far. Because of the large proportion of herbs to vinegar, these vinegars are strongly flavored; you may wish to dilute them with additional vinegar. I usually make them in large juice bottles (such as for cranapple juice), which hold 5 cups of liquid and 4 cups of herbs, but they are so good and useful, you may wish to use gallon jugs. Any of these variations can be used in any of my recipes that call for a lemon herb vinegar.

❧ *Phyl's Lemon Herb Vinegar* ❧

1½ cups lemon basil leaves
1 cup lemon verbena leaves
1 cup lemon balm leaves

½ cup lemon thyme sprigs
Lemon peel from 1 fresh lemon
4 cups white wine vinegar

Place the rinsed and dried herbs and the lemon peel in a sterilized, 5- to 6-cup bottle. Heat the vinegar to the boiling point, and pour it into the jar over the herbs and lemon peel. Allow to cool. Cap with nonmetallic lid. In a week or two, strain and rebottle into smaller, sterilized containers. Label, and store in cool, dark place.

Lemon Herb and Garlic Vinegar

Use the same ingredients and instructions as for Phyl's Lemon Herb Vinegar, but add 4 large cloves of garlic, minced with a knife or garlic press. Use in any recipes in which you want a lemony-garlic flavor.

Lemon Thyme Vinegar

2 cups lemon thyme sprigs
1 cup lemon balm leaves
1 cup lemon verbena leaves
Lemon peel from a fresh lemon

Follow the same procedures as for Phyl's Lemon Herb Vinegar. This is especially nice in chicken or fish recipes, and it is also good to have on hand as an insect repellent for the skin.

& *Phyl's Marinated Flounder* &
YIELD: SERVES 6

This tasty dish is just as good served cold as it is hot! Plan to serve three people for dinner, and save the leftovers for a delicious cold lunch for three.

1 cup safflower oil
1 cup Lemon Thyme Vinegar
1 teaspoon salt
1 teaspoon freshly ground pepper
3 large cloves garlic, pressed
1 large onion, sliced
1 fresh lemon, sliced
2 pounds flounder fillets
Paprika

Whisk the oil, vinegar, and salt and pepper together. Add the garlic, onion, and lemon pieces. Cover the fish with the marinade, and refrigerate several hours or overnight, carefully stirring once or twice. With a slotted spoon, place the fish in a 3-quart, microwave-safe baking dish, and layer it with the garlic, onion, and lemon pieces. Allow some of the marinade to remain on the fish and accumulate in the baking dish. Sprinkle with paprika. Cover with waxed paper and microwave on high for 10 minutes.

& *Shaudyses' Garden Vegetable Stir-Fry* &
YIELD: SERVES 6

Kim and I created this recipe to utilize our garden produce. The veggies are crisp and tasty!

Peanut oil
5 or 6 baby zucchini, sliced
2 inner stalks Chinese cabbage, sliced
3 or 4 cups sugar peas (in pods)
Salt and pepper, to taste
Lemon Herb Vinegar

Coat a large skillet with peanut oil, and heat to medium high. Add the zucchini, Chinese cabbage, and peas, in that order, cooking each for only a minute or two, and stirring with each addition. Sprinkle the sautéed vegetables with salt and freshly ground pepper, to taste, and Lemon Herb Vinegar. Cook 2 or 3 minutes longer, tossing and blending the ingredients. Serve immediately. Freshly picked zucchini blossoms make a delightful, edible garnish for this dish. Add them to the pan at the last moment of cooking. Remove from heat, cover, and let stand for a minute or two to steam the flowers.

& *Kim and Tom's Pasta Sauté* &

My daughter and her fiancé created this recipe one night when they were in the mood for pasta and my cupboards were rather bare! Throughout their engagement they embellished the recipe and added the variations. This is great as a side dish (without meat), or as the main dish with the addition of either chicken or shrimp.

Olive oil
2 tablespoons butter (optional)
4 cloves garlic, minced
Juice of 1 lemon
½ cup white wine
2 tablespoons fresh sweet basil, minced
1 pound broccoli florets
1 pound pasta (twists), cooked
Parmesan cheese

Preheat a large skillet on medium-high heat. Add enough olive oil to fill skillet to ½ inch. Add the butter for flavor, if desired. Add the garlic, lemon juice, wine, and basil. Cook and stir until everything is blended. Add broccoli and sauté until tender crisp. Mix with the cooked pasta. Sprinkle with Parmesan cheese. Voilà!

Variation I
Add a pinch of oregano and/or savory along with the basil, and 2 or 3 cups of cooked chicken, cut into bite-sized pieces, when you add the broccoli.

Variation II
Substitute snow peas for the broccoli, and add 2 or 3 cups of cooked shrimp.

Variation III (Mom's!)
Substitute 1 cup of Lemon Herb Vinegar or Lemon Herb Garlic Vinegar for the lemon juice and white wine, for any of these three recipes!

Ways to Use Herb, Fruit, and Floral Vinegars

by Shirley B. Young

❤

Delicious Combinations Using Flavored Vinegars

BASIL	Stir-fried asparagus; tomato salad; tomato soup; "overnight pickles" of marinated slices of carrot, cucumber, squash, green pepper; salad greens
BLACKBERRY	Basting for chicken; add to mayonnaise as dip for fruits and vegetables; add to yogurt for fruit salad; add to fruit punch or pie filling; steamed puddings
CARAWAY SEED	Coleslaw; red cabbage
CHIVE BLOSSOM	Wherever onion flavor is desired: egg salad, cooked broccoli or Brussels sprouts, marinades
DILL	Cooked beets or cabbage; three-bean salad; coleslaw; potato salad; poaching eggs or fish; cucumber salad
FENNEL SEED	Avocado, grapefruit, and mushroom salad
FLORAL VINEGAR	Fruit or cream dishes; fruit salads; green salads; use vinegared flowers to garnish winter salads (flowers to use: violets, carnations, elderberries, roses, or lavender)
GARLIC	Green salads; vegetable salads; spinach; marinade for sauerbraten
HERB-GARDEN	Crisp, green salads; bean soup; cooked green beans (see recipe on page 168)
ITALIAN	Antipasto vegetables; tossed salad; marinade for meats before grilling; broccoli
LEMON THYME	Mayonnaise; fish and fish salad; stir-fry vegetables such as asparagus, broccoli, zucchini, pea pods
MINT	Stir into mayonnaise or whipped cream for fruit salads; sauce for lamb; fruit gelatin; fruit punch
NASTURTIUM	Wherever peppery flavor is desired: pickled eggs, meats before grilling, green bean salad
OREGANO	Scrambled eggs; salads; pizza
RED-RASPBERRY	Spinach salad; baked pears or apples; hot chicken; meat marinade; add to yogurt for fruit salad; add club soda, seltzer, or tonic for a refreshing drink (1 tablespoon per glass)
ROSEMARY	Pork or lamb marinade; tomato and cucumber salad; orange and onion salad; fried potatoes; fruits
SALAD BURNET	Cucumber flavor without indigestion; salads; clear or potato soup
SAVORY	Beans and bean soup; cabbage; mushrooms; meat marinade
TARRAGON	Chicken, crabmeat, and tuna salads; vegetable juice cocktail; chicken gravy; hollandaise and béarnaise sauces; peas and onions combined; green salad
TARRAGON AND GARLIC	Robust salads like kidney bean or chef's (use red wine vinegar)

CULINARY USES FOR HOMEMADE VINEGARS

❤ Sprinkle over fruit, vegetable, fish, or poultry salads, or simple, crisp greens.

❤ Make a salad dressing by mixing herb vinegar with olive oil and shaking well, or, for a creamy dressing, blending it with mayonnaise.

❤ For extra zip, add a splash to soups, stews, sauces, gravies, aspics, or scrambled eggs.

❤ Use as a marinade or basting liquid for meat, poultry, or fish.

❤ Sprinkle over cooked vegetables, especially cabbage, broccoli,

Shirley Young is one of those gregarious souls who wanted to find herb friends when she moved to a new locality, so she started an herb group. As a result, there is an active herb society in the Pocono Mountains! This article is from one of her many lecture-demonstrations at local historical events.

❧ *Herb-Garden Vinegar* ❧

*1 cup of mixed fresh herbs, such as
    savory, marjoram, chives, parsley*
2 cups white wine vinegar

Bruise the herbs. Warm the vinegar, and pour it over the herbs. Steep for 2 weeks, shaking jar occasionally. Strain, bottle, and label. Add fresh herb sprigs, if desired. Use on mixed green salads.

❧ *Dilly-Mint Vinegar* ❧

2 cups cider or white wine vinegar
3 cloves garlic, minced
*3 heads fresh dill (or 2 teaspoons dill
    seed)*
6 long, leafy spearmint sprigs

Combine all ingredients in a glass jar. Let stand 4 to 6 weeks, shaking jar occasionally. Strain and bottle. Add a fresh dill sprig to each bottle. Use for potato salad, coleslaw, oil and vinegar dressing, or deviled eggs.

Brussels sprouts, and spinach.
❤ Use in stir-fry cooking, and as a base for sweet-sour dishes.
❤ Use as a poaching liquid for fish or eggs.
❤ Add to ground-meat dishes and stuffings for meat and poultry.

COSMETIC USES OF HOMEMADE VINEGARS

Mouthwash. Add 1 ounce chamomile, sage, comfrey, lavender, or rosemary to 2 cups heated vinegar. Steep for 10 days. Strain.

Facial rinse. Steep 2 cups chopped leaves or petals of appropriate herbs (sage, yarrow, plantain, or lemon balm as an astringent for *oily* skin; chamomile, comfrey, or elderflower to soothe *dry* skin) in 1 pint of white or cider vinegar for 2 weeks. Strain. *Dilute* (2 tablespoons in washbasin of water), and splash onto skin.

After-shave lotion. Steep 2 cups of chopped leaves of thyme, sage, rosemary, basil, dill, marjoram, or lavender in 1 pint of cider vinegar for 2 weeks. Strain. Invigorating and healing.

Underarm deodorant. Splash underarms with thyme or sage vinegar.

Hair rinse. Add ¼ cup aromatic vinegar, such as lavender or rose petal to 1 quart of warm water. Removes all traces of soap, and leaves hair soft and lustrous.

Dandruff treatment. Steep nettles, southernwood, horsetail, or a combination of rosemary and mint in cider vinegar for 2 weeks. Strain. Rub 2 tablespoons into scalp twice a week to control dandruff.

SHIRLEY B. YOUNG, SCIOTA, PA 18354

TIPS ON USING VERSATILE HERBAL VINEGARS

by Linda Fry Kenzle

❤ Make your windows shine with a spritz made by combining herbal vinegar and hot water; wipe dry.
❤ Spray a fragrant, herb vinegar on your dog (not in the face, please) to get rid of doggy odor.
❤ Excellent salad vinegars are made with orange mint, tarragon, or salad burnet.
❤ Keep a bottle of salad burnet vinegar in the refrigerator for a refreshing body splash after a day at the beach.
❤ Dip a piece of cheesecloth in herb vinegar, wring it out, and wrap it around cheese to prevent molding.
❤ An herbal hair rinse (chamomile/white vinegar for blondes, rosemary/apple-cider vinegar for brunettes, orange mint/wine vinegar for redheads) removes excess shampoo residue. Mix in equal parts with warm water before use.

❤ Instead of using a plain herbal vinegar on your salad, whip up a simple vinaigrette (salad dressing made with oil and vinegar) with 1 cup olive oil; ⅔ cup herbal vinegar; 1 clove garlic, minced; ½ teaspoon sugar; ¼ teaspoon salt (optional); and ⅛ teaspoon lemon balm. Mix in a jar and shake just before using.

♥ A lavender/white vinegar reduced with warm water makes a very Victorian herbal rinsing water for doilies and other linens.

♥ Make an ***Old-fashioned Vinegar Pie:*** Cream together ½ cup sugar and 2 tablespoons butter. Add 3 tablespoons flour, 1 teaspoon cinnamon, ¼ teaspoon cloves, ¼ teaspoon allspice, ⅛ teaspoon salt, 1 egg, 2 tablespoons rosemary vinegar, and 1 cup of water. Cook these ingredients together in double boiler, stirring constantly, until thickened. Line a pie pan with the pie crust. Pour in the filling, and bake at 350° F. until crust is browned, 8 to 12 minutes.

♥ Thymol, an acidic compound found in thyme, is a powerful antiseptic. Use a thyme/white vinegar splash on insect bites. This vinegar will also repel insects if you put it on just before going outdoors.

LINDA FRY KENZLE, FOX RIVER GROVE, IL 60021

HERBAL VINEGARS

by Alma Otto

My favorite way of making herb vinegar is to put fresh herbs into a jar and cover them with red or white wine vinegar. I date the jar and put it on a windowsill with *some* sun, or on the screened porch in the summer; 2 to 3 weeks are usually enough time for the herb flavors to take hold. Always taste it before straining for rebottling to be sure it is strong enough. You can also pour room-temperature vinegar over your herbs in the selected jar and let it stand in the pantry or on a shelf for 1 or 2 months. Many persons use only heated (*almost* boiling) vinegar to pour over the herbs. This method is the quickest, since the vinegar can be ready in 9 or 10 days.

Here are some of my favorite recipes.

Savory/basil/garlic
½ cup summer savory or tender sprigs of winter savory; ¼ cup basil leaves; 2 small cloves garlic (or more, if desired); and 1 quart red-wine vinegar.

French tarragon
Place three 3-inch tarragon sprigs into each pint jar. Fill with white-wine vinegar. This is the best way to preserve the flavor of tarragon. Never use dried tarragon.

Dill
Place ½ cup of fresh dillweed in a pint jar, cover it with white wine vinegar, and place the jar in a sunny window.

Dark opal basil
This is delicious as well as beautiful — it's fun to watch the color develop. Use three 3-inch clusters of the basil, and cover with white-wine vinegar. In 2 or 3 days a lovely pink color will begin to show. The taste is just a little different from sweet basil vinegar.

Burnet/garlic/chives
Use the outside leaves of burnet and leaves of chives in even amounts, and cover with white wine vinegar.

ALMA OTTO, LARGO, FL 34644

❧ *Rose-Petal Vinegar* ❧

Into 4 cups of hot white vinegar, place 2 cups of your reddest roses; allow to steep for a week. Strain. This vinegar, with its beautiful, rosy color, can be used as an after-shampoo rinse, in your bath (1 cup) to neutralize the skin, as a soothing headache remedy (soak a cloth in the vinegar, wring it out, and place it on your forehead), or to dress a fruit salad!

FROM *A BOUNTIFUL COLLECTION* (PENN-CUMBERLAND GARDEN CLUB) BERTHA REPPERT, THE ROSEMARY HOUSE, MECHANICSBURG, PA 17055

MARSHA'S GOURMET OREGON VINEGARS

by Marsha Peters Johnson

If you want the very latest advice on making and using flavored vinegars, here's a must *for your kitchen library:* Gourmet Vinegars: How to Make and Cook With Them *by MARSHA PETERS JOHNSON (Lake Oswego, OR: Culinary Arts, Ltd.). The author founded and operated the very successful firm, Oregon's Own Gourmet Vinegars (which are now marketed under the label of Oregon Trails Gourmet Vinegars). In the book are secrets for making her vinegars, along with fifty-seven step-by-step vinegar recipes and many outstanding recipes for using them. Here are some of Marsha's gems and surprises. (Although most of Marsha's recipes call for aging unheated blends in a cool, dark place for about a month, she recommends the heating process when spices, some fruits, or dried herbs are used.)*

Aging time. Certain recipes that require heating will be ready for use at once, but the majority of my vinegars require about a month to fully develop their unique flavors. I believe in cold processing as opposed to hot processing. Treating the fruit or herbs gently and combining them with vinegar in its prime makes a great finished product, full of the natural vitamins and nutrients leached from the fruit or herbs during the aging process.

Shelf life of finished vinegar. Flavored vinegars will keep up to 18 months, possibly longer, if stored in proper containers in a cool, dark place. Some fruit sugars, like strawberry or blueberry, tend to caramelize after a while and turn slightly brown, which isn't as attractive as a clear red or violet liquid. Use these vinegars in 3 months to avoid this problem. Since high-acid vinegar is often used as a preservative itself, spoilage just isn't a problem. Usually, you'll end up wishing you'd made twice as much because it disappears so quickly.

❧ Dilled Garlic Vinegar ❧

This is a very easy recipe for the beginning vinegar-maker, since the aging and bottling are done in one step.

6 to 9 whole garlic cloves
Sprigs of fresh dillweed, thoroughly washed
1 quart fine white- or red-wine vinegar

Cut garlic cloves in half lengthwise. Place 4 to 6 garlic halves and 1 or 2 sprigs dillweed in three 8-ounce bottles. Fill with vinegar, and seal with corks and wax or plastic screw lids. Label and age 4 weeks before using.

❧ Marinated Fresh Vegetables ❧
YIELD: SERVES 4 TO 6

¾ cup salad oil, preferably safflower
½ cup any flavored vinegar
2 tablespoons lemon juice (omit if using lemon vinegar)
3 tablespoons finely chopped sweet onion
1 teaspoon dried tarragon
1 teaspoon salt or salt substitute

½ tablespoon granulated sugar, if desired (omit if using a sweet fruit vinegar)
3 to 4 cups cut-up fresh vegetables, such as carrots, onion rings, zucchini, cherry tomatoes, pea pods, celery slices, diced sunchokes, broccoli, cauliflower, celery root, and olives.

In a bowl, whisk all ingredients except vegetables. Pour marinade over fresh vegetables in a flat, shallow container. Cover and marinate for at least 3 hours or overnight. Drain and serve.

❧ *Raspberry Pork Chops* ❧
YIELD: SERVES 4

I print this recipe on the label of my Oregon Raspberry Vinegar. When you taste it, you'll know why.

4 lean pork chops
2 tablespoons flour, if desired
1½ tablespoons butter
1 tablespoon oil

6 tablespoons raspberry vinegar
¾ cup chicken broth
½ cup heavy cream

Coat chops with flour, if desired. In a skillet, brown the chops in butter and oil, turning once. Remove chops, and add vinegar and broth to pan drippings. Stir over low heat until well combined. Return chops to pan. Simmer until cooked, about 10 minutes each side. Remove pork to a serving platter. Raise heat, and boil sauce until thickened slightly, about 5 minutes. Add cream, stirring until thick. Pour over pork chops and serve at once.

❧ *Creamy Cucumber Salad* ❧
YIELD: SERVES 4

This smooth, creamy dish is Scandinavian in origin. Perfect with baked fish, especially salmon.

2 cucumbers, peeled and sliced
1 teaspoon salt
1 cup sour cream

3 tablespoons gourmet vinegar
   (blackberry, dilled, pepper, or
   rosemary)
4 teaspoons minced green onions

In a colander, sprinkle the cucumbers with the salt, and allow to drain for 1 hour. Rinse with clear water and drain for 5 minutes. Mix the sour cream, vinegar, and green onions in a serving bowl. Add the cucumber slices. Refrigerate 2 or 3 hours before serving.

Variation
For Raspberry Chicken, use four, split and boned chicken breasts instead of pork chops.

FROM *GOURMET VINEGARS* BY MARSHA PETERS JOHNSON (LAKE OSWEGO, OR: CULINARY ARTS, LTD.)

RECIPES FROM PINE CREEK HERBS

by Kathleen Gips

❧ *Herbal Pasta Sauce* ❧
Herbal vinegar sparks the taste of this easy-to-make sauce for pasta lovers.

1 cup sour cream
¼ cup grated parmesan cheese
2 tablespoons chive-garlic-basil or basil herb vinegar
2 tablespoons fresh, chopped basil (or 1 tablespoon dried)

Combine ingredients and toss with warm pasta.

Seafood Marinade

1 cup salad oil
1 medium onion, thinly sliced
⅔ cup bouquet garni or tarragon
*   or chive-garlic-basil Vinegar*
Juice of 1 lemon

Whisk ingredients to blend. Toss with cold seafood, and refrigerate several hours or overnight. Baste fish fillets before grilling, or sauté in marinade.

KATHLEEN GIPS, PINE CREEK HERBS, CHAGRIN FALLS, OH 44022

Kathleen's Rose-Petal Jam

1 quart fragrant rose petals, tightly
*   packed* (pesticide-free)
3 cups water
1 package Sure-Jell

2 tablespoons lemon juice
Red food coloring (optional)
4 cups sugar

Heat the petals and water to boiling. Steep for 20 minutes, pushing petals into the liquid occasionally. Strain, and reserve petals. Measure liquid, and add water to make 3 cups. Mix liquid with Sure-Jell, lemon juice, and a few drops of red food coloring, if desired. In a large, stainless-steel pot, bring the mixture to a boil over high heat. Add the sugar, bring to a hard, rolling boil, and boil for exactly 1 minute. Immediately remove from heat, and stir in reserved rose petals. Stir for a few minutes to prevent petals from floating. Pour into sterilized jars, and seal.

Raspberry Fruit Dressing

1 cup sour cream (or plain yogurt)
3 tablespoons honey
3 tablespoons raspberry vinegar
1 tablespoon raspberry jam

Mix all ingredients together, and refrigerate in a covered container for 3 hours. Serve over mixed fruit salad (orange, apple, kiwi, or banana slices, halved green grapes, pineapple chunks, coconut, and so on).

ALYCE P. NADEAU, GOLDENROD MOUNTAIN HERBS, DEEP GAP, NC 28618

FLAVORED VINEGAR RECIPES

by Alyce Nadeau

Splendid Raspberry Vinegar

Gently wash fresh raspberries and drain them in a colander. Loosely fill a 1-quart Mason jar with raspberries to within 2 inches of the top. Heat white vinegar until the first bubbles appear, and add it to the raspberries until the jar is filled. Cover the jar with plastic wrap (to prevent acid build-up and rust from the metal top), and screw on the top. Store the jar in a dark, cool place for 6 weeks. Strain the vinegar through a tea strainer lined with coffee-filter paper (a *must* to remove infinitesimal debris), pour it into a fresh bottle, insert a cork, and label. The recipe at the left is a heavenly way to use this vinegar.

Alyce's Herbal Salad Dressing

½ cup mayonnaise
½ cup sour cream (or plain yogurt)
2 tablespoons herb vinegar
½ teaspoon dry oregano

½ teaspoon sugar
Dash salt
Dash pepper
Garlic (optional)

Blend all ingredients. Place in a covered container in the refrigerator for about 4 hours. Can be used as dip, or thinned with 3 tablespoons of milk for salad dressing.

Mary Michael's Vinegars

❧ Spicy Blueberry Vinegar ❧

3 cups blueberries, rinsed and dried
   (can use frozen)
2 cinnamon sticks

1 whole nutmeg, bruised
4 cups white vinegar
2 tablespoons (to ½ cup) sugar

Place blueberries, cinnamon sticks, and nutmeg in a 6-cup container. Combine the vinegar and sugar in a saucepan and bring almost to a boil, stirring to dissolve sugar. Pour hot vinegar over the berry mixture. Cover jar tightly and let stand for 48 hours. Strain and rebottle. Use on fruit salads, for an exotic tuna salad, or on grilled fish or chicken, steamed vegetables, or tossed salad.

❧ Berry Vinaigrette ❧

5 tablespoons berry vinegar
½ cup oil
2 tablespoons minced shallots

1 teaspoon Dijon mustard
1 teaspoon honey
Pepper to taste

Combine all ingredients, and shake to mix. Cover tightly. Chill. Good for greens and other vegetables (especially spinach or butter lettuce). Keeps for about 2 weeks.

❧ Fruity Cream Dressing ❧

1 cup sour cream (or yogurt)
¼ cup whipping cream
1 tablespoon confectioners' sugar

¼ cup blueberry, raspberry, or
   peach vinegar
Pinch of salt
¼ cup vegetable oil

Whisk together all ingredients but the oil. Add the oil in a slow, steady stream until blended. Refrigerate. Use within 3 days on spinach-cucumber salad.

❧ Gourmet Chicken-Thyme from Hampton Herbs ❧

I like to add cooked carrots and celery to my chicken broth in this recipe.

4 chicken breasts (boned or
   unboned)
3 tablespoons butter or margarine
1 onion, chopped

6 tablespoons thyme vinegar
1½ cups chicken broth
Salt and pepper, to taste
Dash of fresh or dried thyme

Brown the chicken breasts in the butter or margarine. Cover the skillet while chicken cooks. When chicken is browned and almost done, add the onion. Turn heat to low and continue cooking until onion is done. Remove the chicken, and add the thyme vinegar and chicken broth. Turn heat to medium, return chicken, and cook until almost all liquid has evaporated and thickened.

Peach- or blueberry-spiced vinegar, combined with 1 tablespoon sour cream, plain yogurt, or mayonnaise, is great on a fruit salad.

❤

After sautéing fresh mushrooms, add dark opal basil vinegar, a tablespoon at a time, to taste.

❧ Dilled Mustard Sauce ❧
YIELD: 1¼ CUPS

½ cup Dijon mustard
2 tablespoons dry mustard
¼ cup tarragon vinegar
⅓ cup salad oil
¼ cup chopped fresh dill (or 1
   tablespoon dried)

Combine all ingredients. Mix well.

Mary Michael, Millsboro, DE 19966

Betty Leonard, Hampton Herbs, New Carlisle, OH 45344

BURNET-LOVAGE-CHIVES VINEGAR

Even those not fond of celery or cucumbers may enjoy a vinegar flavored with burnet, lovage, and chives. The taste is similar to celery and cukes, almost peppery and quite nice.

SYLVIA VOGLER'S HERB VINEGARS

Sylvia's Spiced Cherry Vinegar

Great with pork and in Waldorf salad!

2 to 3 quarts pie cherries (with pits)
Two 3-inch cinnamon sticks
8 to 10 allspice berries
6 tablespoons honey
3 to 3 ½ quarts white vinegar

Place the cherries in a gallon jar. Add the cinnamon sticks, allspice berries, and honey to the vinegar, and bring them almost to a boil. Pour vinegar mixture over the cherries. Cover, and let sit in a cool, dark place for 2 to 3 weeks. Strain thoroughly and rebottle.

Peachy Pineapple-Sage Vinegar

3 peaches, peeled, pitted, and sliced
5 hefty sprigs of pineapple sage
15 whole cloves
10 whole allspice berries
3 crushed cinnamon sticks
White vinegar, to cover

Place the peaches, pineapple sage, cloves, allspice, and cinnamon sticks in a gallon jar. Cover with white vinegar, and set aside for a month or two. Strain. Very delicate and delicious!

SYLVIA AND KEN VOGLER, MAERRIE MEADOWS FARM, PHILOMATH, OR 97370

Tarragon and Fennel Vinegar

Pack equal amounts of fennel and tarragon in a jar, and pour a combination of hot, white wine and cider vinegars over the herbs. Store in a cool, dark place for 2 to 3 weeks before straining and rebottling. This vinegar adds a very nice flavor to boiled shrimp or any fish entrée. We make aluminum foil "fish boats," into which we place fish fillets, topped with some butter, sprigs of fennel and/or tarragon, and a liberal sprinkling of the tarragon-fennel vinegar. We then gently fold the packets and barbecue them on the grill. (Even I like these, and I am not a fish lover — maybe because the vinegar eliminates the smelly fish odor!)

Herby Barbecued (Smoked) Turkey or Pork

Cut up a whole turkey. Cut large branches of sage, rosemary, or thyme; wash, and leave wet. Put half the herbs on the hot coals and the other half on the grill wires. Place the turkey pieces on top and turn every 15 minutes or so. In about 1 hour, the smoked turkey is perfectly moist — without basting, salt, or pepper. Leftovers freeze well. This technique also works for other poultry.

For pork loin roast, make cuts 1 inch apart down to the bone and stuff these full of rosemary or thyme and orange bergamot branches. Tie the roast back together with long branches of mint. Barbecue on a bed of the same herbs.

HERBAL VINEGARS IN BEVERAGES

Use a dash of

- Basil vinegar in Bloody Marys or tomato juice
- Lemon vinegar in pineapple juice
- Mint vinegar in apple juice

HERBAL VINEGAR GARNISHES

Place any of the following in a bottle of homemade vinegar:

- Dried chile peppers, small chunks of peeled ginger or garlic, or spirals of lemon or orange peels impaled on bamboo skewers
- Flower petals (edible varieties only; see pages 182-84)
- Dried seeds and spices such as coriander, peppercorns, cloves, bay, chiles, fennel, allspice, and dill (lightly crush or bruise with a mortar and pestle and use 2 tablespoons per quart of vinegar)

FROM *THE HERB GARDEN COOKBOOK,* LUCINDA HUTSON, AUSTIN, TX 78756

RECIPES FROM BACK OF THE BEYOND

by Shash Georgi

❧ *Nature's Lite Drink* ❧

One of my original, and best selling, vinegars is Mixed Herb Vinegar. When I tell people I drink it with honey and water, my healthy appearance makes them decide they want to drink it, too. My recipe for this drink, which I call "Nature's Lite Drink," is as follows:

1 cup boiling water
1 tablespoon honey

1 tablespoon herb vinegar (made with apple-cider vinegar)

Fill a cup with boiling water to dissolve the honey. Serve hot or iced for a low-calorie, winelike drink. In days of yore, this energy refresher was called a "switchel" and drunk as a thirst quencher. It also acts as a diuretic, and its potassium gives added energy. Dr. Jarvis mentions most of this in his book, *Vermont Folk Medicine*.

❧ *Herb Salt* ❧

A recipe for dried herbs.

1 cup sea salt or kelp
4 tablespoons each parsley and basil
2 tablespoons each mint, rosemary, tarragon, thyme, dillweed, lemon balm, and paprika

Place ingredients in a medium-sized bowl and mix well. Blend, in batches, in a blender or food processor. Store in a glass container or in decorative shakers. This herb salt is a concentrated mélange of flavors and is good on any dish that requires several herbs.

SHASH GEORGI, BACK OF THE BEYOND, COLDEN, NY 14033

❧ *Minted Pea Salad* ❧

Two 10-ounce packages frozen peas, or equivalent amount of sugar snap peas
½ cup sour cream
6 green onions (scallions), sliced
Herb Salt, to taste
¼ cup chopped, fresh mint (or 2 tablespoons dried mint)
6 slices of cooked, drained, and crumbled bacon

Thaw peas, if frozen, or steam gently, if fresh. Drain thoroughly. Combine with remaining ingredients. Chill. Garnish with fresh sprigs of mint.

❧ *Basil-Chile-Garlic Vinegar* ❧

Fill a jar two-thirds full of fresh basil (experiment with different varieties of basil), the peeled cloves of 2 or 3 heads of garlic, and about 6 to 15 dried red chiles. Cover with heated red-wine vinegar. This is fabulous sprinkled over slices of garden-fresh tomatoes; used to make a zesty salad dressing, or with the addition of olive oil, a beef or chicken marinade; sprinkled over vegetables, steaks, or grilled chicken; added to beef stew, spaghetti sauce, or tomato soup; or splashed into tomato beverages.

FROM *THE HERB GARDEN COOKBOOK* LUCINDA HUTSON, AUSTIN, TX 78756

Readers who have attended open houses at Back of the Beyond have been enchanted and keep returning regularly. SHASH GEORGI and her husband offer a chalet as a bed-and-breakfast at their herbal retreat, where you can enjoy the herb gardens, her herb shop, and an herbal breakfast.

BARBECUE BRUSH

When barbecuing, baste your meat with a brush made from parsley, sage, rosemary, and thyme sprigs tied onto the handle of a wooden spoon.

MINT COOLER

Steep 2 cups of boiling water and 8 mint teabags. Add 1½ cups lemonade, 2 cups orange juice, 2 cups crushed ice, and two 12-ounce cans ginger ale. Garnish with orange slices and mint sprigs. Serve over ice.

SANDI MORAN, HERBPATCH PLEASANTRIES, DES MOINES, IA 50313

Midsummer Projects

PAT AND JON BOURDO offer herb charts and information sheets with varied titles, such as "Special Poisonous Plant Chart," "Seasonings Hint Chart," and "The Pleasures of Making Your Own Potpourri." The latter contains ten potpourri recipes, including these two, as well as a list of herbal symbolism (see pages 142 and 150). Each chart or sheet is unique. The Bourdos specialize in culinary herbs and edible flowers, and sell herb and spice labels, herb vinegars, rice blends, salt-free seasonings, herb teas, and jellies and chutneys, as well as potpourri, wreaths, herbal bath blends, and more. At the farm, over 150 varieties of perennial herbs are available from mid-May to mid-July. Pat is the author of Culinary Uses for Herbs and Spices, *a marvelous cookbook of quick and delicious, salt-free recipes.*

* Hungarian Potpourri *

3 cups rosemary
3 cups dried, yellow rose petals
1½ cups orange blossoms
1½ cups mint leaves
1 cup dried, yellow zinnia petals
2 ounces calamus root
2 ounces crushed vetiver root
Dried and ground peel of 1 lemon
2 drops rose oil, or oil of choice

* American Potpourri *

1 cup each of dried blue salvia, red salvia, blue hydrangea blossoms, rose petals, pinks, and Queen-Anne's-lace, broken into florets
½ teaspoon coarse-ground cloves
⅓ teaspoon coarse-ground mace
¼ teaspoon cinnamon
⅓ cup orrisroot powder
10 drops bergamot oil
20 drops eucalyptus oil
4 drops rose oil

PAT AND JON BOURDO, WOODLAND HERB FARM, NORTHPORT, MI 49670

Expecting company that includes smokers? Instead of putting out regular ashtrays, use decorative bowls filled with white sand and baking soda in which a few drops of essential oil are mixed. This will both help to absorb the odor and add a pleasant fragrance of its own to the room.

SUMMER SCENTS

by Bob Clark

Scented Stationery

Cut a piece of blotter paper and a piece of shirt cardboard to fit your stationery box. Drop some essential oils onto the blotter paper and place it on the shirt cardboard. Cover the blotting paper with a couple of layers of cheesecloth, then with a print fabric. Glue the fabric edges around to the back of the cardboard. Put this in the bottom of the box and replace the stationery. The layers of cloth prevent the writing paper from becoming spotted with oil. This makes a nice gift.

❧ *Lemon Verbena Potpourri* ❧

20 drops lemon verbena or lemongrass oil
10 drops bergamot oil
5 drops honeysuckle oil
⅓ cup orrisroot
3 cups whole lemon verbena leaves
2 cups yellow flowers, such as roses or calendula
2 cups fragrant leaves, such as lemon thyme, thyme,
lemon-scented geranium, or bay
1 cup orange or mock-orange petals
¾ cup lemon peel
⅓ cup gingerroot, cut and sifted
2 nutmegs, crushed

Add the oils to the orrisroot. Add remaining ingredients, mix well.

❧ *Bye-Bye Bugs Potpourri* ❧

This is a versatile mixture: Simmer it at a picnic, use it to deter moths in drawers or closets, or strew it on the ground at outdoor craft fairs, even beside the food stand, to repel bugs — and also to attract attention! Add or substitute other insect-repelling herbs if you wish.

40 drops pennyroyal oil
20 drops eucalyptus oil
20 drops citronella oil
1 cup cedar chips
2 tablespoons cloves
2 tablespoons cinnamon chips
2 cups feverfew flowers and foliage
2 cups scented geranium leaves
1 cup calendula flowers
1 cup lemongrass
½ cup tansy
½ cup southernwood
½ cup patchouli leaves

Add the oils to the cedar chips, cloves, and cinnamon chips. Shake often while allowing scents to mingle for 48 hours, then add the remaining ingredients.

Even in the hot days of summer, it is necessary sometimes to use our clothes-driers when it is rainy or humid. When the clothes are practically dry, empty the lint trap. Add a few drops of essential oils to an old washcloth, place this in the lint trap, and re-insert it. When the clothes finish drying they will smell heavenly! Be certain to remove the washcloth before the next load.

❧ *Vanilla-Cream Potpourri* ❧

4 drops vanilla oil
1½ drops tonka oil
1½ drops musk oil
¼ cup vetiver
¼ cup angelica root
1½ cups white flowers, such as roses or globe amaranth
1½ cups deer's-tongue leaves
1 cup orange petals
1 cup red clover blossoms
1 cup sweet woodruff
⅓ cup orange peel
2 or 3 tonka beans, diced
1 vanilla bean, minced

Add the oils to the vetiver and angelica root. Allow these to intermix and become absorbed, then add remaining ingredients.

To add a nice taste to frozen concentrate or fresh-squeezed lemonade, add fresh sprigs of lemon verbena and orange bergamot mint. Refreshing!

BOB CLARK, LANCASTER, OH 43130

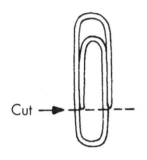

Cut →

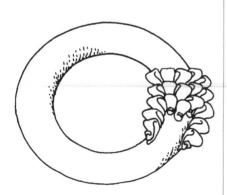

Barbara L. Wade, Herb 'n Ewe,
Thornville, OH 43076

As your flowers and herbs start to bloom, gather small bunches to dry for making herbal or Victorian wreaths (see February and October). PVS

Lamb's-Ears Wreath

by Barbara L. Wade

Like most shepherds, I'm fond of lamb's-ears *(Stachys byzantina)*, as the soft leaves so closely resemble sheep's wool. Once used medicinally as a wound bandage and poultice, these can still be soothing to cuts that occur when shearing your flock. Charmed by the ornamental value of this plant, I strive to create new ways of using lamb's-ears to justify to my co-proprietor and sister, Susan, its place in several of our gardens. This wreath is one of the results.

Instead of wreath pins, I cut and use small paper clips, because unlike wreath pins, which must be placed at an extreme angle so that they won't push through the back of the leaves, paper clips pierce the leaves with little damage. You will need 50 to 100, fresh, dew-free lamb's-ears leaves, depending on the size of your wreath. Select various-sized leaves. To create an effect of depth, I use the larger leaves on the outer edge and the smaller ones on the inside edge. Be sure to use white glue to make the bow; hot glue will singe the lamb's-ears.

Styrofoam wreath of desired size
Wreath pins
Lamb's-ears leaves
White glue
Clear, florist spray sealer

1. Place the tip of the leaf to the stem end to form a loop, fuzzy side out.

2. Place the looped leaf *slightly past* the outer edge of the wreath base. (It is important that this row extends around the outer edge, as lamb's-ear shrinks somewhat as it dries.)

3. Lap another leaf into a loop and place it over the first leaf, taking care to cover the pin. Continue in this manner, until you have completed a row all around the wreath.

4. Using small leaves, make a row of loops around the inside edge of the wreath. Follow this row with another row beside the one on the outer edge, and then with a row beside the one on the inside edge. Make a fifth and final row on the center of the base to add dimension.

5. Spray with sealer, and place on a flat tray or a piece of cardboard to dry for approximately one week. The wreath is delicate and must be handled gently. Hang it in a protected area; direct sun will spoil the gray foliage. It is not easily kept for the next season, so ignore the teasing protests and joyfully plant and divide more lamb's-ears plants for next year!

LAMB'S-EARS BOWS

by Joan Lenon

To make one bow, you will need two short and two long (about 1-inch difference) lamb's-ears leaves, stems included.

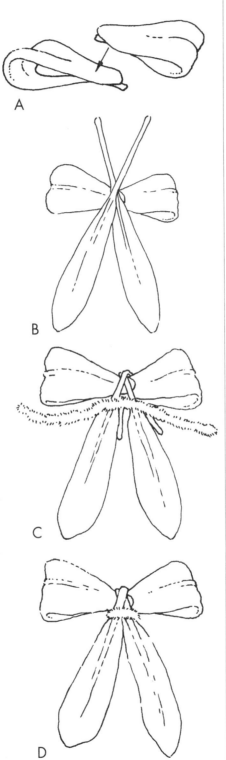

1. To form the loops of the bow, fold the tip of one short leaf to the base of its stem — fuzzy side out. Do the same with the other short leaf, and place it on top of the first leaf, with loops going in opposite directions and with stems hidden (A).

2. To form the "tie" ends of the bow, place the two long leaves on the center of the bow at a slight angle and fold the stems to the back (B).

3. Wrap white pipe cleaner around the two long leaves just under the bow and twist the ends at the back (C and D).

4. Trim off excess stems. Place bow in your favorite drying spot. (The top of the refrigerator is mine!) You can leave the pipe cleaner long in back to make a hook for hanging on the Christmas tree. This bow dries to a silvery, fuzzy white-gray.

JOAN LENON, THE SUMAC SHOP, GRAND RAPIDS, MI 49504

❧ Old-Time Horehound Candy ☙

Use summer's harvest to prepare for winter's colds — horehound candy is an old-fashioned remedy to soothe sore throats.

2 cups fresh horehound, including leaves, stems, and flowers (or 1 cup dried)
2½ quarts water
3 cups brown sugar
½ cup corn syrup
1 teaspoon cream of tartar
1 teaspoon butter
1 teaspoon lemon juice (or 1 sprig lemon balm)

In a large saucepan, cover the horehound with the water. Bring to a boil, then simmer 10 minutes. Strain through cheese-cloth and allow the tea to settle.

Ladle 2 cups of the horehound tea into a large kettle. Add the brown sugar, corn syrup, and cream of tartar. Boil, stirring often, until the mixture reaches 240° F. Add the butter. Continue to boil until the candy reaches 300° F. (hard crack). Remove from the heat, and add the lemon juice. Pour at once into a buttered, 8-inch square pan. As the candy cools, score it into squares. Remove from the pan as soon as candy is cool. Store in aluminum foil or ziplock plastic bags.

RUTH AGEE EKSTROM, BITTERSWEET HERB FARM, TUSCUMBIA, MO 65082

Glaze

1 tablespoon butter, melted
2 tablespoons milk
¼ teaspoon nutmeg
1 cup confectioners' sugar
1 teaspoon vanilla
1 cup chopped pecans

To prepare Glaze, combine the melted butter, milk, vanilla, nutmeg, and confectioners' sugar in a medium-sized bowl. Glaze may also be served on top of a lemon crème anglaise.

JEAN FRENCH
BRONZE MEDAL, "DESSERTS"
FROM *THE CHEF'S HERB FESTIVAL COOKBOOK* (HERBS'88, INTERNATIONAL HERB GROWERS AND MARKETERS ASSOCIATION)

Geranium-Zucchini Cake
YIELD: THIRTY-FIVE 3" x 2½" BARS

¾ cup butter or margarine
½ cup granulated sugar
½ cup brown sugar, firmly packed
Zest of one lemon
2 eggs
1 teaspoon vanilla
1¾ cups all-purpose flour
½ teaspoon salt
½ teaspoon baking powder
¾ cup flaked coconut
¾ cup dates
¾ cup raisins
2 cups coarsely shredded zucchini
30 scented geranium leaves (mix of lemon- and peppermint-scented)

Preheat oven to 350° F. In a large bowl, cream the butter and sugars. Add the lemon zest. Beat the eggs with the vanilla. Fold into creamed mixture.

In a separate bowl, stir together the flour, salt, and baking powder. Gradually add dry ingredients to the creamed mixture. Mix in the coconut, dates, raisins, and zucchini. Stir until well blended. Grease and flour a 15" x 19" x 2" baking pan. Place geranium leaves on the bottom of pan. Pour batter over leaves. Bake in the preheated oven for 35 to 40 minutes, or until a knife inserted into the center of the cake comes out clean. Unmold cake on serving plate. Remove geranium leaves. Dribble the Glaze over the warm cake. Sprinkle the pecans on top. Let cool, and cut into 3" x 2½" bars.

AUGUST

After reading these summer chapters, you may think that this is the only time we herb enthusiasts cook! Closer to the truth is the fact that August is our most creative month in the kitchen, because the herbal harvest is at its peak and we want to save as much of it as possible for the winter ahead. (Even though there will be fresh herbs in the gardens for a few more months, heavy harvesting of perennials should end several weeks before the average frost date for your region, so the plants can build strength for the winter months.) After spending much of July and August producing herbal vinegars, pestos, and pastes to preserve the fresh-herb flavors of summer, we are anxious to use them. It's an attempt to justify the fact that every countertop, table, and available space in the kitchen and dining room are filled with empty or full jars and bottles of all sizes and descriptions possible for most of the summer! More than that, however, experimenting with

herbal blends and flavors challenges us to find exciting new taste experiences.

Now that the blender and the food processor, along with the herbal renaissance of the eighties, have helped to make "pesto" a household word, the food sections of newspapers and magazines are full of variations on pesto recipes. The word pesto *comes from* pestle — *the ancients mashed basil with a mortar and pestle to make this sauce. I have seen pestos featuring many herbs and vegetables, including spinach, cilantro, oregano, red peppers, and parsley. Modern cooks are using exotic cheeses, as well as Romano, ricotta, and Parmesan, in their pestos. Pine nuts are being replaced by walnuts, pecans, or almonds. And olive oil is no longer the* only *oil to use for pesto; less pungent oils, such as peanut, safflower, sunflower, or vegetable, are commonly seen in present-day pesto recipes.*

You will find some surprises in this chapter, I think — at least, I sure did when I was

researching material for August! You will learn about using vinegar in and on top of pestos, both for a taste sensation and for better preservation. I had originally intended to include several recipes for making herbal oils, but new information on this subject is beginning to surface at this time. The federal Food and Drug Administration has recently issued a warning to consumers that some commercial and homemade, chopped garlic-and-oil mixtures — which contain no acidifying agents such as phosphoric or citric acid and which have not been refrigerated at all times from production to consumption — have caused potentially fatal botulism food poisoning in at least two documented instances. According to the FDA report, "Clos-tridium botulinum bacteria are widespread in the environment and may be found on various produce, including garlic, but their spores are harmless when there is oxygen in the environment. However, the spores can produce a deadly toxin when in an oxygen-free, low-acid environment. Recent FDA studies have shown that garlic in an oil mixture can support bacterial growth and toxin production even when very few Clostridium botulinum spores are present."

Cooperative Extension Services in the Northeast have cautioned my publisher that some homemade flavored oils may have caused illness in their regions, even though there is no written documentation of this yet. Because there are differences of opinion among even the experts regarding how long homemade flavored oils may be safely stored in your refrigerator, we have decided not to include herbal oil recipes in this text. Nevertheless, until more is learned about this subject, there are still many ways you can create your own special flavors with your favorite herbs.

A fun family project is to save the scraps of herb stems, blemished leaves, and other leftovers. Toss a pile of similar-scented scraps in the crockpot with water to cover. Add a complementary spice or two. Heat on high, covered, until you can smell the aroma; uncover and turn to low. Some of our favorite simmers are all the lemon herbs, peppermint/bergamot/lime balm, rose geranium/lavender/cinnamon, rosemary/thyme/bay/ cloves.

Adding Edible Flowers to Your Cooking

A BLOOMING CUISINE

Flowers have been used as food in cultures all over the world since antiquity. Odysseus encountered the lotus-eating Sybarites on his way home from Troy. Charlemagne ordered his wine to be flavored with palace garden carnations. The Chinese have used daylilies, lotus, and chrysanthemums in their cuisine for centuries. Elizabethan cooks made "stewed primroses" and "gillyflower fondant," and Queen Bess favored lavender conserve. The American colonists made such delicacies as violet vinegar, Oswego tea with bergamot flowers, and mutton broth with marigolds.

Today one can't read the cooking section of a magazine or dine in a good restaurant without finding fresh flowers somewhere on the menu. This exciting revival of age-old customs offers challenging ways to be creative in the kitchen with our herb and floral harvests.

The best time to pick edible flowers is in the early morning, when the blossoms are fresh and moist. Remove any part of the stem. You will notice that some recipes call for just the petals of the flower. This is because the stamen, sepal, and calyx may be bitter. I have noted on my list when petals are the only part to use. Gently wash the blossoms or petals in cool water. Wrap them in paper towels and place in a plastic bag to be stored in the refrigerator until mealtime. It's best to use them when fresh, but the flowers will keep for a few days this way and may be "crisped" in ice water if revival is necessary.

The flowers of all culinary herbs are safe to use. If the leaf of an herb is edible, then so is the flower. Herb blossoms have the same flavor as their leaves, but, with the exceptions of chamomile and lavender blossoms, the flavor is usually more subtle. A good way to start experimenting is to use the flowers of an herb in recipes calling for that particular herb.

Here are short lists of safe and unsafe flowers for cookery. Neither list is complete, by any means, but I offer them so you can start cooking with flowers without worry before you delve into the subject more thoroughly. For the sake of space, I have not included the dozens of culinary herbs, which would greatly expand the safe list. There are probably many more safe flowers and undoubtedly more toxic blossoms than listed here. It's best not to use flowers you don't know about. **If in doubt, call your local poison center.**

Before you start experimenting with all those pretty blossoms in your yard, it is essential that you become familiar with lists of flowers that are safe and unsafe for human consumption. Sinclair Philip and Ron Zimmerman's List of 84 Safe Edible Flowers is a particularly good resource (see appendix for ordering information). **Be sure your children know the difference between safe and unsafe plants too!** Be certain that the flowers you use in cookery are pesticide-free.

SAFE, EDIBLE FLOWERS

All culinary herbs

Bachelor's-button

Begonia

Calendula (petals)

Carnation (*Dianthus pinks*)(petals)

Chrysanthemum (petals)

Citrus-scented marigold (petals)

Citrus tree blossoms

Cornflower

Dandelion (petals)

Daylily (*Hemerocallis fulva*)

English daisy (petals)

Fuchsia

Gladiola

Hibiscus

Hollyhock

Honeysuckle

Johnny-jump-up

Lily (*Lilium auratum* only)

Nasturtium

Pansy

Peas (*Pisum sativum*)

Purslane

Rose (petals)

Scented geraniums

Snapdragon

Squash (especially male zucchini blossoms)

Tulip

Viola

Violet

Watercress

Water lily (*Nymphaea odorata*)

Yucca

daylily Johnny-jump-up

chives

nasturtium

calendula

violet

begonia

Toxic Flowers

Azalea

Buttercup*

Boxwood

Columbine

Cowslip*

Daffodil

Delphinium

Foxglove

Fritillaria

Goldenrod

Heliotrope*

Hydrangea

Iris

Jack-in-the-pulpit

Jimsonweed

Lily *(Lilium atamasco)*

Lily *(Lilium gloriosa)*

Lily-of-the-valley

Milkweed*

Mistletoe

Monkshood

Narcissus

Nightshade family (Belladonna, bittersweet, white potato, tomato, eggplant)

Oleander

Pennyroyal

Poinsettia

Poppy

Rhododendron

Scarlet pimpernel*

Snowdrops

St.-John's-wort

Tansy*

Yellow jessamine

Wisteria

*These have proven toxic to animals, so I include them as a caution, although I am not sure of their toxicity to humans. I would suggest further research before including them in your cuisine!

Hollyhocks, calendula, and bachelor's-button blossoms are compatible in salads of tossed greens.

Scarlet pimpernel *(Anagallis arvensis)*

The blossom of Queen-Anne's-lace may also be toxic, although it has been used medicinally in the past and sometimes now appears in exotic recipes. Henry Art, author of A Garden of Wildflowers: 101 Native Species and How to Grow Them *(Pownal, VT: Garden Way Publishing, 1986), tells me that the roots of Queen-Anne's-lace are marginally edible, young ones being okay. He could find no evidence that the flower is toxic, but points out that the young plant looks a great deal like poison hemlock (Conium maculatum), which is quite toxic, so that great caution must be used when picking Queen-Anne's-lace for edible purposes. When I published this list in my newsletter, subscribers also wrote that their mothers and grand-mothers had eaten cowslip and milkweed greens, with no appar-ent ill effects. Nevertheless, until I see these plants documented on a safe edible flower list, I feel that readers should be cautioned about them. In my opinion, this is a case where it is most defi-nitely better to be safe, than sorry!*

❧ *Orange Calendula Drop Cookies* ❧
YIELD: 3 TO 4 DOZEN

6 to 8 fresh calendula blossoms
½ cup butter, room temperature
½ cup granulated sugar
Grated rind of 2 oranges
2 tablespoons orange juice concentrate, room temperature

1 teaspoon vanilla
2 eggs, lightly beaten
2 cups flour
2½ teaspoons baking powder
¼ teaspoon salt
1 cup almond halves

Preheat oven to 350°. Rinse calendula blossoms; pull off petals and set aside. Cream butter, sugar, and orange rind until fluffy. Add orange juice concentrate and vanilla. Stir in eggs until blended. Sift together flour, baking powder, and salt. Blend calendula petals and dry ingredients into creamed mixture. Drop dough by teaspoonfuls onto lightly greased cookie sheets. Press an almond half into each cookie. Bake 12 to 15 minutes until golden brown.

❧ *Special-Treasure Chinese Beef with Anise Hyssop* ❧
YIELD: SERVES 4 TO 6

Anise hyssop adds a subtle flavor that enhances all the other ingredients in this simple and delicious dish. Serve with fluffy, white rice.

1 pound flank steak, cut across the grain into 3" x ½" strips
½ cup chopped anise hyssop flowers and leaves
⅓ cup soy sauce
1 tablespoon brown sugar

2 tablespoons sherry
2 tablespoons vegetable oil
¼ cup chicken broth
2 teaspoons cornstarch dissolved in 2 teaspoons water

Combine flank steak with chopped anise hyssop, soy sauce, brown sugar, and sherry. Marinate several hours. Remove meat from marinade, reserving any remaining sauce. Heat wok or large skillet, add oil, and stir-fry meat quickly over medium-high heat until brown. Add chicken broth and remaining marinade, heat through. Blend in cornstarch mixture and cook, stirring until thickened.

❧ *Opal Basil Flowers with Eggplant* ❧

2 tablespoons opal basil flowers and leaves, thyme, rosemary, and oregano
1 tablespoon Italian parsley
1 garlic clove, chopped

Salt and pepper
1 pound eggplant
2 tablespoons olive oil

Preheat oven to 325° F. Mix herbs, garlic, salt and pepper. Cut the eggplant in half, make slits in the flesh, and stuff with the herb mixture. Season with more salt and pepper; brush with olive oil. Bake 25 minutes. Serve, sprinkled with fresh opal basil flowers.

RENEE SHEPHERD'S Garden Seed Catalog of European seeds is full of delightful and useful information, as well as luscious recipes to inspire us to plant the dozens of exotic and new vegetable, herb, and flower seeds that she offers. Her paperback cookbook Recipes from a Kitchen Garden contains flower and herb recipes, including eighteen for the scented basils alone. The catalog, book, and other edible flower recipes are available from Shepherd's Garden Publishing.

Anise hyssop (Agastache foeniculum)

RENEE SHEPHERD, SHEPHERD'S GARDEN SEEDS, FELTON, CA 95018

JAY AND PAMELA NORTH'S Guide to Cooking with Edible Flowers is published by Paradise Farms, the largest producer of fresh flowers for the market today. Their booklet is full of unique recipes and lovely photographs. It may be ordered directly from Paradise Farms (see Appendix for address); quantities are available at a discount.

The flavors of flowers range from fiery to sweet to herbal. In most cases, they are a milder form of their fragrance. Float edible blossoms on soup, toss them into salads, crystallize to decorate desserts, freeze in ice rings or cubes for punch or cold drinks, combine into stir-fried dishes or marinades, chop up and stir into cream cheese for tea sandwiches, or use as a garnish on dinner, salad, or dessert plates. PVS

FROM *GUIDE TO COOKING WITH EDIBLE FLOWERS*
JAY AND PAMELA NORTH, PARADISE FARMS, SUMMERLAND, CA 93067

Anise Hyssop Syrup

Great over fresh fruit or ice cream.

1 cup sugar
1 cup water

5 anise hyssop flowers, chopped

Combine all ingredients in a pan, and cook over medium heat until thickened, stirring while cooking. Simmer for a few more minutes. May be stored in jars in the refrigerator for future use.

Nasturtium Aspic
YIELD: 4 TO 6 SERVINGS

1 dozen nasturtium blossoms
6-ounce package lemon-flavored gelatin

1 cup finely shredded green cabbage

Rinse the nasturtium blossoms. Pinch off stems; set aside. Prepare the gelatin according to package directions, and cool in refrigerator until thick and syrupy. Rinse a 4-cup ring mold with cool water, and pour in the gelatin to a depth of ½ inch. Chill until firm. (Leave the remaining thickened gelatin out of the refrigerator.) Arrange the blossoms face down on this layer all around the ring. Pour in enough gelatin to cover, and chill until firm. Distribute the shredded cabbage evenly around the ring. Pour the remaining gelatin on top. Chill until firm. Unmold onto a platter and garnish with additional nasturtium blossoms and leaves.

Linda's Lemon Summer Salad

Eye-catching, floral salads are a specialty at Linda Morgan's herb-tasting buffets! This dressing is especially lovely with a salad of loose-leaf (both green- and red-tipped) and Romaine lettuces, spinach, salad burnet, lemon basil, lemon bergamot mint, French sorrel, endive, and whatever of the following are blooming: nasturtiums, chive blossoms, borage flowers, rose petals, heartsease, or calendula.

¼ cup fresh lemon juice
1 small clove garlic, crushed
1½ teaspoons grated lemon peel
1 teaspoon minced fresh thyme
1 teaspoon minced fresh lemon thyme
1½ teaspoons sugar (more, if lemon is very tart)

¾ cup oil (we use a blend of safflower, olive, and/or vegetable oils)
Freshly ground black pepper, to taste
½ teaspoon salt, or to taste
⅓ cup finely chopped parsley

LINDA BALTIMORE MORGAN, ANTIQUE ORCHID HERBARY, ABINGDON, VA 24210

Place in a salad jar all ingredients, except the parsley (its fresh color and taste will be better preserved if you wait until close to serving time to add it). Shake the mixture until it is opaque. Refrigerate and let set at least 2 hours to blend the flavors. About ½ hour before serving, add the parsley. Shake well before using.

❧ *Applemint Sorbet* ❧
YIELD: 4 SERVINGS

7 large sprigs applemint
6 tablespoons sugar
1 ¼ cups water

Juice of 1 large lemon
1 egg white
Mint sprigs for decoration

Wash mint, and carefully pat it dry. Place sugar and water in a large pan, and boil until all the sugar has been absorbed. Add the mint, cover the pan, and remove from heat. Let steep for 20 minutes. Taste. If you desire a stronger flavor, bring the liquid to a boil once more, cover, remove from heat, and let sit for another 10 minutes. Strain the liquid into a bowl, and add the lemon juice. Let the mixture cool. When cool, place in the freezer until semi-frozen (45 to 60 minutes). Beat the egg white in a separate bowl until the white is stiff. Gently fold it into the semi-frozen mixture, and return the sorbet to the freezer until it is frozen to a firm consistency (about 1 hour). To serve, spoon into four champagne glasses. Decorate each with a sprig of applemint.

LINDA BALTIMORE MORGAN, ANTIQUE ORCHID HERBARY, ABINGDON, VA 24210

EDIBLE FLOWERS AND HERB DECORATIONS ON CHEESE

by Theresa Neff

Edible flowers can be combined with herbs to make plain, dull cheese look spectacular. In this recipe, the flowers are held in place with an aspic glaze, and the whole creates a shimmering presentation. The cheese can be prepared up to 36 hours ahead of time with very little effort. You can decorate any flat cheese that has an edible rind, but it is best to choose a variety of shapes, colors, and textures, such as Cheddar, Jack, gourmandise, or Camembert. After you select your cheese, you can decide on your decorating material. Just about any edible flower or herb can be used — roses, pansies, violets, nasturtiums, sage, rosemary, thyme, lemon verbena, lemon balm, dill, chives, tarragon, parsley, or cilantro.

THERESA NEFF'S newsletter, Country Thyme Gazette, *is a bi-monthly publication specializing in herbal entertaining, cooking, and gardening, California-style.*

Edible flowers and herbs
Flat cheese with edible rind
2 cups dry white wine (or regular-strength chicken broth)
1 envelope unflavored gelatin

Lay the flowers and herbs flat on top of the cheese and experiment with different combinations until you have an arrangement that suits you. Rinse all the herbs and flowers with cool water, blot them dry, and set them aside until the aspic glaze is ready.
Combine the wine and gelatin in a medium-sized saucepan.

♥

Decorated cheese makes a wonderful presentation at herbal weddings. We serve it on an appetizer table covered with fresh-cut herbs. This cheese can also be served at parties, bridal showers, and other festive occasions.

♥

THERESA NEFF, COUNTRY THYME GAZETTE, EL SEGUNDO, CA 90245

♥ ♥ ♥ ♥ ♥ ♥ ♥ ♥ ♥

In 1980, when LANE ("MISSY") FURNEAUX led a one-woman campaign to inspire Dallas supermarkets to carry fresh herbs, her success was due, in part, to a booklet she wrote telling shoppers how to cook with fresh herbs. Much to Lane's surprise, the booklet was so popular that she had to keep reprinting it, and now she and her charming co-author, Lady-bug, have an expanded fifth edition, entitled Heavenly Herbs.... Enjoy Them! *The booklet can be obtained directly from Lane (see Appendix for address); wholesale rates are available. In the new version, the authors added information about Lane's special tussie mussies (she made these for Nancy Reagan, as well as for the Queen of England!), herbscaping techniques, and tips on growing and using herbs. Mrs. Furneaux is known for her "Mint Alley," which she maintained next to her*

Stir over medium heat until the gelatin is completely dissolved and the mixture is clear. Remove from the heat, and set the saucepan into a larger container filled with ice. Stir the mixture slowly so that bubbles are not created. Continue stirring occasionally until the mixture begins to thicken. (If it becomes too thick, you can reheat and repeat the process.)

Place the cheese in a shallow dish to catch the drippings from the glaze. Carefully spoon some of the aspic glaze onto the cheese and spread evenly. After approximately 3 minutes the glaze will become tacky to the touch. At that time, carefully arrange the decorations on top of the cheese. Refrigerate the shallow dish and cheese for 15 minutes. Remove from the refrigerator and spoon more glaze over the decorations. Return the cheese to the refrigerator until the coating is tacky. Two or three coats of glaze are sometimes necessary for thick decorations. If the aspic glaze becomes too thick during the decorating process, just reheat it and place it in the ice until it thickens again.

MISSY AND LADYBUG DO IT AGAIN!

❧ Pine-a-Mint Salad ❧

This is my favorite molded salad. Its colors are especially exciting when nasturtiums are blooming. But its minty and dilly taste is what makes it so popular.

20-ounce can crushed pineapple (including its juice)
4-ounce jar pimientos (including juice), finely chopped
½ cup dill pickles, finely chopped
10 leaves of spearmint or ginger mint, finely minced

3 ¼ tablespoons dill vinegar (or plain vinegar and minced dill)
¾ cup sugar
2 tablespoons plain gelatin
¾ cup cold water

In a large bowl, mix together the pineapple, pimientos, dill pickles, mint, vinegar, and sugar. Stir thoroughly, cover, and refrigerate at least 1 hour to blend the flavors. Dissolve the plain gelatin in the cold water. Melt it over hot water and stir it into the pineapple mixture. Pour into eight, individual molds or a 6-cup mold.

When this pretty salad is unmolded, your head will reel with ideas for garnishing. A wreath of salad burnet (for a merry heart) is pretty, especially when paired with nasturtiums or other edible blossoms. My favorite flower for a fruit salad like this is begonia. Variegated pineapple mint and peppermint-scented geranium leaves are also wonderful. I always serve this salad with a green-tinted mayonnaise to which I have added minced leaves of mint and dill, as well as some dill vinegar and pineapple juice. I call it "Rockingchair Mayonnaise," because I like to rest and rock in my favorite kitchen chair while I use scissors to mince the herbs into a cup.

The colors of this salad make it a great holiday dish, especially if you decorate it with dill foliage in imitation of little Christmas trees.

FROM *HEAVENLY HERBS...ENJOY THEM!*
LANE FURNEAUX, LADYBUG PRESS, DALLAS, TX 75225

property — with scissors nearby so joggers and passers-by would help themselves! In this chapter, are a few recipes from her charming 50-page, herbal cooking treasure.

Basils for All Seasons

WHAT A BOY, BASIL!

Marilyn Hampstead, who owns an herb plant mail-order business, became well-known through her "Oh Boy, Basil! Festivals." Her Basil Book *is thoroughly entertaining and informative from cover to cover. Did you know that there are 150 species of basil worldwide? Only about four species, however, generate the many varieties that are economically or historically important. In her book, Marilyn gives personality profiles for the fourteen or so varieties that are good to eat or fun to do things with; her profiles include descriptions, origins, propagation methods, and uses.*

Ocimum basilicum *is the basic basil. Marilyn describes it as voluptuous, robust, and stimulating, with a complex aroma that is at once pungent and sweet, clovelike and aniselike, with a hint of mint. I was surprised to learn that the* **French fine-leaf basil** *is the basil reputed to repel flies; it is so well-suited to pot culture that when treated as a tender perennial and pruned and repotted regularly, it will last for years.*

Lettuce-leaf basil *is especially nice to use as a salad green and a finger-food wrapper.* **Piccolo verde fino basil** *is reputed to be the authentic pesto basil; its sweetness is outstanding. The true, sweet, lemony flavor of* **lemon basil** *almost overshadows the typical basil taste; Marilyn suggests it be used for fish dishes or stir-fried with shelled, young peas in sweet butter. Because* **thrysiflora basil's** *sweetness is almost overpowering, it is used for floral bouquets as well as in cooking.* **Nano compatto vero basil** *is a trim and pert "knockout" in the garden.* **Camphor basil** *can be used in moth-repelling blends.* **Licorice basil** *is very nice in fruit salads and with poultry, as well as being lovely for potpourri.* **Cinnamon basil** *is a pleasant addition to desserts and to rhubarb.* **"Tulasi" holy basil** *can be used in fruit dishes, jellies, sweet yeast breads, and potpourris.* **Genovese basil**, *"a beautiful harlequin of sleek green and deep purple," is delightful in floral bouquets; it is excellent, as well, in tomato-based dishes, as*

a salad green, and in potpourri. This is only a small portion of what Marilyn tells about each type — and I've left one or two out. She sells all of these basils, plus four other varieties, from her mail-order brochure (see Appendix for address).

The Basil Book *includes numerous basil recipes, as well as whole menus of basil treats, planting and growing instructions, and delightful garden plans. I am enchanted with her Basic Medallion Knot Garden, which will "gleam like a jewel when set in the expanse of a lawn." Best of all, she shows how to plot out a circular knot garden and suggests three different plant combinations, two of basils, one of perennials. She suggests many ways of preserving basil, and ends with a chapter called "Basil Beyond the Palate: Things To Do with Basil When You're Not Eating."*

Here are a few samples from the book to whet your appetite, hungry or not. The first four recipes are part of a "Simple Breakfast Menu."

❧ *Linda's Quick Basil Beer Bread* ❧

3 cups self-rising flour
3 tablespoons granulated sugar
12 ounces warm beer
½ cup sweet basil, chopped

Mix all the ingredients together, and pour into a well-greased, 5" x 9" loaf pan. Place in an *unheated* oven. Set temperature to 350° F., and bake 50 minutes. Remove from pan, cool on a wire rack, and slice.

❧ *Hot Holy Basil Tea* ❧

Place 6 to 8 sprigs of holy basil and 4 to 6 cups of rapidly boiling water into a preheated teapot. Cover pot with a tea cozy, and let steep for 10 minutes. Serve (without cream, sugar, or lemon) in bone china teacups or mugs.

Cinnamon basil

❧ *Pesto Omelette* ❧
YIELD: SERVES 2 OR 3

6 large fresh eggs
Salt and pepper to taste
2 tablespoons water

2 tablespoons butter
2 tablespoons olive oil
¼ cup pesto sauce (see page 194)

Preheat a heavy, 8-inch frying pan or omelette pan over a high flame. Add the butter and oil, melt, and swirl to coat the surface of the pan. While the pan is heating, separate the eggs. Beat the egg whites to a soft-peak stage; beat the egg yolks until lemon colored. Add the salt, pepper, and water to the yolks, and blend. Quickly fold the egg whites into the yolk mixture. Pour the egg mixture into the hot pan. Let edges get firm. With a spatula, gently lift an edge and allow the unset eggs to drift underneath. When eggs are just firm, spread the pesto sauce (thinned with a bit of milk or cream, if necessary) in a thin strip over the eggs. Fold in the traditional manner, and serve hot.

❧ *Icy Cinnamon-Basil Fruit Compote* ❧
YIELD: SERVES 6
PREPARATION TIME: 30 MINUTES

1 cup cinnamon basil
6 sprigs sweet woodruff
3 sprigs spearmint
2 cups Simple Syrup
1 small cantaloupe
1 small honeydew

2 crisp, firm apples
15-ounce can kumquats or litchi nuts
1 quart blackberries
6 large, firm pears

In a small bowl, mix together the basil, sweet woodruff, spearmint, and Simple Syrup. Refrigerate for 24 to 48 hours. Remove the herbs. Peel and seed the cantaloupe, honeydew, and apples; cut them into bite-sized pieces. Drain kumquats or litchi nuts, reserving liquid; add reserved liquid to herbed Simple Syrup. Destem and clean blackberries. Combine prepared fruit with herbed syrup. Mix and refrigerate several hours to improve flavors. Remove the necks, seeds, and all but ½ inch of the flesh from the pears. Spoon the fruit mixture into the pear "cups." Garnish with cinnamon-basil flower spikes.

Simple Syrup

1 cup sugar
2 cups water
⅛ teaspoon salt (optional)

In a medium-sized saucepan, combine sugar, water, and salt. Stir over moderate heat until sugar is dissolved and mixture becomes syrupy. Chill.

❧ *Basil Butter* ❧

Try substituting lemon basil or other basils for French fine-leaf basil.

½ pound fresh, sweet cream butter
1 cup French fine-leaf basil, destemmed

Method 1. Melt butter in a heavy, 6-inch fry pan. Carefully pour off any clear fluid. Allow to cool. Quickly stir in the basil (which should be finely chopped if large-leafed basils are used). Place in a covered butter crock and refrigerate. Let stand at least overnight before using.

Method 2. Soften the butter to room temperature, and then cream it with a wooden spoon. Thoroughly blend in the basil. Form mixture into a log and, if desired, roll in additional destemmed basil. Wrap tightly in plastic wrap or foil, and refrigerate. Use on basil bread or buns, sauté blanched vegetables in it, or stir it into pan juices for flavor.

French fine-leaf basil

❧ *Artichoke and Crab with Lemon Basil Butter* ❧
YIELD: SERVES 3

3 large, fresh whole artichokes
⅔ pound fresh crab or lobster meat

¼ pound lemon-basil butter
1 clove garlic, minced

Trim the artichokes, and cook them in rapidly boiling water until tender. Place them upside down in a colander and drain well. Remove the thistle choke and discard. Boil the crab or lobster meat until just cooked. Place the butter and garlic in a small saucepan and warm over low heat; keep hot.

To assemble, gently open the artichoke leaves and fill the cavity with the cooked seafood. Pour one-third of the hot butter over each artichoke. Nice with a very crisp, light red wine.

FROM *THE BASIL BOOK*
MARILYN HAMPSTEAD, FOX HILL
FARM, PARMA, MI 49269-0007

❧ *Opal Basil Cheddar Crisps* ❧
YIELD: 40 SNACKS

We haven't met anyone yet who didn't enjoy snacking on these. They make good appetizers, too!

8 ounces medium-sharp cheddar
   cheese, grated
½ cup butter, room temperature
½ teaspoon Tabasco sauce
1 teaspoon prepared mustard

1 cup flour
2 tablespoons chopped purple opal
   basil
1½ cups crisp rice cereal

Preheat oven to 350°. In a large bowl mix the cheese, butter, Tabasco sauce, and mustard. Blend in the flour and basil. When combined, stir in the cereal, and blend well. Shape into small balls. Place on a greased baking sheet and flatten with the bottom of a lightly floured glass. Bake in the preheated oven for 15 minutes. Serve hot. The crisps may be stored for several days in an airtight container or frozen. Reheat for 5 minutes as needed.

Purple opal basil

RENEE SHEPHERD, SHEPHERD'S
GARDEN SEEDS, FELTON, CA 95018

❦ *Pasta Nola* ❦

YIELD: SERVES 8

¼ cup olive oil
1 pound onions, julienned
3 pounds tomatoes, peeled, seeded, and diced
1½ pounds prosciutto, julienned
8 large garlic cloves, crushed
3 cups heavy cream
4 tablespoons chopped fresh oregano
4 tablespoons chopped fresh basil
3½ pounds fresh egg fettuccine
Whole basil leaves, for garnish
Freshly ground pepper

In a skillet, heat the oil and sauté the onions and tomatoes until the onion is soft and translucent. Add the prosciutto and garlic, and sauté lightly for 2 to 3 minutes. Add the cream and the chopped herbs. Simmer for 30 minutes. Cook the fettuccine in salted boiling water, until *al dente*. Drain the pasta and place it in a warm serving bowl. Pour the sauce over the hot pasta and serve, garnished with whole basil leaves and lots of freshly ground pepper.

CREATED BY CHEF ROCKY PARCHARD AT THE SANTACAFÉ IN SANTA FE, NM. FROM *HERBS* BY EMELIE TOLLEY (NY: CLARKSON N. POTTER, INC.,1985)

Lemon basil

❦ *Aunt Lane's Mustard* ❦

This is a sweet-and-hot, "does-everything" recipe, loaded with sweet basil and hot mint! Mix it with mayonnaise for stuffed eggs, potato salad, and some pasta salads. Try a dash with hot vegetables, especially green beans and broccoli. It is excellent in dips or as is with a sliver of mild cheese or cold meat on toast or crackers.

3 tablespoons cornstarch
1 teaspoon salt
7 tablespoons sugar
⅔ cup mint vinegar
¾ cup water
½ cup dry mustard

⅛ teaspoon turmeric
2 tablespoons butter
1 tablespoon finely minced ginger mint
1 tablespoon minced sweet basil

Blend together the cornstarch, salt, sugar, vinegar, and ½ cup of the water. Combine the mustard and remaining ¼ cup water into a smooth mixture, and stir it into the vinegar mixture. Add the turmeric and butter. Stir in the mint and basil.

FROM *HEAVENLY HERBS*, LANE FURNEAUX, LADYBUG PRESS, DALLAS, TX 75225

❦ *Scented Basil Jellies* ❦

YIELD: FOUR 8-OUNCE JARS

These delicate jellies are unusual, delicious, and easily made. Their clear, jewel-like colors of rose pink, deep garnet, and champagne are quite beautiful. You'll find they are delicious with cream cheese and crackers or bagels, and they make wonderful presents for others — and yourself!

1½ cups packed, fresh anise, cinnamon, opal, or lemon basil (choose one)
2 cups water

2 tablespoons rice vinegar
Pinch of salt
3½ cups sugar
3 ounces liquid pectin

Wash the basil, and dry it in paper towels. Finely chop the basil or process it in a food processor. Put it in a large saucepan, and crush the chopped leaves, using the bottom of a glass. Add the water, bring slowly to a boil, and boil for 10 seconds. Remove the saucepan from the heat; cover and steep for 15 minutes. Strain 1½ cups of liquid from the saucepan, and pour through a fine strainer into another saucepan. Add the vinegar, salt, and sugar, and bring to a hard boil, stirring. When the boil can't be stirred down, add the pectin. Again return to a hard boil that can't be stirred down, and boil for exactly 1 minute. Remove saucepan from heat. Skim off the foam. Pour the hot jelly into hot, sterilized, 8-ounce jelly jars. Leave ½-inch headspace, and seal at once with sterilized two-piece lids or melted paraffin.

FROM *RECIPES FROM A KITCHEN GARDEN*
RENEE SHEPHERD, SHEPHERD'S GARDEN SEEDS, FELTON, CA 95018

❧ *Spicy Basil Potpourri with Scented Geraniums, Patchouli, and Clevelandii Sage* ❧

1 quart licorice basil leaves
1 quart sweet basil leaves
1 quart French fine-leaf basil leaves
2 cups apple geranium leaves
2 cups old spice or nutmeg geranium leaves
2 cups patchouli leaves
1 cup thyme
1 cup lemon eucalyptus leaves or lemon verbena
1 cup Clevelandii sage leaves
3 ounces vetiver

Make sure all plant material is dry. Carefully mix all dried leaves, tossing gently. Slowly sprinkle on vetiver. Toss again. Place in an airtight container, and store for a couple of months, stirring occasionally.

FROM *THE BASIL BOOK* (NEW YORK: LONG SHADOW BOOKS, 1984)
MARILYN HAMPSTEAD, FOX HILL FARM, PARMA, MI 49269-0007

❧ *Sweet Basils with Roses, Lavender, and Orrisroot: A Potpourri* ❧

1 quart sweet basil leaves and flowering spikes
2 cups each of dark opal basil leaves, dark opal basil flowering spikes, thrysiflora flowering spikes, rose petals, rosebuds, and attar-of-roses geranium leaves
1 cup lavender blossoms
1 ounce each of orrisroot and sweet flag powder

Creating Pestos

PESTO SAUCES AND RECIPES FROM HERBAL ACRES

Here are some new pesto variations from my kitchen, which I developed while experimenting with herbal vinegars. I had learned from Marilyn Hampstead's Basil Book *to add vinegar, as well as oil, to the finished pesto to form an airtight seal before capping and freezing it. I liked the flavor of the thawed pesto after I had mixed in the oil and vinegar seal, so I began adding vinegar to my pesto blends, as well as on top of them.*

Two of the following recipes
utilize herb vinegars, which we think add a new taste sensation and a special zip! (The third pesto, which contains ricotta cheese, does not have vinegar in the recipe, as I think it might curdle the cheese.)

We were also delighted to discover that those pestos that contained vinegar did not turn dark after exposure to air. I assume that the preservative quality of vinegar had something to do with that. Here are the pesto recipes, as well as ways to use them.

SOME REMINDERS FOR PESTO-MAKERS

❤ *Herbs for pesto must be clean and dry (see page 163).*

❤ *The containers for storing pesto must be sterile and dry.*

❤ *All air bubbles must be eliminated from the pesto before the oil and vinegar "seal" are added. (For my recipes that include vinegar, use a wooden or porcelain spoon or spoon handle to accomplish this.)*

❧ *Phyl's Pesto Sauce for Any Pasta* ❧

To make machine processing easier, slice one handful of basil leaves at a time, placing the stems crosswise on a bread board, before putting them in the blender. This pesto can be used with any pasta, but we prefer crinkly rotini or rotelle, as it absorbs the sauce readily and evenly.

3 tablespoons olive oil and 3 tablespoons melted butter or 6 tablespoons olive oil
3 tablespoons herb vinegar (lemon-herb, basil, or garlic)
3 tablespoons pine nuts, blanched almonds, or walnuts
2 large cloves garlic, sliced
½ teaspoon salt
¼ teaspoon freshly ground pepper

¼ teaspoon cayenne powder
1½ cups fresh basil leaves
½ cup fresh oregano leaves
¼ cup garlic chives, in 1-inch pieces
1 cup grated Parmesan cheese or ½ cup Parmesan and ½ cup Romano cheeses
1 pound pasta, cooked and drained

If you are using butter, melt it in the oven or microwave. Let it cool a bit while assembling other ingredients.

Place in the blender, in this order, the oil, herb vinegar, nuts, garlic, salt and pepper, and cayenne. Add the herbs and then, if you are using it, the melted butter. Blend all together until smooth and creamy, wiping down the sides of the blender at least once with a rubber spatula.

Pour mixture into a 3-cup bowl, and stir in the cheese(s). Drain the pasta, and immediately stir the pesto into it while it is still hot.

Note: It may be blasphemous, but we prefer to mellow the pesto taste with butter. By adding it to the pesto, I eliminate the step of adding it separately to the hot pasta. I do not add butter to the batches I will be freezing. PVS

❤

TO FREEZE PESTO

Pack pesto firmly down into sterilized jars, getting rid of any air bubbles by drawing a wooden or porcelain spoon handle through it. Drizzle enough olive oil on top to cover and seal it. Add 1 teaspoon of herb vinegar to the oil. Screw on the lid. (If the lid is metallic, cover the jar top with plastic wrap before screwing on the lid.) Label and date the jar, and freeze. Use within 3 to 10 months.

FROM THE BASIL BOOK MARILYN HAMPSTEAD, FOX HILL FARM, PARMA, MI 49269-0007

❤

❧ *Lemon-Herb Pesto Sauce* ❧

With basting instructions for fish or chicken.

3 tablespoons oil (safflower or olive)
3 tablespoons Lemon-Herb Vinegar (page 165)
2 large or 4 small cloves garlic, sliced in pieces
1 cup clean, dry lemon basil leaves

¼ cup lemon thyme leaves
½ teaspoon freshly ground pepper
1 cup grated Parmesan cheese
2 pounds fish fillets or chicken pieces

Place the oil, vinegar, garlic, basil, thyme, and pepper into a blender, in the order they are listed. Blend until thoroughly smooth, wiping down sides of blender at least once during the process. Pour into a small (3-cup) bowl, and stir in the cheese. Brush a portion of the pesto sauce on top of the fish and place on a greased baking sheet. Broil 4 inches from heat for 3 minutes. Turn fillets over, brush remaining pesto on top, and broil for another 3 minutes, or until tender. If using chicken, place in a baking pan, and bake at 350° F. for 20 minutes on each side, or until tender, topping each side with pesto, as above.

❧ *Ricotta Pesto* ❧

I created this originally for stuffing pasta shells (see Pesto-Stuffed Shells, below) but discovered that it is excellent in any recipes calling for pesto. This pale green sauce is especially attractive and tasty, and freezes well.

8 ounces ricotta cheese
1 cup sweet basil leaves
½ cup grated Parmesan cheese
⅓ cup chopped scallions

⅓ cup walnuts, blanched almonds, or pine nuts
¼ cup virgin olive oil
2 large or 4 small cloves garlic

Place all ingredients together in a blender, and run on "Liquefy." Stop two or three times to scrape down the sides of the blender.

❧ *Pesto-Stuffed Shells* ❧

YIELD: 6 TO 8 SERVINGS

When I cook, it's always double-duty — enough for at least two meals. I serve these stuffed shells plain one night, and then dress them up with the sautéed Vegetable Sauce two nights later!

12-ounce box jumbo shells (38 to 40 shells)
3 cups Ricotta Pesto Sauce or Ricotta Pesto Dip

Olive oil
1 cup grated Parmesan or Romano cheese

Cook the pasta shells according to directions on box. Drain, return to pot, and drizzle with olive oil, stirring to coat the shells and keep them from sticking together. When shells are cool, fill them with the pesto or pesto dip. Sprinkle the cheese over the stuffed shells. Place upright in two oiled baking pans, cover with aluminum foil, and bake at 350° F. for 20 minutes, or until cheese is bubbly.

❧ *Pesto, Pasta, and Tomato Salad* ❧

YIELD: 6 TO 8 SERVINGS AS A MAIN DISH; 8 TO 10 AS A SIDE DISH

This refreshing dish is very different, and is equally good served hot or cold. The pesto ingredients may be mixed and frozen for later use with tomatoes and orzo.

1 cup sweet basil leaves
1 cup lemon basil leaves
½ cup light olive oil
½ cup balsamic vinegar
4 large cloves garlic

Salt and freshly ground pepper, to taste
8 large fresh tomatoes, skinned and quartered
1 pound orzo (rice-like) pasta

Chop up and blend the basils, oil, vinegar, garlic, and salt and pepper in a food processor. Add the tomatoes, and chop coarsely. Chill, covered, in refrigerator. Cook the pasta according to box instructions. Drain. While still hot, gently toss with the chilled, pestoed tomatoes. Serve warm or chilled.

❧ *Ricotta Pesto Dip* ❧

1 cup Ricotta Pesto
6 ounces cream cheese, softened
½ to 1 cup ricotta cheese

In a mixer, blender, or food processor, blend all ingredients until the desired consistency is reached. The amount of ricotta you add is determined by whether you are using the mixture as a dip or a stuffing. One-half cup is adequate for dishes to be heated; 1 cup is good for a dip for raw veggies or crackers.

Vegetable Sauce

Sauté in olive oil or butter, in any available amounts, sliced onions, sweet peppers, tomatoes, mushrooms, and zucchini until the peppers and zucchini are tender-crisp, about 10 minutes. Season with salt and pepper, if desired. Add this to stuffed shells after they are thoroughly heated.

❤

When making pesto in a food processor, add the cheese to the other ingredients once they are blended, and mix together in the processor.

❤

FROM PESTOS TO PASTES AND BACK AGAIN!

Preserving the flavor of basil in pesto has evolved naturally into making pastes of other herbs to get a fresh herb taste in winter recipes. Highly concentrated and using a minimum of oil, herb pastes are now considered to be the best way to preserve the fresh herb flavor. I first learned of this method from Marilyn Hampstead's booklet "Preserving the Herbal Harvest" (1980). In her Basil Book, *Marilyn tells how to make basil paste for making out-of-season pesto (recipes follow). So we have come full circle — from pestos we learned to make pastes in order to make pestos! Other pioneers in the development of this method of preservation include Madelene Hill and her daughter, Gwen Barclay, who tell of their findings about herbal pastes, after many years of refining their methods and recipes, in* Southern Herb Growing *(Fredericksburg, TX: Shearer Publishing, 1987).*

❧ Lemon Balm Pesto ❧

Chop and blend together 2 cups fresh lemon balm, ½ cup olive oil and 3 or 4 cloves garlic. Use as a baste for broiled or grilled fish.

❧ Spearmint Pesto ❧

Chop and blend together 2 cups fresh spearmint, ½ cup safflower or olive oil, and 3 or 4 cloves garlic. Use as a baste for broiled or grilled lamb chops, or serve with lamb patties.

GENERAL RULE FOR MAKING HERB PASTE

Start with clean, dry herbs and sterile, wide-mouthed jars of several sizes. (Being a new grandmother, I use baby-food jars, especially the junior size, and recycled jars from peanut butter, processed cheese, artichokes, pickles, and so on.) Use approximately the same proportions of oil and herbs called for in pesto recipes (⅓ cup oil to 2 cups herbs). Place oil and herbs in a blender, and chop until you have a smooth paste, scraping down the sides of the blender as needed, until all the bits of herbs are coated with oil. Use as little of the oil as necessary to accomplish this. (If you chop the herbs by hand first, the process will be hastened.) The oil is a carrier only and will not add an oil flavor to the herbs, especially if you use a bland type, like corn, safflower, or sunflower, rather than olive oil. Place the mixture immediately into jars, remove air bubbles, seal with oil and vinegar (as in pesto instructions, page 194), cap, label, and date. Refrigerate (for use within a week), or freeze (for several months). Always keep mixture refrigerated or frozen.

Suggested Herbs for Herb Pastes

basil

chervil

cilantro

dill

fennel

coriander

marjoram

mints

parsley

rosemary

sage

savory

tarragon

HOW TO USE HERB PASTES

Always start with small amounts, as these are highly concentrated. They can be floated in hot soup; added to dressings for salads; added to sauces, gravies, and marinades; used as a baste for meat and fish; used to flavor hot vegetables, to sauté meats or vegetables, or to make wintertime, fresh-tasting pestos!

❧ *Basil Paste in Oil* ❧

Work fast when making herb pastes and do them in small batches to avoid basil burn — the darkening that occurs during oxidation when the volatile essential oils are released.

5 cups of any variety of basil leaves, soft stems, and flowers
½ cup or so of your favorite salad oil
1 teaspoon distilled vinegar or basil vinegar

Use your preferred grinding apparatus (mortar and pestle, food processor, blender, or a very sharp knife and cutting board), and reduce 2 cups of the basil to a coarse chop. Add another 2 cups of basil, and reduce to a medium chop. Add the final cup of basil and reduce to a medium chop. Slowly drizzle in oil until all cut leaf surfaces are lightly coated with oil. Pack the basil paste firmly into small (10-ounce), wide-mouthed, tight-sealing jars, filling jars to within 1½ inches of the rim. Draw a knife through the mixture to remove, carefully and thoroughly, all the air bubbles. Float one inch of oil and 1 teaspoon of vinegar on top of the paste, to form an airtight seal. Refrigerate immediately, or label, date, and freeze.

FROM *THE BASIL BOOK* (NEW YORK: LONG SHADOW BOOKS, 1984)
MARILYN HAMPSTEAD, FOX HILL FARM, PARMA, MI 49269-0007

❧ *Out-of-Season Pesto* ❧
YIELD: SERVES 4 TO 6

3 tablespoons pine nuts, walnuts, or sunflower seeds
2 cloves garlic, peeled
½ cup Basil Paste
½ to ¾ cup grated Parmesan, Sardo, Asiago, or Romano cheeses
Pinch of salt
½ to ¾ cup olive or salad oil
1 pound vermicelli, trennette, or linguini

In a food processor or blender, grind the nuts. Add garlic, and grind again. Add basil paste and process very briefly. Add cheese and salt. With processor running, slowly incorporate oil until the sauce is of your favorite consistency. Cook pasta until just tender. Toss the pesto sauce with the hot pasta.

Other Late Summer Recipes

❧ *Poached Salmon* ❧

Whether served hot or cold, poached salmon is my favorite food from the sea.

3 cups water (or more, if needed, to cover the fish)
1 cup white wine
6 dill sprigs
3 parsley sprigs
Leaves from 2 ribs of celery
3 spears of onion chives
6 peppercorns
Salmon steaks

In a large, shallow pan, bring to a boil all of the above ingredients, except the salmon. Place the salmon steaks in the pan; liquid should cover. Barely simmer for 20 minutes. Cool, and then chill salmon in the liquid. To serve, drain and accompany with heavily dilled mayonnaise.

FROM *HEAVENLY HERBS...ENJOY THEM!*
LANE FURNEAUX, LADYBUG PRESS, DALLAS, TX 75225

❧ *Joy's Iced Mint Tea* ❧

In 10 cups boiling water, steep the following for about 15 minutes: 5 sprigs spearmint, 3 sprigs red-stem applemint, 2 sprigs red bee-balm flowers, and 1 sprig peppermint. Use ice cubes made of lemon balm tea, which improve the flavor of the mint tea as they melt!

FROM *HEAVENLY HERBS...ENJOY THEM!*
LANE FURNEAUX, LADYBUG PRESS, DALLAS, TX 75225

❧ *Minted Beets with Apricots* ❧

Steam young beets until barely tender. Skin and slice (or, if beets are tiny, leave whole). Place in a casserole, and dot with apricot jam. Cover with a blanket of mint sprigs. Dot with butter. Pour frozen lemonade concentrate over all. Cover casserole tightly. Cook in a moderate oven (325° F.) until tender (about 20 minutes). Remove cooked herb before serving, and garnish with a light sprinkling of minced, fresh mint leaves (try curly spearmint or orange bergamot mint).

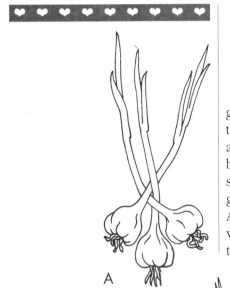

A

B   C

BRAIDING GARLIC

by Donna Metcalfe

Braiding garlic is easy — plus it's the perfect way to preserve garlic and ensure that it gets proper air circulation. It is important to use garlic fresh from the garden, so that the leaves are attached and pliable. Rinse the plants off, and choose the fullest heads for a better-looking braid. Take three large heads and arrange them as shown at A. Braid the leaves together once or twice, close to the garlic heads; braid tightly so that the leaves don't show in between. Add a fourth head of garlic above the center one; include its leaves with any one of the others and braid a little more (B). Next, add two more heads, this time to the side. Include their leaves with the others and keep braiding (C). Add one, then two, then one again until the braid is as long as you want — or until you run out of garlic. For the best appearance, keep the heads close together. (When I am doing this for myself, however, I braid loosely, to make it easier to break off the garlic heads as I use them; I don't care how it looks.) To finish, braid the remaining leaves together, tie with twine, and trim the ends. Hang to dry.

DONNA METCALFE, GOOD SCENTS, RIALTO, CA 92376

SEPTEMBER

THIS IS THE TIME OF YEAR to begin creating lovely fragrant blends from the dried flowers and herbs of summer's harvest to use as gifts or to sell at fall bazaars or in shops. A great deal has happened to potpourri in the past 5 years. Large fragrance firms have very successfully cornered the market with bags of dyed, scented wood chips or shavings in every conceivable color and aroma, which they call potpourri. This has caused a furor in the herb world and great consternation to the traditionalists among us. In the pages ahead, you will see how several experts in the field feel about it, as well as my own reactions and suggestions for coping with this new form of fragrance or adapting to it in authentic, traditional ways.

In recent years, there has been an increasing awareness of the sensitivity to orrisroot that allergy-prone individuals may experience. Most large cosmetic firms have long since stopped using orrisroot in dry shampoos,

powders, perfumes, and other potions, but the cautions have just recently begun to filter down to small businesses and individual crafters. Although I have researched this in the computer data banks of hospital libraries, I have found no recent studies to verify what percentage of the population is affected, or how seriously. With increasing numbers of people making or using potpourri in the past decade, however, the number of complaints from afflicted people at potpourri workshops and in herbal publications has escalated. This has important implications for those who make potpourri to give to others or to sell. Many have started using alternative fixatives and are offering customers a choice of potpourris made with or without orrisroot. Responsible crafters are listing the ingredients of their potpourris on the packaging, so that alert customers can be selective. You will thus find many potpourri recipes in this book that do not call for orrisroot.

Apparently, allergy-prone people can experience swollen eyes, an itchy nose, and other discomforts from exposure to orris, especially the powdered form. None of my family members is bothered by it, so I will continue to use it in potpourris just for our use. If I were still selling potpourri, however, I would not use orrisroot without putting a warning on the label to caution those with allergies. You will find herein excellent alternative methods to using orrisroot to make long-lasting fragrances, such as blending liquid or crystal fixatives with your oils to give them more "body," strengthening synthetic oils (so much in use now), and using more oils, fixatives, and spices than called for in older recipes.

One of the most startling developments since 1987 is the use of ground-up corn cobs as a fixative! Called by any number of brand names, this is usually described as natural cellulose fiber, *and is heralded as the new replacement for orrisroot. It is much cheaper, is lightweight, and seems to be free of any substances that could cause allergic reactions. As far as I'm concerned, however, the jury is still out regarding the ability of this to replace orrisroot's excellent quality of making a* long-lasting *fragrance. Most of my early potpourris, made with orris 30 years ago, and unchanged in any way since then, are still fragrant. It will be interesting to see, many years from now, how well the cellulose fixative really works to* maintain the scent of potpourris. In my own experiments with cellulose *fiber granules, I found it necessary to use nearly twice the amounts of the fixative and oil to achieve and maintain the desired aroma over a several-month period. To test the effectiveness of fixatives yourself, use equal amounts of the same oil on equal amounts of different fixatives in separate jars. Cover and shake occasionally, comparing the strengths of the aromas at weekly intervals over several months. Equal amounts of the same botanicals could be added to each jar in the beginning, if desired. Similarly, one can test the quality of oils by using the same amounts of different oils on equal portions of one fixative in separate jars.*

Another exciting inroad of potpourri-making is the development of crystals that can be colored and scented with oils for potpourri fixation and/or for simmering blends. This is so newly available to everyone, that I haven't had time to try it. See the Appendix for more information.

Now a household word, "simmering" potpourri is sold in just about every kind of store and in every fragrance. A large number of herb businesses are using scented crystals alone for simmer pots, and many crafters are making botanical blends that can be used both as a dry fragrance and as a simmering potpourri. In general, a botanical simmering potpourri will consist of less expensive ingredients than those used for a long-lasting dry fragrance. Powdered forms of spices and fixatives are not *used for simmering, as they would float to the top. Instead, whole sections of fragrant woods, barks, roots, twigs, gums, spices, citrus peel, and dried fruits, such as apples, are likely to be found in blends meant to be soaked in water. Oils or synthetic fragrances are often included, but usually one does not use the most expensive oils, fixatives, flowers, or spices for these potpourris, at least in large amounts, since the ingredients will soon be used and discarded. Flowers are often added for color.*

My own Citruswood Potpourri (page 218) is a very colorful blend of natural fragrant woods and wood shavings. It shows how you can use new products and alternatives to orrisroot, add ingredients from your garden to make a long-lasting blend that is suitable for both dry and wet (simmering) use, and, if you are making potpourri to sell, be flexible with potpourri recipes in order to be competitive in the marketplace. In addition, this potpourri can be utilized outdoors as an insect deterrent!

I hope that you enjoy reading more about these recent changes in the art of fragrance blending from several experts in the field, and that you will feel inspired and challenged, accordingly, to create your own new aromatic blends. I am proud to include at the end of this chapter one of the most popular and most original herbal ideas in the 11-year history of my newsletter — an herbal church service!

New Developments in Potpourri-Making

AROMATIC WOOD SHAVINGS — A CONTROVERSIAL POTPOURRI

Wishing to improve the fragrance in a new shop, an interior designer experimented with soaking the available wood shavings from the carpentry work in essential oils — and the rest is history. In 1986, wood chips turned into gold for some very enterprising folks! But, is it really potpourri? Undoubtedly, these aromatics are behind a report in Newsweek *(January 11, 1987) that the sales of potpourri were expected to reach $100 million in 1988 — double the 1986 total! And, "simmering" potpourri alone was already a multimillion-dollar business.*

I first discovered this product in an exotic shop in Cape May, New Jersey, where the essence of the colorful cellophane-bagged wood-shaving fragrances permeated the entire two-room boutique. The aura was so enticing that it was difficult to limit my purchases to my available cash. I was enchanted, as I react strongly to fragrances and colors. I guess I'm one of those housewives targeted by the marketers of this product. I chose a Holiday Spice fragrance, gaudy bright red, but, when placed in bowls around the house, a startling success during the Christmas season. For several days, a whiff of the scent was noticeable when passing by a bowl of it. After that, guests had to hold it up to their noses for the fragrance — which

everyone did, because they were curious. If nothing else, it was a colorful and sensual conversation piece. By the next holiday season, after a year of closed storage, the aroma was nearly gone. I added my favorite Christmas oils to it, however, and restored it for further enjoyment. It contained brilliant red wood shavings, bay leaves, tiny pine cones, rosemary, cloves, hibiscus, small berries, twigs, and cranberries, plus a bayberry aroma. I would have to say that this most certainly was a potpourri, lacking only a large amount of flowers and a visible fixative. It was most certainly a fragrant blend of herbs, spices, woods, berries, and oils.

Later, I was drawn to another mixture of this type because it smelled like my favorite perfume, and the faded, teal-blue wood shavings matched some of my living room slipcovers. More delicately scented, this one came from England and contained many more flowers and herbs than the other, such as rosebuds, glove amaranth, small pine cones, lemongrass, pearly everlasting, and uva-ursi leaves. To me, these new versions of potpourri are more like decorating accessories, and I do love to blend in natural products with the color schemes in my home, for the visual as well as aromatic effect. So, the chips are

dyed — they match my living room!

In all fairness to the staunch traditionalists among us, many of these new-fangled concoctions are 98 percent oil-soaked wood pieces. They should not be called potpourri, which, according to the Oxford American Dictionary *is "a scented blend of dried petals and spices." There is no doubt that this novelty line is very competitive with the potpourri that we know and love, and it has certainly hurt the sales of traditional potpourri in the marketplace. In many cases, the public is paying $8.00 or more for a package, which, except for the oil, is little more than wood shavings! I feel that one of the best ways for herb businesses to deal with this problem is for them, and other interested individuals, to make a concerted effort to educate the public about the main differences between authentic potpourri and the new "pretender," those differences being, for the most part, the lack of fixatives for a lasting fragrance and the disproportionate amount of (sometimes gaudy) wood bulk, compared to the natural essences of flowers, herbs, and spices. In labeling, lectures, publicity, and writings, professionals can try to capitalize on the weaknesses of the new product in comparison to the strengths of traditional potpourri. And, whether we are* *making potpourri for ourselves, for gifts, or for profit, we could also take advantage of the new trend and incorporate some of its charm into our own blends. Why not add more herbal woods, pre-soaked in oil, to our potpourris? Such potpourris would be more naturally redolent, because they would contain such materials as cedarwood, sandalwood, and the woody twigs of lavender, thyme, southernwood, or rosemary. And, why not color-coordinate our potpourris to be used for interior decorating? By using brighter flowers in larger proportions, and by making a variety of*

colorful blends, traditional potpourri can be promoted for interior decorating, too. Most important, herb businesses can now announce to the world that they offer "Authentic" or "Old-Fashioned" or "Traditional" Long-Lasting Potpourri! Or, they could emphasize Victorian or Colonial potpourris.

I know that I am probably putting myself out on a limb with my ambivalent feelings about this. In a sense, it is because I think that we all benefit from the larger fragrance industry's heavy promotion of the delights of using potpourris in the home to create an aura or

a look. Even if we don't like the mass-produced products from big business and their cheap imitations of potpourris, big business is enticing the general public to buy fragrances for home use. What we now have to do is to expose the public to quality essences, to the real and natural fragrances. My apologies to you traditionalists for my propensity for the visual and sensual stimulation that is created by vivid color and scent. You will undoubtedly be more pleased to read what others have to say on the subject in the pages to come!

ROSELLA MATHIEU has become a dear friend over the years, especially since we collaborated on a presentation for the fragrance panel at the International Herb Growers and Marketers Association conference in Indianapolis. At that time, I became more familiar with her expertise on quality oils and potpourri, and had the privilege of seeing her workrooms and enjoying the hospitality of the Mathieus. Her high-quality oils have long been a favorite of mine; we used her Magic Garden oil as the base of Kim's wedding potpourri of herbs and flowers from our gardens. Rosella is a pioneer among us, as she established her Fragrant Herb Farm and was selling herb blends and fragrances in the 1940s! I value her expertise.

AN ALTERNATIVE TO ORRISROOT: ADVICE FOR HERB BUSINESSES

by Rosella F. Mathieu

"Fixation is *the* question of importance in the manufacture of perfumes," according to W.A. Poucher, a foremost authority in the field of perfume and cosmetics. This is just as true of the fragrance used in the making of potpourri, for if your potpourri lasts only a short time after your customer buys it, you are not building good will.

From the earliest times of potpourri-making, orrisroot has been a favorite fixative. It has been found, however, that persons who are allergic to orrisroot have unpleasant reactions to it. I am one of these, and when someone sends me a potpourri or sachet made with orris, I can't wait to get it out of the house. Although many people experience discomfort without realizing that they have an allergy, persons who are aware of the source of their discomfort tell me they are so glad I don't use orrisroot in my recipes. Orris oil, which is distilled from the root of the plant, was commonly used to scent dry shampoo, sachets, toothpaste, dusting powder, and many other cosmetics for years, but because of many allergic reactions ("including infantile eczema, hay fever, stuffy nose, red eyes, and asthma" — from Ruth Winter, *A Consumer's Dictionary of Cosmetic Ingredients*), it has been discontinued in this country.

So, what do I use instead of orrisroot? Here are some of many alternatives that will give lasting performance:

Method 1. The fragrance oils may be placed directly on barks like cinnamon chips, leaves such as deer's-tongue (cut and sifted), and gums like frankincense, which will absorb the oils and serve as fixatives.

Method 2. Oils of selected resins or gums, and liquid or crystal synthetics may be added to the fragrance oils *directly*, to fix, blend, or modify a weak oil into one that is more lasting. Often the scent itself is improved. This is the method used by perfume chemists.

Method 3. I use method 2, but in line with method 1, I make what I call a *high concentrate*, which is merely a mixture of ground spices like cinnamon and cloves, with a high percentage of finished oils added to it, which *already* contain a number of fixatives. I place the high concentrate on the bottom of a clear glass container, so that the petals and herbs will not be clouded by the spices. Scent is volatile and travels, and in a short time the aroma will permeate the whole potpourri. I make potpourri that will go into a clear cellophane bag in the same way, placing the spice mixture on the bottom of the bag and then adding other ingredients. In an opaque container, I simply combine the spice/oil mixture with the other ingredients.

If you have had no experience with adding liquid or crystal fixatives to fragrance oils to provide more body and permanence of scent, start with ½ ounce of the fragrance oil, placed in a screw-top bottle. Proceed very slowly, adding only a few drops of the fixative at a time and being sure to shake well after each addition. Take notes, or you will never remember what you did — this *is* a trial-and-error method because of the different odors and strengths of the original fragrances with which you are working. If you are using a crystal like heliotropin, use just a tiny bit on the tip of a spoon. Shake well, let it rest for a day or two, and then test again. Keep adding oils or aromatics until there is a perceptible difference and the oil has developed a body.

True civet, ambergris, and musk oils are not available except to the creators of the most expensive perfumes — those who can spend many thousands of dollars for a supply. Many synthetics, however, use some of the following ingredients, as well as others. Heliotropin crystals, which are used to flavor vanilla ice cream, are one of my favorite fixatives. They are light and sweet, and go with almost any scent to make it more long-lasting. Musk xylol crystals are a lighter musk than musk oil. Vanillin is a very good vanilla substitute and useful in perfumery. When I add heliotropin, artificial musk, or vanillin crystals to an oil, I begin by placing the bottle in warm water; most of the crystals are dissolved within an hour, after being shaken occasionally during that time. If the crystals are not completely dissolved, I shake the bottle well before adding the oil to dry materials, so the undissolved particles will be included.

Liquid styrax *(Liquidambar styraciflua)* is another of my favorites — useful when a scent is too sweet and soaplike. Benzoin *(Styrax benzoin)* is a gum or a tincture. I use tincture of benzoin,

---

❤

But is it Potpourri?

I am accustomed to making the modern equivalent of recipes for potpourri with a nostalgic aura, handed down from pre-Victorian times and consisting of flowers, herbs, spices, and fixatives combined with good oils. It came as quite a shock to me, therefore, to see a package of orange-dyed wood shavings, five peach pits, a couple of broken bay leaves, and two tiny leaves of some sort, passing as a "potpourri"! At best, the scent resembled what imitation peach ice cream tastes like. One cannot quarrel with the market success of this new version of potpourri, but we traditionalists should be concerned when the public equates this with all potpourri and does not realize that quality potpourri will have a long-lasting fragrance and that it will not consist primarily of sawdust shavings!

❤

❧ *Rosella's Lemon Verbena Bouquet* ❧
(Using her "high-concentrate" method.)

3 tablespoons ground cinnamon
3 tablespoons ground cloves
1 eyedropper Lemon Verbena Bouquet Potpourri Oil*
1 eyedropper Magic Garden Potpourri Oil*
2 cups lemon verbena
1 cup lavender
1 cup marigold petals
1 cup bergamot mint leaves

Blend together the cinnamon, cloves, and oils to make a "high concentrate." Mix with the dry ingredients.

ROSELLA F. MATHIEU, HERB GARDEN FRAGRANCES, CINCINNATI, OH 45236

which is 10 percent alcohol; it is available in any drugstore. Add in drops to perfume oil for scent and body. The gum is so strong that it must be used with care in order not to overpower other scents.

Some of my favorite plant materials to use as fixatives are the following: oakmoss, in the cut-and-sifted form, which offers good retention and interesting color and quality to potpourri; cedar chips, shavings, or granules from the red cedar tree, which are attractive additions, with a persistent but unobtrusive scent of their own; and powdered vetiver root (also available in chips), although this is very strong and therefore not appropriate for delicate floral scents.

I urge potpourri-makers always to advise on the label of sachets and potpourris, "Crush to activate scent." A recipient unfamiliar with potpourris cannot otherwise enjoy the full benefits of a lasting fragrance.

❧ *Evening Song : A Layered Potpourri* ❧

Make a *"high concentrate"* (see Method 3, page 203) of 2 tablespoons ground cinnamon, 1 tablespoon ground cloves, and 1 full eyedropper of Magic Garden Potpourri Oil (from Herb Garden Fragrances). Place this blend in the bottom of an attractive quart glass jar. With two sheets of 8½″ x 11″ paper, make a cone, through which to pour the layers of scant cups of mixed mints, then sandalwood chips, mixed herbs, orange marigold, cedar chips, lavender, orange marigold, and more sandalwood chips. Top with 2 drops of Magnolia Oil. Add Charles de Mills Old Roses and a few hydrangea blossoms, and top with 2 drops of Magnolia Oil and 2 drops of Gardenia Oil. The scent from the high concentrate will soon permeate the whole potpourri and make it a lasting treasure to enjoy.

*These high-quality oils are available from Herb Garden Fragrances. See Author's Directory for address.

LAYERED POTPOURRI

I first saw layered potpourri in 1987 when Rosella Mathieu included a stunning decorative jar of it in her exhibit for the fragrance panel of the International Herb Growers and Marketers Association conference in Indianapolis. I purchased it before anyone else had a chance at it. I show it whenever I give lectures or demonstrations, and it is a crowd-pleaser! "Layering is fun and easy," says Rosella, "and you can make many different patterns." Later, when I visited her, she gave me a smaller version of layered potpourri, equally as beautiful and made with red and white roses and flowers and mixed green herbs. If I had the time to go into business again, I'd concentrate on customized layered potpourris for interior design! At the left is how she made the potpourri I purchased — my prized possession. PVS

SOME NOTES ON FIXATIVES FOR POTPOURRI

by Dody Lyness

A *fixative* is a substance used to give permanence to the main scent of a potpourri. In contrast, a *blender* is a substance with a distinct aroma of its own, used to enhance the main scent. Fixatives come in many forms, from many sources. The more common ones — oakmoss, orrisroot, and calamus root — are available from potpourri supplies dealers. Of these, oakmoss is my favorite fixative for most dry-type potpourris. Its natural aroma is pleasing, and it adds both bulk and beauty to the mixture. Prepare it 48 hours before adding it to the other potpourri ingredients, using ⅛-ounce fragrance oil to each 2 cups moss. Stir together in a bowl, then store in a glass, screw-top container. Cut-and-sifted or pin-head forms of orrisroot or calamus root should also be prepared 48 hours in advance of using; use ⅛-ounce oil to each ¼ cup of the root.

In the last few years, many new substances have emerged as fixatives. One such is processed corn cobs (sometimes called "natural cellulose fiber"), which can be added to the remaining potpourri ingredients 48 hours after pre-mixing with oil; use 1 ounce oil to 1 cup cellulose fiber. Processed corn cobs are a boon to those, like myself, who are allergic to orrisroot. You can find this and other fixative substances, such as clay pellets for your vacuum scenter mixes and cedar chips for fireplace blends, in the bedding section of your local pet store. At your garden center you can find vermiculite, also for vacuum blends.

I have used the pet-store variety of cedar chips in my Fireside Potpourri mixtures of various leftover spices and botanicals. To make these, I leave the cedar chips in the plastic bag and squirt allspice oil over them. I then stir or shake the mix, and add more oil until I am satisfied with the heavy scent. I add the remaining ingredients immediately. Fireside Potpourri, a hit during the holiday season, can be bagged and given to others or marketed, without being aged.

Even though the cellulose content of wood places it in the category of a fixative for fragrance oil, it is certainly unsettling to see more wood chips than botanicals in packages of dry "potpourri" on the market — especially when the chips are dyed in garish colors, and are certainly not meant for burning! Wood chips should not be the focal point of a fragrant potpourri. Both the color and texture of undyed wood chips, however, serve well in blends that showcase the bounty of our forests, orchards, and farms. Hibiscus flowers and very small pine cones make nice fixatives when prepared as follows: Place them in a glass jar that has a screw-top lid, cover the cones completely with fragrance oil, and let steep 2 days. Drain off and save the oil for re-use. Baby pome-

In the late 1970s, DODY LYNESS and I were among the first to suggest pre-mixing oils and fixatives before mixing them with dried botanicals for potpourri — she on the West Coast, and I on the East end. We shared a friendship by mail for a decade before we had the joy of meeting each other in Baton Rouge a few years ago. I consider Dody the West Coast expert on dried-floral arrangements — the West Coast "Betsy Williams." Her vivacious, full-of-fun personality shines in all her writings, such as her booklet Potpourri, Easy as One...Two...Three, *and her quarterly newsleter,* Potpourri Party-Line.

KITTY LITTER IN POTPOURRI

Although neither Dody nor I have experimented with dousing kitty litter with fragrant oil and using it as a fixative, she suggests that since it is highly absorbent, it should be treated like processed corncobs, which have the same characteristic. I have seen scented kitty litter used in ceramic pomanders, and also in the snakelike door-stoppers created to prevent drafts. One should not, however, use kitty litter in a potpourri intended to be enjoyed for its visual beauty.

Peek ahead to the October and December chapters for holiday potpourris and projects. PVS

FROM *POTPOURRI PARTY-LINE*
DODY LYNESS, BERRY HILL PRESS,
PALOS VERDES, CA 90274

♥ ♥ ♥ ♥ ♥ ♥ ♥ ♥ ♥

Some suppliers of potpourri botanicals now offer scent in pebble-shaped crystal form. Colored and long-lasting in fragrance, these replace botanical fixatives and are environmentally safe. The fragrances, however, are limited to the suppliers' expertise and selection. One's personal creativity is thus inhibited, and that fact alone would keep me from considering such a product. A limited number of oil additives designed to make the fragrance last longer are also available. Micro-encapsulation, such as is used on "scratch-and-sniff" paper, is another possible source of scenting potpourri with tiny scent capsules.

---

granates, whole senna pods, clove-studded citrus rinds, star anise, cinnamon sticks, and the like can be forced into the role of fixative in this manner, and their very appearance lends itself nicely to any mixture of nature's benedictions. I have no quarrel with adding a few dyed wood chips to a blend to enhance its hue, especially for bright holiday potpourri. It's the way-out-of-proportion use of wood chips to other ingredients that I find objectionable.

Remember, a fixative is a substance used to give permanence to the main scent. Don't be afraid to try new substances and new methods for maintaining your fragrances!

RECENT INNOVATIONS IN POTPOURRI SUPPLIES

by Ronda Schooley Bretz

In recent years, many new botanicals have appeared on potpourri supply lists. A few of the various and colorful botanical newcomers are angel wings, harp flowers, moon flowers, zernantheum, and dyed mosses, as well as fruits and their seeds and peels, including apple pieces and carrot slices, coconut ribbons, peach (pits, pieces, and slices), grapefruit strips, orange-peel ribbons, and colorful mushrooms.

In order to produce low-cost materials, particularly for the wholesaler, many manufacturers have begun the innovative processing of some common by-products for use in potpourri of the 1990s. Two such items are wood shavings and chips dyed a rainbow of colors, and corncob cut and processed for use as a fixative in place of orrisroot. The corncob is referred to as *cellulose* and is available in cut sizes, the same as orrisroot. Colored wood chips can make a potpourri look very attractive, if just a small amount is used; when one must search for the flowers and spices in such a blend, I am reluctant to call it potpourri. The cellulose is economical and attractive, but less effective than orrisroot as a fixative. Because it is soft and porous, corncob soaks up fragrance oils. Orrisroot, on the other hand, lends a special aroma of its own, and because of its density, is very hard and absorbs oil slowly. Absorption time is a clue to the effectiveness of a fixative, because it is parallel to the volatility of fragrance in potpourri. The lasting quality of an aroma is determined by the fixative you use. Sandalwood chips and calamus root are also suggested for fixing a potpourri scent. The choice of fixative is in part determined by what fragrance materials you choose.

In the 1950s, a perfumer's palette was enriched with a new array of synthetic products, which are referred to as fragrance oils or aroma chemicals. Today's fragrance industry has been strongly affected by escalating costs, regulatory guidelines, and a shrinking selection of true ingredients, all of which have taxed creative resources. It is not possible to extract the essence from many botanicals, and the cost to extract an oil from others is exorbitant.

Fragrance development now incorporates a blending of traditional techniques and modern technology in order to produce a vast spectrum of aromas that duplicate very well the fragrances they imitate. It is good, however, to know the "naturals" before smelling the synthetics. The best fragrances are those whose aromas are most like natural scents — and these also make very successful potpourris. Quality is often adversely affected when oils are thinned with unscented viscous oils, a practice that benefits only the dealer who wants to increase volume. The fragrance quality is diffused with the amount of additive given to it. My rule of thumb is to test by placing each oil on a blotter for several days and then evaluating its volatility.

When all of these varied materials for potpourri-making are reviewed and considered, I find only a few that satisfy my traditional taste for what is a beautiful medley of flowers, herbs, spices, and aroma to please the eye and nose.

✿ *An Old-Fashioned Potpourri* ✿

Ronda adapted this recipe from her studies of potpourri-making 50 years ago and says it makes a gallon of wonderful potpourri.

¾ cup cut orrisroot
140 drops lavender oil
140 drops rose geranium oil
1 dram plus 45 drops sweet rose oil
1 dram plus 45 drops heliotrope oil
1 cup calendula flowers
1 cup cornflowers
1 cup blue bachelor's-buttons
1 cup calcatrippae
1 cup lavender buds
1 cup yellow rose petals
1 cup red rosebuds
1 cup pink rosebuds
1 cup jasmine flowers
1 cup pink statice flowers
1 cup scented geranium leaves
2 cups lemon verbena leaves
1 tablespoon each bruised allspice berries and bruised cloves
¼ cup cinnamon, broken into small pieces
½ teaspoon ground nutmeg
2 tablespoons gum benzoin powder (optional)

Combine the orrisroot, lavender, rose geranium, sweet rose, and heliotrope oils, and allow them to set until the orrisroot has absorbed all of the oil. Combine the flowers, leaves, and spices (except for gum benzoin) with the orris/oil mixture. Store in a glass jar for 6 weeks, shaking or stirring three or four times a week. For more lasting quality, add the gum benzoin powder, distributing well, after the first 5 days of aging.

BLOTTER TEST

To test the quality of oils, dip the tips of thin strips of blotter paper in the oils. Label and date each strip. Air-dry on a paper towel, and compare the strengths of the fragrances at weekly intervals. The blotters that retain the scents the longest (at least 2 or 3 weeks) will indicate which oils will create quality potpourri. PVS

Woodrose: A Modern Potpourri Recipe for the 90s
YIELD: 1 GALLON

¾ cup cellulose, cut into ⅛-inch pieces
36 drops dark musk oil (must be heavy-scented), synthetic
¼ ounce lavender oil, essential
¼ ounce cinnamon oil, essential or synthetic
¼ ounce clove oil, essential
½ ounce rose oil, synthetic
2 cups yellow wood chips
2 cups pink rosebuds and petals
2 cups rose geranium leaves, whole
1 cup pink wood chips
1 cup lavender buds
1 cup lavender or blue statice flowers
1 cup purple statice flowers
1 cup blue flowers, such as cornflower, delphinium, pansy,
bachelor's-button, violet
1 cup rosemary leaves, whole
1 cup lemon peel, cut in ½- to 1-inch pieces
½ cup sage leaves, whole
½ cup sandalwood chips
½ cup heather flowers
½ cup cinnamon sticks, broken
⅛ cup cloves, whole
⅛ cup cloves, crushed
⅛ cup coriander seeds, crushed slightly
1 nutmeg, cracked
2 tablespoons gum benzoin powder

Mix the cellulose and oils in a small jar, and allow cellulose to be saturated with the oils. Shake several times. The fixative blend is ready to use when it no longer clings to the inside of the jar.

Gently mix the dry chips, flowers, leaves, and spices in a large bowl. Add the fixative blend. Transfer to a 1-gallon jar or crock. Your container should allow some air space so that the potpourri can be shaken and the ingredients moved about. Cover tightly. Do not use aluminum or plastic as this will affect the fragrance quality. Place your potpourri in a cool, dark place to age for six weeks. It should be shaken or stirred daily the first two weeks. During the second week, add the gum benzoin powder. Be sure it is well-distributed throughout the potpourri.

After the aging process is complete, your Woodrose will be ready to display and use. Covered dishes are suitable because they keep the fragrance fresh inside and the lid can be removed when you wish the scent to waft into a room. Sachet bags filled with potpourri are lovely to use and to give. Always keep potpourri out of direct sunlight, as light will fade the colors and the aroma.

RONDA SCHOOLEY BRETZ, SILVER SPRING, PA 17575

Decorating Your Home with Potpourri: A Sensual Accessory

by Linda Gannon

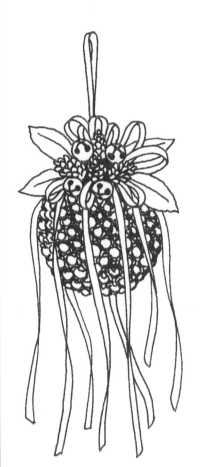

Few things spark pleasant memories as readily as fragrance. For centuries, men and women have sought to surround themselves with pleasing scents. In China, various scents are believed to stimulate specific human emotions and states of mind in six basic fragrance categories: beautiful, tranquil, luxurious, refined, recluse, and noble. Even in the United States, fragrance is used to create a sense of well-being and peacefulness in the home.

In the past few years, methods by which those aromas are presented have become much more sophisticated, innovative, and available. New products must now do more than just smell good — they must also *look* good! They have become the final decorating touch. Of course, my biggest seller is still dry potpourri, but recently I've had requests to create blends to match home accessories. Dyed wood chips or shavings make this an easy process, and they also hold the fragrance for a long time, if good oils have been added to them. I still prefer the traditional "posies-and-herbs" potpourris myself, but it is fun to experiment with what you can add to blends to keep up with the market demand. I have a very magical blend to which I've added silver confetti stars so that it sparkles and is wonderful! To my very earthy Enchanted Forest Potpourri, I've added tiny pine cones, seeds, pods, nuts, and chunks of cinnamon sticks and other spices. I spread my newest Christmas potpourri all out on an old sheet and spray it with a fine gold mist, petals and all!

It's great fun experimenting. You could add shells, small crystals, and all kinds of unusual plant materials. And don't forget the presentation, which is a fashion statement in itself! Old baskets, wine goblets, crockery, sugar bowls and creamers (those wonderful garage-sale items you don't know what to do with), your children's clay projects, or anything copper or tin are great containers for potpourri.

Pomanders and sachets no longer need to be stuck away in closets and drawers. With a little decorating pizzazz, they can become gorgeous fashion pieces. Tie your clove pomander with lots of delicate ribbon, and add rosebuds and baby's-breath. Or affix tiny pine cones, mini-bells, and bay leaves at the top. Sachets can be made in heart, butterfly, moon, or star shapes with lace around the edges, and tied with fancy ribbon. Voilà! — nice enough to add among the pillows on the love seat. With just a little imagination, every room in the house can be scent-sational!

Linda Gannon, The Magick Garden, McFarland, WI 53558

DONNA MADORA MITCHELL was one of the first to introduce cellulose fiber as a fixative. Her own brand is called Potpourri Magic (to order see Appendix for address), which she recommends using in a ratio of ⅛ ounce oil to 1 cup of Potpourri Magic for long-lasting fragrance. That 1 cup of fixative will scent up to 1 gallon of potpourri. This allergy-free, orrisroot alternative is also quite cheap. Donna sells over 80 essential and fragrance oils in all quantities, even by the pound, with no minimum order necessary.

FROM CRAFTING WITH FRAGRANCE MAKES SCENTS
DONNA MADORA MITCHELL, LAVENDER LANE, CITRUS HEIGHTS, CA 95621-7265

SCENTED GERANIUM POTPOURRI

Variation 1

4 cups citrus-scented geranium leaves
2 cups mint-scented geranium leaves
2 cups rose- or nutmeg-scented geranium leaves

Variation 2

2 cups coconut-scented geranium leaves
2 cups apple-scented geranium leaves
2 cups old spice- or nutmeg-scented geranium leaves

❧ Fixative ❧

3 tablespoons Potpourri Magic, orrisroot, or gum benzoin
or ½ cup patchouli leaves, dried and crushed
2 tablespoons coriander, cloves, and/or allspice

Mix together the dry, scented geranium leaves (either Variation 1 or 2). Add the Potpourri Magic, orrisroot, gum benzoin, or the patchouli leaves, and the coriander, cloves, and/or allspice. Mix ingredients thoroughly. Put in an airtight container for 6 to 8 weeks to blend fully. For use as air fresheners, place in decorative glass or ceramic containers with lids, or put into sachets or pillows to tuck in your bed for sweet dreams.

MEASUREMENT OF DROPS OF VARIOUS OILS

Measurements of oils can only be approximate, because the differences in the viscosity of oils determines the number of drops in an eyedropper. Eyedroppers, too, are varied — glass or plastic, with small holes or large, and from half-ounce, ounce, or even larger-sized bottles. Thus the following numbers are approximate, and each person must experiment with the dropper in use. Remember, too, the fullest dropper is only about three-quarters full.

½-dram bottle = ¹⁄₁₆ ounce = 60 drops
⅛-ounce bottle = 120 drops
¼-ounce bottle = 240 drops
½-ounce bottle = 480 drops

Using a glass dropper with a small opening and a 1-ounce bottle, ¾ dropper equals about ¼ teaspoon or 35 to 42 drops, depending on the oil. Using a plastic dropper with a plastic bulb (much stiffer than rubber), and a ½-ounce bottle, ¾ scant dropper equals about ⅛ teaspoon plus 10 drops (or 23 drops), depending on the oil.

BASED IN PART ON INFORMATION PROVIDED BY ROSELLA F. MATHIEU, HERB GARDEN FRAGRANCES, CINCINNATI, OH 45236

THE DEFINITIVE BOOK ON POTPOURRI

❧ Herb Base ❧
YIELD: 16 CUPS

A very pungent, herbal, almost mentholated fragrance with a clean, refreshing scent. If it is too strong, reduce the oils by one half.

2½ cups sage
2 cups bay leaves
2 cups lavender flowers
1 cup lemon thyme
1 cup rosemary
¾ cup patchouli
½ cup coriander seed
¼ cup each hyssop, licorice mint
(anise hyssop), tansy, thyme

Fixatives: 1 cup angelica root, ¼ cup calamus root

Oils: 1 teaspoon lavender, ½ teaspoon rosemary, ¼ teaspoon each bay and marjoram

Color and Texture: 1½ cups each calcatrippae, blue malva, and 1 cup yarrow flowers

❧ Hellacious Herbal (herb and wood) ❧

An aromatic cedarwood fragrance softened by oakmoss. The title of this potpourri refers to its moth-repellent properties, not its fragrance. Add feverfew flowers, tansy, and pennyroyal for increased effect.

2 cups Herb Base
3 cups cedar chips
1 cup lavender flowers
1 cup oakmoss
½ cup wormwood
½ cup southernwood
20 drops each of lavender, patchouli, and rosemary oils
10 drops each of cedarwood, clove, and vetiver oils

❧ Heartfelt Herbal ❧
(herb and spice)

A dry and aromatic scent that could be sweetened with tonka, vanilla, or oakmoss. Increase the dryness and pungency with white thyme oil or bay and other herbs.

2 cups Herb Base
2 cups gingerroot
1 cup each of cinnamon chips, mace, and star anise
½ cup each of nutmeg and angelica root
10 drops allspice oil

❧ Hallelujah Herbal ❧
(herb and resin)

An aromatic, resinous fragrance suitable for the addition of floral oils or for burning as incense. Herbal oils and herbs such as sage, bay, and rose geranium would be compatible.

2 cups Herb Base
1½ cups frankincense
1½ cups myrrh gum
1 cup patchouli
1 cup lavender flowers
½ cup mace
½ cup gingerroot

LOUISE GRUENBERG's Potpourri: The Art of Fragrance Crafting *has recently been revised and reprinted by Frontier Herbs (to order, see Appendix for address). The book is an in-depth guide with complete base formulas for blending potpourris, perfumes, sachets, and more. The section that utterly intrigues me (and makes me ache to dabble in fragrances and oils again) is the one containing formulas for the base blends in ten fragrance categories (animal musk, citrus, floral, fruity, hay-scented, herb, menthol, resin, spice, and woody) and then gives five variations of each base blend, with suggestions for adding compatible materials to make it your very own potpourri. This is a very sophisticated and much more complete presentation of my original and simple suggestions in* The Pleasure of Herbs *where I discussed basic rose and lavender potpourris, divided into batches and varied with additional materials. The possibilities are endless!*

FROM *POTPOURRI: THE ART OF FRAGRANCE CRAFTING*, BY LOUISE GRUENBERG (NORWAY, IA: FRONTIER COOPERATIVE HERBS)

❧ *Country Spice Potpourri* ❧

1 teaspoon whole cloves
1 teaspoon whole allspice
1 teaspoon star anise
1 teaspoon cinnamon stick
2 cups rock salt
½ vanilla bean, snipped
1 teaspoon vanilla extract
½ teaspoon almond extract

Coarsely grind the cloves, allspice, star anise, and cinnamon stick with a mortar and pestle. Combine with the rest of the ingredients. Display in an open container in your kitchen or bath for an unusual air-freshener. This may also be used as a simmering mix by adding 2 tablespoons mix to ½ cup *(or more, PVS)* water.

FROM *AN HERBAL CELEBRATION COOKBOOK* (THE HERB GUILD)

LAYERED SPICE POTPOURRI

by Madeleine H. Siegler

Inspired by the Herb Guild's Country Spice Potpourri, I created unusual potpourris consisting of whole spices layered in glass jars with the salty Country Spice playing a leading role in each. I first mixed a batch of Country Spice Potpourri, using an old blender reserved just for grinding spices, instead of mortar and pestle. (That blender is so redolent of many spices that I would not dare use it for anything else!) Since I did not have almond extract, I substituted bitter almond oil. I was a bit too generous with the bitter almond, but the end result smelled wonderful, if somewhat strong on almond! I found two tall, quart-sized, glass canisters with glass covers. I then got out about seven kinds of whole spices. In one jar, I first poured about 1 inch of the potpourri blend, and then a layer of rich brown, whole allspice. This was followed by an inch of reddish brown, whole mace; then a layer of large, whole cloves; next, an inch of light brown coriander seeds; a layer of star anise pieces; and a layer of orange rind, cut fine. The whole thing was topped off with cloves with their tree stems attached, which I had been saving ever since a visit to Grenada. The total effect is both pleasing to look at and very fragrant. The Country Spice aroma finds its way up to the top, helped along occasionally by stirring from the center with a slender chopstick.

I gave the second jar a definite snowy-winter look by layering the spicy blend between each layer of the many-colored spices. The white, salty mix runs down into the whole spices somewhat for an equally pleasing appearance. I topped this jar with whole mace and strips of vanilla bean.

MADELEINE H. SIEGLER, MONK'S HILL HERBS, WINTHROP, ME 04364

CLASSIC POTPOURRI RECIPES

by Madeleine H. Siegler

Making potpourri has been one of the greatest pleasures I've had working with herbs. Getting to know such exotic plant materials as vetiver root, patchouli, oakmoss, and sandalwood has been an educational experience as well as a sensory delight. Two books that served me well when I began this adventure were the easily available paperback by Ann Tucker Fettner, *Potpourri, Incense and Other Fragrant Concoctions* (New York: Workman, 1977, 1972) and the difficult-to-find hardcover book by Jacqueline Heriteau, *Potpourris and Other Fragrant Delights* (New York: Simon & Schuster, 1973; revised by Lutterworth, 1975). These books, along with a small booklet entitled *Creating Potpourri,* by Evelyn Varga, taught me all I would ever really need to know. I was fortunate to have them, as my need for knowledge pre-dated the wonderful herbal books, magazines, and newsletters of today.

I'm sorry to report that *Creating Potpourri* has been out of print for some time. In ten little pages, Mrs. Varga covered the mysteries of making moist and dry potpourris; explained all about spices, oils, and fixatives; and gave several good recipes for traditional blends. Mrs. Varga was an active member of the New England Unit of the Herb Society of America for many years. When I met her at a meeting and was able to tell her how much her booklet meant to me, her shy and quiet manner gave no hint of the vast knowledge she possessed. Later, when I was teaching classes, she very kindly gave me permission to reprint her material for my students. From her booklet came a recipe for a potpourri fixative that is very handy to keep on hand. At the right is a slightly updated variation of it.

You will soon find that many recipes call for freshly cracked spices. I consigned an old, two-speed blender to this task and for years it has served me well for just this function. The fragrance in the kitchen is marvelous as this old machine works its way through allspice, cloves, and even whole tonka beans with no grumbling. When I have all the spices assembled for this fixative, I usually make several batches while the blender is out. Then, at the next session, I round up all the botanicals and oils, and enjoy a long morning making potpourris.

Many old recipes call for pure coarse salt, which will absorb the oils, as well as any possible moisture in the botanicals. I found, however, that the salt tends to sift out of potpourri enclosed in lace or net sachets, so I have stopped using it. My blends seem to remain just as fragrant without salt.

In my first attempts at making potpourri, I faithfully followed recipes to the letter. As I became more comfortable with these new materials, I found I could improvise, as long as I stayed with the basic principles. I now approach potpourri-making with the same

❧ *Mrs. Varga's Fixative* ❧

¾ cup cinnamon bark
1 tablespoon whole cloves
4 tonka beans
¼ cup orrisroot or calamus root chunks
2 tablespoons frankincense
½ teaspoon myrrh

Coarsely grind the cinnamon bark, cloves, and tonka beans. Add the remaining ingredients, and mix well. Store in a tightly covered jar. Use about 2 tablespoons, mixed with appropriate oils, for 2 quarts of dried flowers and leaves.

❧ *Memorable Potpourri* ❧

This potpourri has a rich, earthy aroma without any flowery fragrance, a feature that makes it popular with men. It contains many oils and is quite expensive to make, but I promise you will make it again and again.

In a wide-mouth jar or crock, put 3 cups rose petals or buds, 1½ cups lavender flowers, 2 cups whole coriander, and 1 cup fine-cut orrisroot. Add ½ cup whole cloves, 1 cup soft cinnamon, finely shredded, and ½ cup mace blades. If you lack the mace, 2 crushed nutmegs could be used, although mace gives a softer aroma. Stir well and add oils, stirring again after each addition. Use ½ ounce *each* of oils of rose, lavender, cinnamon, and cloves, and 1 ounce musk. Age for 3 weeks; shake or stir frequently.

My method of stirring any large batch is to pour the contents back and forth a few times from the jar to a large paper bag. It adds a fair amount of dust to the kitchen (my version of a still room), but does a thorough job of blending all my ingredients.

VICTORIAN SACHET

Add 2 tablespoons calamus root to finely crushed lemon verbena and rose geranium leaves (½ cup each) and 1¼ cups crushed lavender flowers.

If at all possible, dry your own rose petals and lavender for the most fragrance in your potpourri. Not all recipes depend so heavily on the oils; many rely on the botanicals for their scent, with the oil only serving to enhance. Do not spare the budget when shopping for oils. Only the best quality will give you results you will be proud to give to your friends or sell in your shop.

MADELEINE H. SIEGLER, MONK'S HILL HERBS, WINTHROP, ME 04364

attitude I have long used in cooking: "Use it up, make it do." Lemon balm can substitute for lemon verbena, although it crumbles to dust rather quickly; rose geranium leaves can take the place of rose geranium oil. Changing the *amount* of oils makes a dramatic difference. Most of my results have been good; some have been spectacular. One of my best — which I named "Persian Garden" — is lost to me because I failed to jot down the combination of oils that went into it.

While it is true that lavender flowers hold their fragrance almost forever, I found that some of my lavender potpourris lacked "oomph." It was necessary to remind my customers to squeeze the sachets to get the fragrance. After studying many recipes I put together one that has had staying power. Let me share it with you:

❧ *Lavender Forever* ❧

Put four big handfuls of lavender flowers into a wide-mouth gallon jar. Add one handful of oakmoss. Crack 1 ounce of cloves and ½ ounce of allspice with 1 ounce of soft cinnamon in the blender, and add this mixture to the jar. Pull apart one luscious, fresh vanilla bean, snip it into small pieces, and add. Stir in 2 ounces fine-cut orrisroot, and scatter ⅛ ounce *each* of pure lavender and bergamot oils over the surface. Stir well, and age for three weeks.

❧ *Old-Fashioned Rose Potpourri* ❧

This is another of my old standbys for a never-fail rose potpourri. It started out as Evelyn Varga's recipe, but I enlarged on it and altered the scent into something my customers said should be worn behind the ear, not buried in a jar!

1 quart rose petals
2 cups each lavender flowers and rose geranium leaves
½ cup each patchouli leaves and freshly cut vetiver root
¼ cup sandalwood chips
1 cup rosemary
2 teaspoons each frankincense and freshly cracked cloves
1 teaspoon myrrh
6 tonka beans, cracked or ground
2 cups fine-cut orrisroot
⅛ ounce each rose, bergamot, sandalwood, rose geranium,
and lavender oils
½ ounce each of musk and ambergris oils
¼ ounce lemon oil

Combine the rose, lavender, rose geranium, patchouli, vetiver, sandalwood, and rosemary. Add the frankincense, cloves, myrrh, and tonka beans. Add the orrisroot, and stir it all well. Add the oils, mixing well after each one. (When I cannot find a good-quality ambergris oil, I substitute patchouli, and add a bit more musk.) Let this mixture age, with frequent stirring. In 3 weeks, it will tone down and retain a mellow richness for years.

Ann Tucker Fettner's Brown Sugar Potpourri

For several years I have been hunting the source of a brown-sugar potpourri recipe called "Half-Century Potpourri" that appeared in a newspaper article. Lo and behold, when I was preparing Madeleine's article on classic potpourris, I hunted up my copy of Ann Tucker Fettner's book (she was just Ann Tucker when I purchased it!), and there was the recipe right in front of me.

Alternate two gallons of *partially* dried rose petals, with layers of salt in a crock (or use bay salt, described at the right). Measure the salt to be used and make up an equal quantity of a mixture of allspice, cloves, and brown sugar, ¼ pound of gum benzoin, and 2 ounces of crushed orrisroot. This goes in with the salt layers. Add ¼ pint of brandy and any sort of fragrant flowers you have on hand. Citrus leaves, lemon verbena, and rose geranium leaves can also be added. Make sure they have all been partially dried first. Allow this mixture to age for a month, stirring every day. Once it has matured, turn it out into a large pan, mix thoroughly, and fill about four good-sized containers. This is an old recipe and is said to retain its perfume for at least 50 years with the occasional addition of some French brandy.

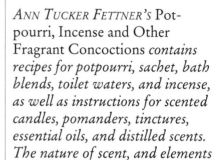

Ann Tucker Fettner's Potpourri, Incense and Other Fragrant Concoctions contains recipes for potpourri, sachet, bath blends, toilet waters, and incense, as well as instructions for scented candles, pomanders, tinctures, essential oils, and distilled scents. The nature of scent, and elements of perfume, are all spelled out.

❤

Bay salt. *To about 1 pound of common (non-iodized) salt add 6 torn bay leaves. With a wooden spoon, or mortar and pestle, crush the salt over the leaves until the leaves are exhausted. The salt picks up a pleasant, slight bay scent.*

❤

Potpourri Pleasantries from Sandi Moran

Sandi Moran, the mother of five growing children, has an herb workshop in her backyard, which is her "refuge" when she needs peace and quiet. Sandi has a mail-order catalog offering her home-made herbal crafts, also loves to teach classes, as well as to design crafts for Better Homes and Gardens *publications.*

❧ Just Peachy Potpourri ❧

¼ cup orrisroot or calamus root
15 drops peach oil
5 drops mango oil
¾ cup pale pink rosebuds
½ cup each *peach-tinted wood chips and senna pods*
¼ cup each *uva-ursi leaves, rose leaves, tilia starflowers, cinnamon bark, allspice, and life-everlasting flowers*
2 tablespoons each *rosemary and star anise*

Blend the oils together with the orrisroot or calamus root, and allow to set. Mix in the remaining ingredients.

❧ Sandi's Kitchen Simmer ❧

2 tablespoons calamus root
6 drops orange oil
4 drops cinnamon oil
2 drops clove oil
½ cup broken cinnamon sticks
½ cup lemon verbena or peppermint
¼ cup orange peel
¼ cup cloves
2 tablespoons allspice
2 tablespoons star anise
1 nutmeg, crushed
½ cup bay leaves, torn

Blend the calamus root with the oils. Mix in the remaining ingredients immediately.

❧ Herb-Patch Exotic Rose ❧

¼ cup calamus root
8 drops rose oil
6 drops lavender oil
4 drops sandalwood oil
2 drops patchouli oil
1 cup rose petals
1 cup lavender
½ cup lemon verbena
½ cup hibiscus
½ cup uva-ursi leaves
¼ cup rosehips
¼ cup sandalwood
¼ cup citrus peel
3 tablespoons patchouli
1 tablespoon each *cloves and cinnamon*

Pre-mix calamus root with the oils. Add remaining ingredients.

Sandi Moran, Herbpatch Pleasantries, Des Moines, IA 50313

Woodstove Potpourri

½ cup each of whole cloves, whole allspice, whole coriander, broken cinnamon stick, dried orange peel pieces, and dried lemon peel bits.

Mix well, and add a tablespoon to a kettle or pot on the back of the woodstove.

BARBARA RADCLIFFE ROGERS, HERBITAGE FARM, RICHMOND, NH 03470

PAT BROWN, COUNTRY POTPOURRI, AUSTIN, CO 81410

How to Use a Simmering Potpourri

Use 2 or 3 tablespoons of potpourri per pint of water in a pot on the stove. Be sure to get a good sampling of everything in the potpourri — even the small spices at the bottom of the bag. Add water as needed when it evaporates. If the resulting aroma is not strong enough, try doubling the amount of potpourri. PVS

TWO EXCELLENT CLUB FUND-RAISERS

by Pat Brown

Cinnamon Cones

*8 pounds white spruce cones
2 pounds large cinnamon chips
1 pound 1-inch cinnamon sticks
1 pound 3-inch cinnamon sticks
2 ounces cinnamon oil*

Mix cones and cinnamon sticks in a large, plastic garbage bag. Drop oil on cones. Leave in bag for a few months, tossing occasionally to blend. When ready to sell, package in plastic bags of various sizes, and tie with red or green ribbon. Makes a lot!

Peaches 'n Cream Simmer

*1½ cups sandalwood
1 ounce peach oil
½ ounce vanilla oil
1 pound dried, cut peaches (from "drops" or blemished fruit)
6 ounces deer's-tongue leaves
½ cup crushed, whole nutmeg
¼ cup whole cloves
6 cups peach-colored statice flowers*

Mix together the sandalwood and oils. Mix in remaining ingredients, and stir occasionally for a few weeks. Bag.

Amaretto-Almond Simmering Potpourri

This potpourri calls for kesu flowers, which, although they have no fragrance, add a peachy tan color to the mixture. They are available from Frontier Cooperative Herbs (see Appendix for address).

*4 cups kesu flowers
1½ cups chamomile flowers
1 cup calendula flowers
1 cup orange peel
½ cup broken cinnamon sticks
¼ cup gingerroot
6 crushed nutmegs
2 ounces sliced almonds
½ cup calamus root
2 droppers bitter almond oil
1 dropper fruit oil (your choice)*

Blend the calamus root with the oils. Mix in remaining ingredients.

JANIE DUTTWEILER, GEORGETOWN, TX 78626

DEER'S-TONGUE: A POTPOURRI-CREATOR'S DELIGHT

by Eve Elliott

Deer's-tongue *(Trilisa odoratissima)* is a common, native southern, flatwoods herb that (similarly to sweet woodruff) contains coumarin, a fixative used in setting potpourris. The leaves give off a strong, vanilla-like fragrance when crushed, and especially when dried. Collected in Florida for the past 50 years, this herb is used in the blending of pipe and cigarette tobaccos, since, in addition to flavoring the tobacco, it also absorbs unwanted flavors and sustains the burning. The tobacco industry market for deer's-tongue has recently declined because many newer types of cigarettes use artificial flavoring. Deer's-tongue has also been used in the manufacture of artificial vanilla.

Also called vanilla leaf, vanilla plant, dog's-tongue, or hound's-tongue, deer's-tongue is a perennial herb that grows from 2 to 4 feet tall. Its single, center stem rises above basal leaves and has a large, purple, flower-head cluster about the size of a large grapefruit, which blooms in the fall. Since deer's-tongue grows only in low, damp, pine flatwoods areas, it does not thrive on high and dry land or in very swampy locations. Today, the last few commercial growers are in central Florida, near the Deland area. The Florida Native Plant Society has included it in their native garden located in Orlando.

Harvest begins in early May and lasts throughout fall. Pickers harvest the leaves by stripping the basal leaves from the plant by hand — while at the same time watching out for the rattlesnakes that also live in the flatwoods areas! The leaves are dried by spreading them on the floor or on drying racks out of the sun. They are turned several times a day, and then bundled in bales when dry. They sell for 5 to 8 cents a pound fresh, or 55 cents a pound dried. It takes about 5 pounds of green leaves to produce 1 pound of dried.

For sources of deer's-tongue see Appendix.

Many people ask about growing their own deer's-tongue because of its heavenly fragrance. Seeds do not seem to be available, and EVE ELLIOTT*'s article helps us understand why growing this plant is confined to limited areas. I guess most of us will have to settle for buying it! This article first appeared in Eve's now discontinued newsletter,* Southern Herbs.

EVE ELLIOTT, CAPE CORAL, FLORIDA

HARVESTING ORRISROOT

This is the month to dig up and divide Iris germanica. *Of the two or three roots from each plant, save the larger rhizomes to use as a fixative, and replant the smaller ones. Clean and peel the skin off the root with a knife or potato peeler. Chop into coarse pieces and allow to air dry for a few days before chopping them more finely in a food processor. Dry completely before using. Or, try this suggestion from Roberta Bashor (Elizabethton, TN): Scrub the freshly dug root, and chip it on a potato chipper. After the chips dry, they will be about the size of rose petals, curve a little, stay white, and look pretty in potpourri. PVS*

Phyl's Citruswood Potpourri

YIELD: APPROXIMATELY 1½ GALLONS

This is a colorful and fragrant dry potpourri, which can also be used as a simmering blend for indoors or outside. Steamed on the grill with the dying embers, this will keep the insects at bay! Use completely dry ingredients, and cut all stems into 3-inch pieces. Two gallon-sized jars, with lids, are helpful for this project, as well as a very large mixing bowl or plastic tub (18-inch width works well). Or, you may prefer to halve or quarter the recipe. Divide equally between gallon jars, and you will have plenty of room for shaking and blending.

1 cup calamus root pieces*
1 cup angelica root pieces*
2 tablespoons sweet orange oil
2 tablespoons lemon oil
2 tablespoons citronella oil**
2 cups citrus peel spirals from oranges, lemons, limes, and grapefruit
2 cups cedar shavings
½ cup whole cloves
4 cups lemon and lime balm leaves and stems
2 cups yellow and orange marigold flowers for color (optional)
2 cups lemon-scented marigold flowers, leaves, and stems
(for color and scent)
2 cups tangerine-scented marigold flowers, leaves, and stems
(for color and scent)
1 cup lemon basil leaves and stems
1 cup lemon verbena leaves and stems
1 cup lemongrass, snipped into 3-inch pieces
1 cup whole bay leaves

Blend the calamus and angelica root and the sweet orange, lemon, and citronella oils together in a gallon jar. Cover and let set for 2 or 3 days, shaking often. Add the citrus peel spirals, cedar shavings, and cloves to the jar of fixatives and oils. Cover and allow to blend for 2 more days, shaking occasionally.

Pour half of the fixative/oil/spice mix into another gallon jar. Mix together the remaining ingredients and place half of these dried materials into each jar. Mellow for 4 to 6 weeks, shaking often to coat the botanicals evenly with the oiled spices and fixatives.

*You may substitute cellulose fixative for the calamus and angelica. Use 4 cups cellulose fixative and 4 or 5 tablespoons of *each* oil.

**If making this primarily for outdoor use, increase citronella oil to 3 tablespoons and decrease the other two oils to 1½ tablespoons each. Also, purchase cheap cedar shavings from a pet store.

For more potpourri recipes that use natural ingredients in bulk in order to compete with the new versions on the market, see Scented Pine-Cone Mix and Apple Harvest in the October chapter. PVS

Other Fall Crafts

HERB PILLOWS

by Barbara Radcliffe Rogers

There is no luxury quite akin to laying a tired head upon a pillow filled with herbs and fragrant flowers. The scent of a spring garden or of the woods on a summer afternoon is sure to conjure up dreams of happy times. While any pillow feels better if it carries a pleasant fragrance, certain herbs comfort in special ways. Hops, for example, have been known for centuries to help induce a normal, natural sleep. We now know that it is because of the lupulin they contain. The Kings of England are said to have slept on pillows of hops when the headaches of state robbed them of sleep.

Dill is known to have a calming effect on cranky babies, and its very name is thought to come from a word meaning "to lull." Lavender will soothe a headache, although its invigorating scent does not promote sleep. It could be used for a headache pillow, but, in my opinion, not for one meant to induce slumber.

As a pillow *stuffing,* however, herbs are way behind feathers! We must find a way, therefore, to put the potpourri in the pillow without filling it with rustling, often bumpy and bristly leaves and flowers. The herb pillow doesn't *replace* the big bed pillow — it supplements it. Our favorite slumber pillows are made for the guest room. They are small, flat packets, like large sachets, lace-edged and stitched of quilted fabric to pad against any sharp little stems. We make up the guest-room bed with one on each pillow. They can be as small as 6 inches square or up to 8 by 10 inches. The lace can be any soft variety, narrow for the smaller pillows and wider for the larger sizes. The fabric is always a pastel, usually a soft, elegant floral. Look for remnants of chintz or other cotton decorator fabrics, and line them with a layer of quilt batting sandwiched between the outer fabric and a muslin lining. Use plenty of potpourri but don't fill it so it bulges; it should be fairly flat. In England, some pillows are filled with hops alone, and they smell terrible! Unfortunately, hops are not sweet-smelling, but instead have an almost acrid odor, like a campfire of poplarwood. Hops should be mixed, therefore, with at least equal parts of a potpourri strong enough to let it blend in. Since strong, invigorating herbs like mint and lavender cannot be used, lemon verbena saves the night, with its fresh, lemon scent that lasts forever.

We mix lemon verbena, rose petals (removing the lumpy buds to be used in blends where they'll be seen and not felt), chamomile, and rosemary, and add a little rose oil and *very* little chipped orrisroot. Because of its possibly irritating nature and the allergic reactions some folks experience, orrisroot should be used sparingly, if at all, and never in powdered form in herb pillows. Equal parts of this potpourri and hops create a pleasant, fragrant blend for pillows. Less fancy, but equally effective, flat, muslin packets of this potpourri may be placed inside the pillow cover. It is best to tack them to the center with a stitch or two so the packets won't slip about.

A dill pillow for the baby should be a very flat little packet of dillweed. If you use lace, be sure it is narrow and quite soft. I wash eyelet edging for the pillows before sewing, but no ribbons or bows should be put on these, or on the adult pillows meant to be slept on.

Headache pillows were very popular in Victorian times and have a number of variations. My favorite is an elongated, hour-glass shape, which is filled with lavender and placed under the back of the neck. A few moments repose with head thus propped should revive one's spirit and send a headache well on its way.

Not all herb pillows have such particular uses — many are frankly frivolous, such as ours made of flowered calico and shaped like a Chinese ginger jar. A white label, with "Potpourri" embroidered on it in script, is appliquéd to its center. Since I use a predominately violet fabric, the pillow, stuffed with polyfibre, encloses a generous, muslin packet of French lavender.

Botanic print fabrics with framed designs (available at fabric stores) make perfect herb pillows. Choose a backing fabric to match either the border frame or the main color in the flowers. I use a matching, corded piping along the edge. Just before hand-stitching the pillow closed, I tuck a packet of pink rose petals right behind the print. I made one featuring a damask rose, and people are always quite surprised to lean on it and actually smell the roses. You needn't be limited to florals, however. These squares are available with Christmas scenes (which would be nice filled with balsam), with seashells (a perfect setting for a seashore potpourri of bay, thyme, rosemary, balsam, and beach roses), or with wild bird or duck prints (suitable for a man's study, filled with a packet of cedar shavings, balsam, lemon verbena, oakmoss, and whole cloves).

Barbara Radcliffe Rogers, Herbitage Farm, Richmond, NH 03470

Artsy Herb Baskets

by Linda Fry Kenzle

Baskets are currently enjoying a welcome revival. A look into any gallery, upscale craft shop, or country store reveals baskets of every shape and design imaginable, of both manmade and natural materials. Herb crafters should accept the challenge to wander into the field of basketry — it's a natural progression. One of my favorites is made of southernwood, using a secondhand, cheaply made basket as an armature (form). Discarded baskets of all sizes and shapes can be had for a song at flea markets, garage sales, and thrift shops. The armature basket doesn't need to be in pristine condition either; as long as it is strong, you can use it.

If you are familiar with traditional basketmaking, you'll notice that this method is a bit different — it's easier, fast, and exciting! Begin at the bottom by wrapping a branch of southernwood around the armature basket. The branch should go all the way around the basket so that its tips overlap its base. Wire the tip to the base at the overlap, and then secure the branch by weaving the ends snugly through the armature basket. The wire ends should face the inside of the basket. Continue weaving and wiring branches around the armature basket, until you reach the top.

If the basket has no handle and you want to add one, braid three long branches of southernwood together. Gently bend the braid into an arc, set the ends in place at the top inside edge of the basket, and wire them securely in place. (If you'd like a thicker handle, braid together six branches or, for that matter, any multiple of 3.) To cover an already existing handle, simply wind branches of southernwood around the handle, adding as many branches as necessary to give good coverage. Wire the branch ends to the main basket. You can also leave the basket without a handle.

To finish the inside of the basket and cover the wires, I glue pieces of sheet moss in place with a hot-glue gun. The moss can be gathered from shaded places in the woods (be sure to leave some for regrowth). Remove the dirt from the back of the moss, and it's ready to use. Or, sheet moss can be purchased from most suppliers of floral craft materials.

Cover the top edge of the basket with annual statice and yarrow flower heads. Glue the flowers in place with a hot-glue gun. If you've added a handle, spot glue to hold it securely in place. The final touch to the basket is a bird's nest fashioned from a ball of Spanish moss fitted with a purchased feathered bird and a big bow. Glue all in place.

Once you've completed your first southernwood basket, venture out in your own direction by experimenting with other herbs. Consider incorporating feathers, beads, pine cones, cloth strips, lichens, ribbons, and so on. Incorporate the spirit of your land into your herbal baskets!

❤

The shrubby herb southernwood is excellent for basketmaking. Its fernlike leaves stay on its branches and retain their color well. The herb branches are easier to work with when they are fresh and pliable, so set aside time in the fall for creating baskets. Cut large bunches of southernwood, making the stems as long as possible.

❤

Linda Fry Kenzle, Fox River Grove, IL 60013

A Biblical Harvest

HERBS OF THE BIBLE

by Jane Dole

I have had more requests for reprints of this article than for any other in the 11-year history of my newsletter! JANE DOLE'S so original and unique development of a church service revolving around the herbs of the Bible has been the inspiration for similar programs in dozens of churches since she shared it with my readers.

Taking note of the fact that herbs are frequently mentioned in the Bible, our church centered a Sunday worship service around "The Herbs of the Bible." Herbs were the theme of the scripture, hymns and other music, and sermon. Assisted by garden club members, we hung eight herb wreaths on the doors of the sanctuary, and spent all day Saturday making tussie mussies of fresh herbs, with a rosebud or saffron blossom in the center of each, and white paper doilies enveloping the herbs. These were refrigerated overnight, and during the service, we distributed them from baskets to every member of the congregation. A sprig of rosemary was added to the rosebuds for the ushers' boutonnieres, and artemisia and wormwood supplemented the altar bouquet. The minister's sermon, entitled "A Celebration of God's Good Creation," compared the individual characteristics of herbs — their colors, shapes, textures, flavors, and scents — to our own individuality. He expanded this herbal metaphor by suggesting the ways in which we change when "mixed together" — as in a potpourri.

At the social hour after the service, we served herb punch and herb tea as well as herb sandwiches and herb cookies. The room was decorated with bouquets of roses and herbs, and bowls of potpourri.

The following appeared in the morning bulletin on our herb Sunday:

HERBS OF THE BIBLE

Historically, herbs like spices, are rich in legend, fact, lore, romance — and good business. They can be traced back through the Bible to the Garden of Eden. Wars have been fought, trade routes established, lives sold, and cultures, countries, and businesses founded, all in the name of the plants we call herbs. An ancient record, the *Ebers Papyrus,* reports that in Egypt, 2000 years before Christ, there were many herb doctors, and the Bible makes repeated references to herbs. Below is a listing of herbs mentioned in the Bible or associated with the Christian religion.

Aloe *(Aquilari agalloche)* is called "Paradise Wood" or the "Shoot of Paradise," for it is believed to be the only tree descended to man from the Garden of Eden (Numbers 24:6).

Anise *(Pimpinella anisum).* Mentioned in Matthew 23:23,

Anise *(Pimpinella anisum)*

"Woe unto you, scribes, and Pharisees, hypocrites: for ye pay tithe of mint and anise and have omitted the weightier matters of the law, judgment, mercy and faith." This famous herbal quotation is a mistranslation, for the original Greek was "anethon" or dill *(Anethum graveolens)* and not anise.

Coriander (Coriandrum sativum) is one of the most ancient of herbs, with several Old Testament references. The fruit is similar to the manna that God showered upon the Israelites (Exodus 16:31).

Cumin (Cuminum cyminum) is an herb native to the upper areas of the Nile, mentioned in the Bible when Jesus reproved the scribes (Matthew 23:23).

Frankincense (Boswellia thurifera) and myrrh *(Cistus creticus)*. The wisemen from the East brought these gifts of great value to the Christ Child: gold, a token of kingship; frankincense for holiness; and myrrh to symbolize the suffering the newborn infant would have to endure.

Gall (Papaver somniferum) was added to vinegar and offered to Jesus on the cross, but he refused it. Gall, the juice of the opium poppy, provided a narcotic that induces sleep so heavy that the person becomes insensible (Matthew 27:32-34).

Garlic (Allium sativum) is mentioned only once in the Bible (Numbers 11:5). It was held in great esteem by the ancient Egyptians. In one of the pyramids is an inscription stating that 100,000 slaves spent 30 years in its construction, and ate garlic, leeks *(A. porrum)*, and onions *(A. cepa)* to the value of 1600 talents of silver.

Hyssop (Sorghum vulgare), known as the holy herb, was used by the Egyptians to cleanse the temples and other sacred places. In Psalms 51:7, David says in a prayer, "Purge me with hyssop and I shall be clean."

Mint (Mentha, various species), mentioned only in the New Testament (Matthew 23:23 and Luke 11:42), grows wild throughout the Holy Land. A writing from A.D. 37 states that mint was mentioned often in a book of cooking recipes of that date.

Mustard (Brassica nigra) is described in Matthew 13:31 as "the least of all seeds: but when it is grown, it is the greatest among herbs, and becometh a tree, so that the birds of the air come and lodge in the branches thereof."

Rose (Rosa, various species). The name for a rose is almost the same in every European language, an indication of its antiquity. Early poets all sang praises of the rose; dried roses have been found in Egyptian tombs. (Isaiah 35:1)

Rue (Ruta graveolens) is known as the "herb of grace," for brushes made from rue were at one time used to sprinkle holy water at the ceremony preceding High Mass. (Luke 11:42)

Saffron (Crocus sativus). In biblical times, this herb was very important to the people of the East as a condiment and sweet perfume. (Song of Solomon 4:13)

Wormwood (Artemisia judaica) is frequently mentioned in Scripture, always for its bitterness. (Jeremiah 23:15)

❤

ORGAN PRELUDES: Intermezzo ("Seed Time and Harvest") and West Pastorale ("Forest Green"), arr. Purvis

ORGAN POSTLUDE: "The Heavens Are Telling" from The Creation, *Haydn*

HYMNS: "Let the Whole Creation Cry," Monkland; "For the Beauty of the Earth," Dix; "At the River," Copland

OLD TESTAMENT LESSON: Psalm 104

NEW TESTAMENT LESSON: Mark 1:9-13

❤

Hyssop *(Hyssopus officinalis)*

Costmary *(Chrysanthemum balsamita)*

JANE DOLE, INDIANA, PA 15701

Rosemary *(Rosmarinus officinalis)* is an herb steeped in religious tradition from ancient times. A symbol of fidelity and remembrance, it was used in two of the holiest of Christian ceremonies — the wedding and the funeral.

Lady's-bedstraw *(Galium verum)* is a strewing herb. Christian legend has it that it was used to provide a bed for the Christ Child in the manger in Bethlehem.

Costmary *(Chrysanthemum balsamita)*. This aromatic herb has always had a special place in Christianity, for it derives its name from the Latin word *costus* and Mary, the mother of Jesus. In Colonial times, a costmary leaf served as a bookmark in Bibles and prayer books, thus it is also known as "Bible leaf." When the long sermon became boring and drowsiness set in, the sleeper treated himself or herself to the minty leaf in an effort to stay awake.

Fennel *(Foeniculum vulgare)*, caraway *(Carum carvi)*, and dill *(Anethum graveolens)* in Colonial times were carried to prayer meetings in small pouches, for they were a natural to curb the appetite. They were called "meeting seeds."

OCTOBER

NOW THAT WEATHER dictates our being in the gardens less and in the house more, October is a good month to start making gifts from the harvest for the holiday season. There is something very special about homemade gifts of beauty and fragrance that come from the heart and hearth, and give pleasure for months, or even years, to come. The beautiful herb and spice wreaths that launch this chapter, as well as the dried floral topiary and pomander projects, would thrill any Mrs. Santa on your Christmas list. Some of the pine cone and dried apple crafts make excellent bazaar items for school, community, or craft fairs. Of course, all of the projects herein are worth your consideration for selling in a shop.

Several kinds of wreaths are described in the pages ahead. Two of my favorite creations are table wreaths made with sweet Annie bases — one a lively green hue (harvested in the early stage of blooming) and the other a rich reddish-brown shade (harvested at its last stage of life). The green wreath is decorated with golden tansy buds and strawflowers (to match the sweet Annie blossoms) and gold satin ribbon woven around the wreath. We use this as a table centerpiece with a thick gold candle in the center, covered with a hurricane lampshade for safety when we light the candle. The brown base is adorned with deep red and rust strawflowers, spice "cookies" (see December), and burgundy ribbon and candle. This sits on the end of my kitchen counter each year. Both wreaths are brought out of storage in November and used until January or February. Somehow, seeing our favorite decorations early in the season brings back happy memories, helps to set the holiday mood, and inspires us toward a relaxed preparation for the weeks to come.

Sweet Annie (Artemisia annua) is a favorite of mine, so I was sorry to learn from a few of my readers that they have had *allergic reactions (sneezing, coughing, tearing up) to the pollen when working with the plant. One person has had to stop growing it altogether; another has found that if she harvests it just before it blooms, there is no problem; and another mists his harvest and works with it in the damp stage, thus cutting down on the pollen dust in the air. One subscriber to my*

newsletter suggests spraying the blossoms with hair spray to prevent the pollen from dispersing so readily in the air as it is handled, a particularly good idea, I think, for sweet Annie wreaths that one might sell or give away. You could protect most of the foliage from the spray by covering it (with plastic, for instance), so that the wreath would still be aromatic. Where

there's a will, there seems to be a way. I do, however, want to caution allergy-prone readers about this potential problem and share these solutions.

At the end of the chapter, you will find some delicious foods to try on the chilly nights of fall — among them the Shaudys family's favorite meat marinade. Bon appetit!

Herb, Spice, Pine-Cone, and Apple Wreaths and Other Projects

THE FINE ART OF CRAFTING AN HERBAL WREATH MASTERPIECE

by Linda Fry Kenzle

When your herb gardens are bulging with large, vigorous plants, it's time to begin selecting the tussie bundles for a masterpiece herbal wreath. Variety is the key to creating an exciting herbal wreath. For variety in *color*, collect a number of different greens, from the bright hue of Italian parsley to the dark emerald greens of the mints. For variety in *texture*, the soft, woolly lamb's-ears and pebble-patterned sage are good examples. Sharp accents add spark and excitement. The silvery artemisias combined with opal basil make an excellent eye-pleaser.

Another important consideration is *scent*. This notion came from the gentle urging of one of my best customers, who was dismayed that my wreaths "didn't smell as wonderful as they looked." I began adding scented geraniums, cinnamon and licorice basils, sweet Annie, and the scented southernwoods, and was quite

This is the month to plant garlic bulbs and saffron corms in sunny areas and sandy garden loam with good drainage. Garlic bulbs are available from Nichols Rare Plants and Seeds (OR) and saffron corms from The Rosemary House (PA). PVS

pleased with the new textures and colors, as well as the fragrance they added. Wreaths could also be scented with essential oils.

To prepare herbs for drying, gather them in bundles of five to seven stems, each about 4 or 5 inches long. Wrap each bundle together with a rubber band, and fasten it over a wire coat hanger. Add wrapped herb bundles to the hanger until it is full, and then hang in an airy, dark place to dry. Do not overcrowd the herbs on the hanger or they will dry unevenly, or possibly mildew. Nine herb bundles per hanger dry well. An 18-inch diameter wreath — very full and lush, with no skimping — will require about five or six hangers full of herbs.

The herb bundles, when thoroughly dry and papery to the touch, are attached to a straw base with fern pins. The day before you plan to make the wreath, insert a fern pin, with the notch facing upward, into a spot on the back of a wreath form that has been slathered with tacky glue. About ¾ inch of the pin should be left exposed for ease in hanging. Let the glue dry thoroughly before beginning the wreath. This hanger is sufficiently strong to hold any herb- or flower-based wreath up to 24 inches in diameter. Larger wreaths, or those employing heavier materials, will require a wire hanger looped and twisted around the straw wreath base.

In the early seventies, I studied with wreathmaker Guri Henderson, who covered her straw wreath bases with Spanish moss, before decorating them with dried flowers. I no longer find this necessary, since I can get very full coverage with the herbs alone. Another excellent wreathmaker of my acquaintance cuts a circle of corrugated cardboard to cover the back of the wreath base. I share these ideas with you for your own experimentation. Each master wreathmaker uses some special design element in all of his or her wreaths — try to develop your own such "signature."

To begin, lay the straw base on newspaper (you can save for your next potpourri any loose herbs that crumble off as you work) and take all the dried herb bundles off the hangers. Remove the rubber bands; once dried, each herb bundle will remain intact. Take note of all the different colors, textures, and "sparks," or accents, you have available, and begin to formulate your design in your mind. These are two basic rules of wreathmaking:

❤ Work the herb material in a random fashion around the wreath, contrasting the colors, textures, and accents by placing smooth leaves next to fuzzy ones, bright greens next to silvers, and so on.
❤ Face all of the herb bundles in the same direction, generously overlapping the herbs. This method covers the fern pins and gives fluidity and consistency to the final form.

Working within these parameters, begin in the center, or face,

Field mice can damage woody herbs such as lavender, santolina, southernwood, and hyssop. To keep them from dining on the heavier stems of these plants, mound used kitty litter around their bases just before the heavy snows.
PAT AND JON BOURDO, WOODLAND HERB FARM, NORTHPORT, MI 49670

Salad Burnet (*Poterium sanguisorba*)

of the ring by using fern pins to fasten the herb bundles in place. This is a reverse of the technique required for constructing a pine-cone wreath, where the cones are attached first to the inside of the ring and then to the outside of the ring, and finally, the center, or face, is filled in. The fragility of the herb bundles necessitates changing this order so that the herbs are less likely to be crushed. Continue adding bundles to the outside of the ring, and then the inside of the ring. Keep the wreath lush and full. No bare spots, please!

If you wish to add a focal point to your wreath, attach a flourish of comfrey leaves clustered with Chinese-lanterns and sprigs of sweet Annie. The comfrey leaves eventually turn a lovely bronze. Any cluster of color or unusual dried materials can provide a focal point wherever you wish it on the wreath. Don't be afraid to experiment.

When the wreath is completed, hang it, and fill in any spots you might have missed. Work carefully with the dried materials at this point. When the wreath is hung, gravity tends to pull materials down on the left side and at the bottom, making these trouble spots on many wreaths. There are two remedies: First, you can hold materials up with small dabs of tacky glue, very sparingly, in strategic spots. Or, you can pin through the edge of the stray plant material, pushing the pin in only to the point where the herb should be positioned. Cover the pin by pulling some of the neighboring herb over it to conceal it. Occasionally, you may wish to neaten the final wreath by snipping away any small, stray herb sprigs. Try not to overdo this, or your wreath will look unnatural. That's it! Hang the wreath away from bright light, and you will receive years of pleasure from it.

WREATHMAKING BOTANICALS

Artemisias – all varieties (*Artemisia* species)
Basil – all varieties (*Ocimum basilicum*)
Bergamot (*Monarda didyma*)
Boxwood (*Buxus*)
Burnet (*Poterium sanguisorba*)
Catnip (*Nepeta cataria*)
Comfrey (*Symphytum officinale*)
Coriander (*Coriandrum sativum*)
Costmary (*Chrysanthemum balsamita*)
Curry plant (*Helichrysum angustifolium*)
Fennel (*Foeniculum vulgare*)

Germander (*Teucrium chamaedrys*)
Horehound (*Marrubium vulgare*)
Hyssop (*Hyssopus officinalis*)
Lamb's-ears (*Stachys byzantina*)
Lavender – all varieties (*Lavendula* species)
Lemon balm (*Melissa officinalis*)
Lemon verbena (*Aloysia triphylla*)
Lovage (*Levisticum officinale*)
Marjoram (*Origanum majorana*)
Mint – all varieties (*Mentha* species)
Oregano (*Origanum vulgare*)

Patchouli (*Pogostemon patchouli*)
Rosemary (*Rosmarinus officinalis*)
Sage – all varieties (*Salvia* species)
Santolina (*Santolina* species)
Scented geraniums – all varieties (*Pelargonium* species)
Sweet woodruff (*Galium odoratum*)
Tansy (*Tanacetum vulgare*)
Thyme – all varieties (*Thymus* species)
Winter savory (*Satureja montana*)
Yarrow (*Achillea millefolium*)

Live Herbal Wreaths

by Barbara Radcliffe Rogers

Living herbal wreaths are a wonderful way to grow herbs after the weather becomes too severe to enjoy them outdoors. Not difficult to make, a live wreath can be a stunning centerpiece by itself or used as a surrounding decoration for a punch bowl, fruit bowl, or candle. I decide the size of my living wreaths according to the plates I have available. Large, round trays work well for bigger wreaths; saucers make good containers for wreaths intended to surround candles.

A box-wreath frame (the double-wire type made in two layers) slightly smaller than your plate is ideal, but not absolutely necessary. Fill the box frame with sphagnum moss, or wrap pieces of sphagnum around a single-wire frame, and tie the moss loosely with heavy thread to hold it in place. For a candle wreath, you can use a macramé ring or a plastic coffee-can lid with the center cut away. The ring base will be completely covered, so it doesn't matter what it looks like. Whatever you use, don't pack the sphagnum too tightly.

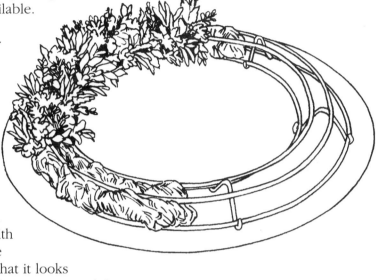

Gather herbs, especially those with soft stems that propagate by layering, such as creeping thyme. This excellent base can be supplemented with stems of rosemary, boxwood, germander, lavender, mint, marjoram, savory, and sage. Begin with the thyme, or whatever soft-stemmed herb you have. Try to have some roots on the plants, if possible. Press the roots or the stem ends into the moss as firmly as possible, winding the herb stems into the shape of the wreath. How you do this will depend on the herbs you have, their length, and how easily they bend. Save those herbs with larger leaves for last and use them as accents.

If you are making your wreath at a time of year when you have small plants, you can tuck their roots, with a small ball of potting soil still attached, into the sphagnum. Basil, chamomile, and even violets or small salad burnet plants may be used; small-rooted, scented geraniums work well. These plants, or any others whose cuttings have roots, will continue to live in the moist sphagnum.

When your wreath is the way you like it, fill the base plate or tray with water and set the wreath in it. After a few hours, check it. If the plate still has water in it, but the sphagnum is not wet through, leave it another few hours. If the sphagnum is completely wet, pour out the excess water. If there's not water in the plate, but the moss still isn't wet, add more.

Live wreaths made in mid- to late October will be lush for the holidays. I suggest keeping the freshly made wreath out of direct light for the first few days, especially if you want the cuttings to take root. A rooting hormone and frequent mistings are beneficial. Gradually move the wreath under more light, either a sunny window or indoor lights; apply weak feedings of fertilizer when watering. These procedures will definitely prolong the life of the wreath, as the sphagnum moss is a sterile soil and any rooted plants will have the same requirements inside as they do outside. Bring the wreath to the dining or coffee table for special occasions. PVS

For special occasions, push fresh flowers with a few inches of stem into the moss. They will keep as they would in a vase. Over a period of time, some things in your wreath will grow and need to be pruned or woven back into the wreath; others will wilt and need to be replaced. A living wreath, like a living garden, requires some care — but brings much pleasure indoors when there's little greenery outside!

Barbara Radcliffe Rogers, Herbitage Farm, Richmond, NH 03470

A Spice Wreath

by Grace M. Wakefield

The perfect accent for a kitchen, this wreath is a fragrant, attractive decoration, as well as a conversation piece. The Creative Twist paper ribbon loops give the wreath a nice, plump and airy aspect. You might want to make up half a dozen of these for delightful Christmas presents. The materials list includes enough ingredients to make six wreaths.

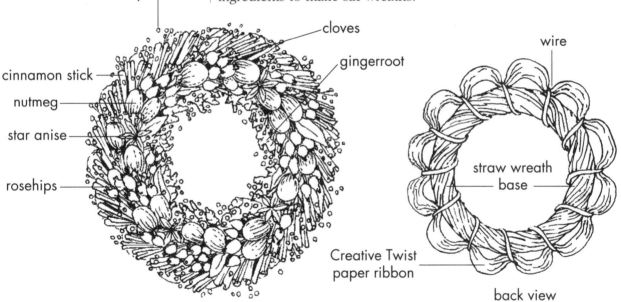

baby's-breath — cloves — gingerroot — cinnamon stick — nutmeg — star anise — rosehips — wire — straw wreath base — Creative Twist paper ribbon — back view

Six 6-inch straw wreath bases
Six 48-inch lengths Creative Twist paper ribbon, in colors of your choice
Fine wire (or nylon thread in several thicknesses)
Hot glue
1 bunch baby's-breath
8 ounces whole nutmeg
8 ounces 3-inch cinnamon sticks
8 ounces gingerroot
8 ounces star anise
4 ounces rosehips, whole
4 ounces whole cloves
4 ounces whole allspice

1. Unravel the Creative Twist ribbon.

2. Attach the end of a 48-inch (approximately) piece of wire securely around a starting point on the wreath base.

3. Fasten the Creative Twist paper to the outside of the wreath with the wire, wrapping the wire around the wreath at about 1-inch intervals, and pulling up the paper to make 1-inch loops. The wreath will be encircled by about twelve paper loops when you are done. Bind off the end of the wire securely.

4. With wire, make a hanging device at the top back of the wreath.

5. Hot-glue the cinnamon sticks all around the surface of the wreath in a slanted fashion going in one direction. Fill in any spaces with cinnamon sticks that have been cracked in half crosswise (use a hammer to crack the sticks).

6. Hot-glue the gingerroot pieces to the inner surface of the wreath.

7. Use hot glue to attach the nutmeg, star anise, clusters of cloves and allspice, and groupings of three rose hips. Space these spices in attractive clusters on top of the cinnamon sticks.

8. Pinch off 1½ - to 2-inch long clusters of baby's-breath, and hot-glue them in between the Creative Twist paper loops on the outer edge of the wreath. Glue more clusters of baby's-breath to the surface of the wreath, sparingly, to fill gaps.

9. The wreath may be sprayed with hair spray to help preserve it, *or* you may prefer to brush cinnamon oil on the cinnamon sticks and other spices to enhance and preserve the fragrance.

FROM *HERBAL CRAFTS QUARTERLY NEWSLETTER*
GRACE WAKEFIELD, TOM THUMB WORKSHOPS, MAPPSVILLE, VA 23407

A SPICE NECKLACE

by Madeleine H. Siegler

My version of a spice necklace originated in 1975 when I saw a photograph in *The Herb Grower,* that wonderful small magazine published for years by Gertrude and Philip Foster and now out of print. The original necklace had fewer spices but credit for the idea perhaps belongs with the reader who sent it to Mrs. Foster. A spice necklace will keep its fragrance for years, it will not stain your clothing, and it is not fragile. Should the center star break, it can be repaired with any household glue.

My design calls for allspice, cloves, cinnamon stick, cardamom, nutmeg, vanilla bean, tonka bean, star anise pieces, and a large, perfect star anise for the center front. Did you know that cinnamon is the bark of a tree? And cloves are flower buds? Star anise and cardamom are seed pods and allspice is a berry, while nutmeg and tonka beans are fruit pits. Vanilla bean is the seed pod of a tropical orchid that is common, but the bee that pollinates its

You may purchase a completed spice necklace from Madeleine Siegler (see Appendix for address).

flower is rare. Because none of these spices can grow in our temperate climate, all are imported from tropical countries.

Finished length: 28 inches

2 tablespoons whole allspice
1 teaspoon cloves
12 or more pieces of star anise
2 tonka beans
6 cardamom pods
One 3-inch cinnamon stick
2 whole nutmegs
1 whole star anise
Four 1-inch pieces of vanilla bean
36 inches heavy-duty (carpet) brown thread, dental floss, or monofilament
    line
2 sewing needles

1. Soak the allspice and cloves with the star anise and tonka beans for about 8 hours. Because the cardamom pods may discolor if soaked with the other spices, soak them separately for about 4 hours. (While cardamom pods are expensive, the white makes a nice contrast with the many shades of brown, and they add another fragrance.) Strain the soaked spices and spread them on an old towel.

2. If you own a small power tool with drill and saw attachments, use it to cut the cinnamon stick into 2 pieces, each about 1¼ inches in length. Use a drill to put holes through these pieces as well as through the nutmegs and the large center star. (If you don't have a power tool, you can soak the cinnamon, cut it with scissors, and then re-roll it to its original curled shape, and use a large sewing machine needle to put holes in the tough nutmegs. I made my first 100 necklaces this way, but it was not easy!)

3. Begin by threading each end of your thread through a needle. Run one needle through the hole in your large center-front star anise, and pull it to the center of the length of thread. Now, pierce a nice plump allspice and slide it on. Next, a white cardamom, another allspice, a clove, an allspice. Pierce a flat side of a soaked tonka bean and slide it on. Repeat these six on the other needle. Beginning to look good already, right? Continuing to use 2 allspice and a clove for spacers, build your design as follows: the nutmeg, then the cinnamon stick, then the 2 pieces of vanilla bean (no need to soak this). Repeat on the other side. It may take you half an hour to get both sides to the vanilla bean mark. Push all the wet spices closely together as you work, as they will shrink a little when they dry. Next, add an allspice snug against the vanilla, another white cardamom, and then work out a design alternating with cloves and a few pieces of star anise. My pattern uses eleven pieces before the last cardamom goes on.

❤

If you teach geography, try wearing this in the classroom — you'll find it will spark interest in the faraway places where all these spices grow. One teacher confides, too, that she wears hers to class whenever she expects a harrowing day — the continual fragrance from it relieves her stress.

❤

4. All that remains is to add about 3½ inches of allspice on each side. When each side measures 14 inches to the star center, tie the ends of thread tightly, pull on the knot to make sure it won't slip, and hang the necklace to dry. (Bet you will slip it over your head and go look in the mirror while it is still wet!)

You may feel utterly exhausted when you finish your hour's work, but your second necklace will come easier — you will know what you are doing! Perhaps you do not care for my design; be creative, change it to suit your taste. A big chunk of dry gingerroot is wonderful for a center, and vanilla can easily be eliminated. The technique is always the same, however — soak all small spices, drill or cut the heavier pieces, and experiment to your heart's content.

Sources for spices include Gingham 'n' Spice, Potpourri Party Line, and The Rosemary House. See Appendix for addresses.

MADELEINE H. SIEGLER, MONK'S HILL HERBS, WINTHROP, ME 04364

SPICE-FILLED TRIVETS AND MUG MATS

by Sally Booth-Brezina

To make a 9" x 9" trivet, use the following directions; to make a 4" x 4" mug mat use measurements in parentheses. The pattern features a lap seam so that the spice pouch can be easily removed when the cases need laundering. This recipe for spice oil makes 60 drops, or 1 dram of oil — enough to scent 1 pound of spices. To make half again this amount, see page 234. If you wish to stencil, silk-screen, or embroider a design on your trivet (mat), plan the design to fit a 6-inch (3-inch) square centered top to bottom and end to end.

Several weeks before you put your trivet or mat together, make the spice and oil mixture. Using the ingredients listed at the right, combine oils and spices, and let set, covered, for 3 weeks.

Case

One fabric piece 10" x 24" (5" x 13½") for case
One fabric piece 7" x 13" (3½" x 7") for spice pouch

1. On short ends of case fabric piece, fold over ½ inch (½ inch) twice, and press. No need to sew, as topstitching in Step 3 will hold these in place.

2. Fold piece into thirds, with end folds facing out and with the lefthand end overlapping the righthand end by the width of the folds. The overlap should occur at the center of the piece. Press flat.

❤ ◆ ❤ ◆ ❤ ◆ ❤ ◆ ❤ ◆ ❤

Spice Mix
YIELD: 1 POUND

4 ounces cinnamon pieces, ¼ inch or smaller
3 ounces whole allspice
2 ounces orange peel, potpourri-cut or smaller
1 ounce whole cloves
1 ounce rosemary leaves
1 ounce star anise, broken into pieces
1 ounce oakmoss, cut and sifted
½ ounce crushed nutmeg
½ ounce ginger, cut and sifted

Spice Oil
YIELD: ENOUGH TO SCENT 1 POUND OF SPICES

14 drops each of cinnamon, allspice, and sweet orange (or bergamot) oils
10 drops clove oil
8 drops nutmeg oil

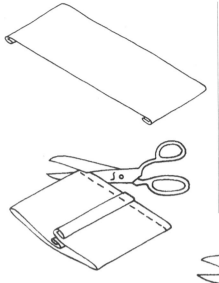

3. Sew ½ inch (¼ inch) seams along the sides. Trim corners, turn inside out, and press. Topstitch 1½ inch (½ inch) all the way around.

4. To make spice pouch, make ½ inch (½ inch) folds in each short end of the fabric piece, and press. Fold the entire piece in half at the center, with the end folds facing out; press.

5. Stitch long edges in ½ inch (¼ inch) seams, leaving short end open. Trim corners and turn inside out.

6. Insert up to 1 cup (¼ cup) of the spice mixture into the inside pouch. Whip stitch or machine stitch closed. Tuck pouch into case.

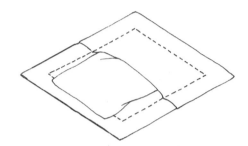

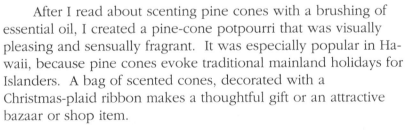

SCENTED PINE-CONE MIX

by Sally Booth-Brezina

After I read about scenting pine cones with a brushing of essential oil, I created a pine-cone potpourri that was visually pleasing and sensually fragrant. It was especially popular in Hawaii, because pine cones evoke traditional mainland holidays for Islanders. A bag of scented cones, decorated with a Christmas-plaid ribbon makes a thoughtful gift or an attractive bazaar or shop item.

6 ounces assorted cones (red pine, spruce, hemlock, tamarack, or other
*   medium- to small-sized cones)*
2 ounces orange peel, dried (large-cut or cut in long strips)
1½ ounces orrisroot, in as large chunks as possible
1 ounce cinnamon pieces, 1- to 3-inch
1 ounce whole hibiscus flowers (for color, texture, and a weak fixative)
½ ounce bay leaves (or lemon eucalyptus)
*1½ drams Spice Mix Oil: 21 drops **each** of cinnamon, allspice, and sweet*
*   orange or bergamot oils, 15 drops of clove oil, and 12 drops of nutmeg oil*

Mix all together and let set, covered, for 3 weeks. Shake often.

Before drying apple slices, dip them in a solution of lemon juice and citric acid (available in the canning section of the grocery store) to help preserve the natural color of the apples.

Green apples make beautiful decorations, too!

Theresa Neff, Country Thyme Gazette, El Segundo, CA 90245

❧ *Dried Apple Wreath* ❧

¼ cup lemon juice
1 teaspoon salt
2 pounds small apples (Jonathans work well!)
1 coat hanger (or other wire of comparable size or thinner)
½ ounce pomander rolling mix (powdered spices and fixatives)
Small cinnamon sticks and star anise for decoration
Narrow ribbon, twine, or raffia

1. Mix together the lemon juice and salt. Leaving the core in place, slice apples ⅛- to ³⁄₁₆-inch thick. Dip each slice into the lemon juice mixture. Drain the slices in a colander, saving the juice for more dipping.

2. Dry slices on racks in 200° oven. This will take up to 6 hours depending on your oven. Leave a small opening in the oven during the first 2 or 3 hours to let the moisture escape. A wooden spoon handle will prop the door open nicely. When the apples feel leathery, they are dry enough. Any softness in the apple is a sign that further drying is necessary. If the apples get crisp, they can still be used.

3. If using a coat hanger, remove the top. Shape the wire into a circle or a heart. Leave at least 1 inch extra wire on each end and do not yet join. String the apples onto the wire until all but 1 to 1½ inches of wire on each end is covered. With pliers, form a hook on each end, and link the hooks together. Push the apples over the hook ends to cover this space, if you wish, or cover it with a ribbon, twine, or raffia bow.

4. Place the pomander rolling mix into a bag with the wreath and shake it until coated. The spices deter insects and add a delightful aroma of their own. The fixative in the mix helps preserve the apple and spice scents.

5. Decorate the wreath with cinnamon sticks and star anise.

6. Attach narrow ribbon, twine, or raffia at the top of the wreath for hanging.

For an easy apple pomander that children enjoy making, see December. PVS

Sally Booth-Brezina

CHERYL TAYLOR started making eucalyptus cones at Christmas time last year. She wanted to make one for her cousin to put on her desk at work, but remembered her cousin disliked eucalyptus. So, Cheryl created an apple cone for her. Within a few days of her cousin's taking it to work, Cheryl had fifty orders for apple cones! Heartfelt Farms (see Appendix for address) offers large pine cones, completed cones, or kits for both pine and eucalyptus cones.

CHERYL TAYLOR, HEARTFELT FARMS, SALEM, VA 24153

APPLE (OR EUCALYPTUS) CONES

by Cheryl Taylor

Apple (or eucalyptus) cones are delightful gifts for brides, co-workers, teachers — or for yourself! By changing the color of the apples or eucalyptus and the ribbon, you can make a decorated cone fit any reason or any season. A touch of essential oil on the edges of the cone "petals" (scales) will make the cone a treat for *all* the senses.

1 large (6 to 8 inches tall) pine cone
Dried apple slices (approximately 1½ cups)
Small sprays of baby's-breath
3 or more 6-inch lengths of ⅛-inch ribbon
Glue gun and glue sticks

1. Level your cone by rocking it gently back and forth on a solid surface. Remove any loose petals from the bottom of the cone.

2. Cut a large, dried apple slice in half and fold to form a cone shape. Put a small drop of glue where pieces overlap. Allow to dry. Apply hot glue to the tip of the cone, and place the dried-apple cone over the tip.

3. Starting at the top of the pine cone and using the smallest apple slices first, insert the apple slices between the cone petals, skin side out, to test for fit before gluing. To glue, run a small bead of hot glue along the edge of the apple slice and insert the slice between the cone petals.

4. Glue small sprays of baby's-breath scattered around the cone. Tie 6-inch lengths of ribbon into small bows and glue them on the edges of the cone petals. You can also tie ribbon onto small pieces of cinnamon sticks, and glue the sticks onto the cone.

5. Scent the cone by placing a few drops of essential oil along the edges of the cone petals.

❤

If your dried apple slices have not been sprayed with a sealer, keep the apple cone away from areas of high humidity. I prefer not to spray mine, as I like the natural, soft look.

❤

BETSY WILLIAMS'S DRIED TOPIARY CONSTRUCTION

Dried topiaries are a big hit in Europe and are fast making their way across the Atlantic, and Betsy Williams (The Proper Season, Andover, MA 01810) has been abroad to study the art of dried topiary-making. Her creations are priceless and elegant works of art. The natural trunk material used by Betsy is one of the reasons her topiaries stand apart from those made by others, who often use dowels. Her demonstrations at events such as the International Herb Growers and Marketers Association and the North Carolina Herb Association conferences draw standing-room-only audiences. The following is taken from a report by Cricket Hefner in the NCHA newsletter, along with some new procedures that Betsy has added since her lecture.

Collect lilac stems or other suitable "trunk" material. Assemble the flowers, herbs, and foliage you wish to use, and fill a clear plastic basket liner with plaster of paris. This liner should fit snugly into the container into which the topiary will be placed. As soon as the plaster begins to harden, stick the "trunk" piece into it. When the plaster is hard, use hot glue to secure it into the desired container (such as a terra cotta pot or a basket).

Use a Styrofoam ball or cone as a form for the top of the topiary. Shove the top of the trunk up into the Styrofoam, and then remove the form in order to fill the hole with hot glue. Replace the form onto the trunk. Cover the plaster base with such material as sheet moss, stones, or flower petals, to camouflage the plaster. Cover the Styrofoam with sheet moss, if desired. Establish the basic shape of the topiary with hydrangea, statice, or baby's-breath. Cover the form loosely with this base material so that other materials, such as flowers for color, contrast, and interest, may be tucked in with it. Build up layers to achieve an in-and-out, or three-dimensional effect. Ferns and boxwood work nicely in this project. Finish off with loads of narrow ribbon streamers for a festive touch!

KEEPING ROSEMARY ALIVE THROUGH THE WINTER

We northerners usually have to buy new rosemary plants each spring, as bringing them inside for the winter seldom results in lush, thriving plants by the next April. I have found a solution that has worked for me, however. I use a red clay pot large enough to give the roots room to grow. I then line a larger plastic or ceramic pot on the inside with damp sphagnum moss and place the pot of rosemary into it, making sure that both pots have good drainage. I place the pots under fluorescent lights in a fairly cool (or unheated) room, for best results. Whenever the moss starts to dry out, I water it enough to moisten it well; the soil containing the rosemary plant needs watering only when it is dry.

BOB CLARK, LANCASTER, OH

FRAGRANT POTPOURRI POMANDER

by Grace Wakefield

This decoration, with its sweet, old-fashioned look, makes a delightful gift. It can be hung in a bedroom or kitchen window, or from a protruding wall hook, or on the Christmas tree. Or, it can be placed in an antique bowl with other fragrant pomanders.

Crochet yarn or fine wire of a length sufficient to suspend the pomander (doubled)
3-inch Styrofoam ball
Clove or toothpick
Oakmoss
Elmer's glue
Velvet ribbon for a bow
⅛ ounce fragrant oil
An assortment of potpourri flowers and spices, such as whole allspice, balm-of-Gilead buds, blue hydrangea flowers (dried in silica gel), 1-inch cinnamon sticks, tiny heather flowers, whole rosehips, sandalwood chips (for scent), sunflower petals, tilia starflowers, and other flowers you have dried in silica gel, as well as Assortment A or B at the left

Assortment A

Rosebuds and petals (pink), star anise (brown), cloves (brown), French lavender (purple), life everlasting (yellow), and malva flowers (black)

Assortment B

Hibiscus flowers (maroon), calcitrippae flowers (deep blue), statice flowers (purple/pink), Roman chamomile (cream), white cardamom seeds (cream), and uva-ursi leaves (green)

1. Thread the crochet yarn through a long darning needle, knot the two ends together, and push the needle through the center of the Styrofoam ball. Push a clove or a 1-inch piece of toothpick through the knot at the end of the yarn, and pull this end up against the ball to prevent the string from pulling through. (If you use wire, double it, and force the center folded end through the ball to use for hanging. Fold back 1 inch of wire on each of the two loose ends and tuck these up into the ball securely to keep the wire in place.)

2. Place oakmoss on a sheet of newspaper. Cover the ball with Elmer's glue, and roll it in the oakmoss until completely covered. Allow this to dry before adding more material.

3. Arrange the rest of the botanical material all over the oakmoss, using plenty of Elmer's glue.

4. Make a dainty, multi-looped bow out of the ribbon. Add long streamers, if you wish. Attach the bow to the top or bottom of the pomander.

5. Add a few drops of fragrant oil in several places over the surface. The oakmoss will act as a fixative. Refresh with oil from time to time.

FROM *FRAGRANT WREATHS AND OTHER AROMATIC BOTANICAL CREATIONS* GRACE WAKEFIELD, TOM THUMB WORKSHOPS, MAPPSVILLE, VA 23407

AUTUMN POTPOURRIS

by Bob Clark

❧ *Ember-Glow Simmering Potpourri* ❧

Incorporates the reds, golds, oranges, and browns of a wood fire with the spicy fragrance of fall cooking.

½ cup calamus root
20 drops rose geranium oil
10 drops lemon oil
10 drops cinnamon oil
3 cups red rosebuds and petals
3 cups orange and yellow flowers
(such as calendula, marigold, nasturtiums, and starflowers)
1 cup red hibiscus flowers
1 cup orange peel
½ cup gingerroot
½ cup red or natural sandalwood
2 tablespoons allspice berries
2 tablespoons cinnamon chips

Store the calamus and oils together in a covered jar for at least 2 days, shaking occasionally. Add to the other ingredients. Allow to mellow, shaking regularly.

❧ *Apple Harvest Potpourri* ❧

Use red-skinned apples or a combination of red-, green-, and yellow-skinned apples, depending on the color scheme desired. These will form the bulk of this potpourri, making it "larger than life" to compete with bulky potpourris on the market, but entirely natural!

1 cup calamus root chunks
4 cups dried apple slices (see page 235 for suggested drying methods)
1 cup whole cloves (bruised)
1 cup 3-inch cinnamon sticks
½ cup tonka bean pieces
½ cup sandalwood and/or sassafras
3 tablespoons apple oil
1 tablespoon cinnamon oil
3 cups chamomile flowers
3 cups applemint or spearmint
3 cups red or yellow flowers
2 cups lemon balm
Harvest decorations, such as nuts, acorns, or small buckeyes

Mix together the calamus root, apple slices, cloves, cinnamon, tonka beans, and sandalwood. Add the oils. When the oils are absorbed, add the mix to the crisp-dry flowers and herbs, and the harvest decorations.

❧ *Woodland Treasures Potpourri* ❧

A good blend to simmer, if you don't mind "steaming up" your good oils.

30 drops patchouli oil
30 drops sandalwood oil
10 drops vanilla oil or extract
½ cup santal chips
½ cup oakmoss
½ cup cinnamon chips (or broken cinnamon sticks)
1½ cups patchouli
1½ cups deer's-tongue
1 cup hibiscus flowers
¾ cup orange peel
¾ cup balsam fir
½ cup star anise
½ cup sassafras root bark

Add the oils to the santal chips, oakmoss, and cinnamon chips. Stir in remaining ingredients.

❧ *Apples-and-Spice Simmering Potpourri* ❧

Add 40 drops spiced apple oil and 10 drops bitter almond and cinnamon oils to ¼ cup calamus root in a lidded glass jar. Shaking occasionally, let the fixative absorb the oils for at least 2 days. Add this mixture to 2½ cups chamomile flowers, 1½ cups red rosebuds, 2 cups whole applemint or spearmint leaves, ⅔ cup whole lemon verbena or lemon balm leaves, ½ cup patchouli, 1 cup dried-apple pieces, ⅓ cup sassafras root bark, 4 or 5 nutmegs (broken), and a handful of whole or broken cinnamon sticks.

BOB CLARK, LANCASTER, OH

Meat Marinades and Other Fall Recipes

A marinade is a tenderizing bath of wine, vinegar, or citrus juice, combined with herbs, spices, and oil. It both flavors the meat and breaks up muscle fiber, making the meat tastier and more tender. Because of the acid in the marinade, always use nonmetallic containers for marinating. With a long-tyned fork, poke holes evenly throughout the meat, so juices will permeate deeply.

Chicken and fish seldom need tenderizing but may be marinated for added flavor; less time is required for this process than for tenderizing. Always cover and refrigerate meat, fowl, and fish while marinating. Leave pierced meats in marinade for 4 to 24 hours, turning the food occasionally to coat evenly.

Sherried Gingerroot

Preserve fresh gingerroot for up to a year by cutting it into pieces, covering it with dry sherry, and then refrigerating the lidded jar. To use, peel and shred, grate, or mince the desired amount. The gingered sherry may also be used, but leave enough liquid so that the remaining ginger is covered with sherry. Add Sherried Gingerroot to marinades, soups, stews, or salad dressings, or to the cooking water for sweet potatoes, carrots, or onions.

SWIMMING IN FLAVOR

❧ Shaudys London Broil: A Family Favorite ❧
YIELD: SERVES 8 TO 10

The amount of marinade this recipe makes is usually enough for one steak. If you need marinade for additional steaks, add a little more liquid to the ingredients.

1½ cups red cooking wine
½ cup tamari (or soy) sauce
¼ cup olive oil
2 bunches chopped scallions
4 garlic cloves, pressed

2 tablespoons Sherried Gingerroot (a 2" x 2" piece, peeled and grated)
1 tablespoon fresh rosemary (1½ teaspoons dry)
One or two 2-pound London broil cuts, 3 inches thick

With a cooking fork, pierce the meat evenly throughout, on all sides. Whisk together (or use a blender to mix) the wine, tamari, and oil. Stir in the scallions, garlic, Sherried Gingerroot, and rosemary. Place the meat in a glass or stainless steel dish. Pour the marinade over the meat, cover, and refrigerate for several hours or overnight, turning the meat several times during this time. Drain the meat a tad (I leave some of the marinade on the meat), and broil or grill to taste. Let the meat stand (covered with foil) for a few minutes before carving. Slice diagonally at a 40° angle, against the grain, in thin strips. Enjoy!

❧ Marinated Salmon Broil ❧

⅓ cup tamari (or soy) sauce
⅓ cup safflower oil
⅓ cup white wine
6 tablespoons Sherried Gingerroot, grated
3 cloves garlic, pressed

2 tablespoons minced fresh chives
2 tablespoons minced fresh parsley
2 tablespoons minced fresh dill
2 teaspoons freshly ground pepper
1 teaspoon cayenne pepper
4 salmon fillets

Blend all the marinade ingredients together. Rinse fillets under cold water and pat dry on paper towel. Place fish in a single layer in a shallow glass dish. Pour marinade over fillets, turning fish to coat evenly. Cover with plastic wrap, and refrigerate for 1 to 3 hours, turning the fish at least once. Drain salmon and broil or grill, about 10 minutes per inch of thickness, or until done. Brush with marinade when turning.

RECIPES FROM THE NEW THYMES

(a quarterly newsletter from Rathdowney Herbs and Crafts)

❧ Microwave Savory Herbed Rice ❧

A versatile recipe that can be used for a main dish, a side dish, or a stuffing, this rice goes nicely with Fish Fillets Salsa.

2 cups water	2 teaspoons parsley
2 vegetable bouillon cubes	Pinch of thyme
1 cup long-grain rice	Dash of pepper
1 tablespoon onion flakes	1½ tablespoons butter or marga-
1 tablespoon celery flakes	rine, if the bouillon is fat-free

Mix all ingredients together in a 2-quart, microwave-safe casserole. In a microwave, cook, covered, on High for 4 to 6 minutes or until mixture begins to boil. Stir. Cook, covered, on Medium for 15 to 20 minutes, or until rice is just tender. Let stand covered for 5 minutes. (See Variations at right.)

❧ Microwave Fish Fillets Salsa ❧

YIELD: SERVES 4

Low in cholesterol, fat, and sodium!

1 pound fish fillets, about ½-inch thick	2 tablespoons lemon juice
	2 teaspoons minced parsley
14½ ounce can low-sodium, stewed tomatoes, drained	1 clove garlic, minced
	½ teaspoon thyme
¼ cup dry, white wine	Dash or so of tabasco, to taste
3 tablespoons chile sauce	

Place fish in a single layer in a 12" x 7" x 2" glass baking dish. Cover with vented, microwave-safe plastic wrap. Cook in a microwave on High for 4 to 7 minutes, or until fish flakes easily when tested with a fork, rotating the dish a half-turn after 4 minutes. Drain off liquid.

Mix the remaining ingredients and pour over fish. Cook, covered, on High for 2 or 3 minutes, until sauce is heated.

❧ Rathdowney Chicken Breasts ❧

½ cup olive oil	1 teaspoon dry mustard
¼ cup low-salt soy sauce	2 pounds boneless chicken breasts
1 cup dry sherry or vermouth	2 tablespoons olive oil

Combine the olive oil, soy sauce, sherry, and mustard to make a marinade. Split the chicken breasts into halves, and marinate them, refrigerated, at least 1 hour. Drain. Over medium-high heat, sauté the chicken in the 2 tablespoons olive oil about 8 or 9 minutes on each side.

Herbed Rice Variations

- ❤ Add ½ cup fresh, or a drained, 4-ounce can, button mushrooms during the last few minutes of cooking.
- ❤ Replace up to half the long-grain rice with wild rice.
- ❤ Add 1 to 2 cups of finely cut-up, cooked chicken, cooked small shrimp, or chopped, cooked vegetables.

❧ Creamy Potato-Dill Soup ❧

3 pounds potatoes
Salt to taste
1 large onion, chopped
1 tablespoon dillweed
1 to 2 teaspoons freshly ground pepper
2 tablespoons butter
1 cup sour cream or sour milk
Chives, parsley, or dill for garnish

Wash the potatoes and cut them into 1-inch cubes. Place them in a large pot and cover them with water; add salt to taste. Bring to a boil, and simmer for 10 minutes. Add the onion. Simmer an additional 15 minutes, or until the potatoes are soft and falling apart. Add the remaining ingredients, stirring well after each addition. Bring back up to a simmer. Serve, garnished with chives, parsley, or dill.

FROM THE NEW THYMES, A QUARTERLY NEWSLETTER
LOUISE DOWNEY-BUTLER, RATHDOWNEY HERBS, LTD., BETHEL, VT 05032

TERRY'S ROSEHIP CONCENTRATE

Rosehips are said to contain thirty times more vitamin C (before they are dried), than equal amounts of orange juice! Because the vitamin C is easily destroyed by contact with copper or aluminum, be sure to use only wood, glass, stainless steel, enamel, or plastic cooking utensils when preparing rosehips. Rosehips also contain high amounts of other vitamins and several minerals. The most nutritious rosehips are those from shrub roses, such as Rosa rugosa *(available from Wayside Garden Catalog). PVS*

Caution: Be sure that the rosehips you harvest have not been sprayed with poisonous chemicals.

For a warming treat on cool fall evenings, add this to hot apple cider, or for a refreshing, hot-weather drink, add it to sparkling water or soda on ice. Or, use it as a base for jellies and jams, especially wild grape jam, or as a syrup for pancakes or as a fruit leather. Since some of the high vitamin-C content in rosehips is lost in the cooking process, you may prefer to freeze the syrup rather than process it under high heat. Refrigerate, after opening.

5 pounds fresh or dried rosehips
3 broken cinnamon sticks
Cloves and grated nutmeg to taste

½ cup brown sugar (optional)
1 cup honey (optional)

Clean the rosehips and place them in a large enamel pot, with just enough water to cover. Simmer for 2 hours or until soft and mushy. (Or, soak the hips in water to cover overnight, then simmer slowly until soft, about 1 hour.) Mash hips with a potato masher, and strain through a sieve. To the thick juice, add the cinnamon sticks, cloves, and nutmeg. Cook until the mixture is a thick syrup. Strain. Add sugar or honey, if desired, stirring to dissolve. Place in small, hot, sterilized jelly jars. Seal. Process in a boiling water bath for 5 minutes. Cool, and check seal.

TERRY KEMP, GOD'S GREEN ACRE HERBARY, ONALASKA, WI 54650

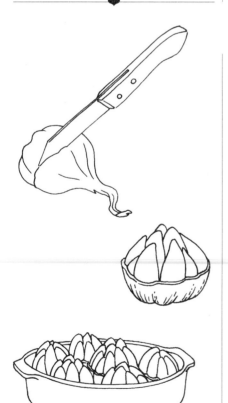

❧ Roasted Garlic ❧

A deliciously different, surprisingly mild-flavored appetizer. (Leftovers may be warmed in the microwave and spread on chicken, beef, or lamb. PVS)

1 cup olive oil
8 whole garlic heads
1 teaspoon salt
¼ teaspoon ground black pepper

1 pound, round loaf of dark pumpernickel bread, torn into eight pieces

Use 1 tablespoon of the olive oil to grease the bottom of an 8-inch baking pan. Make a shallow incision all around each garlic head, halfway between top and bottom, cutting through the skin but not into the meat of the garlic. Lift off the pointed top of each head. Arrange the garlic in the prepared pan. Pour the remaining olive oil over the garlic heads. Sprinkle with salt and pepper. Bake uncovered in a 200° F. oven for 15 minutes. Cover the pan with foil, and continue to bake for 1 to 1½ hours, or until garlic is tender. Serve warm, spread on bread.

FROM *AN HERBAL CELEBRATION*, THE HERB GUILD

NOVEMBER

By NOVEMBER OUR tender perennials, such as bay, lemon verbena, rosemary, and scented geraniums, have been taken in from the garden and are becoming acclimated to their indoor locations on windowsills, under lights, or in the greenhouse. Annual or perennial herbs, potted up in late summer, may also be thriving inside now. If you haven't yet brought plants in for winter enjoyment, however, it is not too late. Scented geraniums are some of the nicest plants for indoor culture and can be ordered in the fall before freezing temperatures inhibit their delivery by mail. These make lovely gifts for yourself and others to savor during the bleak winter months.

There's another method of having fresh-cut herbs at your fingertips all winter long — hydroponics, or growing plants in water! Chefs in large, elegant restaurants are now growing their own herbs in water gardens close to their kitchens for the freshest flavor. Although they use elaborate and costly equipment (pioneered by General Electric or a Montreal-based company, Applied Hydroponics of Canada), you will learn in this chapter how to grow culinary herbs in water at home for very little cost! A restaurant kitchen can grow, in twelve 3-foot containers of water, the amount of herbs one could harvest from a 3' x 36' soil garden outdoors. White fluorescent-tube lighting is used, because tinted lights encourage blooming, and from herbs, chefs want the foliage most of all. (Although this attitude might have changed recently, with the rage for edible flowers on menus!) A fish-tank-type pump is used to provide continuous nutrients through the water to the plant roots. Basil, dill, fennel, peppermint, and spearmint are said to be the most vigorous growers under hydroponic conditions, with all but fennel supplying repeated harvests for up to 5 months. Some growers report just moderate luck with marjoram, thyme,

and oregano in water, and the least success with rosemary and savory. As with any method of indoor herb gardening, if you have an insect problem, it can be controlled with Safer's Insecticidal Soap (5 tablespoons to a gallon of water), sprayed weekly. Hydroponics could have far-reaching implications. The method could revolutionize herb production where the growing season is short or garden space is limited!

This chapter also includes tips for starting an herb business, for exhibiting at craft fairs, and for informing others about herbs, whether by teaching or giving lectures or demonstrations. This last information is not just for professionals, as there are so many of you "lay" people who educate others about herbs, whether in adult education classes, lectures to your garden club and other organizations, or with informative tours through your own gardens. The public is eager to learn about herbs and many experienced herb gardeners are called upon to share their expertise. I always enjoyed giving lecture-demonstrations to garden clubs or civic organizations, because there are so many sensual and surprising things to share about herbs that delight an unknowing audience! I include herein the format I used, and some tips from my experiences over a 25-year period.

You'll find here, as well, some unique ways to use herbs for the Thanksgiving season. Herbs are indeed for every season, every holiday, every occasion!

Herbs Indoors

PLAN A FRAGRANT WINTER!

It's a little early to be discussing the "January Blues" that usually afflict us gardeners in the colder climates. But you can plan ahead to eliminate this annual let-down by giving yourself and others a winter of indoor fragrance and delight! If you have a sunny window with a southern (or southeastern or -western) exposure or an indoor garden under lights, order now the superior full-color catalog from Logee's Greenhouses (see March, Herb Seed and Plant Catalogs in the Appendix for address), which features begonias, rare plants, geraniums, and herbs. They sell over 60 varieties of scented geraniums at very reasonable prices, and ship plants all year, but at the customer's risk in severe weather, so don't tarry!

Select from the following most fragrant of the scented geraniums, the leaves of which can be used for tea, baking, and potpourri:

- ❤ *Rose scents: Attar of Roses, Rober's Lemon Rose, and True Rose*
- ❤ *Lemon scents: Dr. Livingston, lemon balm, Mable Gray (heaven itself), Prince Rupert, and lemon crispum (the fingerbowl geranium)*
- ❤ *Fruit and Spice scents: apple (great for hanging baskets), apricot, cinnamon, ginger, lime, Logeei (spicy), nutmeg, orange, and strawberry*
- ❤ *Peppermint scents: chocolate mint, Joy Lucille*
- ❤ *Pungent scents: Godfrey's Pride, Mrs. Kingsley, pine, and Pretty Polly (almond fragrance)*

Scented geraniums make exquisite houseplants, provided they receive good sun or light, are not overwatered (once a week usually sufficient), have firm, loamy soil, and receive occasional fertilization. I grow them for the foliage, not the tiny flowering blooms, so I use the 20-20-20 variety of Peter's Plant Food, following the directions for indoor plants. They love misting and occasional spray showers in the tub or kitchen sink. I guarantee you plenty of sensual pleasure as you care for these alive-with-fragrance plants in the dead of winter!

When growth is lush, as the sun warms the plants up in the spring, trim the top third of the branches and root the prunings in water or a sandy loam to increase your crop. For large summer harvests, place them in your gardens in the summer (after last frost). Or, leave them in their pots and put them outside — just be sure they don't dry out in the hot sun, more of a danger when left potted up. Make cuttings late in the summer to pot up for gifts, and bring both cuttings and mother plants inside before frost. The re-potted, tired mother plants will need a rest, so don't feed them for a few weeks. Water them lightly and keep them out of the direct sun for the dormant period, just as we do with rosemary and lemon verbena when first brought inside each fall.

Although many of the hard-to-find herbs from Logee's — such as black peppermint (Mentha piperita), *which so many ask me about, and its variation, chocolate mint — should be ordered in the spring, another super Christmas gift from Logee's for yourself and others would be the sweet bay* (Laurus nobilis). *My first one* thrived for 8 years, surviving all but the last of five transplantings to bigger pots. It lived for 9 months a year in our bay window with a southern exposure, and outside for the summer months; it grew from 6 inches to 4 feet in those years. Of course, I've replaced it! The Logees have been in business for over 95 years. Try to visit them when you're in the Danielson, CT, area. Meanwhile, plan now — enjoy January!

GROW A POT OF GINGER

by Madeleine H. Siegler

Safe to say that most of us have at least one herb on the windowsill in winter. Maybe it is rosemary, maybe a cherished bay tree, or perhaps a pot of chives. Why not grow a spice? As we know, herbs grow in our temperate climate, while spices need the hot tropics. We cannot grow cloves, nutmegs, or mace, but we *can* grow ginger! And although we may never harvest fat, juicy roots, such as we can buy in nearly any supermarket, we can have the pleasure of growing the plant. That pleasure just might help us to fight the winter blahs — and will be far less expensive than a trip to the West Indies, where the very air is fragrant with spices.

I first learned the joys of ginger-growing at an herb symposium at Merry Gardens in Camden, Maine, many years ago. Joy Logee Martin of Logee's Greenhouses was one of the featured speakers, and she shared the following with us. Search out the freshest, plumpest gingerroot in the exotic-vegetable section of your supermarket. One piece is all you need. Cut a small piece the size of a walnut. Make sure it has an "eye," or sprouting spot, such as is found on potatoes; if in doubt, plant the whole thing! Fill a 4-inch pot with potting soil or plain peat moss, and bury the ginger 1 inch below the surface, cut side down. Water well, and keep moist. Place the pot in a warm spot and practice patience, for it will take about a month for the first sprout to appear. Put the plant in a sunny window, keep it watered, and just watch the bright green, linear leaves appear in opposite positions on the round, central stem. They are extremely soft to the touch and quite fragrant — rather a fruity smell.

The first year I grew ginger, I put the well-started plants into the garden in June. They objected to the full sun, but flourished in part shade. No — I never did harvest my very own gingerroot, but

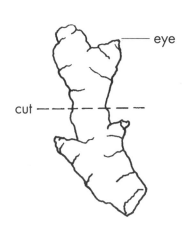

❧ Monk's Hill Spicy Chicken ❧

2 small pieces dried gingerroot
2 star anise
1 chile pepper
1 cup boiling water
1 chicken bouillon cube
4 to 6 chicken pieces
2 cloves garlic, minced
4 tablespoons soy sauce
¼ teaspoon sugar

Soak the gingerroot, star anise, and chile pepper in the boiling water to which you've added the chicken bouillon cube. While they all get acquainted, put the chicken pieces in a shallow casserole. Add the garlic, soy sauce, and sugar to the spicy broth, and pour it all over the chicken. Bake at 350° F. for an hour, more or less, turning once.

I feel quite sure that had I taken the plants into the greenhouse in the fall, I could have. As it was, I grew a spice and that was nice.

Those who live in southern Florida can easily grow and harvest ginger outdoors. *Wyman's Gardening Encyclopedia* states that it is hardy in zone 10, and that it takes 10 to 12 months for sizable rhizomes to form. This ginger *(Zingiber officinale)* is not to be confused with the asarums, which are so lovely and so hardy in zone 3 (the northern parts of Vermont, New Hampshire, Maine, North Dakota, and Minnesota, plus small sections of Idaho, Colorado, and Wyoming. Wild American ginger *(Asarum canadense)* puts up its twin, heart-shaped leaves in early spring. Every year, without fail, I am down on my knees, pulling away pine needles to find that very curious, chocolate-brown blossom hugging the ground. This is the plant that all the books tell us served the colonists as a ginger substitute. I have tried it, and a poor substitute it is. The tubers are very small, and the aroma and flavor very mild in the fresh root, although somewhat stronger when dry.

I often use dried chunks of gingerroot along with another exotic spice — star anise — for one of our favorite chicken dishes. You might like to try the recipe, which is fat-free and salt-free except for the soy sauce. You can usually find star anise and dried ginger at your favorite herb shop or in a Chinese grocery store.

MADELEINE H. SIEGLER, MONK'S HILL HERBS, WINTHROP, ME 04364

♥ ♥ ♥ ♥ ♥ ♥ ♥ ♥ ♥ ♥

GROWING HERBS HYDROPONICALLY

by Bertha Reppert

BERTHA REPPERT'S Herbs with Confidence, written in her personalized, friend-to-friend and easy-to-understand style, outlines step-by-step the countless ways you can make herbs work for you — with complete confidence. It includes 135 tried-and-true recipes, 55 herb crafts, 50 herbs in-depth, garden plans, and Bertha's accumulated experience over the years. You will love it! To order, see Appendix for address; you may also wish to order a copy of The Rosemary House's catalog, featuring everything herbal.

When indoor gardening beckons, the thought of green, growing plants draws me from my armchair to my window. Alas, visions of lush, redolent, green herbs on sunny windowsills rarely come true, especially during short or sunless days. Although growing herbs indoors in soil in pots is not always satisfying, I have had phenomenal success with growing herbs hydroponically. They are healthy, dark green, fast-growing, productive, and tasty. Although herbs do not like wet feet in the garden, they flourish under water culture simply because no soil is involved. In the garden, soil acts as an anchor for plants, and nutrients must be converted to liquid to be absorbed by the roots. Without soil, no conversion need take place, and herbs thrive. Another plus to soilless gardening is the absence of weeds and, generally, of insects, diseases, and other soilborne organisms (or, at least, they are easily controlled). Hydroponics is everybody's dream of carefree gardening.

As in other hobbies, you can make a big investment in hydroponic gardening equipment, but it is possible to grow herb bouquets through hydroculture with a few, simple household tools. A list of necessary supplies appears to the right.

2 pans (such as plastic wash basins) that fit into each other (the bottom of the upper pan should clear the bottom of the lower pan by at least 2 inches when the two are fitted together)

Six 6-inch strips of cloth about 1-inch wide (use polyester; it won't rot)

A well-balanced, water-soluble houseplant fertilizer (such as Peter's House Plant Special 15-30-15)

Vermiculite, or any other sterile growing medium

Several sturdy herb plants, such as parsley, chives, rosemary, sage, and thyme

If you wish to begin with seeds, you will need to germinate them first in separate containers before transferring the baby seedlings to your hydroculture garden. Seeds tend to rot when exposed to the constant wetness of hydroponics, but cuttings and long shoots develop roots rapidly in the water.

To set up your hydroponic garden, first drill six, ½-inch drainage holes in the bottom of the smaller (upper) pan. Draw the lengths of fabric through the holes, leaving them half in and half out, to act as wicks for carrying the nutrient-growing solution to your herbs. Fill the same pan with a sterile growing medium such as vermiculite, sand, pebbles, gravel, or sphagnum moss. Cover the all-important wicks with the growing medium. Next, mix 2 quarts of the houseplant fertilizer according to instructions on the label. Nest the filled, upper pan in the lower one, and pour the solution through the growing medium. The liquid will drip through the holes into the bottom pan. Be sure that only the wicks hang in the liquid, not the bottom of the upper pan. You've now created the life-support system that will carry food to the roots of the herbs.

Wash all soil from your herb plant roots by gently tapping each root ball and soaking it. This step is *important*. It is best to wash the roots in a bucket so as not to clog your household drains. (Pour the muddy water onto your nearest drought-stricken shrub.)

As soon as your growing medium is thoroughly dampened, gently tuck the herbs into the upper basin. Because of the intensive feeding process, the herbs can be crowded together to grow twice the number of plants usually possible in the same amount of space.

All you need to do for your easy-care water garden is to pour fresh fertilizer solution (always mixed with tepid tap water) through the growing medium every week, or as often as needed to keep an inch or two in the bottom pan. The fertilizer provides the oxygen essential to plants that are accustomed to life in soil. The wicks keep a supply of oxygen flowing to your herbs, causing them to grow at an amazing rate.

Herbs thrive in our cool, energy-wise home, but if your home is hot and dry, humidity will need to be provided. Because misting helps a lot, keep a filled mister handy to supply moisture daily. Also, frequently check the water level in the bottom pan. I also advise scratching the surface of the medium occasionally to allow air to reach the roots and to discourage fertilizer salt buildup. In fact, you might even poke a dowel through the drainage holes to supply more oxygen to the roots.

Place your hydroponic garden on your sunniest (southern) windowsill. Or, do as I do and assure their success in the most unlikely locations by growing them under lights. Use fluorescent horticultural lights, or insert a grow-light bulb in any regular lamp fixture. The light source should be less than a foot above the plants. You may eventually want to put the lights on an automatic timer so that the unit turns on in the morning and off at night, 12 hours later. The cost of the electricity is negligible, and the rewards justify the expense. A great place for a water garden is right under your kitchen cabinets. Highly decorative, the lights will brighten your darkest space, while growing fragrant, flavorful *bouquet garnis* for the cook's delight. Under hydroculture, the herbs will grow fast, so keep them trimmed and enjoy your handy harvest!

FROM *Herbs with Confidence* by Bertha Reppert (Remembrance Press, 1986)
Bertha Reppert, The Rosemary House, Mechanicsburg, PA 17055

❧ CORRECTING THE SOIL IN YOUR GARDEN ❧

Every 2 or 3 years, in November, is an excellent time to have the soil in your herb beds tested and corrected for the proper pH level. This is also the best time to dig up new beds for spring planting. Lime should be applied no less than 3 months before seeding a new bed, so the preceding November is the best time to prepare these. The soil is more likely to be dry and workable now than in the next 4 or 5 months, and the melting snows will help the soil to absorb the lime.

The pH is a measurement of the relative acidity and alkalinity of soil on a scale of 1 to 14. Optimum growth for most herbs occurs in a soil with a pH level of 6.0 to 7.0, which is slightly acid to neutral (7.0). Soil-testing kits are available at garden nurseries or from your local County Cooperative Extension Service. To raise the pH level, use lime; to lower a too-sweet (alkaline) soil, use sulphur.

Another advantage to correcting the soil in November is that you can use the best types of lime now — either crushed limestone, which is slow-acting and long-lasting, or dolomitic limestone, which contains the important trace element, magnesium, and is also slow-acting. The lime should be tilled or worked into the bed at a 3-inch depth. Hydrated lime or Quicklime must be used if you wait until the beginning of a growing season. These types of lime are fast-acting in the soil, but their effects are short-lived. They are caustic materials and can cause leaf-burn on contact with wet foliage of existing herbs in beds.

Wood ashes will neutralize an acid soil quickly, but need to be applied at twice the volume of limestone.

Anise, fennel, lavender, and winter savory are happiest with a pH of 7.0, and will not tolerate a level below 6.0. Sage, sweet basil, and watercress will tolerate a pH of 4.0, and sweet woodruff requires a pH of 4.5 to 5.0. All of the other common herbs in home gardens will do very well in a soil with a pH no lower than 6.0 and on up to 7.0. No herbs will survive a pH below 4.0 or above 8.5.

THIS INFORMATION IS CULLED FROM *HERBS: 1001 GARDENING QUESTIONS ANSWERED* (POWNAL, VT: GARDEN WAY PUBLISHING, 1990) AND FROM ALLEN V. BARKER'S ARTICLE ENTITLED "LIMING OF SOILS FOR PRODUCTION OF HERBS," IN THE WINTER 1989 ISSUE OF *THE HERB, SPICE, AND MEDICINAL PLANT DIGEST*, COOPERATIVE EXTENSION OF U.S. DEPARTMENT OF AGRICULTURE, UNIVERSITY OF MASSACHUSETTS, AMHERST, MA 01003 (SEE APPENDIX FOR SUBSCRIPTION RATES).

Thanksgiving Herbs

A *THANKSGIVING* FROM "*NATIVE HARVESTS*"

❧ *Turkey with Oyster-Cornbread-Raisin Stuffing* ❧
YIELD: SERVES 12

12-pound turkey, dressed
Giblets
8 cups crumbled cornbread or
*   johnnycakes*
5 scallions, diced (including tops)
10 medium-sized fresh mushrooms,
*   chopped*
1 cup shelled, dried black walnuts
1 cup raisins
2 tablespoons chopped fresh parsley
½ teaspoon chopped fresh savory

18 oysters, shucked and chopped
*   (reserve liquid)*
1 egg
1 clove garlic, crushed
5 tablespoons giblet broth
½ cup drippings
1 cup Sunflower Seed Butter
5 tablespoons oyster liquid for
*   basting*
3 tablespoons cornmeal

Prepare the cleaned, dressed turkey for stuffing.

In a covered saucepan, simmer the giblets in 1½ cups water for 30 minutes. Remove, cool, and chop. Return to the cooled broth and save for gravy.

Preheat the oven to 325° F.

I met the lovely BARRIE KAVASCH at a Michigan State University conference, where she inspired us all regarding the culture and herbalism of Native Americans. A charismatic lecturer, Barrie is an ethnobotanist, an herb grower and researcher, a culinary historian, and a very talented freelance writer and illustrator. Craig Claiborne, in The New York Times, *described her book* Native Harvests: Recipes and Botanicals of the American Indian, *from which these recipes are shared, as "the most intelligent and brilliantly researched book on the food of the American Indian." Barrie invites us to enjoy the wild harvests, "with caution, moderation, and correct identification of paramount importance"; her beautiful sketches make identification an easy task.*

Thoroughly mix the cornbread, scallions, mushrooms, walnuts, raisins, parsley, savory, oysters, egg, garlic, and 5 tablespoons giblet broth together in a large bowl. Lightly stuff the neck and body cavities of the turkey; do not pack. Skewer the openings closed and truss the legs together.

Place the turkey, breast side up, in a large roasting pan. Rub the bird generously with ¼ cup of the Sunflower Seed Butter. Roast the turkey, uncovered, in the preheated oven, basting every 30 minutes with a mixture of 5 tablespoons of the oyster liquid and the juices from the bird. Every hour or so, dot with spoonfuls of the remaining ¾ cup Sunflower Seed Butter. Roast for approximately 6 hours, allowing 40 minutes per pound as a guide. The bird is done when the legs move easily at the joint.

Giblet gravy should be made in a saucepan over medium heat, after the turkey is finished and being carved. Add ½ cup of the seasoned drippings from the turkey to the giblets and broth. Bring to a boil, add the cornmeal, and simmer, stirring continually until the gravy thickens and is creamy. Serve hot.

❧ *Sunflower Seed Butter* ❧

Sunflower seeds (*Helianthus* spp.) from the native North American annual plant were used extensively by many tribes. The seeds are an excellent protein source, raw or roasted. Sunflower seed oil is extracted by bruising and boiling the seeds, then skimming the oily residue off the broth. The ground paste from the seeds retains their natural oil and makes a fine butter. The roasted seeds and shells make an interesting coffee drink. To make *Sunflower Seed Butter*, using stones, a mortar and pestle, or a blender, grind 1 cup or more of the seeds into a paste. Refrigerate.

COURTESY OF ELLA THOMAS/SEKATAU OF THE NARRAGANSET PEOPLES.

❧ *Lovage Tea* ❧

Lovage *(Levisticum officinale)* and the wild plant, Scotch lovage *(Ligustrum scoticum),* are smooth, perennial herbs that provide excellent food and tea resources. Both the celerylike foliage and the large, aromatic roots may be enjoyed fresh or dried (in moderate amounts). Add a small handful of leaves and roots to a quart of boiling water; steep, covered, for 15 minutes. Sweetening is hardly necessary. This pale, fragrant, mineral-rich tea is a digestive aid.

FROM *NATIVE HARVESTS: RECIPES AND BOTANICALS OF THE AMERICAN INDIAN* BY BARRIE KAVASCH (NEW YORK: RANDOM HOUSE, 1979)

Lovage *(Levisticum officinale)*

❧ *Thanksgiving Potpourri* ❧

A potpourri recipe with a twist — one for the birds!

1 cup sage leaves
1 cup lovage leaves
½ cup pumpkin seeds
½ cup squash seeds
1 cup Indian corn
2 cups goldenrod
½ cup sunflower seed
1 cup evening primrose pods
2 cups basil leaves and flowers
2 cups hickory nuts
2 cups acorns

This large quantity makes a colorful, crisp, and fresh-scented mixture that is decorative in open, glass containers for the holidays. After the festivities, it can be stored for later use as winter bird feed. The leaves will blow away, and the remaining nuts and seeds are attractive to foraging birds.

FROM *LIVING WITH POTPOURRI* BY KATE JAYNE AND CLAUDETTE MAUTOR (WHITE PLAINS, NY: PETER PAUPER PRESS)

KATE JAYNE, of Sandy Mush Herb Nursery, has collaborated with CLAUDETTE MAUTOR, also of the farm, to write a delightful, 64-page primer on the art and history of potpourri. Their book traces the course of scents and fragrances from earliest recorded history to present times. Living with Potpourri (White Plains, NY: Peter Pauper Press) includes recipes for holiday potpourris, and mixes for the bath, bedroom, and linen closet, as well as for the teapot and soup kettle. Flower and color meanings enhance the recipes for Valentine, wedding, and birth potpourris. This is the first account I have seen of the significance and symbolism of color in potpourri.

❧ *Margaret's Turkey-Herb Baste* ❧

Once you try this, you'll never bake another turkey without it!

¼ teaspoon dry mustard	1 teaspoon fennel seed
¼ teaspoon nutmeg	1 teaspoon salt (optional)
¼ teaspoon allspice	1 teaspoon pepper
2 teaspoons dried parsley	½ cup white wine (such as Chablis)
1 teaspoon sage	2 tablespoons lemon juice

Using a mortar and pestle, grind all the herbs and spices together. Add to the wine and lemon juice, and blend together. Before baking, brush the inside and rub the outside of the turkey with the mixture. Stuff with your favorite dressing. Use remaining mixture to baste the turkey as it cooks.

MRS. MARGARET J. SPRINGER, WEBSTER, NY 14580-0213

SAGE YOUR TURKEY OR MINT YOUR CHICKEN!

Starting from the rear of the uncooked poultry, carefully slip your fingers under the breast skin and separate it from the meat. Place rinsed and dried whole sage leaves under the skin on both sides of the turkey or chicken. This will not only add flavor to the meat, but also be quite decorative. Or, for a refreshing taste change, use fresh spearmint leaves, and add salt, 2 or 3 tablespoons butter, and a cupful of additional spearmint to the cavity before trussing the chicken. Garnish the platter with mint sprigs. PVS

❧ *Kim's Limed Turkey Sauce* ❧

A unique way to use turkey leftovers.

4 cloves garlic, minced
Butter or oil for sauté
1 cup turkey or chicken broth
4 tablespoons brown sugar
3 tablespoons tamari sauce
 4 limes, peeled and cut up (reserve
    the pulp and juice)

½ cup raspberry vinegar
¼ cup sherry
2½ to 3½ cups cooked turkey cubes
1 tablespoon fresh sage leaves,
    minced (1½ teaspoons dried)
Rice for 3 or 4, depending on
    amount of meat

Sauté garlic in butter or oil in skillet. Reserving ¾ cup of broth, add the ¼ cup broth, brown sugar, tamari, lime pulp, vinegar, and sherry to the skillet. Mix well, and simmer, covered, for 15 minutes. Add ½ cup more broth (for 2½ cups turkey) or ¾ cup broth (for 3½ cups turkey) to the skillet, along with the turkey pieces. Simmer another 10 minutes, uncovered, stirring a few times. Add the sage and simmer another 5 minutes. Serve on hot rice.

Dry leftover lime peel from Kim's recipe, and use in citrus potpourris or hot herbal teas. PVS

Herb Businesses and Lectures

SO YOU'D LIKE TO START A LITTLE HERB BUSINESS?

by Jim Long

Have you been thinking it would be fun to start a little herb business in your back yard — something that would supplement your income and not take much additional time? After all, you're in the garden anyway; why not grow some extra herbs and flowers and get paid for doing it? Let's say that in this fantasy of yours you would like a tiny, quaint shop where you could work up your herb crafts and give back the kitchen and living room to your family. You convince the family that they'd have more space, more headroom if the bundles of drying flowers and herbs were in their own place. The family will probably be supportive, even enthusiastic at this point, in order to regain normalcy in the house.

A site for the shop is found; maybe you choose an existing structure to remodel or maybe you decide to build a new one — just something small. After all, you don't really *need* much space, because most of your crafts are being stored in closets and cupboards now anyway. You forge ahead, family or friends helping with the building project. You order a little bit of stock to supplement what you have — some books, ribbon for your wreaths, bottles for oils, decorative storage jars for potpourri and bulk materials, some baskets.

The day arrives and you move in with excitement. Your family is pleased, as it is like having a whole new room in the house. Into the new shop you move the bundles of larkspur, cornflower, lamb's-ears, statice, and chive blossoms from the rafters in the kitchen and the baskets of dried rosemary, poppyseed, lavender, and basil from family living space. Ah, what roominess you've put back into your home! The shop fills up quickly, and you arrange it to look homey. Here it is, your dream fulfilled — a real herb shop, and only steps from the house!

Your next step is to advertise. You put up signs on the shop and on the road. You invite garden clubs to visit, serve them tea, and sell your wares. You demonstrate your crafts and go on speaking engagements to build your reputation. Newspaper reporters come for interviews and articles, which bring more customers to your shop. You're dedicated to having the shop open on Fridays and Saturdays *only*, and you always advertise that. The other days are for maintaining your home and family, for errands, and for time for yourself. Of course, because you are open two days each week, your lectures and demonstrations come out of your other time. And, garden clubs usually have specific meeting days, so they always require that they come on their regular day. This means that you open on a special day for them, but that's only an occasional thing. Fridays and Saturdays find you busy, so you have to have some help with running the cash register, serving tea, and keeping the shop neat and orderly.

Say that you've put between $5,000 and $20,000 into your building — even remodeling costs a sizable amount. You must have shelving, a counter, display areas. As the shop gains a reputation, you no longer have the space in your little shop to fill orders, make wreaths, pot up herbs, dry herbs and flowers, and make your crafts (which probably is being done in the house again!). The shop must be kept presentable, so the messes go back to the basement or kitchen. You need a workroom added on to the shop. And a small kitchen would help with the refreshment preparations for your customers. The groups are larger than you'd anticipated, and sometimes you have two groups at one time, so a screened deck with tables would be beneficial. At this point you need an accountant to look at your sales and expenditures and give you some advice about expansion.

"Open Friday and Saturday, 9 to 5 only" sounded good in the beginning, but you find that people call during the week with, "I know you're closed today, but my sister is visiting from Vermont and has to leave before Friday; so could we please come out for just a few minutes? We won't stay long and won't interrupt what you are doing." Naturally, this is one of your good customers calling. So, even though it is Wednesday and you'd planned to weed the garden while composing your lecture for Thursday evening, you seem to have little choice but to say, "Sure, come

It sounds as though your fantasy has come true. You've started your herb business, it's within walking distance from your home and garden, and it is successful. It sounds perfect! Can this fantasy become a reality? Certainly it can, and has for lots of people. But is this the whole picture, or could there be more to the story? Let's look further.

over." To get ready for visitors, you must run in and change your clothes. One way or the other, you don't want a good customer who is bringing her sister to see you in whatever you are wearing (or *not* wearing!) in the garden on your day off. But first you need to tidy up the shop. You had emptied the herb dryer into baskets, planning to do some mixing in the afternoon, and some of it spilled on the floor. You need to give the floor the old "lick and a promise" once-over, as well as to sweep the grass clippings from the lawn mower off the porch.

The phone rings. Darn. You've left the portable phone in the house. You can make it to the house in four rings. Just as you get through the door on the third ring, they hang up. (When will city- and townspeople learn that gardeners need several rings in order to reach the receiver in time?) You shower and dress, or rather are still dressing, as the customers arrive. One glance in the mirror just before darting out the door shows you that you put on the shirt that's missing some buttons. Back you run, turning on the teakettle for the tea you advertise will be on if visitors call first. You change your top garment, and run out to greet your guests.

They're impressed, say nice things, and of course, want a tour. You give your tour, encouraging them to taste, smell, and look at the plants you have. You answer their questions about herbs. They have this friend back in Vermont whom you must meet and would dearly love. You hear about that person's life story, complete with divorces and broken legs. They're nice people, however, and you are relaxing a bit now. The phone rings again. Great. It's still back in the house. If you've had the business long, you have by now worn a path to the house across the shortest route to the phone. When you return, the visitors are in the shop. They have picked out some things they want to take back home for gifts. The good customer says she'll come back to get *her* things on your regular business day, to save you the trouble of writing up an order on your day off. Her sister spends $21.78. They thank you, and are gone, after staying an hour and a quarter. You can't count the time you spent getting ready, or the time you lost in the garden working on the weeds and your lecture. But you've lost your momentum and your gardening mood, and need a cup of tea for reflection. All in all, the better part of the afternoon is shot.

Was the visit worth it? How do you estimate the profit or cost of having customers drop in when you're not open? Are you frustrated by this interruption of your quiet day off? Some business owners feel that this type of thing is a fair trade-off for not having to work away from home or for someone else. Others find that such experiences can lead to burn-out, in which case tact becomes difficult when dealing with demanding customers. Burn-out is a reality in any job, and particularly one in which the outside world is invited into your own private garden space. Some people suggest the safeguard of being firm and saying no when you need to have time for yourself. After all, if you don't take care of yourself first, the business will suffer much more in the long run. Limiting your commitments, sticking to your business hours, giving yourself relaxing time away from the business with family and friends — all help to keep you in good form. Reserving time for those you love should be at the top of your list because they are a lot more important to you than the business. Set time aside for vacations — and that *doesn't* mean dragging your significant other to an herb conference and calling it a vacation!

Look at all the angles before you begin. Don't be afraid to write out a worst-possible scenario, listing the worst aspects of having a business near your home, and then a best-possible outcome, including all the great things that could happen. Compare the lists. Be realistic in what you expect from your business and about the actual *need* for an herb business in your area. Are there several herb farms or shops in the immediate vicinity? Certainly, you would want to consider the existing competition before investing any great amount of money into a business. Are you located in a heavy-traffic area for constant exposure from passing cars; or, at least, are you situated in a place where people would enjoy going out of their way to visit you? Assess the pluses and minuses of your location and consider how you would take advantage of or overcome them. Set goals and write out what you would like your business to be like in 5 years. Make a 5-year plan leading to this achievement, step-by-step. If you decide to proceed, make your "little herb business" something that is a joy to experience on all levels of your own life, as well as the lives of your loved ones.

❤

You are the only one who can control how your "little herb business" proceeds, and you, too, are the only one who can estimate the cost of taking on such a project.

❤

From *The Ozarks Herbalist*
Jim Long, Long Creek Herbs, Oak Grove, AK 72660

Tips on Beginning an Herb Business

If you're thinking of starting an herb business, choose a highly visible location (preferably separate from your home), have an alternate source of income for the first few years, check out zoning and health regulations (particularly if you will sell food products), plan to sell both herb plants and herb products, and maintain a good working relationship with the public by being active and supportive in the life of the community. Anyone who sells herbal culinary products should be aware of the herbs approved or not approved by the Federal Drug Administration for sale for human consumption. For a complete list, see Frontier Herbs' *Herb and Spice Handbook* (to order, see Appendix for address). You will learn in this book, for instance, that lemon verbena, sweet woodruff, and several other commonly used herbs may be sold for human consumption only if the intended use is alcoholic beverages! This does not necessarily mean they are unsafe for other uses, but that the status of these herbs has not been changed since this list was compiled in 1958. Protect yourself by using the guidelines if you are in the business of selling culinary products!

Pat and Jon Bourdo, Woodland Herb Farm, Northport, MI 49670

I've been a fan of BETTY WOLD's ever since, years ago, she shared with me and my newsletter readers her experience, after raising five children, of moving herself and her herbs to Oklahoma and single-handedly chopping through the stony soil on her new farm to create lush herb gardens! By now, her outreach through her lectures, exhibits at craft fairs, and her writings has created many herb enthusiasts in her area of the country. She co-writes a quarterly journal, The Herb Gazette, *and has just written* Speaking of Herbs, *a collection of her lectures and crafts for the would-be speaker (in fact, for anyone interested in herbs). I had the pleasure of spending some time with this talented lady at an herb conference, and I know you will enjoy her wonderful sense of humor and her clever ways to use herbs in her writings.*

❤

TEACHING HERB CLASSES

Portia Meares, a former teacher and TV producer, the founder of The Business of Herbs, and instrumental in the founding of The International Herb Growers and Marketers Association, has prepared an extremely informative sample syllabus for teaching herb classes. For details, send a SASE to Portia Meares, P.O. Box 559-HT, Madison, VA 22727.

❤

WORKING THE CRAFT SHOW CIRCUIT

by Betty Wold

When I was young, my great ambition was to join the circus. I never did, but as the years passed, I found the perfect substitute — working the craft show circuit. It offers everything but the animals: tents, crowds, excitement, novelty, diversity, travel, and income.

For those starting out in the retail side of an herb business, the craft show is a perfect introduction. It requires little initial investment, offers flexible hours, and gives you a choice of time and location. It provides a means of testing and refining your product, and it sharpens your sales and display techniques. It affords the opportunity to meet, and to educate, a large number of potential customers. It introduces you to the bookkeeping and other financial aspects of your business. In short, you have not only a good income, but a solid background should you afterwards desire to open a shop or start a mail-order business.

It goes without saying that you will need dependable transportation, anything from a small economy car to a truck or a van. It is amazing how much you can carry once you decide what you will take and how you will pack. Display tables should be foldable. Six, stacking, plastic shelves take a space only 8" x 8" x 30" when disassembled. Try to carry things in containers that can be stacked to use for display. Sheets, tablecloths, and 60-inch polyester fabric make good covers and are easily washed. Chicken wire stapled to lightweight, folding screens and backed with appropriate fabric provides a good background for hanging your product. Take along lightweight, plastic sheeting to cover your display in case of rain, a cash box or apron with pockets, plenty of change, and a chair — for the rare moments when you can sit. If you are working alone, take a picnic cooler with lunch and beverage. Later, you may wish to invest in a booth cover; you can design your own or buy one of the attractive and convenient setups now on the market.

How do you find out about the craft shows to attend? Contact the Chambers of Commerce and the Department of Tourism in states near you to ask for the listing of events for the year. Read local newspapers, and subscribe to one of the publications that list upcoming shows, such as *Potpourri from Herbal Acres* and *The International Herb Growers and Marketers Association Newsletter* (see Appendix for addresses); newsletters often give important information about the management and customer interests at specific fairs. Plan your schedule early in the year and keep an up-to-date calendar. Send in your application and fees early, and keep all confirmations and information clipped to the appropriate calendar page. Fees can vary from $10 with no commission to $100 with 10 percent commission. Usually, the more expensive shows require you to submit photos or samples of your work before they accept you as an exhibitor. Experience will tell you which shows are best for your product, so keep good records.

Obviously, you are taking a product you expect to sell. Listen to the comments of your customers *and* non-customers. Don't sit down while you talk with customers unless you use a folding stool that puts you at eye level with them. Constantly evaluate your product in terms of customer interest and new trends. Try to develop at least one product that is original. If it is a good selling item, you can be sure others will copy it, but yours will be first and best. Try for newspaper publicity covering your work, and display a copy of the article at your booth. Tailor your product and your display to the upcoming season. If possible, have something to demonstrate. Nothing attracts a crowd like a crowd. Don't display too many of the same handcrafted item, as this allows customers to think they can come back later to pick up what they want — but they seldom do return. Provide a sign-up sheet for news of future products, workshops, or lectures. Offer handouts explaining the uses of your product. Include your name and address on all your printed material. Keep lists of customers, including type of merchandise purchased and amount of sale. Copy information from any checks. These lists will be invaluable if you wish to expand to a shop or mail-order business or to offer workshops or lectures.

Apply for a resale number; most wholesalers require one. To avoid dealing with pennies, or customer resentment for an added tax, it is best to set your craft show prices so that tax is included. Keep accurate records, not only for tax purposes, but more important, so that you know whether or not you are actually making money. List all expenses: transportation, licenses, fees, taxes, cost of materials, meals, and motels. Balance against sales. Are you making a reasonable wage for your time? The first year or two you may realistically expect this wage to be low, but consider the experience and exposure you are getting.

❤

You can learn from your fellow exhibitors, even those with whom you feel you are competing. Approach them with the attitude that you are willing to share and most times you will find them equally agreeable. Above all, enjoy yourself.

❤

FROM A LECTURE AT *HERBS '88* IN BATON ROUGE, LOUISIANA; REPRINTED WITH THE PERMISSION OF THE INTERNATIONAL HERB GROWERS AND MARKETERS ASSOCIATION BETTY WOLD, SEQUOYAH GARDENS, GORE, OK 74435

SPEAK UP!...FOR HERBS

by Bertha Reppert

Lecturing is a natural byproduct of being in the herb business. Speaking engagements can add revenue, as well as bring in new customers. No matter which aspect of the remarkable world of herbs is your chosen field, if you become known as an herb "expert," you will be asked many questions and, inevitably, invited to answer them in a public forum.

Public speaking has been elected "the most-feared activity" by many Americans. We shy people (to quote Garrison Keillor) need more practice. Contrary to popular opinion, I have found that one really never gets "used to hanging," so brace yourself for the challenge with the knowledge that speakers are made, not born.

BERTHA REPPERT'S advice about lecturing on herbs can be just as useful to the herb gardener who loves to share herbal knowledge with the public, as to someone in the herb business. Bertha charms her audiences wherever she appears. Her expert knowledge of herbs, combined with her down-home stance, unquestionable enthusiasm, and great sense

of humor, all keep the audience spellbound and rapt in attention. When I have heard her speak, I've found myself disappointed that her talk was over — she left me hungry for more! This article first appeared in the September/ October 1989 issue of The Business of Herbs, *an absolutely essential bi-monthly periodical for anyone in the herb business. (See Appendix for address and ordering information.) There is much to be learned from the herb experts included in this periodical, whether you are contemplating an herb business or not.*

Your first venture may be a small group at church or the local Friends of the Library. Size, you quickly learn, has nothing to do with intimidation. Remember, you *need* to be nervous; it's that extra rush of adrenalin that will get you through.

Building confidence. The secret is thorough preparation. Self-confidence develops in direct relationship to advance preparation. For complete self-assurance, do your homework well. Until you develop an easy delivery, plan to speak only on what you know and understand very well. Prepare a lengthy outline listing all your favorite herbal ideas, anything that has struck you at one time or another as particularly remarkable. You'll be amazed at how quickly you fill your worksheet.

If gardening is your strong suit, play on that important strength. Your high level of personal knowledge and lively enthusiasm will inspire even those with brown thumbs. Cooking or crafts, lore or home remedies, plant drying or symbolism, insecticides or potpourri — all are possible subjects to consider. After you've completed your list, reduce it by half and start working on your patter. The rest of the list will become Talk No. 2. Offer several topics. Be sure to give the program chairperson a choice and let him or her know you can be invited back another year.

Presentation. Come the appointed time, pick up your basket of goodies and sally forth. The more you lecture, the better you become at packing. Your bag of tricks becomes rather like the lively hoard of clowns emerging from a compact car, a number of fascinating items to "show and tell." Play put-and-take with your display, changing and honing your presentation each time.

Props can serve as your notes as well as display. However, no one will fault you for reading from a carefully prepared and well-rehearsed text, if necessary. On the other hand, you *will* be criticized for muddling along, rambling like mint in all directions, and speaking on and on.

Mr. Malloy (of *Dress for Success* fame) says an expensive wrist watch and good shoes are requisites for center stage. I wear a bit more than that, sometimes a long shirt and decorated hat, a fresh herb bouquet, my spice necklace *(See pages 231-33 for how to make your own spice necklace. PVS)*, or my plant-dyed sweater. If the mood strikes, I may even don my rosemary halo. Fortunately, Mr. Malloy approves of dressing to represent the product. Of course, I put on The Rosemary House apron for a class in cooking. As for my old gardening Timex, it may not meet high standards, but keeping track of the time is absolutely crucial to good speaking. Know when to stop! For this, an egg timer will serve as well as a Rolex.

The stage. Be sure to tell the program chair your exact requirements: tables and covers, lavaliere microphone, a glass of water, assistance to unload or pack, parking near the entrance, time necessary to set up. Whatever your needs may be, spell them out very carefully. Confirm it in writing, too. Then, arrive prepared to search for the janitor and set up your own tables, anyway. Don't let glitches ruffle your calm. I have arrived at an important engagement and found assorted-sized, unattractive card tables set up, uncovered. "Be prepared" is a very good motto. I have learned to carry a few extra tablecovers and to allow extra time for things that go wrong.

Slides. I had a professional photographer capture one of my lectures on film, but I rarely use it. When I do use my slides, I first pass around a very large bunch of fresh herbs or a bowl of fragrant potpourri to touch and smell in the darkened room. "Caress them!" I urge. The room is instantly fragranced, and my audience's senses are alert. The slides I use most often are those of herb gardens and plants in their prime.

Payment. You work hard at a lecture — preparing, packing, performing. There's more to a good road show than meets the eye, so you absolutely must charge (except perhaps for your church or local service club). If you don't, there's no limit to the programs you will be asked to perform for nothing. If you don't know what to charge, ask "What is your usual program honorarium?" You may be pleasantly surprised. If no one mentions price, always say, firmly and clearly, "I have a fee," and establish what it is before you put the date on your calendar. It took me a while to learn to do that, but I have forced myself. It can save misunderstandings and worse, bad feelings.

What you charge is determined by where you live, how far you travel, and the size of the group. It can be a modest $15 or $25, a moderate $50 or $100, or up into megabucks in metropolitan areas where even parking is expensive. My usual fee within our area is $50. Remember, please, we're talking Mechanicsburg, Pennsylvania, a very small town with small program budgets and penny parking meters. Speaking fees are fraught with variables and I can only tell you my own personal guidelines. I figure it's good advertising for The Rosemary House that should pay off eventually. For me, it's getting out the message that counts.

Beyond the county line, I charge $75 because of the distance and time elements. To go a hundred miles, which means 4 hours or more of travel time, my fee jumps to $100, plus 25 cents a mile. Beyond that I quote additional increments plus mileage, tolls, meals for two, hotels, and whatever other expenses are involved for me and friend husband. This can mean that the lecture fee is a fraction of the total cost. Sometimes we agree to put a cap on the total, say $500 to go several states away, especially if it's to raise money for a worthy project. I suggest selling tickets both to swell the crowd and ease the strain on the treasury. This has proven a very successful gambit, especially for small groups willing to host an herb tea party and publicize the event as open to the public. I gladly provide advice, recipes, and free herb tea. All of this, in other words, is negotiable and entirely up to you. You might also bear in mind this rule of thumb: Preparation and stress grow in direct proportion to the size and the cost of the show. Personally, I always feel the more it costs, the harder I must work!

❤

HOLDING ATTENTION

Nodding off in the audience is a problem for any speaker; there are those who habitually settle into their seats and promptly close their eyes against the possibility of learning something new. I seek out the brightest eyes in the audience, establish contact, and plunge in. Humor comes to the rescue. After five or six hearty guffaws, the nodder knows there's something going on that's not to be missed.

❤

Sales. It is also good to bear in mind that "show and *sell*" can increase the final figure considerably. Only twice have I been refused permission to sell my books afterwards — and I promptly doubled my fee. Book sales can easily make up for any amount of time and trouble you have expended. You have a captive audience, an appealing product, and no real competition. People like souvenirs, especially if it's something new and wonderful, inexpensive and useful, too.

Luncheon and convention committees like it when I suggest offering herbal favors and centerpieces, all in coordinating colors — and I offer to do the work involved, too. If they are willing to sell chances, door prizes from The Rosemary House, such as our big Baskets of Love or Herbs of the Zodiak, can net them many times the cost — as much as $1,000 at a large convention.

Promotion. I like to give the audience something free to take home. Recipes are always popular, as well as a handy list of herbal ideas for the household, an herb chart, or perfumed bookmarks; even a brochure on all the services you offer will suffice. Be sure it bears your name, so that it is an ad that will continue to speak for you, your business, or your book.

One program, you'll learn, quickly leads to another and another in ever-widening circles, with higher level affairs like symposiums in the offing. How busy do you want to be? Certainly, there's a tidy sum to be realized lecturing on herbs. By such public exposure, an otherwise obscure herb business well off the beaten track can be propelled into fame and fortune. Trust me!

Although word of mouth is great advertising, you may have to beat the bushes yourself to achieve this plateau. Contact all the local Chambers of Commerce to acquire the names of garden clubs, women's clubs, and other organizations and their presidents. Club announcements in the social pages of local papers will also offer leads. Large hotels and convention centers have entertainment directors who coordinate many meetings. They are always looking for something different and will welcome your input. These places can be found in your yellow pages or listed in the large newspapers or travel magazines under resorts. We have done many such "ladies' programs," and they are always lucrative.

If you are really serious about hopping on the lecture circuit, you might want to develop an effective triple-fold brochure complete with your picture, a biographical profile, some testimonials, and information on your subjects. Have it printed (even designed) professionally for mass distribution through the mail or at your programs. "Lectures and Luncheons" is a format that has become quite popular at our various local hostelries. On a fee-per-person basis, a restaurant or inn advertises an herbal luncheon by reservation only, and I am featured as part of the dessert. Changing topics with the seasons has made this a prestigious form of popular entertainment. The ladies — and some gents, too — love a special luncheon. These super audiences are unique in that they are there by choice and are out for a good time, and the day becomes a party. They are among my best contacts and always the most pleasant assignments. Don't overlook garden centers and cooking schools. They are open to suggestion and always seeking a dynamic, new speaker, especially one whose specialty is herbs.

One last bit of advice. Be smart! Demonstrate something herbal to which your audience can relate — and which they can taste or smell or touch. These senses are sometimes hard to awaken with words. Such a touch of showmanship will lure your audience up to your display afterwards, give them an opportunity for pleasant participation, and effectively demonstrate the magic of herbs.

So, go for it! Grab your basket of herbs (read that "notes") and step forthrightly into the limelight with the sure knowledge that there is no right or wrong way, only *your* way. Good luck!

BERTHA REPPERT, THE ROSEMARY HOUSE, MECHANICSBURG, PA 17055

✎ A "SHOW-AND-TELL, SEE-AND-SMELL, AND TAKE-HOME-TO-TASTE" ✎ LECTURE-DEMONSTRATION

Well, who could follow Bertha Reppert — the prototype of herb speakers, the very best there is! So as not to put anyone else in this spot, I'll volunteer. I have very little to add to what she said about the preparation for giving a lecture, except to stress the importance of good oral and written communication between you and your contact from the group about your needs and expectations concerning the event, as well as a couple of little extras. I always wanted an estimate of how many might attend, for the sake of providing enough handouts if the group was not willing to do the photocopying, and to figure out proportions for herbal tea or punch if I were providing the herbal recipes for the refreshments. And, if a microphone was going to be necessary (such as in large auditoriums) I always requested the lavaliere type, which fits around your neck, leaving your hands free to

concentrate on the props (or, to assist you in a slow death, if things aren't going well).

I had done no public speaking before an adult audience, when a fellow member of my garden club asked me to speak to the club on herbs. I was nervous about doing it, therefore, until she said, "Just tell everybody what you told me last month about your fascination with herbs!" That made it sound easy, so I accepted, hoping that my enthusiasm on a one-to-one basis would do the trick with a crowd. I didn't want my talk to seem like a rehearsed lecture (although I had rehearsed it in front of the mirror and with a tape recorder many times!), so I took three or four tablefuls of herbal "props," and lined them up in the order in which I wanted to present them. This negated the need for copious notes (although I did use a 3" x 5" card at each table with key words to remind me to define

and explain important details), because if I had a total lapse of memory, I could simply move on to the next prop. In early lectures, I found spontaneous questions from the audience distracting; so after I had developed enough self-confidence to make my own rules, I asked that questions be deferred until after the demonstration.

Soon other garden clubs, libraries, garden centers, schools, and civic organizations within a 100-mile radius were calling me to speak on herbs, so I guess the "enthusiasm" was working. By the time I was writing about herbs and selling herbal crafts to thirteen stores, I had to limit the number of public engagements, as it took a great deal of time preparing for my kind of lecture-demonstration and packing up as well as putting away again, which was by no means limited to the day of the lecture. I found a quick and easy way to cut down; I charged a fee, based on a 3-day loss of time away from my businesses, as I had found that the day before, the day during, and the day after each event were shot to me for doing anything else. From then on, my presentations were limited to two or three a year — the very interested groups.

The basics were the same for each of my demonstrations; only the emphasis changed to fit the season. I began by saying that this would be a Show-and-Tell, See-and-Smell, and Take-Home-to-Taste experience, as I wanted the audience to learn about the many sensual aspects of herbs. I always provided labeled baskets of fresh or dried herbs (usually black peppermint, lemon verbena, scented geraniums, and basils) to be passed around and squeezed and sniffed, and I gave favors of labeled fresh or dried herbs to take home for tea.

Card tables were my preference (over long tables) for easier thematic groupings; to cover them, I brought my own tablecloths, chosen to more or less match the table contents. For example, I placed my artemisia tree on a lacy, gray cloth with a purple liner; Christmas projects were displayed on red; and potted herbs, on oilcloth.

*Most of my lecturing took place at the first two tables, which contained **culinary and potpourri groupings.** To anticipate the most oft-asked questions, as I showed my quart jars of dried culinary herbs and mixes, I defined herbs ("mostly the leaves or seeds of plants useful to man for flavoring, fragrance, dyes, medicines, or decorations and grown in*

temperate climates") as contrasted with spices ("mostly the roots, barks, pods, or seeds of flavorful or fragrant plants grown in tropical climates"). I then pointed out the significant differences in flavor between fresh or home-dried herbs compared to those found in tins at the market, and explained why one uses at least twice the amount of fresh herbs as dried ("because, when dried, herbs shrink in bulk, but retain the same amount of oil as when fresh"). I then demonstrated the hand-defoliation of a dried stem of rosemary or thyme. The second grouping contained numerous samples of labeled fixatives, spices, and oils, with several jars of potpourri for examination by the audience later. Using my mortar and pestle, I blended an oil with a fixative; the aroma always permeated the air. The method of making potpourri was described and at least one sample was an unusual one (such as lemon-scented daffodils and citrus peels), to show the effectiveness of oils and fixatives. Several exotic ingredients were shown, such as patchouli, sandalwood, and vetivert.

*The next two groupings were primarily displays for close scrutiny afterwards, but I held up two or three examples from each table and discussed these in the talk. The **fragrance table** held a large variety of sachets, sweet pillows, and decorative ornaments for the home or holidays, while the **decorative herbs grouping** consisted of branches of the silvery artemisias, as well as pungent herbs such as tansy, the southern-*

woods, and sweet Annie and/or the scented basils, which participants could take home and cull the seeds from for their own gardens. At each lecture, I had a table of potted herbs to be touched and enjoyed, always including at least a bay, a lemon verbena, and some scented geraniums. Any extra potted plants were awarded as door prizes. My goal was for everyone to have something flavorful and something fragrant to take home and enjoy. I also distributed handout sheets with instructions for growing herbs, a list of mail-order herb farms selling plants, and recipes related to the potpourri demonstration and the herbal refreshments that were served.

As to the question-and-answer period, if I was stumped, I would explain that I had not experienced that herb or that problem, but would gladly research the answer and provide it by mail to be shared with everyone. Although I think that anyone who gives a presentation on herbs should have thorough knowledge of the subject matter, it is impossible to know everything about the world of many herbs, and one needn't feel apologetic about having to research an answer later.

I tried to show the audiences the many ways in which herbs had enriched my life, and after each lecture, all the jitters and all the hustle and bustle of preparation were forgotten. I was on a heady high for days because of the responses and thank yous from those in attendance. Feel free to copy my format!

A POTPOURRI BUFFET WORKSHOP

by Barbara Radcliffe Rogers

While lectures and demonstrations can be useful and informative, there is no substitute for getting right in there up to your elbows! Workshops and classes, however, are practical only for groups small enough to fit around work tables. When I was asked to give a program on potpourri-making for a group of sixty, I wondered how I could possibly give so many people any notion of how pleasant it is to blend fragrant flowers, herbs, and spices when they couldn't sniff and poke at each one. I couldn't pass bags of each around the room as I spoke, as the distraction would be counterproductive. Clearly, this called for innovative methods.

It was then that I came up with the "potpourri buffet," and it has been my most popular program ever since. Here's how it works. Half fill large, square-bottomed, plastic freezer bags with potpourri ingredients, one kind of ingredient to a bag. Label the bags with large, white labels printed in heavy, felt-tip pen. These bags will, with a little coaxing, sit up straight, but the unfilled top of the bag is long enough to seal with a plastic tie while you are traveling. Pack all these in carrying boxes.

Several weeks before the workshop, half fill a number of pint-size canning jars (or well-scrubbed jelly jars) with orrisroot chips. Into each jar, pour a tablespoon or two of essential oil, one scent to each jar. Cover, and shake well each day for a week. Be sure to label each jar with the name of the oil used.

When you pack for the workshop, take along as many teaspoons as you have jars, 3" x 5" index cards, and a large quantity of pint freezer bags or zip-top sandwich bags.

When you arrive at the workshop, set all the large bags of herbs and flowers along the front of the demonstration table. If there are too many, line them up around the ends and back as well, with all the labels facing outward. I group like things together — all the fragrant flowers, all the herbs, all the spices, and all the bulk and color ingredients. At a separate, small table, line up the scented orrisroot jars, each with its own spoon.

After you have given the basic instructions for potpourri making, begin at one end of the table and open each bag of ingredients, folding down its top as you describe the characteristics of that particular herb or flower. Tell what it contributes to the blend, what it goes well with, and what sort of scent it has. Then, describe the various oils and explain how you have pre-mixed them with the orrisroot. Explain how to shake and blend the potpourri for two weeks before using or giving it.

Ask the audience to come up, a row at a time, or any other orderly way, and create their own little bags of potpourri. Explain the procedure: Each one will get a little bag, which they should fill no more than half full (to allow blending space). As they sniff and

A FUND-RAISING POTPOURRI

Years ago, I presided over a workshop to teach members of my garden club how to make potpourri for our fall fund-raiser. Our summer newsletter told what flowers the members should save and how to dry them. The club ordered the fixatives and oils that I suggested, and I provided the herbs and spices. A dozen very excited gals turned up in September with large canning jars and scads of dried flowers. We made lavender and rose potpourri (in kitchen garbage bags), and used the remaining flowers for my Frankincense and Myrrh Potpourri (in The Pleasure of Herbs*). I discussed the art of the craft as we mixed and stirred and blended the ingredients. Each student took home one-twelfth of the results in the jars she had brought. After the potpourri had "settled," members made their own attractive containers or sachets for their blends. All were quickly sold out at the benefit. A great way for an organization to learn and benefit financially from the same process. PVS* add a pinch of this and a bit of that, they should write each ingredient on their 3" x 5" cards. Since some ingredients such as whole cloves as compared to mint leaves, are costly, it is wise to put a limit on the amount of the expensive materials allowed in each bag. You might explain that this way there will be enough to go around. When they have a blend they like, they bring their bags and cards to you at the oil-and-orris table, and *you* add the orris. Look at the ingredients and discuss what scent they wish to be predominant. Be sure they write the name of the oil, or oils, on their "recipe" cards. Seal the bag, leaving a good amount of air space.

You will be amazed at how orderly this process can be, even with large groups. People may have to wait a little, but the scents from the table are so fragrant that no one will mind.

There are several possible ways to charge for the ingredients that are used. The easiest for everyone is to charge the sponsoring group your regular speaker's fee, plus a surcharge of one or two dollars (or more, depending on how large your bags are) per person attending. The group can collect that at the door as a fee or charge more for tickets to cover it. The alternative is to charge each participant as they come through the line. If you do this, be sure to bring someone with you to collect the money, or ask the host group to provide someone, so that you won't have to do that, as well as concentrate on the oils. Make some provision for those people who want to make more potpourri while the fine array of materials is available. Set a price for extra bags and charge that separately. (Or, simply explain that you have only enough for one bag each.) Have fun offering your own "potpourri buffet"!

Barbara Radcliffe Rogers,
Herbitage Farm, Richmond,
NH 03470

DECEMBER

DEALLY, YOU WILL HAVE perused this chapter in advance of the holiday season, so that projects requiring an early start will already be in progress. You will find many lovely holiday potpourris here, as well as herbal crafts, ornaments, and recipes for holiday giving, decorating, baking, and all-around enjoyment.

Our Christmas tree is filled each year with fragrant sachets of potpourri-stuffed stars, teddy bears, hearts, butterflies, fans, cone-shaped trees, candy canes, and miniature tussie mussies, plus lavender wands and apple pomanders. What fun it is to add new shapes and fragrances each year! Start doing this now for and with your children. When, as adults, they leave home, they can take some as mementoes for their own trees, and you can add new ones each year as gifts. Adding fresh oils to the fabrics (in unnoticeable places) will revive the fragrances, as needed. This tradition makes each of their adult Christmases filled with happy

memories of home and childhood.

Use the "Christmas herbs" in your decorating and on your wreaths: bedstraw, chamomile, horehound, lavender, rosemary, thyme, and sweet woodruff. We adorn our crèche with a straw base and tiny bunches of some of these herbs that are associated with the manger legends. The dried sprigs resemble shrubbery at this scale, and make the manger scene look very natural and real. It is said that all of the above herbs, except for lavender and rosemary (which were nearby), were mixed with sweet grasses in the manger. The legend is that Mary draped her wash to dry over lavender and rosemary plants. As a result, the swaddling clothes of the Babe Jesus gave the previously scentless lavender its lovely fragrance, and Mary's cloak changed the color of the rosemary blossoms from white to blue. Rosemary, the herb of remembrance, is so appropriate to include in Christmas cards and gifts. Rue and pennyroyal, too, are part of the

Christmas traditions, in Sweden and Sicily, respectively.

After the holidays, save and dry some of your fragrant greens! This chapter ends with two blends for the New Year. Greens are optional for the one blend, and required for the other.

I wish for each of you a warm and cozy holiday season and a new year filled with all the things that really count — love, health, sustenance, and fulfillment.

Scents of the Season

A FRAGRANT CHRISTMAS

by Madeleine H. Siegler

The prettiest Christmas tree we ever had was a 5-foot, tubbed rosemary trimmed with fragrant, homemade ornaments. It represented a dramatic break with Maine tradition, where one of the earliest rites of the holiday season is the annual trip to our nearby woods to find the perfect balsam fir. The rosemary tree had been a gift, and since its arrival pre-dated our solar greenhouse, it was already occupying the living room in December.

First, I strung a set of tiny, white lights on the aromatic branches. The trimmings were white snowflakes made from pressed Queen-Anne's lace; spice balls hung from narrow, red velvet ribbon; and tiny, red or green calico hearts filled with sachet. It was a tree to please all the senses, with air currents twirling the lacy snowflakes, heat releasing the fragrance of spices, and scented hearts speaking of love for all. To this day it remains in my memory as the first Christmas tree I ever hated to dismantle.

We have trimmed other rosemary trees of my own growing in the years since that first one. Carefully dug from the garden in September, planted in huge tubs, and moved into the greenhouse by late October, they are painfully hoisted into the adjoining living room in December to give their special touch to our Christmas celebration. In the few areas of the U.S. where rosemary survives outside year round, it seems to be taken for granted and rarely thought of as something special for the holidays. Although in the North it may take several years for a rosemary to grow to be a 3- or 4-foot tree, smaller rosemaries that we dig from the garden to keep inside for the winter make charming tabletop decorations when trimmed with smaller versions of the ornaments we used on our large tree.

THE ORNAMENTS

Snowflakes. These must be prepared in late summer. Simply gather newly opened flowers of Queen-Anne's lace, remove the stems, and place the flower heads face down on the centerfold of yesterday's newspaper. Fold the other half of the paper over them, and slide the whole thing under a heavy rug — even one that you walk on! In a month, the flowers will have dried to a very sturdy hardness and will truly resemble snowflakes. Use purchased ornament hangers to suspend them from the tree. A dozen of these, carefully packaged along with some hangers, would be a nice gift for a city friend. Not exactly from your herb garden, but from the field next to it!

Spice balls. Fun to make, these are an ideal project for children who want to give gifts of their own doing. To make about twenty small balls, you will need 1 cup of unsweetened applesauce, 1½ cups ground spices, and 2 teaspoons of orrisroot (optional). I use homemade sauce from cull apples, and ½ cup each of cinnamon, nutmeg, and cloves. The orrisroot will help hold the fragrance, but the balls are strongly scented without it. Commercially canned applesauce with sugar can be used, if you find that more convenient. *These are for smelling, not eating!*

Gradually stir the spices and orrisroot into the cold applesauce. The dough should be thick enough to roll into balls without having it stick to your fingers. If the dough is crumbly, add a few drops of water. Using your hands, form small balls from the mixture, and place them on waxed-paper-lined cookie sheets to air dry. In a few days they will be dry and hard. (Do *not* bake them.) A few of these individually wrapped in netting make an attractive trim for holiday gifts, or several may be tied with cord to resemble a bunch of grapes, and hung as air fresheners in any room.

For use as tree ornaments, the balls should be larger — about the size of a golf ball. Pierce them through the middle with a skewer and let them partially dry. Carefully insert through the hole a length of narrow ribbon, folded in the middle. Pull the folded end up to form a hanging loop, and tie a small bow with the two ends at the bottom of the ball. Hang the ornaments on a coat hanger with the ends bent up until they have finished drying. An egg carton makes a fine container for storage or for gift giving. These spice balls will hold their fragrance for many years if packed away in a covered container.

SPICE "COOKIES"

To make other fragrant tree ornaments, roll the applesauce mixture between sheets of waxed paper to about ¼ inch thickness and cut with fancy cookie cutters, such as hearts, stars, trees, and gingerbread people. Trim them while moist with bits of cloves, allspice, star anise, or herb seeds such as coriander or fennel. Make a hole for a hanger before you set them aside to dry. Heavy spices that fall off when the "cookies" are dry can be glued on with household glue.

MADELEINE H. SIEGLER, MONK'S HILL HERBS, WINTHROP, ME 04364

Calico hearts. Scented with sachet, these are the finishing touch for our fragrant Christmas tree. Using a heart-shaped cookie cutter for a pattern, trace the design on two thicknesses of fabric remnants, wrong sides together, and, using pinking shears, cut out the hearts. Insert a loop of light cord in the cleft of the heart for a hanger, and stitch around three sides, leaving a 2-inch opening on a flat side for filling. Stuff with any fragrant blend of your choice, then machine stitch closed. I make some quite fat hearts for the tree, as well as some slim ones to enclose with my Christmas cards. You may prefer to use organdy or any other suitable fabric, if calico does not suit your decor.

The potpourri that I most often use for this project contains vetiver root, patchouli leaves, rosemary, lavender, sandalwood chips, tonka beans, frankincense, myrrh, and rose geranium leaves. It is a rich mixture and quite expensive to make. Another rich and spicy potpourri is made with Mrs. Varga's Fixative (see page 213). Any fragrant potpourri would be nice for the Christmas tree hearts or to use in sachets for gifts from your garden. Old candy jars make good containers for your prettiest potpourris, as do odd sugar bowls if they have covers. If you enjoy making patchwork or crewel pillows, you might enclose some potpourri in a square of cloth and include it in the pillow stuffing.

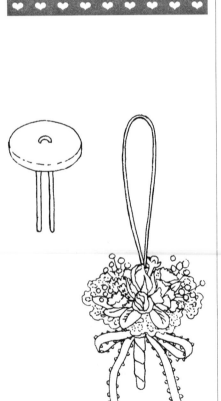

HERBAL CHRISTMAS TREE ORNAMENTS

by Barbara Radcliffe Rogers

You can make fragrant and lovely Christmas tree ornaments by following these instructions, or experimenting with other designs made from tender herb tips.

TINY TUSSIES FOR THE TREE

Miniature tussie mussies make elegant Christmas tree ornaments and are easily made from tiny, dried rosebuds, little sprigs of baby's-breath, pieces of statice, and other dried flowers. This is a perfect way to use the pieces that have broken off in the process of making herbal wreaths.

Cut a piece of sheet Styrofoam (well-washed meat trays work perfectly) about the size of a nickel. Push a 4-inch length of doubled florist's wire through it to make a handle in the center. Push the stems of herbs into the Styrofoam, using a single little rosebud in the center and other rosebuds or tiny sprigs around it. Use single florets of statice, tansy, and so on to make a tiny bouquet, and then fill in the spaces with little whole cloves, tiny sprigs of baby's-breath, leaves of boxwood, or other tiny blossoms. Glue these in place with tacky glue. When the bouquet is dry, you can glue around the edge a small piece of narrow gathered lace or little ruffles cut from paper doilies. Cover the back with a circle of white paper, first snipping off any stem ends that come through the Styrofoam. Wrap the florist's wire stem with florist's tape, and finish off with a tiny bow of ¼-inch wide, satin picot ribbon, in a complementary or matching color. Add a loop of nylon thread for a hanger.

If you don't have rosebuds, you can use a very small strawflower for your center or you can simply group your other flowers. If the flowers have stems ½ inch or longer, you can bundle your blossoms into a bouquet, tie with heavy thread, and wrap with florist's tape. To the base of the stem, glue a ruffle of slightly wider lace or eyelet gathered into a circle. Although full-sized tussie mussies can be used on the tree, these miniature ones are so delicate and dainty that they are certain to steal the show.

MINIATURE LACE WREATHS

Form a 1½- to 2-inch diameter circle using a white, florist-weight wire. (The circle may be formed around a bottle or other round object of the desired size.) Do not fasten the wire ends, but allow them to overlap about 1 inch. Using one end of the wire as though it were a needle (you may have to smooth it slightly with steel wool), thread ½- to ¾-inch wide ecru or white lace onto the circle. Use about ½ yard of lace, or enough to form a full-gathered circle. Loop the ends of the wire together, and trim off excess. If the lace is not fairly stiff, give the wreath a quick spray of starch and allow it to dry thoroughly. Decorate by gluing on tiny, dried herb blossoms, such as individual chive blossom florets, little clusters of marjoram flowers, tansy or costmary buttons, feverfew, leaves of thyme, germander, boxwood, and seeds or berries such as bay and coriander. Finish by attaching a loop for hanging and a bow of ⅛-inch satin ribbon in a complementary color.

PRESSED HERB ORNAMENTS

As herbs bloom, save the tiny blossoms and a few leaves in a flower press. Good subjects for this are thyme, sage, lavender, marjoram (especially pot marjoram, with its bright magenta flowers), the individual florets of chive and bee balm, rue, hyssop, and the smaller leaves of bay and costmary. Arrange these carefully on a microscope slide, and secure with tiny droplets of glue applied with the point of a pin. When glue is dry, cover with another slide and secure at the corners with additional glue droplets. Press until dry. Using a piece of ⅛-inch wide, satin or grosgrain ribbon in a color to match or blend well with the flowers and foliage, make a 1-inch loop and glue it to the very edge at the top center. When the loop is dry, make a border with the ribbon, covering the raw edges of the glass. Beginning at the top center, glue the ribbon in

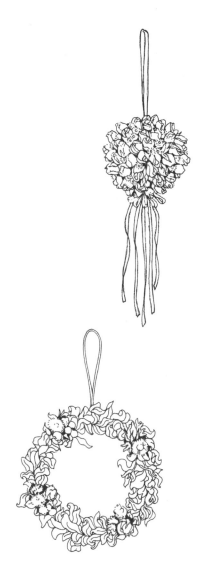

place, all the way around, ending at the center and leaving 4 or 5 inches of ribbon at each end. When the glue is thoroughly dry, tie the ends in a bow around the hanging loop and trim ends to an attractive length.

ROSE BALLS

Although we don't normally use potpourri glued onto polystyrene shapes, we have conceded that a Styrofoam ball is the only base suitable for our rose pomanders. You will need a lot of perfect, dried rosebuds, preferably small ones, and a supply of dried pearly everlasting. Push the rose stems into the ball, as closely as you can, until the ball is covered. Fill in the spaces with single everlasting blossoms, glued in place. For a hanger, make a ribbon loop, and fasten it to the ball with a hairpin; finish with a long-tailed bow. Not only do these look elegant, but the scent of the roses will combine beautifully with the evergreen and spice scents of the other herbal ornaments and the tree itself.

MINIATURE HERB WREATHS

Tiny herbal wreaths can be made from Silver King or Silver Queen artemisia when it is fresh and pliable. Use about 6 or 8 inches, as far down as the stem will bend in a round shape without being too stiff. Wrap several of these around one or two fingers, entwining them or tying them with gray sewing thread or invisible plastic thread. When they have dried, decorate them by gluing on very small flowers, florets, and leaves. If you have a microwave oven, try tying several sprigs of upright thyme into a ring in the same manner to create a very full, but tiny wreath. Place it inside a folded paper towel, and microwave for 15 seconds. Check results and continue to microwave in 5- to 10-second intervals until leaves are crisp and dry. They will retain a fresh green color and may be decorated with tiny sprigs of red, or other colored, dried flowers. A tiny satin bow may be added to any of these wreaths, along with a loop of nylon thread for hanging.

BARBARA RADCLIFFE ROGERS, HERBITAGE FARM, RICHMOND, NH 03470

CAROL JO MORSE, A STITCH 'N' THYME, WESTBROOK, ME 04092

SCENTED CRANBERRY HEART

Shape 18-gauge wire into a heart of the desired size. String fresh cranberries tightly onto the wire (they will shrink considerably). Air-dry flat in a very warm, dry place. I place mine in a drying box made with a portable heater. Using this method, it takes up to 6 days for the fruit to dry completely. Insert a hanging wire or thread, and hot-glue the wire ends together. Adorn with baby's-breath and ½-inch satin ribbon. I dot some of mine with Cape Cod Cranberry oil from Gingham 'n' Spice (see Appendix for address).

Symbolic Tussie Mussies for the Christmas Tree

by Beverly Anderson

Think about a Christmas tree whose branches have tucked in among them little nosegays surrounded by wisps of baby's-breath. If you want to create such a Victorian-style Christmas tree, use tussie mussies made with herbs and flowers that symbolize the true meaning of Christmas. Tussie mussies are nosegays made with herbs and flowers that carry a message for a special occasion. Christmas tussie mussies can be used as table favors and gift decorations, as well as ornaments on the Christmas tree.

The strongest symbol should be associated with the plant material used at the center of the tussie mussie. An appropriate Christmas symbol is a red rose, for it symbolizes not only love, but martyred love. A white rose could also be used, as it symbolizes the messianic promise. Surrounding the rose, use the following herbs: thyme, marjoram, rosemary, and sage. Thyme was believed to be one of the manger herbs, and it symbolizes strength and courage. Marjoram means happiness. Rosemary is used not only for remembrance, but also because it is part of the legend of the Holy Family's Flight to Egypt. Sage leaves represent the Wisemen. Add baby's-breath for the Christ Child. The gold of the tansy flowers reminds us of the gifts of the Wisemen, and tansy symbolizes immortality. Other materials that could be used are lady's-bedstraw and lady's-mantle, both of which represent the Virgin Mary. In addition, bedstraw was believed to be one of the manger herbs. Herbs that symbolize joy and hope are most appropriate. Surround the tussie mussie with white German statice, which means everlasting love. Complete the tussie mussie by backing it with a white, gold, or silver doily, depending on the color scheme desired.

Christmas tussie mussies add beauty, fragrance, and symbolism to holiday decorating and entertaining. As gifts they will be cherished remembrances that last long after the Christmas tree is gone.

From *The Herb Journal* of the Michigan Herb Associates Beverly S. Anderson, Illusions in Thyme, Williamston, MI 48895

Cinnamon Stick Hotplate

Make a fragrant Cinnamon Stick Hotplate by gluing 3-inch cinnamon sticks onto a 6" x 6", ¼-inch thick plywood base. Sticks may be arranged in any design of your choice. Use a good glue that is not affected by heat (such as Dow Corning Silicone Glue) and is nonflammable. Cover the bottom of the plywood with self-adhesive flannel or stick-on, cork "feet."

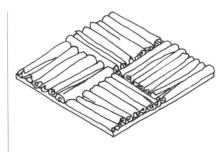

Bob Clark, Lancaster, OH

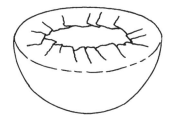

STIFFENED LACE SACHET

by Bob Clark

In this project, lace treated with stiffener is stretched over a round form, which is removed once the lace has dried. The result — an airy, lacy confection — is filled with potpourri. Depending on the ball's size and the manner in which it is decorated, the sachet may be used as a tree ornament, a decorative hanging, or a closet scenter. It is important to use stainless steel pins for this project, or your lace may get rust spots.

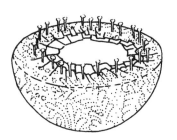

100 percent cotton lace fabric
Styrofoam or Dylite ball, bell, or egg
Aluminum foil
Stainless steel or nickel-plated pins, or T-pins
Strong, sharp scissors
Knife, fine-toothed saw, or hot-wire foam cutter
Fabric stiffener
Silicone glue
Decorative trims, ribbon, potpourri, and a 5-inch square of fine tulle
  (netting)

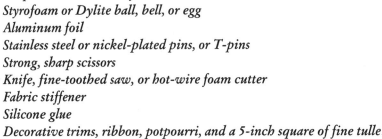

1. Using a thin, sharp knife, hot wire, or fine saw, carefully cut the Styrofoam or Dylite form in half. Wrap each half with aluminum foil, folding the excess to the flat side.

2. Cut the lace fabric slightly larger than necessary to cover the foil. Soak the lace for 2 or 3 minutes in a dish of fabric stiffener. (Do *not* use diluted glue!)

3. Remove excess stiffener by stripping the fabric between your fingers. Wrap the fabric around the foil-covered form, folding edges to the flat side. Pin in place, making it slightly taut and smoothing out all wrinkles. Dry in a low (175° F.) oven with the door ajar. Repeat with other half.

4. When the lace is totally dry, remove the pins. Use sharp scissors to cut excess foil and lace flush with flat side of ball half. Repeat with other half. Carefully remove the foam form, and peel the foil away from the lace.

5. Place the potpourri on the tulle, gather up the corners, and fasten with fine cord to make a little packet. Place the packet in one stiffened lace half. Apply silicone glue liberally, and put the halves together. When dry, remove excess glue with a razor blade or knife.

6. Use thick craft glue or hot glue to affix ribbon over the seam where the two halves are joined. Decorate with a bow, dried flowers, lace motifs, rickrack, and so on.

BOB CLARK, LANCASTER, OH

FRAGRANT POTPOURRI CANDLES

by Bob Clark

Transform homemade or purchased candles into exquisite, fragrant gifts and decorations. If you wish to try your hand at making your own scented candles, I recommend that you rely on a good book on the subject and purchase supplies made for that purpose. (Crayons for color and string for wick simply do not work!) You can scent the wax by adding fragrance or essential oils sparingly just before casting the candle.

When lit, the heat from this candle will release the oils and fragrance of the potpourri. As it burns down, its light will dramatically silhouette the potpourri pattern. For an attractive candle holder, use an inverted glass goblet, filled with potpourri. Or, simply place the candle on a piece of lace.

Candle, at least 2½ inches in diameter and not more than 6 inches high
Clear spray paint or hair spray
Paper and scissors
White glue (such as Designer Tacky Glue)
Potpourri
Decorations such as tiny whole flowers (ammobium and acroclinium are
   nice), spices, tiny pine cones, small bows
Ice pick (or similar tool)
Essential oil
Paraffin, with 143° to 145° F. melting point
2 large cans (tall enough to accommodate the candle), saucepan, strong
   cord, nylon stocking

1. Spray the candle with clear spray paint or hair spray to help the glue adhere.

2. Plan your design, using a wreath, tree, or bell for Christmas (or appropriate symbols for other holidays, such as a heart for Valentine's Day). Cut from paper a silhouette of your chosen motif, and attach it to the candle. This makes a kind of reverse stencil — potpourri will adhere everywhere *but* where the motif is attached.

3. Apply thick, white glue to the candle where you want the potpourri to adhere. Work a section at a time, pressing the potpourri on to the glued areas. *Do not* glue potpourri to the top or bottom of the candle. When glue is dry, remove the reverse stencil and glue on the additional decorations, such as small flowers or cones, to outline and ornament the holiday motif. Allow glue to dry for 12 to 24 hours. Shake off excess potpourri.

4. To scent the candle, heat the ice pick and make five holes about 1 inch deep around the wick. Place a couple of drops of essential

Before attempting the project detailed here, follow these precautions:

- ❤ *Never heat the wax directly on a burner or flame.*
- ❤ *Never leave the room while the wax is heating.*
- ❤ *Never leave hot materials within a child's reach.*
- ❤ *Always protect yourself and your clothing from hot molten wax.*
- ❤ *Always cover the floor and counters with plenty of newspapers.*
- ❤ *Always keep a cover, a box of salt, and/or a fire extinguisher at hand.*

CITRUS PEEL POMANDERS

Grind up fresh citrus peels in a good grinder or blender. If necessary, fresh peels may be saved in a bag in the freezer until enough are collected (about 1 quart). Add powdered spices, such as cinnamon, cloves, nutmeg, ginger, and/or allspice, in amounts as desired (about 6 tablespoons). Add calamus, sandalwood, orris, or other fixative powders or oils and other related fragrance oils as desired until the mixture is the consistency of dough; if it does not hold together, mix in a few drops of glycerin as a binder. Roll the dough into balls, and allow to dry. This recipe is fine for pomanders, but it does not hold together well enough to roll out and cut with cookie cutters.

BOB CLARK, LANCASTER, OH

oil in each hole; the same oil can be added to the molten wax before dipping (see Step 5).

5. Place a large can full of cool tap water in readiness. Melt the paraffin in a large can set in a pan of boiling water. Use only enough water to melt the wax; do not allow the water to overflow. If the wick is short, tightly tie a 6- to 8-inch piece of strong cord to it. When the wax has totally melted and reached a temperature of 185° to 200° F., you may add a few drops of essential oils. Place the container of hot wax and the container of cool water next to each other. Pick up the candle by its extended wick and lower it into the molten paraffin for a couple of seconds. Take it out of the hot wax, and immediately lower it into the cool water. Repeat this procedure once or twice. If desired, you can build up a thicker coating by repeated dippings, but the potpourri will not show as well. For taller candles, you may have to dip the bottom half, invert, and then dip the top.

6. Untie the wick extension, and admire! When cooled, polish with an old nylon stocking, if desired.

❧ *Fragrant Decorative Yule Log* ❧
This looks wonderful in front of the fireplace or on top of a woodstove.

Oakmoss, or other moss
Small log (real or artificial)
White glue, such as Tacky or Velveret
Frankincense and myrrh potpourri
Two 10-inch cinnamon sticks
Star anise
Whole cloves
Pine cones in various sizes
Fragrant oils
Red or green satin bow
Feathered dove or cardinal
Sprigs of fresh holly

Glue the moss onto the log; because this log is meant to be burned do *not* use hot glue. Cover the moss with the frankincense and myrrh potpourri. Glue on the cinnamon sticks, star anise, whole cloves, and pine cones. Drop the related fragrant oils onto the moss and spices. Add a red or green satin bow, a little feathered dove or cardinal (to be removed before burning, of course), and sprigs of fresh holly.

BALSAM FIR: CHERISHED FOR ITS EVERLASTING SCENT

by Wendy J. Newmeyer

Balsam *(Abies balsamea)*, in the language of herbs, stands for warm friendship. It was a veritable dispensary for the Native Americans, who used almost every part of the tree medicinally. The aromatic resin served them as a salve for cuts, sores, and burns; as a cement for canoe building and repairs; and as an internal medicine for colds and coughs. When brewed into a tea, the inner bark served as a remedy for chest pains, and the twigs, as a laxative. Handfuls of needles were thrown on live coals in saunas, so that the vapors could be inhaled to clear up the congestion of colds and coughs, and as a benefit for sore muscles. Balsam was effective enough to attract the attention of frontier doctors, eventually finding its way into the U.S. pharmacopeia.

Nowadays, balsam is important in pulp manufacture in the U.S. Northeast. Because of its fragrance and the fact that it holds its needles much longer than most conifers, it is also widely used for Christmas trees and wreaths. The young foliage serves as winter food for deer and moose. Canadian balsam, an aromatic oleoresin obtained from "swelling" or resin blisters in the bark, is used for mounting microscopic specimens and for optical cement; it is also a source for turpentine. The essential oil distilled from the needles and twigs is used to a small extent in flavoring candy, baked goods, and beverages, as well as in perfumes and household sprays.

One way to enjoy its spicy redolence is to make a balsam pillow or "sweet bag." Encased in fabric, the fragrance will last for many years; just fluff it up, or moisten it occasionally with water to revive the scent. As with any herb pillow, don't stuff it too full, as the herb needs some air space to produce the best scent. Another way to enjoy the woodsy aroma is to mix it with other herbs and spices in a potpourri for a favorite jar or basket, or for sachets. Our recipe follows, or you may enjoy creating your own variation.

❧ *Balsam Woods Potpourri* ❧

3 cups balsam fir tips
1 cup rosebuds and petals
½ cup lavender blossoms
½ cup lemon or orange peel
½ cup oakmoss
1 teaspoon whole cloves
1 teaspoon whole allspice
3-inch stick cinnamon, broken
2 tablespoons orrisroot
A few drops of essential oils

Mix all ingredients together. Let cure in a dark place for 4 to 6 weeks, stirring weekly.

"I pine for you and sometimes balsam!"

—*E.B. WHITE,* STUART LITTLE

❤

An evergreen tree growing 40 to 80 feet tall, balsam has dark, shiny green, flattened needles, 1 to 1½ inches long, which look as if they were arranged in two rows but actually grow all around the branch. It may be found in swamps and bogs, as well as in well-drained soils.

❤

WENDY J. NEWMEYER, MAINE BALSAM FIR PRODUCTS, WEST PARIS, ME 04289

BALSAM: PERFECT FOR A NATIVE AMERICAN WREATH

by Bertha Reppert

I buy balsam wreaths every year. An American native, balsam grows best from Maine to the tundra. Because my token balsam tree would never make a sizable wreath, I purchase the wreaths from people who can grow, make, and ship them best — mail-order firms in New England (for sources, see Appendix). Ex-easterners now living in California or Florida should order one just for nostalgia's sake — aaah, that holiday fragrance! I buy three every year — one for the front door, one for the back, and the third for our small powder room that has no ventilation. Even in August, the humid air is unbelievably perfumed by it.

It is my contention that if balsam had been known to the Pharaohs of ancient Egypt, the first scent that would have assailed the archeologists who opened the pyramids would have been aromatic balsam, rather than sandalwood, frankincense, and myrrh. This evergreen is the exotic oil of our continent. Its needles are loaded with built-in resins, fragrant oils that never go away. Perhaps that's why the needles hang on so long. When my wreaths arrive in early December, they are dewy fresh and bright green. They come with a few pine cones and a red velvet bow, and, since it's the busiest time of the year, that's the way we hang them. They just shout *Merry Christmas!* In mid-January, we add big red hearts to celebrate Valentine's Day. On the first of March we remove the red ornaments, change to pastel bows recycled from gifts, and add bunnies and eggs on picks, and a few silk daffodils or a bunch of violets. In early May, we again transform the wreath; red-white-and-blue ribbons and small flags hold sway through Memorial Day to the 4th of July. In summer, our wreath makes a tan background for a big bunch of silk daisies that can pass for real.

During the summer, the balsam, still refreshing the air, is gradually changing colors as the aromatic resins heat and bake in the sun — and so tightly packed with thick boughs, it provides a network of cavities to capture and hold anything you poke in. But, the best is yet to come! By fall, the wreath will have turned a deep, dark russet — unmatched by any color I have ever encountered elsewhere — shiny with surface resins, *more* fragrant than ever. It is at this stage that I use this treasure to create a lesson in what the first settlers found on the new continent (native plants are my specialty). I begin with one of my year-old wreaths, now aged to a rich, dark brown and still pouring its fragrant oils out to scent the air. As the summer progresses, I ornament it with plant material from the garden and fields, until I have what I consider the "Cadillac" of all wreaths. Silica-dried dogwood blossoms are glued in place. Brilliant orange butterfly weed provides colorful accents. Other ingredients include red velvet sumac, milkweed, dried black elderberries, gray bayberry from the beach, black-eyed Susans and their *Echinacea* cousins (both flowers and centers alone), lots of boneset from the fields, small red chile peppers from the supermarket, bee balm in both red and lavender, bright orange clusters of American mountain ash berries, cattails, brown dock, goldenrod, oakleaf hydrangea and American hollies, unbelievably yellow jasmine, mauve Joe-Pyeweed (sprayed to keep it from shattering), sweet fern, senna pods, sweet pepperbush (dried by hanging), sycamore balls (dipped in shellac to prevent shattering), and large clusters of yucca pods placed at strategic spots. When completed, it forms a big, bold, all-native wreath of great distinction that is itself a lesson in native plant varieties.

FROM *WREATHS...OF ALL SORTS*
BERTHA REPPERT, THE ROSEMARY
HOUSE, MECHANICSBURG, PA 17055

❧ *Balsam Bouquet* ❧
YIELD: 1 GALLON
Since this winter holiday potpourri must be aged for 6 weeks, make it in the fall so that you can enjoy it in December.

¾ cup orrisroot, cut and sifted
or ¾ cup ¼-inch cellulose, cut and sifted from corncobs
2 drams plus 90 drops balsam oil
1 dram plus 45 drops pine oil
1 dram plus 45 drops bayberry oil
3 cups balsam needles
1 cup tilia starflowers
2 cups tiny pine cones (larch or hemlock)
2 cups Roman chamomile
¼ cup juniper berries
¼ cup myrrh and frankincense crystals, mixed
2 cups spina cristi flowers
2 cups pink rosebuds and petals
1 cup purple globe amaranth flowers
2 handfuls lemon verbena leaves, whole

Combine the orrisroot or cellulose and oils, and allow them to set in a tightly covered glass jar until the oils have been completely absorbed. Gently toss the bulk ingredients with the fixative/oil mixture. Store the potpourri in a glass, stainless steel, or graniteware container. Shake the storage container frequently to redistribute the ingredients while aging for about 6 weeks.

RONDA SCHOOLEY BRETZ, SILVER SPRING, PA 17575

❧ *Christmas Potpourri* ❧
1 cup red roses
1 cup balsam tips
1 cup hemlock cones
1 cup red and white strawflowers
½ cup whole allspice
1 cup bay leaves
1 cup broken cinnamon
¼ cup whole cloves
¼ cup orrisroot chips
⅛ ounce balsam oil

Mix this potpourri in September. By the first Sunday of Advent, it will be ready and may be left in an open bowl or basket until Twelfth Night without having to be covered at night. Be sure you use balsam oil — pine oil will make it smell like deodorant! If you would like it to be more floral, add a few drops of rose oil.

BARBARA RADCLIFFE ROGERS, HERBITAGE FARM, RICHMOND, NH 03470

FRAGRANT HOLIDAY BOUGHS

Decorate a tree with orange- and apple-peel wreaths, cinnamon stick garlands, apple pulp pomanders, and long garlands of dried herbs and flowers, highlighted with Queen-Anne's-lace, lightly pearlized with spray. Crown the tree with a tussie mussie of baby's-breath, blue salvia, lavender, and pepper berries.

BARBARA SAUSSER, BARB'S COUNTRY HERBS, RIVERSIDE, CA 92504

ORANGE-PEEL WREATHS FOR THE HOLIDAY TREE

by Barbara Sausser

I love to make use of sunny California's bounty at holiday time. A favorite centerpiece is made of oranges, partially studded with cloves, and arranged on a three-tier tray adorned with herbs, flowers, and ribbons. Another specialty is my orange-peel wreaths, which I make and sell as mementoes of Woodcrest (my area) in Riverside, California (the center of orange growing). Customers send them to others or buy them to take home as reminders of California.

For a small citrus-peel wreath to use as an ornament on the tree, you will need a 12-inch piece of 22-gauge wire and pieces of fresh orange, lemon, tangerine, or grapefruit peel. You can make any size wreath you wish; this one will be about 4 inches across at its widest part.

I use a potato peeler to remove the skin in long strips, going around and around the fruit. (An electric appliance that will spiral fruit peel makes this job much easier!) I then cut the strips into pieces about 1 inch in size. For a larger wreath you might want to cut larger pieces.

Next, I bend the wire into a heart shape, with the ends left free. Pushing the peel together tightly, because it shrinks as it dries, I thread the peel onto the wire. I fill the wire completely, except for 1 inch at each end. I then twist the two ends together, and hang the wreath to dry. I hang my wreaths up high to take advantage of the fact that warm air rises, for it is best to dry the wreath as quickly as possible, so that it does not mold. This is especially important because the fruit peel pieces are so close together.

To finish the wreath, I tie raffia around the twisted part of the wire to cover it from view, and then I add a raffia bow. You can use ribbon if you prefer it, but we feel that raffia is most suitable for the texture of the peelings — kind of a homey feeling for a humble commodity. Depending on the season, I glue in small flowers or alder cones as an accent. Blue makes a particularly nice contrast to the citrus colors.

I always feel virtuous using the peels in this manner, for the same reason that I find it hard to make things out of food that someone else might be able to eat. I use the same technique to make apple peel wreaths out of red, green, or yellow fruit.

Herbs and Spices for the Holidays

FRUITCAKE: A SPICY HOLIDAY TREAT

by Isabelle M. Wiand

Fruitcake — dark, moist, and spicy, with more fruit than cake — is a holiday tradition at Seven Oaks. Recipes for fruitcake vary from family to family and from one part of the country to another. They also differ in complexity, from those requiring a whole shopping cart full of ingredients that must be cracked, chopped, and diced, to the quickie recipes based on boxes of cake mix. What they all have in common, besides calories, dried fruit, and nuts, are the spices — allspice, cinnamon, nutmeg, and cloves — at one time available only from the Orient and so costly only the very rich could afford them. In fact, spices were once stored in special boxes and cabinets under lock and key!

Set aside at least 1 hour to mix the following recipe, and be prepared to bake the resulting cakes for 3 or 4 hours. Assemble all the ingredients, put on a long-playing record or tape of holiday music, and begin by placing the following ingredients in a very large bowl. I use a big, blue, enamel canning kettle, which allows ample room for mixing without spilling over the edge.

Fruitcake tends to improve with age, as the spices and fruit flavors meld and blend. If not stored in the refrigerator or freezer, each cake should be wrapped first in brandy- or wine-soaked cheesecloth or linen, and then in foil, and kept in a cool place. For very long storage, Irma Rombauer and Marion Rombauer Becker, authors of The Joy of Cooking, *recommend burying the liquor-soaked cake in powdered sugar in a tin before storing in a cool place. (I use the root cellar.)*

❧ *Seven Oaks Fruitcake* ❧

4 cups cracked and broken nuts, including pecans, blanched sliced almonds, Brazil nuts, and walnuts
3 pounds mixed candied fruits (the commercial mix of peels, citron, and so on)
1 pound whole dates, pitted
2 pounds dark, seedless raisins
1 pound dried currants
10-ounce jar maraschino cherries, including the juice

¼ cup candied angelica (optional)
18-ounce jar of apricot preserves
3½ cups white flour
4 teaspoons ground cinnamon
½ teaspoon allspice
2 teaspoons nutmeg
½ teaspoon cloves
2 teaspoons salt
1 pound butter, room temperature
1 pound brown sugar
12 eggs, beaten until foamy
1 cup molasses

Mix together the nuts, candied fruits, dates, raisins, currants, cherries, angelica, and apricot preserves. Sift the flour, cinnamon, allspice, nutmeg, cloves, and salt over the fruits and nuts, stirring until all the ingredients are well coated.

In a separate bowl, use a heavy-duty, electric mixer to cream together the butter and brown sugar. Beat the eggs until foamy, and add them and the molasses to the butter and sugar mixture. Combine well, and pour over the dried fruits and nuts. Stir until well mixed. Mixture will be stiff. Spoon into well-greased baking pans lined with waxed paper and greased. Bake at 275° F. This recipe makes about 12 pounds of batter, enough to fill two 9-inch tube pans, plus two 8-inch loaf pans two-thirds full. Baking times will be about 4 hours for larger cakes and 3 hours for smaller ones, or until a cake tester inserted into the center of each cake comes out clean. Remove cakes from oven. Let cool on a rack for about 5 minutes, and then turn out of the pans, carefully peeling waxed paper from each one.

Make the Lemon Glaze, prick each hot fruitcake with the tines of a fork to allow the glaze to penetrate the interior of the cakes, and use a small pitcher or measuring cup to pour the hot glaze slowly over the hot fruit cakes. When cool, wrap in plastic wrap or wine- or brandy-soaked cloth, and store in a cool place.

Lemon Glaze

¼ pound butter
¾ cup white sugar
½ cup lemon juice (3 large lemons)
Grated rind from 3 fresh lemons (or 1 tablespoon dried lemon rind)

Combine the butter, sugar, lemon juice, and lemon rind in a medium-sized saucepan, and heat until butter has melted and sugar has completely dissolved into the lemon mixture. Pour over cake while both cake and glaze are hot.

ISABELLE M. WIAND, SEVEN OAKS, WEEKS MILLS, ME 04361

& *Ruth's Herb-Cheese Biscuits* &

1 cup whole wheat flour
1 cup unbleached, all-purpose flour
3 teaspoons baking powder
¼ teaspoon each dried marjoram, parsley, oregano, thyme (or to taste)
½ cup shredded brick or cheddar cheese
5 tablespoons soft butter
½ cup milk

Preheat oven to 450° F. Mix flours, baking powder, herbs, and cheese in a large bowl with a fork. Cut in the butter with a pastry blender until the mixture forms coarse crumbs. Add the milk, and stir until mixture clings together. If too dry, add a bit more milk. Form the dough into a ball, and turn out onto a lightly floured surface. Knead gently, not more than 5 turns of the dough. Roll out to a ½-inch thickness, and cut with a biscuit or cookie cutter. Place on a baking sheet 1 inch apart. Bake for 12 to 15 minutes.

RUTH AGEE EKSTROM, BITTERSWEET HERB FARM, TUSCUMBIA, MO 65082

& *Ozarks Treats Cookies* &

YIELD: APPROX. 100 COOKIES

These are delicious and moist — and good keepers. A favorite cookie to make for gifts, as they pack and keep so well.

1 cup lard (preferred) or margarine	*1 teaspoon cinnamon*
2 cups brown sugar	*Pinch of nutmeg*
2 tablespoons cocoa	*1 cup cold, black coffee*
3 cups flour	*2 beaten eggs*
1 teaspoon baking soda	*2 cups raisins*
1 teaspoon baking powder	*1 cup chopped black walnuts*

Preheat the oven to 375° F. Cream the lard and sugar. Sift together the cocoa, flour, baking soda, baking powder, cinnamon, and nutmeg. Add the coffee and eggs to the lard and sugar mixture along with the sifted ingredients. Mix in the raisins and walnuts. Drop by spoonfuls onto a greased cookie sheet. Bake 10 to 12 minutes in preheated oven.

RUTH AGEE EKSTROM, BITTERSWEET HERB FARM, TUSCUMBIA, MO 65082

BREAD RECIPES FROM
AN HERBAL CELEBRATION COOKBOOK

The Herb Guild's 250-page collection of the favorite recipes of their members would make a lovely gift, as would any of the creations it contains. It may be ordered from The Herb Guild (see Appendix for address). These recipes are sure to whet your appetite!

❧ *Pimiento Bread Wreath* ❧
YIELD: 12 SERVINGS
A holiday dinner bread.

1-pound loaf frozen, white bread dough, thawed 15 minutes at room temperature
Vegetable oil
Pimiento Butter
2 tablespoons grated Parmesan cheese
2 tablespoons parsley, finely chopped

Lightly grease a cookie sheet. Using a sharp knife, cut the bread crosswise into twelve ¾-inch slices. Arrange on prepared cookie sheet in a 10-inch circle with sides touching but not overlapping. Lightly brush dough with oil. Let stand, uncovered, in a warm place about 45 minutes until thawed and doubled. While the dough is rising, preheat oven to 400° F. Bake bread 12 minutes, or until lightly browned. Remove from oven. Spread with 3 tablespoons of the Pimiento Butter, and then sprinkle with the cheese. Return to oven, and bake 2 to 4 minutes until cheese is lightly golden. Sprinkle with chopped parsley. Serve on a bread board. Invite guests to break off pieces.

Pimiento Butter

½ cup butter or margarine, room temperature
4-ounce jar pimientos, drained and patted dry
2½ tablespoons grated onion
1 teaspoon dried marjoram leaves
1 teaspoon dried basil

Process all ingredients in blender or food processor until *almost* smooth — small pieces of pimiento should be visible.

KAREN SEIDLITZ

❧ *Banana Anise Bread* ❧

¾ cup buttermilk
2 tablespoons butter
1 large egg
¾ cup honey
3 ripe bananas, mashed
3 cups flour
1½ teaspoons baking soda
1 teaspoon salt
1 cup dates, chopped
1 cup broken walnuts
4 teaspoons anise seed

Preheat oven to 350° F. Mix together the buttermilk, butter, egg, honey, and bananas. Add the flour, baking soda, and salt. Mix well. Add the dates, nuts, and anise seed. Pour into two, greased loaf pans (9" x 5" x 3"). Bake in preheated oven for 45 to 55 minutes, or until tester comes out clean.

MARY KAY FILIPIAK

❧ *Mint Nut Bread* ❧
This bread slices more easily and has a better flavor the day after it is baked. It also freezes well.

2 cups unbleached flour
¾ cup brown sugar
1 tablespoon baking powder
½ teaspoon baking soda
1 teaspoon salt
½ teaspoon nutmeg
1 cup nutmeats
Fresh or dried mint, to flavor
1 egg, beaten
1 cup applesauce
¼ cup salad oil

Preheat oven to 350° F. Mix together the flour, sugar, baking powder, baking soda, salt, nutmeg, and nuts. Combine the mint, egg, applesauce, and oil, and add to dry ingredients. Stir just until blended. Pour batter into two, greased loaf pans (8" x 4" x 2"). Bake in preheated oven for about 45 minutes. Cool on a rack.

MARY M. PITONYAK

❧ Herb Bread ❧

YIELD: 1 LOAF

Keep a loaf of this herb bread in the freezer. Take out a few slices at a time for delicious, toasted cheese sandwiches. If you are using fresh herbs, use twice the dry amount.

½ cup warm milk
½ cup warm water
2 tablespoons sugar
1 tablespoon dry yeast
2 tablespoons unsalted butter, soft
1 teaspoon salt

1 tablespoon dried parsley
½ teaspoon dried tarragon
½ teaspoon dried dill weed
¼ teaspoon dried minced onion
2½ to 2¾ cups bread flour
½ cup chopped pecans

Heat the milk and water to between 105° and 115° F., and combine with sugar in a large mixing bowl. Add the dry yeast. Stir to dissolve. Let stand. Add the softened butter, salt, parsley, tarragon, dill weed, and onion. Add half the flour and mix well. Add the nuts. Mix in enough of the remaining flour to make the dough easy to handle. Turn the dough onto a floured bread board, and knead for 8 minutes, adding additional flour, if necessary. Place in a greased bowl and turn to grease the top. Cover, and let rise until double in size, about 1 hour.

While dough is rising, preheat oven to 375° F. Form dough and place in a greased 9" x 5" or 8¼" x 4" loaf pan. Bake in preheated oven for 25 to 30 minutes, or until the top sounds hollow when tapped. Remove from oven, and brush top with melted butter. Cool on a wire rack.

BETTY BARNET
FROM *AN HERBAL CELEBRATION COOKBOOK*, THE HERB GUILD

SPICY BEVERAGE BLENDS FOR GIFTS OR REFRESHMENTS

These blends make lovely holiday gifts, and they are also appropriate for garden or herb club refreshments, for they are so easy to prepare for a large crowd! For gift giving, package instant beverage mixes in tins or plastic-lined, cloth sacks tied closed with a cinnamon-stick-adorned ribbon. Include instructions for use.

❧ Spicy Cocoa Mix ❧

YIELD: 4 CUPS

1 cup cocoa
2 cups sugar
1 cup non-fat dry milk
1 tablespoon grated and dried
   orange peel
1 tablespoon ground cinnamon
¾ teaspoon ground cloves

To use, add ½ tablespoon per cup of hot milk or water.

❧ Instant Herb Tea ❧

YIELD: 2 CUPS

1½ cups instant tea
½ cup dried lemon or orange peel
¼ teaspoon ground cloves
½ teaspoon ground cinnamon

For hot tea, use a teaspoon per cup of boiling water.

FROM *HERBAN LIFESTYLES* NEWSLETTER
CHRIS UTTERBACK, HERBAN LIFESTYLES, NEW HARTFORD, CT 06057

An All-Purpose Holiday Mix

❧ *Holiday House Freshener* ❧
YIELD: 1 BAG

4 pieces whole dried gingerroot
Three 3-inch cinnamon sticks
1 teaspoon whole cloves
1 teaspoon whole allspice
1 teaspoon pickling spice (remove red pepper)

Package all these dry spices in a little muslin bag for a most wondrous holiday house freshener, with a multiplicity of usages:

Air freshener. Combine one bag of mixed spices with 4 cups water. Bring to boil in a large kettle (preferably enamel); boil briskly for 10 minutes. Reduce heat, and simmer to fill your home with a wonderful holiday aroma. Add water as necessary. Spice bag may be re-used; be sure to let it dry completely before storing.

Spiced punch. Add one 46-ounce can pineapple juice and 1 quart apple cider to the simmering spices, and simmer for half an hour. Strain, add water if necessary, and serve cold with clove-studded orange slices. Add honey or sugar, if desired. Dilute with ginger ale or dry white wine to make a holiday party punch.

Spiced holiday tea. Dilute 2 quarts of the simmering spiced water with 2 quarts of your favorite tea. Add one 6-ounce can frozen lemonade and one 6-ounce can frozen orange juice. For a festive occasion, reheat and serve with cinnamon-stick stirrers.

BERTHA REPPERT's Herbal Scrapbook: Christmas Herbs *is just jam- packed with clever and unusual ideas, recipes, and projects for the holidays! Here's a sampling.*

FROM *HERBAL SCRAPBOOK: CHRISTMAS HERBS*
BERTHA REPPERT, THE ROSEMARY HOUSE, MECHANICSBURG, PA 17055

Scenting Cones for a Winter Spice Jar

by Dody Lyness

Dried cones and pods are wonderful media for holding the scent of an essential oil for a long while, and at the same time, they add interest to wintertime mixes. Pick cones while they are tightly closed; spread them on a foil-covered baking sheet and heat them in a 150° F. oven. They'll gradually open to full size, and you'll have nice, shiny, bug-free cones to work with. Laying atop each petal will be the next generation's seed; brush these away before oiling. Apply the oil with any soft brush (most essential oils are too viscous to use in an atomizer), either by dabbing a little on each cone petal or by painting all sides, depending upon how strong a scent you want and how long you want it to keep giving of its fragrance.

To make a winter spice jar, select a large, glass apothecary jar or (easier to work with) a round glass jar with a straight side. Lay several scented pine cones in the bottom. Line the entire inside of the jar with cinnamon bark pieces cut to the size of the jar's height. Add more scented cones as needed to keep the cinnamon sticks upright. Use cones all of one scent, or mix in a variety of differently scented cones, such as orange, lemon, allspice, cinnamon, nutmeg, clove, and bayberry. Crumble cinnamon bark on the top, working the pieces as far down into the pine cones as possible. Once all of this material is firmly in place you can decorate the sides of the jar with a combination of any of the following: whole cloves, whole bay leaves, whole allspice berries, large pieces of colorful, dried citrus rinds, or rock salt. To put the decoration in place, run a knife down the inside of the glass, slide the chosen decoration down the knife, and use its tip to place the piece exactly where you want it. As you remove the knife, the volume from the center of the jar will push against the decorative botanical and hold it in place. Add several drops of essential oil on top of the mix. Like great-gramma's rose jar, open when you enter the room; close when leaving.

FROM *POTPOURRI...EASY AS ONE, TWO, THREE!*
DODY LYNESS, BERRY HILL PRESS, PALOS VERDES, CA 90274

(Each one of these trade-marked oils is absolutely divine! PVS)

❧ *Memories-of-the-Holidays Potpourri* ❧

The basic recipe may be adjusted according to the amount of dried material you have saved. For the essential oil, we have used oil of cinnamon, as well as our own oil mixtures, such as Sleigh Bells and Holly, Cape Cod Cranberry, and New England Bayberry.

1 cup orrisroot to which you have added 1 dram of your favorite oil
6 cups of needles from your holiday tree or greens
(you may also incorporate such things as berried desert juniper, holly, or any appropriate greens)
3 cups of either *dried red roses or any flowers from holiday arrangements,*
or
3 cups dried apple or orange slices (or some of each)
1 cup each of star anise or whole allspice, 3-inch cinnamon sticks, and tiny pine cones or whole nuts (in shells)

Thoroughly combine orrisroot with oil. Add dried ingredients, and seal in a glass or plastic container to age. Stir once a week for approximately 4 weeks. Place the contents in a favorite container. For the finishing touch, top your potpourri with one of the following:

❤ Cinnamon sticks and star anise brushed with gold powder or paint (Gold Leaf from Rub 'n Buff works beautifully!)
❤ Dried apple slices painted with a dot of oil and dusted with ground cinnamon or any ground spice
❤ Homemade pomanders
❤ White, pearl, or opal-type glitter or silver sequin stars (if you like glitz)

NANCY MCFAYDEN, GINGHAM 'N' SPICE, LTD., GARDENVILLE, PA 18926

❧ *Author's Directory* ❧

ANDERSON, BEVERLY. ILLUSIONS IN THYME, WILLIAMSTON, MI 48895

Beverly conducts workshops and lectures on herb use, culture, and legends and lore. Her shop features a variety of potpourri, herb wreaths, seasonal herbcraft, and depression-era antiques. A member of the Herb Society of America and the American Rose Society, she has extensive herb and rose gardens.

BEAN, CAROLEE. NEW HOPE HERB FARM, RTE. 1, BOX 660, SPENCER, IN 47460

Ms. Bean grows hundreds of varieties of herbs, everlastings, perennials, and hard-to-find plants, and shares her skills and love of growing herbs in workshops, articles, and craft shows. Two festivals (2nd Sundays in July and September) feature 6 acres of display gardens, tours, demonstrations, lectures, crafts, and music. Open for plant sales each Sunday in May and June, or to groups by appointment. She has been a professional grower for 11 years, and participates in the Bloomington Farmers' Market each Saturday (May-October).

BECKER, JIM AND DOTTIE. GOODWIN CREEK GARDENS, P.O. BOX 83, WILLIAMS, OR 97544

Specializing in herbs, everlastings, and fragrant plants, the Beckers sell both seeds and plants, as well as products made from herbs and everlastings. They also have a retail nursery and gift shop in Ashland, OR. The Beckers are known nationally because of their excellent book, *A Concise Guide to Growing Everlastings* ($7.70 ppd.), a must for any grower. Their catalog is available for $1.00, refundable with first order.

BETZ, SUSAN. 1100 N. SAND LAKE, HILLS DALE, MI 49242

Susan is the owner and operator of The Little Farm Herb Shop, located in Allen, Michigan. She lectures, writes, and teaches classes on herbal crafts and folklore, and also teaches program and project ideas for the State 4-H program. A member of the Herb Society of America and the Michigan Herb Associates, she has grown and used herbs for the past 9 years.

BLACK, RANDA. BUTTERPLUM BAGS, BASKETS, WREATHS, & DESIGNS, P.O. BOX 57-12, EPHRAIM, UT 84627

Randa makes herbal and dried flower creations, wreaths, and baskets that are sold at boutiques. Her velvet, satin, lace, and cotton drawstring bags for sachets and potpourri are available by mail, wholesale (price sheet, $1.00). Randa has designed several Victorian wreaths, baskets, and accessories that will soon be published by Hot Off The Press, a craft book company in Canby, OR. Her Bath Baskets of natural soaps and bathing products are available in peach, mauve, or blue ($20, ppd.).

BOOTH-BREZINA, SALLY.

Sally has been arranging dried naturals for 13 years and herb crafting for 8, but she has sewn and worked with general crafts for over 30 years. She taught school for 8 years, then worked as the national teaching director for a chain of craft stores located in 19 states before allowing flowers and potpourri to dominate her time and workshop. When she lived in Hawaii, Sally served as president of the Pacific Handcrafters Guild and was an officer in the Kalanianaole Art League.

BOURDO, PAT AND JON. WOODLAND HERB FARM, 7741 NO. MANITOU TRAIL WEST, NORTHPORT, MI 49670

The Bourdos' herb farm is the oldest and largest in northern Michigan. Their products are available at their shop or through their catalog ($1.00, refundable with first order), which features herbal vinegars, wreaths, handcrafted copper fountains and garden windvanes, and many other culinary and decorative delights. Pat is the author of *Culinary Uses for Herbs and Spices*, a cookbook in which 95 percent of the recipes are salt-free (autographed copy, $7.95 ppd.). Send SASE for schedule of events.

BRETZ, RONDA SCHOOLEY. P.O. BOX 264, DEPT. HB, SILVER SPRING, PA 17575

Ronda manufactures an upscale line of environmental aromatiques — potpourris, sachets, perfumes for the air, and scented decorative fancies. She has thoroughly researched herbs, flowers, and essential oils for their fragrant use in scented products. As a freelance writer, Ronda specializes in the subject of perfumery and herbal fragrance, particularly on how to make highest quality potpourri. Her current interests include research, gardening, and writing on herbs of the Bible and on the study of aromachology. For literature regarding Ronda's products and articles, send a SASE along with your request.

BROWN, PAT. COUNTRY POTPOURRI, 2097 J. 25 ROAD, AUSTIN, CO 81410

Pat, a Colorado State University Cooperative Extension Master Gardener, feels fortunate to work with the herbs and flowers that give her so much peace and happiness. Her antique-filled shop features wreaths, potpourri, and custom decorations, using many flowers she has grown. She also enjoys giving holiday workshops and serving herbal teas and cookies to guests. A catalog is not available at this time. Special seasonal hours, or by appointment.

BUCHANAN, RITA. 21 SAND BANK RD., WATERTOWN, CT 06795

Shortly after her book *A Weaver's Garden* was published in 1987, Rita moved to Connecticut to help launch *Fine Gardening* magazine. As well as being Associate Editor, she regularly contributes articles and photographs to the magazine. She served as Guest Editor for a new Brooklyn Botanic Garden handbook on dyes from plants (August 1990). She is actively interested in fiber plants and dye plants; dyes, spins, and weaves; travels to teach seminars and workshops on these crafts; and contributes a regular column to *Spin-Off*, a magazine for handspinners.

CARLIN, CLEMENTINA. THE GINGER TREE, P.O. BOX 1882-P, SCHENECTADY, NY 12301

The Ginger Tree is a mail-order herb business, specializing in essential oils. Clementina also writes about aromatherapy and gives aromatherapy consultations by mail. Her personally designed aromatherapy programs consist of essential oils for the bath, face, massage, and a custom-designed perfume, based on your needs and preferences, which are determined by a questionnaire. She has researched and experimented with essential oils for several years, has owned and operated a health and beauty spa, and has been teaching and lecturing about herbs, essential oils, and nutrition in adult education classes and to professional health organizations for a number of years. Her plans for the future include seminars on aromatherapy for health professionals. Catalog, $1.

CLARK, BOB. FORMERLY OF 901 SHERIDAN DR., LANCASTER, OH 43130

After receiving a Bachelor of Fine Arts degree, Bob Clark turned his lifelong love of arts, crafts, and ceramics into a retail and mail-order business he named Ceramics by Bob. In 1984, his interests broadened to include pot-pourri and other herb projects, which he combined with his unique ceramic creations. This unusual blend of interests and his sharing nature gave him a bountiful harvest of herb friends. Bob died in December of 1989 as a result of complications from an illness dating back to his childhood. Sadly, his death was a shock to most of his fans and customers, for he had kept his constant pain and crippling circulatory problems to himself. Because Bob so enjoyed sharing his crafts, his parents have graciously offered his many contributions to appear here, and he will live on in our hearts and memories through his writing.

DODT, COLLEEN K., AROMATHERAPIST. HERBAL ENDEAVORS, 3618 SOUTH EMMONS AVE., ROCHESTER HILLS, MI 48063

Colleen Dodt, one of the leading authorities on aromatherapy in the U.S., is a well-known writer, lecturer, and radio broadcaster. Her brochure offers the Tisserand Pure Essential Oils, plus all the Robert T. Tisserand books (*The*

Art of Aromatherapy, Aromatherapy for Everyone, Safety Data Manual), and Maggie Tisserand's *Aromatherapy for Women*, as well as Judith Jackson's *A Scentual Touch.* Colleen is also a contributing writer for *The International Journal of Aromatherapy.*

DOLE, JANE. 149 CAMBRIDGE, INDIANA, PA 15701

A long-time gardener, flower-arranger, and herb-crafter, and a former co-owner of a craft-gift shop, Mrs. Dole is now retired in order to spend more time with her grandchildren and her gardens. She is very active in her local Herb Study Group and Garden Club; she has been active in the Federated Garden Clubs of America.

DOWNEY-BUTLER, LOUISE. RATHDOWNEY LTD., 3 RIVER ST., BETHEL, VT 05032

Rathdowney Ltd. is a unique herbal apothecary and gift shop that occupies the entire first floor of a restored, 1850s millowner's house. Surrounding the building are many herb beds and gardens. Rathdowney manufactures their famous herb blends and potpourri in the restored attached carriage house. The shop is open 7 days a week, year round. Mail-order and wholesale inquiries encouraged; a free catalog is available upon request. The New Thymes, an herbal newsletter filled with gardening information, lore, recipes, and healthful hints is published four times a year. Subscriptions: $9.00 for 4 issues; $16.00 for 8 issues (Rathdowney Ltd., P.O. Box 357 PS, Bethel, VT 05032).

DOWNS, DIANE. LOST PRAIRIE HERB FARM, 805 KIENAS RD., DEPT MPOH, KALISPELL, MT 59901 (406-756-7742)

An herb grower for nearly two decades, Diane offers through her catalog over 300 live herb plants, hardy perennials, ground covers, natural pest control products and advice, and safe animal-care products. Diane has written for numerous publications over the past ten years and offers workshops at the farm. Greenhouses and display gardens are open by appointment, April 15 to September 15. Catalog, $1.00.

DUNN, MARY. MOUNTAINVIEW HERB FARM, BOX 104 PHA, MOUNTAINVIEW RD., THORNDIKE, ME 04986 (207-568-3785)

Mary has been growing and using herbs for 10 years. Her Mountainview Herb Farm is a small, organic farm overlooking the mountains of central Maine, where she sells herb plants, fresh-cut herbs, and dried bunches of herbs and everlastings. Formerly operator of a mail-order wreath business, she now lectures and writes on herb-related topics. Her articles have appeared in *The Herb Companion, The Herb Journal of the Western Reserve,* and the *Maine Organic Farmer's and Gardener's Association* and *New Hampshire Herb Association's* newsletters. She offers classes and workshops throughout the year; visitors are welcome to the gardens April to Oct., by appointment.

DUTTWEILER, JANIE. DUTTWEILER'S, 1531 ASH ST., DEPT. B, GEORGETOWN, TX 78626

Janie has been making potpourri and other scented gifts for 11 years. With the encouragement of family and friends, she began selling her items retail and is now testing the market to sell potpourri ingredients such as herbs, spices, and oils, in bulk, to crafters. She also sells her Bath Scrubbies wholesale. For price list send SASE.

EKSTROM, RUTH AGEE. BITTERSWEET HERB FARM, RT. 1, BOX 73, DEPT. 527, TUSCUMBIA, MO 65082

Ruth and her husband, Keith, operate her herb business from their home, a 130-year-old farmhouse on the Osage River. They, and their nephews, grow, gather, and dry flowers and herbs for her dried flower and herb wreaths, arrangements, and swags. She special-izes in potpourri and sachets, using all natural and pure ingredients, mostly gathered from the roadside and gardens at Bittersweet Herb Farm. No catalog. Visitors welcome by appointment.

ELLIOTT, EVE. 1729 UNICE AVE., LEHIGH ACRES, FL 33971

Eve has grown and studied herbs for many years, both in Michigan and Florida. She edited the newsletter *Southern Herbs,* now discontinued.

Since her move to Florida, she has become very interested in tropical plants and trees.

FREDERICK, KATE CARTER. SEVENTH HEAVEN HERB PRODUCTS, 856 TWELFTH AVE. S., ONALASKA, WI 54650

Kate's interest in herbs began with a study of native Midwestern plants and herbal folklore. Through her home-based herb business, she shares her excitement about herbs by crafting a wide variety of herb products, such as aromatic, culinary, and self-care blends. Kate has written about herbs for national magazines and herb trade journals. Catalog: First-class postage.

FURNEAUX, LANE. LADYBUG PRESS, 7348 LANE PARK COURT, DALLAS, TX 75225

Author of the widely acclaimed *Heavenly Herbs...Enjoy Them* (fifth and expanded edition; $7.95 ppd.), and very much in demand as a speaker, Lane has assisted with a number of "benefit" cookbooks. Her work has been published in the official journals of the Dallas Civic Garden Center, the Dallas County Heritage Society, and the British Herb Society; her article on tussie mussies appeared in the journal of England's Royal Horticulture Society, *The Garden*. It was in her genes, she says, to write and to cook, but it was her love of herbs that made it all come together.

GANNON, LINDA. THE MAGICK GARDEN, 5703 COUNTRY WALK, DEPT. PS, MCFARLAND, WI 53558

Linda's new Magical Celebration Baskets are filled with exquisite herbal treats, keyed to special themes and celebrations. Each basket or tin is unique and personalized, based on color and aromatherapy; from $10.00; delivered UPS anywhere in the continental United States. Brochure for SASE.

GEORGI, SHASH. BACK OF THE BEYOND, 7233 LOWER E. HILL, DEPT. PS, COLDEN, NY 14033 (716-652-0427)

Bed-and-breakfast; organic gardens; greenhouse; Herbtique gift shop; open year round. Annual open house in early November; workshops in March and October. Offers organically grown plants, crafts, unusual gifts, and dried everlastings. For 10 years, Shash has written a monthly column on organic gardening/herbs, for *Bestways* magazine; her articles have also appeared in *Flower and Garden, Your Home, Women's World, Health Foods Business, National Gardening,* and *New York Alive.*

GIPS, KATHLEEN MARIE. PINE CREEK HERBS, 152 SOUTH MAIN ST., CHAGRIN FALLS, OH 44022

Kathleen has been growing, using, studying, and writing about herbs for over 15 years. Her primary interests have been the tussie mussie, the language of flowers, and potpourri. Her articles on using herbs have been published nationally, she has been the editor of two herb periodicals, and she has written a dictionary entitled *The Language of Flowers* ($12.45 ppd.). She frequently gives workshops and demonstrations on herbs in the Cleveland, Ohio area. She is an active member of the Western Reserve Unit of the Herb Society of America. She operates a small mail-order business from her home to market tussie mussies and related materials as well as potpourri supplies. Catalog, $1.00. Mail order only.

HAMPSTEAD, MARILYN. FOX HILL FARM, 444 W. MICHIGAN AVE., BOX 9, PARMA, MI 49269-0009

Marilyn Hampstead is well known through her nationally acclaimed Basil Festivals held each summer, as well as her *The Basil Book* and her three *What You Need to Know About* booklets, subtitled *Herbs, Scented Geraniums,* and *Preserving Herbs,* as well as seven videos on these and other subjects. One of the largest herb farms in America, Fox Hill Farm grows 450 varieties of herbs and specialty plants; it was one of the first to provide fresh herbs year round to restaurants. Plants, produce, fancy foods, condiments, and crafted items are available at the farm or through mail order. The Herb Sampler Garden is open to the public from mid-April until mid-October; the Farmhouse-shop is open from April through Christmas. Catalog, $1.00.

HARTMAN, LYNN. HARTMAN'S HERB FARM, OLD DANA RD., BARRE, MA 01005

In business for 15 years, the Hartman family grows and sells over 300 varieties of herbs, perennials, and scented geraniums, which they ship to all states. They also sell potpourri supplies and dried materials as well as wreaths and decorative gifts. Send SASE for current schedule of hours open and special events for the public. Known nationwide for their beautiful annual Herbal Calendar with its useful gardening advice and delicious herb recipes in full color. Catalog, $2.00.

HEFNER, CELIA. HEFNER'S NURSERY, RT. 4, BOX 520, CONOVER, NC 28613 (704-256-5271)

The Hefners grow and sell woody ornaments at their nursery and have an educational herb garden open, by appointment, to individuals and groups. "Cricket" has been president and newsletter editor for the North Carolina Herb Association since it's inception.

HYDE, LOUISE AND CYRUS. WELL-SWEEP HERB FARM, DEPT. HT, 317 MT. BETHEL RD., PORT MURRAY, NJ 07865 (201-852-5390)

Cyrus Hyde grew up with his mother's herbal remedies and herb-enhanced cooking in Totowa Borough, NJ. After their marriage, Louise and he moved to rural Warren County and planted a few culinary herbs and some flowers to dry. Neighbors and friends wanted to know where to get some for themselves and so Well-Sweep Herb Farm was born. The Hydes named their farm for the well-sweep in front of their home. Twenty-eight years later, the farm receives thousands of visitors each year. With three greenhouses, a formal display herb garden, and a cozy gift shop, the Hydes and their three children keep very busy. Mail-order catalog for seed, plants, potpourri supplies: $2.00.

JAYNE, KATE AND FAIRMAN. SANDY MUSH HERB NURSERY, RTE. 2, DEPT. PH2, SURRETT COVE RD., LEICESTER, NC 28748 (704-683-2014)

In 1975, the Jaynes started selling unusual herb plants in Asheville and western North Carolina; in 1977, they shipped their plants through mail-order to meet the growing national market for fragrant and culinary herbs. Their first listing included about 60 plants; the current one contains over 800! Their extremely informative handbook/catalog is full of researched descriptions of herb plants and abundant tips, garden plans, recipes, and ideas for all herb gardeners ($4.00, refundable with the first order).

KEMP, TERRY. GOD'S GREEN ACRES HERBARY/GIFTS, DEPT. PH2, W7201 NORTHSHORE DR., ONALASKA, WI 54650 (608-781-0248)

In view of the majestic Wisconsin bluffsides, prairie meadows, and beautiful Lake Onalaska, the Kemp's family-owned business operates from the loft of Grandpa's Barn and features an array of antiques, collectibles, Victorian and French country keepsakes, aromatic botanical dried creations, and a small herb and flower garden. The majority of Terry's products are grown and fashioned with great love and care from her gardens. The store is open March to December 23rd, Tuesday through Saturday, 10:00 to 5:00. Mail-order (retail and wholesale) catalog, $2.00.

KENZLE, LINDA FRY. 101 BAYVIEWS, FOX RIVER GROVE, IL 60021

Linda has been growing and using herbs for over 20 years. A prolific writer and illustrator, she self-published *Selling Herb and Flower Crafts for Profit* and *The Joy of Herbs* and is currently working on her new book, *Seasonal Herbs.* SASE for current information on publications available.

KING, JUNE B. 7200 C.R. 315, KEYSTONE HEIGHTS, FL 32656

June King is author of *Speak Out for the Environment with a Natural Garden,* which covers soil management, composting, companion planting, fertilizers, natural insect and disease control and resources ($4.00 ppd.)

LENON, JOAN. THE SUMAC SHOP, GRAND RAPIDS, MI 49504

LEONARD, BETTY. HAMPTON HERBS, NEW CARLISLE, OH 45344

LONG, JIM. RTE. 4, BOX 730, OAK GROVE, AR 72660 (417-779-5450)

A landscape designer specializing in naturalistic designs using herbs and native plants, and publisher of *The Ozarks Herbalist,* a quarterly herb journal ($10 per year; sample copy, $3), Jim writes, travels, lectures, and hosts groups at his gardens at Long Creek Herb Farm on Table Rock Lake. He offers an annual Herb Day in May celebration, as well as numerous workshops and other plant events during the warm season; the Herb Shop is open by reservation for groups. Jim is a founding member and past President of the Ozarks Regional Herb Growers and Marketers Association.

LYNESS, DODY. BERRY HILL PRESS, DEPT. P2, 7336 BERRY HILL, PALOS VERDES, CA 90274

A well-known expert on floral and fragrance design, Dody is editor of the newsletter *Potpourri Party-Line* and author of the excellent guide and leading textbook on potpourri-making, *Potpourri...Easy as One, Two, Three!* Catalog of *Dried Floral Home Accessories,* $1.50. For retail price list of potpourri supplies, send a SASE; for wholesale price list of Essential/Fragrance Oils, send business letterhead, with a SASE. See **Resource Directory, SEPTEMBER,** *Books on Potpourri* to order her publications.

MASTEY, PEG. HERITAGE HERBS, CANTERBURY, NH 03224

MATHEWS, DIANE LEA. SALISBURY CENTER, NY 13454

MATHEWS, STEVE AND KATHY. HEAVENLY SCENT HERB FARM, N-13730 WHITE LAKE RD., FENTON, MI 48430

"Come follow the scented path to the herb shoppe overflowing with herbal treasures, and take a journey back in thyme to explore display gardens, which include culinary, fragrant, children, and friendship gardens." The Mathews have a variety of herb plants, mini-herb baskets, garden markers, and herbs or everlastings in dried arrangements. Kathy gives approximately 20 different classes, from topiary to eucalyptus swags. Free brochure and class schedule.

MATHIEU, ROSELLA F. HERB GARDEN FRAGRANCES, 3744 SECTION RD., CINCINNATI, OH 45236

In 1942, when most housewives knew no other herbs than sage, parsley, and bay, Rosella cultivated a quarter acre of herbs with a wheel hoe. When she showed a homemade package of her basil, marjoram, oregano, and thyme to the sophisticated head of Bloomingdale's Gourmet Department in New York, he ordered his designer to create a saleable package and introduced herbs from Rosella's garden, along with a 36-page booklet of Rosella's recipes for use of the five herbs. Shortly afterward, Rosella established Fragrant Herb Farm, one of the first such farms in the country, and offered an original line of nationally distributed gift-wrapped sachets, potpourri, and culinary herb seasonings. (The business was sold in 1956 and renamed the Karen-Carson Line, now greatly extended and available in this country and abroad.) Rosella now compounds high-quality, long-lasting oils for potpourri. She is writing a book, *Herb Business: Potpourri for Pleasure and Profit,* for the home-based, small entrepreneur. SASE for price list.

McFAYDEN, NANCY. GINGHAM 'N' SPICE, LTD., P.O. BOX 88-P2, GARDENVILLE, PA 18926

Nancy has been in the oil and fragrant craft business for over 10 years. She is represented at all major gift shows. A wholesale catalog with a product sample is available for $2.00; requests must be on business letterhead. Retail catalogs are also available for $2.00.

MESCHER, JEN AND MIKE. NATURE'S FINEST, P.O. BOX 10311, DEPT. MP, BURKE, VA 22015

In 1983, the Meschers began Nature's Finest, selling potpourri and supplies from a three-page price list; they currently offer a twenty-page listing of potpourri, supplies, books, and scent-related items. For each potpourri ingredient listed is a short description, its volume per pound, and occasional herb lore, so that the catalog becomes almost a reference booklet. They are also glad to draw from their extensive personal library to answer questions about scents and scent products. Catalog $2.00, refundable with the first purchase. Mail order only.

METCALFE, DONNA. GOOD SCENTS, P.O. BOX 854-P, RIALTO, CA 92377

Donna's love of herbs began when she started growing "a little bit" of mint to use in her potpourri. Like mint, her herb garden grew and spread and now occupies her whole backyard! In 1985, she began Good Scents, now a thriving family-oriented herb business, selling herbal products, books, and supplies by mail, and herb plants at local farmer's markets and craft fairs. She now devotes full time to growing and selling herbs, lecturing, writing, and giving workshops. Author of *A Beginner's Guide to Potpourri,* she enjoys teaching beginners how to grow and use herbs in crafts and in cooking.

MICHAEL, MARY. SUSSEX SPICE, RT. 1, BOX 370, LONG NECK ROAD, MILLSBORO, DE 19966

Visitors are welcome at Mary Michael's garden and home business, selling potpourri, crafts, and candy. A member of Delaware Herbalists and Orchid Hobbyists of Delmarva, and Horticultural Chairman of Sussex Gardeners, Mary lectures on herbs and potpourri, and offers workshops on potpourri, herbal crafts, candy-making, and herbal vinegars. Her latest project is creating remembrance potpourri, using flowers from bridal bouquets or other special occasions, and packaging this in ornate boxes; the containers are color-coordinated to buyer's request.

MITCHELL, DONNA MADORA. LAVENDER LANE, P.O. BOX 7265-P, CITRUS HEIGHTS, CA 95621 (916-334-4400)

Donna lectures and writes on herbs and teaches crafting classes. Her home-based business, Lavender Lane, contains hundreds of decorator jars filled with every conceivable herb, spice, and flower for creating the ultimate in potpourris and other herbal concoctions. From Jamaican Allspice to Malaysian Ylang-Ylang, Donna carries hundreds of the highest-quality essential, fragrance, and designer-type oils. She also sells several sizes of glass vials and high-impact plastic containers for storing, dispensing, and displaying herbs and potpourris. No minimum order; most orders shipped within 48 hours. Visitors welcome at Donna's shop in Sacramento (6715 Donerail Drive); please call first. Catalog, $2.00.

MORAN, SANDI. HERBPATCH PLEASANT-RIES, 420 NW 65TH LANE, DES MOINES, IA 50313

Sandi has been enthralled with the romance, history, and folklore of herbs since her early teens; now a busy mother of five, she regards her backyard herb business as her own little bit of serenity. A free-lance designer for several publications, including *Better Homes and Gardens,* she is also co-crafts editor of *Herban Lifestyles.* She is a member of the Des Moines Herb Study Group and the Victorian Tea and Garden Society. Her business, which offers wreaths, arrangements, and "Pleasantries" gift baskets, is primarily retail, both mail order and by appointment. She prints a quarterly newsletter *Patch-Words* for her customers, and teaches herb classes. Catalog, $1.00, refundable with first order.

MORGAN, LINDA BALTIMORE. ANTIQUE ORCHID HERBARY, SR 6, BOX 734, ABINGDON, VA 24210

Linda's unusual mountainside farm is noted for its Saturday Herb- and-Flower-Tasting Buffets (by reservation) and Sunday Old-fashioned English High Teas, June through September. Linda also has workshops and lectures at the farm throughout the year. The grounds feature more than 350 varieties of organically grown herbs; the farmhouse is filled with culinary treats, potpourris, dried flowers, and a large selection of herb books and quality dried herbs and spices. She also sells a comprehensive Herb Gardening Guide, laminated for carrying in your gardening basket. Potted herbs are available at the farm only. An herb grower for more than 25 years and the president of the Virginia Herb Growers & Marketers Assoc., Linda is a popular lecturer and has published on a wide variety of herbal topics. Open all year, Wednesday thru Saturday; Sundays, April through September. Send SASE for workshop schedule. Catalog, $1.00.

MORSE, CAROL JO. A STITCH 'N' THYME, WESTBROOK, ME 04092 (207-854-8282)

An herb enthusiast for the past 15 or more years, Carol Jo enjoys making herb and floral arrangements and crafts with her young family and for occasional craft fairs. Fellow herb enthusi-

asts are welcome to call her for a planned visit.

NADEAU, ALYCE. GOLDENROD MOUNTAIN HERBS, WILDCAT RD., DEEP GAP, NC 28618 (704-264-2683)

Alyce Nadeau has been called "an artist with flowers." President of the North Carolina Herb Association, she gardens, crafts, conducts herb classes, and does herbal weddings based on the Victorian language of flowers on her tiny herb farm in the Blue Ridge Mountains. Visit for some herb tea, herb cake (if you are lucky), and her "show-and-smell" tour (please phone ahead).

NEFF, THERESA. COUNTRY THYME GAZETTE, P.O. BOX 3090, DEPT. POH, EL SEGUNDO, CA 90245

Theresa Neff's bimonthly herbal newsletter specializes in herbal entertaining, decorating, cooking, and gardening. A one-year subscription (6 issues) is $11.50; sample copy is available for $1.75. Seminars and lectures on herbal entertaining and decorating are offered through CTG in the Southern California area. For information send a legal-size SASE.

NEWMEYER, WENDY AND JACK. MAINE BALSAM FIR PRODUCTS, P.O. BOX 9, MORSE HILL RD., WEST PARIS, ME 04289 (207-674-2094)

Ten years ago, Jack and Wendy moved to their wooded acreage in Maine from New Jersey and soon founded Maine Balsam Fir Products. They now sell their beautiful and fragrant pillows to 1000 shops around the country and are the nation's leading source of balsam and various tree cones. They welcome people to their forest home and shop by appointment or by chance, or you can find them at a variety of fairs and craft shows in New England. SASE for Retail Brochure; wholesale requests on letterhead.

NORTH, JAY AND PAMELA. PARADISE FARMS, P.O. BOX 436, SUMMERLAND, CA 93067

Pioneers in the field of providing fresh culinary herbs and edible flowers to the market, the Norths wrote the *Guide to Cooking with Edible Flowers,* available from them, $7.00 ppd.

OTTO, ALMA W. 14130 ROSEMARY LANE, APT. 1308, LARGO, FL 34644

Mrs. Otto has lectured and written about herbs for many years; most recently she has been engaged in intensive study and experimentation with herbs that some consider to be difficult to grow in Florida. A member of the Herb Society of America and the Florida Herb Society, Alma has redesigned the specimen herb garden on the grounds of the Suncoast Botanical Garden.

POWERS, JAN. STONE-WELL HERBS, 2320 W. MOSS, PEORIA, IL 61604

Jan, Mike, and their three daughters live in a restored, century-old farmhouse that is also the site of Jan's shop and display gardens. The shop is open from April to December, Friday and Saturday from 10 to 4. Annual events include a Spring Herbfest, Fall Harvest Market, and Holiday Open House in December. The shop offers a wide variety of plants and herb-related items, as well as garden tours and workshops. Visitors are always welcome. Stone-Well Herbs offers herb booklets, precut herb stencil designs, herbal needlework kits, and many other original items for the herb-lover. Legal-size SASE for catalog.

REPPERT, BERTHA. THE ROSEMARY HOUSE AND GARDEN, INC., 120 SOUTH MARKET ST., MECHANICSBURG, PA 17055 (717-697-5111)

Many years ago, Bertha found saffron, basil, savory, rosemary, dill, French tarragon, and other herbs crowding out garden space once given to petunias, zinnias, and begonias. The eternal, almost magical usefulness of these quiet, ancient plants grabbed her heart as nothing else ever had. As she devised new and more wonderful ways to use them, The Rosemary House was born. In this delightful place, Bertha markets her beloved herbs — seeds, plants, wreaths, books, seasonings, potpourris, teas, and herbal gifts galore. She also lectures widely on her passion, has written about her practical experiences in several easy-to-read herbals, and teaches many workshops, all with the avowed intention of making herbs an essential part of everyone's present-day lifestyle. She firmly believes that if everyone tended a small herb garden

and breathed deeply of these fragrant, endearing plants, stress would disappear and there would be peace. Lecture brochure available upon request. 24-page catalog, $2.00.

REPPERT, NANCY. SWEET REMEMBRANCES, 118 S. MARKET ST., MECHANICSBURG, PA 17055

A SASE will bring you a listing of Nancy's heavenly homemade Easter and Christmas candy. Nancy now has an Herb Tea Room right next to her mother's famous Rosemary House, with herb gardens in the back. Write to Nancy or to sister Suzanna, who manages The Rosemary House shop, for their annual lecture, luncheon, and workshop schedule of events catered by Nancy in the new Herb Tea House.

ROGERS, BARBARA RADCLIFFE. HERBITAGE FARM, 686-A OLD HOMESTEAD HIGHWAY, RICHMOND, NH 03470

Herb gardener, writer, and lecturer, Barbara has been growing herbs and everlastings for over 15 years. She is the author of *The Encyclopaedia of Everlastings and Fresh Herbs*, as well as several booklets in the Herbitage Farm Herbal Library ("Deck the Halls With Artemisia: Christmas Decorating with Herbs," "Herbs: A Compendium of Household Uses," and "Herbs for Beauty"; $3.00 each, ppd.). Barbara designs and creates kits for herb crafts and other folk arts, such as lavender bags, moth sachets, catnip mice, herb-filled mug coasters, and cornhusk dolls, which she sells retail through her catalog and wholesale to museum shops. Mail order and wholesale only; catalog, $1.00.

ROSE, JEANNE. HERBAL PRACTITIONER, STE/P 219 CARL ST., SAN FRANCISCO, CA 94117

Internationally known herbalist Jeanne Rose has enchanted us for over 20 years with practical information about using herbs for health and beauty. To her original masterpieces (*Herbs & Things* and *The Herbal Body Book*) she has added *The Herbal Food Book, Ask Jeanne Rose, Kitchen Cosmetics, The Modern Herbal, The Cosmetic Aromatherapy Book,* and a mail-order "Herbal Studies Course," which offers certification upon completion. She is a lifetime member of the American

Aromatherapy Association. Articles have been written about Jeanne Rose in many publications, including *Lear's, Women of Power, Redbook,* and *Victoria* magazines. Catalog of New Age Creations, including her Herbal Bodyworks and all her books, $1.00.

SALZLER, DANIEL AND KATHY. HERB HOLLOW, SAFFORD RD., EAST OTTO, NY 14729

Located in rural, western New York State, Herb Hollow consists of 40 theme gardens containing over 600 varieties of herbs. The Salzlers have developed a nonprofit Educational Institute dedicated to using herbs in both homes and agriculture. Mail-order catalog, $1.00.

SAUSSER, BARBARA. BARB'S COUNTRY HERBS, 15665 RUSSELL, DEPT. 3A, RIVERSIDE, CA 92504 (714-780-2694)

Barbara welcomes visitors at her working display garden surrounded by orange groves, set in a choose-and-cut Monterey pine Christmas tree farm (please phone ahead). She has live herb plants for sale in the spring and fall months, fresh and dried flowers and herbs, potpourri, wreaths, seasonal gifts, and herb books and brochures. She offers workshops in wreath-making, herbal honey and vinegar, tea tasting, and using herbal cosmetics. Barbara is a member of the Inland Herb Society and the Riverside Community Flower Show Committee. Her workshop and studio (and the family tree farm) are open from Thanksgiving until Christmas. No catalog.

SHEPHERD, RENEE. SHEPHERD'S GARDEN SEEDS, FELTON, CA 95018

SHIMIZU, HOLLY HARMAR, PUBLIC PROGRAMS SPECIALIST. UNITED STATES BOTANIC GARDEN, 245 FIRST ST., SW, WASHINGTON, DC 20024

Holly Harmar Shimizu has been responsible for educational programs, plant records, signage, public affairs, and public information at the US Botanic Garden since January 1988. After extensive horticultural education and experience, both here and abroad, she was appointed in 1980 as the first curator of the National Herb Garden at the U.S. National Arboretum, Washington, DC, where she made significant contributions in the development of the garden for several years. She is an active lecturer and writer on a variety of horticultural subjects, and was awarded the 1986 Nancy Putnam Howard Award for outstanding achievement in horticulture by The Herb Society of America.

SIEGLER, MADELEINE H. MONK'S HILL HERBS, RFD 2, BOX 8200, WINTHROP, ME 04364

Madeleine planted her first herb seeds in 1971, before she even finished reading Adelma Simmons's book, which she says changed the entire direction of her life. Since then she has conducted a home-based business in herb plants and crafts, taught many classes in knowing and growing herbs, lectured extensively, and written about herb gardening for many Maine newspapers and other publications. Although Monk's Hill Herbs is no longer open to the public, she and her husband continue to cultivate their many gardens, while Madeleine expands her knowledge of herbs. She is a member-at-large of the Herb Society of America.

SOMMERFELD, LEILA RAE. LEILA RAE ENTERPRISES, 64001 TANGLEWOOD, BEND, OR 97701 (503-389-0127)

Leila Rae's interior and floral design services specialize in "instant room makeovers," custom-made dried herb-flower wreaths and swags, and fresh, fat eucalyptus wreaths that dry naturally for years of lasting beauty. She also makes handcrafted gifts, such as Old-World St. Nicholases, delicate Victorian dolls, and English country cottages that can be lighted. Wholesale and retail. Visitors welcome by appointment.

SPRINGER, MARGARET J. 160 FAWN LANE, WEBSTER, NY 14580-2819

Margaret Springer is interested in herbs, astrology and herbs, and herbal cosmetics.

STRUDWICK, DONNA. 2444 ESTES ST., MUSKEGON, MI 49441

While still a kindergarten teacher, Mrs. Strudwick developed the hobby of collecting and planting herbs, and the study and use of herbs became a main interest. Under her instigation and

nurturing, a nucleus of eight friends grew from a small herb study group to the Western Michigan Herb Society, of which she served as president for two years. She grows large quantities of sweet Annie and Silver King artemisia, plus other everlastings on a friend's farm and uses the harvest in herbal crafts (although she does not have a business). She runs an herb booth for a local church bazaar and an herb fair for the WMHS, gives talks and writes articles about herbs, and teaches craft classes. She is a member of the Herb Society of America.

TARSKI, CHRISTINE. ROSEMARY LANE FLOWERS, P.O. BOX 493, DEPT. MP, ROCKWALL, TX 75087 (214-722-4301)

Rosemary Lane specializes in elegant everlastings with a sprinkling of herbs. Topiaries, rosebud pomanders, wreaths, baskets, and arrangements are all carefully crafted with quality dried and preserved herbs and flowers for stores and shops nationwide. Please write for a listing of stores in your area; wholesale catalog requests on letterhead.

TAYLOR, CHERYL. HEARTFELT FARMS, DEPT PS, P.O. BOX 1513, SALEM, VA 24153

Heartfelt Farms, co-owned by Joye Futch and Cheryl Taylor, offers an extensive line of herbs, spices, and dried flowers, as well as a delightful array of herbal wreaths, flower bundles, hand-blended potpourri, herbal and silk weddings, gift baskets, bunnies, bears, and much more. Joye and Cheryl hope to offer Victorian High Tea and herbal workshops at their farm in the future. Catalog, $2.00, refundable with order; mail order only.

TERRY, ANNA LEE. ROUTE 6, BOX 309 I, DEPT. P, FAIRMONT, WV 26554-9806

Since childhood, Anna Lee Terry has studied and used herbs. She now creates new uses for herbal plants and writes and teaches about herbs.

THORSON, JOEL AND MARGARET. THOUSAND FLOWER FARM, WALDRON ISLAND, WA 98297

Located on a small rural island in the San Juan Islands of Puget Sound (no phones; mail delivery by packet boat three times a week!), Thousand Flower

Farm grows and sells everlastings and herbs locally and by mail order through a catalog that also includes other related cottage industries on the island. They offer culinary herbs, statice and other everlasting wreaths, elephant garlic, potpourri, and bouquets of statice or mixed botanicals, as well as Christmas tree decorations, Christmas flower wreaths, and gift items through a special mailing in November. Visitors are very welcome to the farm, but access is only by plane or boat; write for details. Catalog, $0.50; published each September.

UTTERBACH, CHRIS. HERBAN LIFESTYLES, 84 CARPENTER RD., NEW HARTFORD, CT 06057

From a cozy log home in rural Connecticut, Chris edits and publishes her newsletter — a sassy, eclectic, 12-page newsletter that examines how we live, work, and play with herbs. A risk-free subscription to *Herban Lifestyles* is $18.00 a year (with money-back guarantee); sample issue, $3.00. Free brochure.

VOGLER, SYLVIA AND KEN. MAERRIE MEADOWS FARM, 24322 EVERGREEN RD., PHILOMATH, OR 97370

Sylvia and Ken have grown herbs since 1985. When they outgrew their front and back yards in California, they purchased just under 10 acres in Oregon and started Maerrie Meadows Farm, where they grow herbs, vegetables, peppers, fruit, flowers, and everlastings — and colored Romney sheep to their heart's content (and everlasting labor and joy). Many materials used in their simmering potpourris and wreaths are homegrown or found in the wild. They also make pomanders wrapped in lace, dainty Victorian sachets, and more. Visitors welcome on weekends; write ahead for appointment. For catalog send SASE.

WADE, BARBARA L. HERB 'N' EWE FARM, 11755 NATIONAL ROAD S.E., THORNVILLE, OH 43076 (614-323-2264)

Sisters Barbara Wade and Susan Mills have spent the last 10 years gardening and expanding their herbal experiences. Barbara has completed a Master Gardener program at Dawes Arboretum, and Susan has developed a line of sachets and everlastings for the New England craft circuit. Herb 'N' Ewe has herbal workshops, classes, and garden lectures with tea. The farm is available for group tours and presentations. Open long weekends, Friday to Monday, 10 a.m. to 6 p.m. Brochure available with legal-size SASE.

WAKEFIELD, GRACE. TOM THUMB WORKSHOPS - HA, RT. 13, P.O. BOX 357, MAPPSVILLE, VA 23407 (804-824-3507)

For 12 years, Tom Thumb Workshops has offered dried flowers, potpourris, herbs, spices, fragrances, herbal crafting books, and craft accessories through mail order, retail and wholesale. Visitors are welcomed at the retail shop and the herb garden. Mappsville is located near the Chincoteague National Wildlife Refuge and the Assateague Island National Seashore. Mail-order catalog, $1.00.

WHITLEY, JEAN. DEPT. JMI, 311 BUNDY AVE., ENDWELL, NY 13760

Jean Whitley has enjoyed hobby crafting for many years. Most of her creations are special gifts for family and friends, although occasionally she does sell her labors of love.

WIAND, ISABELLE M. PHOTO CRAFT'S THE HERB LADY, DEER HILL ROAD, RR 1, BOX 3090 POH2, WEEKS MILLS, ME 04361

During a 7-month trip around the world 20 years ago, Isabelle's discovery of new foods and flavors started an herbal interest and study that came to fruition in 1982 as a free-lance writing, photography, and lecturing business, Photo Craft's the Herb Lady. Her "Notes from the Herb Lady" column appeared weekly in the *Kennebec Journal* newspaper. Her work has also been in *The Herb Companion, Potpourri Party Line, Herban Lifestyles,* and *Potpourri from Herbal Acres.* Each summer she teaches a 4-week Herbal Breakfast Workshop at a local resort. She teaches workshops throughout the Central Maine area.

WILLIAMS, BETSY. BETSY WILLIAMS/THE PROPER SEASON, 68 PARK ST., ANDOVER, MA 01810

Betsy's retail shop features dried-flower wreaths, arrangements, and garlands; garden accessories; books; and gift items. Open 9:30 to 5:30, Monday through Saturday, and on Sunday afternoons in December. Classes given on a year-round basis. Twenty years in the herb business, Betsy is very much in demand as a lecturer and writer on herbs, herb and floral arrangements, garden lore and seasonal celebrations. She is the author of *Planning a Fresh Herbal Wedding* and *The Herbs of Christmas.* Full-color catalog, free.

WILLSON, CHERYL. BLOSSOMS 'N' SPICE, 314 WATER ST., SHELL ROCK, IA 50670 (319-885-4888)

Cheryl grows and dries most of the herbs and flowers she uses in her wreaths and arrangements. She sells her crafts informally out of her home year round, and holds an annual open house and fall sale at the end of October at her home on the Shell Rock River; she also sells at several other area Christmas shows. No catalog; visitors welcome (please phone ahead).

WOLD, BETTY. SEQUOYAH GARDENS AND GIFTS, RT. 1, BOX 80, GORE, OK 74435 (918-487-5849)

Betty has been growing herbs for 40 years. In cooperation with Barbara Downs, she writes the quarterly *Herbal Gazette*, directed to herb lovers in the southern Midwest (send SASE for sample copy). She has written for national magazines and has been a featured speaker at the International Herb Growers and Marketers Association meetings and the New Zealand Herb Federation Conference. She welcomes visitors (please phone first). Her book, *Speaking of Herbs*, is a must for harried program planners everywhere.

YOUNG, SHIRLEY. 80 VILLAGE DR., STROUDSBURG, PA 18360

A few years ago, when Shirley was the new lady in town, she wanted to find friends with whom to share her love of herbs, so she organized The Pocono Herb Club. She also began lecturing on herbs at the annual Quiet Valley's Harvest Festival.

❧ *Resource Directory* ↝

This section provides a chapter-by-chapter listing of books, periodicals, and catalogs related to themes in the book, including complete addresses and ordering information for sources mentioned in the book. It is very important that you send the required fee, and/or SASE (legal size, #10, self-addressed, and stamped envelope) when requesting a catalog or brochure, or you will very likely waste both your postage and time. Many of the catalogs offer a great variety of herbal products, but they are listed here for either their specialty or a specific item mentioned in an article. For example, several herb-product catalogs also offer herb plants or oils for potpourri, but they may be listed here because they carry specific, hard-to-find items.

If you would like to visit any of the herb farms or shops mentioned in the book, be sure to first order the catalog or brochure, which often includes the times of the day and the months of the year they are open to the public, as well as a map giving directions on how to get there. Catalogs also often list special events, such as open houses, fairs, classes, or workshops, which you might want to fit into your travel plans. I promise you joy as you make contact with these wonderful herb people, whether in person or by mail!

MAIL-ORDER HERB BOOKS

Some sources specialize in mail-order herb books; some offer a very extensive listing of books. My favorite book dealer is WOOD VIOLET BOOKS (*Debra Cravens*, 3814 Sunhill Dr., Madison, WI 53704; catalog, $1.00). Whenever I want to order a new herb book, find out about an older one, or try to locate an out-of-print herbal classic, I turn to Debra. She attends herb conferences and stocks all the new books as they come out. And, she'll try to locate hard-to-find books, upon request. Most of the books mentioned on these pages are in her catalog. Another good source is *Arleen Shannon* of GREENFIELD HERB GARDEN (P.O. Box 437, Shipshewana, IN 46565); send a SASE, plus $0.50 in stamps, for this very extensive listing of herb books by mail. Other good sources are the HERB SOCIETY OF AMERICA *(see write-up under* MAY, *Herb Groups and Organizations)* and HERB BOOKS (*Elisabeth Woodburn*, Booknoll Farm, Box 398, Hopewell, NJ 08525; catalog, $2.00). In addition, many herb catalogs and periodicals sell herb books. Your local bookstore should also be able to order a book for you if it is still in print; supply them with the title, author, publisher, and year of publication.

JANUARY

Essential Oils and Related Aromatherapy Supplies

AROMA-VERA, *Marcel Lavabre*, 2728 S. Robertson, Los Angeles, CA 90034 (213-280-0407)

THE ESSENTIAL OIL COMPANY, *Robert Seidel*, P.O. Box 88, Sandy, OR 97055

FRONTIER COOPERATIVE HERBS, Box 299, Norway, IA 52318 (319-227-7991)

THE GINGER TREE, *Clementina Carlin*, P.O. Box 1882-P2, Schenectady, NY 12301

Offers "Aromatherapy Consultations by Mail," oils, information sheet. Catalog, $1.00.

HARMONY HOLLOW INK, 4005 Canyon Dr., Fair Oaks, CA 95628 catalog, $1.00.

Offers a complete list of aromatherapy books; $1.00

HERBAL ENDEAVORS AND TISSERAND OILS, *Colleen Dodt*, 3618 S. Emmons Ave., Rochester Hills, MI 48063 (313-852-0796)

Offers an "Aromatherapy Kit for Beginners," plus oils, books, and equipment.

LEDET OILS, P.O. Box 2354, Fair Oaks, CA 95628 (916-965-7549)

NATURE'S PRODUCTS, 20020 Conant, Detroit, MI 48234

NATURE'S SYMPHONY, 10 NE First Ave., Boca Raton, FL 33434

NEW AGE CREATIONS, *Jeanne Rose*, Ste P 219 Carl St., San Francisco, CA 94117

ORIGINAL SWISS AROMATICS, P.O. Box 606, San Rafael, CA 94915 (415-459-3998)

SANTA FE FRAGRANCE, P.O. Box 282, Santa Fe, NM 87504 (505-473-1717)

TISSERAND OILS/AROMATHERAPY SUPPLIES, LTD., Unit W3(P), The Knoll Business Center, Old Shoreham Rd., Hove, Sussex, England BN3 7GS

Aromatherapy Books

AROMATHERAPY: AN A-Z by Patricia Davis (C.W. Daniel Company, Ltd., 1988)

AROMATHERAPY FOR WOMEN by Maggie Tisserand (Thorsons, 1985)

AROMATHERAPY TO HEAL AND TEND THE BODY by Robert Tisserand (Lotus Press, 1988). Also published under the title *AROMATHERAPY FOR EVERYONE* (Penguin Books, 1988)

AROMATHERAPY WORKBOOK by Marcel Lavabre (Healing Arts Press, forthcoming)

ART OF AROMATHERAPY by Robert B. Tisserand (Destiny, 1977)

THE COSMETIC AROMATHERAPY BOOK by Jeanne Rose (North Atlantic Books, 1990)

THE HANDBOOK OF AROMATHERAPY by Marcel Lavabre (Marcel Lavabre, 1986)

JEANNE ROSE'S HERBAL BODY BOOK by Jeanne Rose (Grosset and Dunlap, 1976)

KITCHEN COSMETICS by Jeanne Rose (Panjandrum, 1978)

THE POWER OF HOLISTIC AROMATHERAPY by Christine Stead (Javelin Books, 1986)

PRACTICAL AROMATHERAPY by Shirley Price (Thorsons, 1983)

THE PRACTICE OF AROMATHERAPY by Dr. Jean Valnet (C.W. Daniel, 1988)

SCENTUAL TOUCH by Judith Jackson (Fawcett)

Aromatherapy Newsletters, Organizations, and Courses

AMERICAN AROMATHERAPY ASSOCIATION P.O. Box 1222, Fair Oaks, CA 95628

Sponsors conventions and an examination for a "Diploma in Aromatherapy"; Common Scents Newsletter is available to non-members

AROMA VERA, 2728 S. Robertson Blvd. Los Angeles, CA 90034

Sponsors workshops, seminars, and Holistic Aromatherapy Certification Courses, conducted by the leading expert in aromatherapy in America, Marcel Lavabre (president of Aroma Vera and the author of two excellent books, listed above). Offers an Aromatherapy Correspondence Course.

PACIFIC INSTITUTE OF AROMATHERAPY, P.O. Box 903, San Rafael, CA 94915

THE INTERNATIONAL JOURNAL OF AROMATHERAPY, 10 Victoria Grove Second Ave., Hove, East Sussex England BN3 2LJ

This journal is highly recommended to those who are seriously interested in the art and science of aromatherapy

Other Sources of Essential Oils

Many other firms specialize in essential oils and fragrance oils. The most reliable will state if their oils are pure and undiluted, and will list synthetic or fragrance oils separately. You may not want to use the most expensive oils for potpourri, but you must use the pure oils for aromatherapy projects, if they are to be effective.

In addition, you will find oils listed in many of the general catalogs, listed later. If you are past the novice stage and seriously interested in learning more about the chemical aspects of perfumes and aromatics, here are two reference books that might be available from the book dealers on page 285: PERFUMES & COSMETICS, WITH SPECIAL REFERENCE TO SYNTHETICS by W.A. Poucher (New York: Van Nostrand Co., 1923) and THE H & R BOOK: GUIDE TO FRAGRANCE INGREDIENTS (English Edi-

tion; London: Johnson Publications Limited, 1985).

GINGHAM 'N' SPICE, LTD., *Nancy McFayden*, P.O. Box 88/HT, Gardenville, PA 18926

Wholesale or retail catalogs, $2.00. Request wholesale catalog on business letterhead. Excellent-quality blended oils and fragrance products.

HERB GARDEN FRAGRANCES, *Rosella Mathieu*, 3744 Section Rd., Cincinnati, OH 45236

Send a #10 SASE for details. High-quality, long-lasting essences for potpourri.

LAVENDER LANE, *Donna Madora Mitchell*, P.O. Box 7265-HT, Citrus Heights, CA 95621-7265

$2.00 for very informative catalog of fragrance and essential oils and more.

LORANN OILS, P.O. Box 22009, Lansing, MI 48909. 1-800-248-1302; Michigan residents, call 1-800-862-8620

Request retail catalog (Food, Apothecary, & Home Crafting) or wholesale catalog. Many oils for food flavoring, and supplies for soap and candle-making.

NATURE'S FINEST, *Mike and Jen Mescher*, P.O. Box 10311/HT, Burke, VA 22015

Catalog, $2.00. Many unusual oils and products for the bath, plus information sheets about uses.

PENN HERB CO., 603 N. 2nd St., Philadelphia, PA 19123

Interesting fragrance oils, such as peach, apricot, and so on. Catalog, $1.00.

Herbal Bath and Cosmetic Sources

ANDALINA, *Janet S. Garcia*, Tory Hill, Warner, NH 03278-0057
Natural Soaps. Brochure, $1.50.

APHRODISIA, 282 Bleecher St., New York, NY 10014
Catalog, $2.50. Great variety.

AROMA-VERA. *(see* **JANUARY,** ***Aromatherapy Supplies*** *for address)*
Cosmetic supplies.

BOERICKE & TAFEL, INC., 1011 Arch St., Philadelphia, PA 19107
Cosmetic supplies.

BUTTERPLUM PRODUCTS, *Randa Black*, P.O. Box 57-12/HT, Ephraim, UT 84627
Lovely bath gift baskets with natural soaps. SASE for details.

CASWELL-MASSEY CO., Ltd., 21 Fulton St., South St. Seaport, New York, NY 10038
Catalog, $1.00. Large variety of natural soaps and lotions; exquisite potpourri oils.

DUTTWEILLER'S BATH SCRUBBIES, 1531 Ash St., Georgetown, TX 78626
SASE for details. Available by the dozen.

HERBAL BODYWORKS, *Jeanne Rose*, Ste P 219 Carl St., San Francisco, CA 94117
Catalog, $1.00.

INDIANA BOTANIC GARDENS, P.O. Box 5, Hammond, IN 56325
Catalog, $1.00. Cosmetic supplies.

LORANN OILS. *(see* **JANUARY,** ***Aromatherapy Supplies*** *for address)*
Cosmetic supplies.

THE MAGICK GARDEN, 5703 Country Walk, McFarland, WI 53558
Linda's Magical Celebration Baskets. Brochure for SASE.

MARY ROSSIER'S NATURAL SOAPS, RR 1, Box 96B/HT, Danville, VT 05828
SASE.

NATURE'S FINEST. *(see* **JANUARY,** ***Other Sources of Essential Oils*** *for address)*
Cosmetic supplies.

SEVENTH HEAVEN HERB PRODUCTS, *Kate Carter Frederick*, 856-12th Ave. S., Onalaska, WI 54650
$0.25 for listing of natural and fragrant products.

Herbal Bath and Cosmetic Books

THE ART OF SOAPMAKING (Charlotte, VT: Harrowsmith Books, $9.45 ppd.)

JEANNE ROSE'S HERBAL BODY BOOK AND *KITCHEN COSMETICS* by Jeanne Rose
(see **Author's Directory** *for ordering information)*

MAKING POTPOURRI, COLOGNES, AND SOAPS: 102 NATURAL RECIPES by David W. Webb (Blue Ridge Summit, PA: TAB Books, 1988)

PERFUME CRAFTING: THE LORE AND LURE OF PERFUMERY by Grace Wakefield
History, instructions, recipes ($2.50; see **Author's Directory** *for ordering information)*

SOAP: MAKING IT, ENJOYING IT by Ann Bramson (New York: Workman, 1975)

FEBRUARY

Victoriana Books

AMERICAN GARDENS OF THE NINETEENTH CENTURY FOR COMFORT AND AFFLUENCE by Ann Leighton (Amherst, MA: University of Massachusetts Press, 1987)

AN AGE OF FLOWERS by Doris L. Swarthout (Old Greenwich, CT: Chatham Press, 1975)

ANTIQUE FLOWERS by Katherine Whiteside (New York: Villard, 1988)

COTTAGE GARDEN FLOWERS by Margery Fish (London: Faber & Faber, 1961)

CREATING A VICTORIAN FLOWER GARDEN by Stefan Buczacki (New York: Weidenfeld and Nicolson, 1988)

FOR EVERY HOUSE A GARDEN: A GUIDE FOR REPRODUCING PERIOD GARDENS by Rudy and Joy Favretti (Chester, CT: Pequot Press, 1977)

THE GIFT OF CHRISTMAS PAST by Sunny O'Neil (The Victorian House-HT, 600 N. Main St., Mt. Vernon, OH 43050)

The "bible" of Victorian Christmas decorating.

LANGUAGE OF FLOWERS by Kate Greenaway (New York: Gramercy Publishing, 1978; reprint of 1884 edition published by G. Routledge, London)

THE LANGUAGE OF FLOWERS, Second Edition, by Kathleen Gips (Pine Creek Herbs, Chagrin Falls, OH; revised 1990)

Over 600 Victorian meanings of herbs, flowers, shrubs, trees, and even weeds! Send $12.45 ppd. to author (see **Author's Directory** *for address) for autographed copy; quantity prices available upon request.*

THE LANGUAGE OF HERBS AND THEIR COMPANIONS by Paula Johnson (Herb Patch Gardens, 429 Hill Rd., Boxborough, MA 01719; $5.00 ppd.; available wholesale)

A NINETEENTH-CENTURY GARDEN by Charles Van Ravensway (Universe Publishing Co., 1977)

THE SCENTED GARDEN by Rosemary Verey (New York: Van Nostrand Reinhold, 1981)

TUSSIE MUSSIES: VICTORIAN POSEY HOLDERS by Jeri Schwartz (Box 271, Hartsdale, NY 10530; $8.95 ppd.)

A VICTORIAN HERBAL: A COLLECTION OF TEAS, TRADITIONS, AND HEIRLOOM GARDENING by Jan Powers (Peoria, IL: Stone-Well Herbs)

$4.00 ppd. from author (see **Author's Directory** *for address).*

Everlastings Seeds and Plants

THE FLOWERY BRANCH (Herb and Everlasting Seeds), P.O. Box 1330/HT, Flowery Branch, GA 30542

Mail-order division of Catnip Acres Farm; $2.00 for 2-year catalog and updates.

GOODWIN CREEK GARDENS, P.O. Box 83-HT, Williams, OR 97544

Catalog, $1.00.

PARK SEED CO., Cokesbury Rd., Greenwood, SC 29647-0001

SANDY MUSH HERB NURSERY, Dept. HT, Rte. 2, Surrett Cove Rd., Leicester, NC 28748

$1.00 for plant and seed listings; $4.00, refundable, for their terrific handbook.

Dried Flowers

COPE'S POSIE PATCH, *Jean Cope,* 3482 Gingham-Frederick Rd., Tipp City, OH 45371

Both retail and wholesale. SASE for listings.

CRAMER'S POSIE PATCH, Dept. HT, 740 High Ridge Rd., Columbia, PA 17512

GOODWIN CREEK GARDENS, P.O. Box 83-HT, Williams, OR 97544

HARRIS PERENNIALS, Dept. HT, 6750 S. Hollister Rd., Laingsburg, MI 48848

SASE.

ISLAND FARMCRAFTERS, Dept. HT, Waldron Island, WA 98297

Catalog, $0.50.

SILVA FARMS, WHOLESALE FLORIST SUPPLY CO., 1098 Tremont St., No. Dighton, MA 02764

Wholesale only.

SPENCER FARMS (Formerly Countree), 4675 Bender Rd., Middleville, MI 49333

Wholesale only.

SEE ALSO floral supply houses under **NOVEMBER**, *Herb Craft Supplies*;

many sell dried flowers, both retail and wholesale.

Books on Everlastings

A CONCISE GUIDE TO GROWING EVERLASTINGS by Jim and Dottie Becker (Williams, OR: Goodwin Creek Gardens; $7.70 ppd.; see **FEBRUARY,** *Everlastings Seeds and Plants* for address)

COMPLETE BOOK OF DRIED FLOWERS by Patricia Thorpe (New York: Michael Friedman, 1985)

FLORAL KEEPSAKES by Sunny O'Neil (The Victorian House/HT, 600 N. Main St., Mt. Vernon, OH 43050)

Autographed copy from author, $23.50 ppd.

FLOWERS THAT LAST FOREVER: GROWING, HARVESTING, AND PRESERVING by Betty E.M. Jacobs (Pownal, VT: Garden Way Publishing, 1988)

THE ENCYCLOPAEDIA OF EVERLASTINGS by Barbara Radcliffe Rogers (New York: Weidenfeld & Nicolson, 1988)

Autographed copy from author (see **Author's Directory** *); $20.45 ppd.*

MARCH

Landscaping Books

HERB GARDEN DESIGN by Swanson and Rady (Herb Society of America, 1984)

LANDSCAPING WITH HERBS by James Adams (Portland, OR: Timber Press, 1987)

Herb Garden Decorations

THE HERB HOUSE CATALOG, 340 Grove St., Bluffton, OH 45817

Bee skeps, retail and wholesale; catalog, $1.00.

STONE-WELL HERBS, *Jan Powers,* 2320 West Moss, Peoria, IL 61604

Stencils for garden markers; SASE for price list.

DEI TOS ORNAMENTAL CONCRETE, Dept. HT, 501 Cedar St., Freeland, PA 18224

St. Fiacre cast-stone statutes; SASE for brochure.

BECK'S CLAYWORKS, RR 2, Box 356/HT, Sharpsville, IN 46068

St. Francis statutes; SASE.

HERBS 'N' HOMESPUNS, 15898 E. 8th Circle, Aurora, CO 80011

Terra cotta plant markers.

ROCK RIFFLE RUN POTTERY, 14435 Rainbow Lake Rd., Shade, OH 45776

Terra cotta plant markers.

THE COUNTRY BUMPKIN, RR 1, Box 159, St. Paul, IN 47272

Ceramic garden markers.

THE SWINGING BRIDGE POTTERY, S.R. 2, Box 395/HT, Criglersville, VA 22727

Porcelain and stoneware markers; free wholesale and retail brochure.

AMARANTH STONEWARE, LTD., P.O. Box 243, Sydenham, Ontario, Canada KOH 2TO

Exquisite stoneware gardening ornamentation, wholesale and retail.

HEARTHSTONE HOUSE, 1600 Hilltop Rd., Xenia, OH 45385

Beautiful antique slate garden markers and ornaments; retail and wholesale.

Books on Dyeing with Herbs

THE COMPLETE ILLUSTRATED BOOK OF DYES FROM NATURAL SOURCES by Connie and Arnold Krachmal (New York: Doubleday & Co., 1974)

DYES FROM PLANTS by Seonaid Robertson (New York: Van Nostrand Reinhold Co., 1973)

GROWING HERBS AND PLANTS FOR DYEING by Betty E.M. Jacobs (Tarzana, CA: Select Books, 1977)

HANDBOOK ON DYE PLANTS AND DYEING #46 and *HANDBOOK ON NATURAL PLANT DYEING #72* (Brooklyn Botanic Garden,

1000 Washington Ave., Brooklyn, NY 11225; $3.05 each, ppd.)

Herb Seed and Plant Catalogs

Current catalogs of plants are available each new year through at least spring. If you order in the late summer or the fall, you may not receive one until the next year. A good reference for sources is THE HERB GARDENER'S RESOURCE GUIDE by Paula Oliver (Northwind Farm, Rte. 2, Box 246, Shevlin, MN 56676; $7.95 ppd.), which lists over 500 resources for herb plants and seeds, gardening supplies, bulk herbs, herbal products, organizations, publications, and books.

CATNIP ACRES FARM (*see* THE FLOWERY BRANCH)

CLARK'S GREENHOUSE & HERBAL COUNTRY, Dept. HT, RR 1, Box 15B, San Jose, IL 62682

Catalog, $1.00.

COMPANION PLANTS, Dept. HT, 7247 N. Coolville Ridge Rd., Athens, OH 45701

Catalog, $2.00 (retail and wholesale).

THOMAS DEBAGGIO, Dept. HT, 923 North Ivy St., Arlington, VA 22201

Lavender and rosemary specialist; newest varieties. $1.00 for current listing.

THE FLOWERY BRANCH , P.O. Box 1330/HT, Flowery Branch, GA 30542

Mail-order division of Catnip Acres Farm. $2.00 for 2-year catalog and updates.

FOX HILL FARM, *Marilyn Hampstead*, Box 7-PH2, Parma, MI 49269

Catalog, $1.00.

HARTMAN'S HERB FARM, Old Dana Rd., Barre, MA 01005

Catalog, $2.00.

HERB GATHERING, *Paula Winchester*, 5742 Kenwood, Kansas City, MO 64110

Catalog, $2.00, refundable with order.

LOGEE'S GREENHOUSES, 55 North St., Danielson, CT 06239

2-year color catalog, $3.00.

LOST PRAIRIE HERB FARM, *Diane Downs*, 805 Kienas Rd., Kalispell, MT 59901

Catalog, $1.00.

MERRY GARDENS, P.O. Box 595, Camden, ME 04843

Catalog, $1.00.

NEW HOPE HERB FARM, *Carolee Bean*, Rte. 1, Box 660/HT, Spencer, IN 47460

SASE.

NICHOL'S GARDEN NURSERY, Dept. HT, 1190 N. Pacific Hwy., Albany, OR 97321

PARK SEED CO., Cokesbury Rd., Box 31, Greenwood, SC 29647-0001

RASLAND FARM, *The Tippetts*, Dept. HT, NC 82 at US 13, Godwin, NC 28344

Catalog, $2.50.

RICHTER'S HERBS, Goodwood, Ontario, Canada LOC 1A0

Catalog, $2.00.

SANDY MUSH HERB NURSERY, *The Jaynes-HT*, Rte. 2, Surrett Cove Rd., Leicester, NC 28748

HERB HANDBOOK, a marvelous guide, $4.00, refundable with purchase.

SHEPHERD'S GARDEN SEED CATALOG, 7389 W. Zayante Rd., Felton, CA 95018

SPRING VALLEY GARDENS, *Kathy Hyzer/HT*, S 6143, RR 1, Loganville, WI 53943

Catalog, $1.00.

TAYLOR'S HERB GARDENS, 1535 Lone Oak Rd., Vista, CA 92083

Catalog, $1.00.

THOMPSON & MORGAN, P.O. Box 1308, Jackson, NJ 08527

WAYSIDE GARDENS, Hodges, SC 29695

Catalog, $1.00, refundable

WELL-SWEEP HERB FARM, *The Hydes*, Dept. HT, 317 Mt. Bethel Rd., Port Murray, NJ 07865

Catalog, $2.00.

WORMWOOD FARM HERBS, HT, Rte. 9, Ridge Rd., Lisbon Falls, ME 04252

Catalog, $1.00.

Books on Propagation

THE ENCYCLOPEDIA OF HERBS AND HERBALISM, edited by Malcolm Stuart (New York: Crescent Books)

THE HERB GARDEN by Sara Garland with NY Botanical Garden Institute of Urban Horticulture (New York: Penguin Books, 1985)

PLANT PROPAGATION: PRINCIPLES AND PRACTICES by Hartman and Kester (New Jersey: Prentice Hall)

PROPAGATION by Alan Toogood (New York: Stein and Day)

SECRETS OF PLANT PROPAGATION by Lewis Hill (Pownal, VT: Garden Way Publishing, 1985)

Natural Gardening Sources

GARDENER'S SUPPLY, 128 Intervale Rd., Burlington, VT 05401

GARDENS ALIVE!, Natural Gardening Research Ctr., Hwy. 48, P.O. Box 149, Sunman, IN 47041

MEDINA AGRICULTURAL PRODUCTS CO., INC., Box 309, Hondo, TX 78861

NECESSARY TRADING COMPANY, 811 Salem Ave., New Castle, VA 24127

Catalog, $2.00, refundable with order.

NITRON INDUSTRIES, INC., 4605 Johnson Rd., P.O. Box 1447, Fayetteville, AR 72702

PEACEFUL VALLEY FARM SUPPLY, P.O. Box 2209, Grass Valley, CA 95945

Catalog, $2.00, refundable with order.

RINGER NATURAL LAWN AND GARDEN PRODUCTS, 9959 Valley View Rd., Eden Prairie, MN 55344

Natural Gardening Books

SPEAK OUT FOR THE ENVIRONMENT WITH NATURAL GARDENING by June King

Available from author, 7200 CR 315, Keystone Hgts., FL 32656; $4.00 ppd.

APRIL

Children's Gardening Sources

GURNEY SEED & NURSERY, CO., 110 Capitol St., Yankton, SD 57079

MELLINGER'S, North Lima, OH 44452-9731

Children's Gardening Books

GARDENING WITH CHILDREN, Handbook #105 (Brooklyn Botanic Garden, 1000 Washington Ave., Brooklyn, NY 11225; $3.05 ppd.)

Includes activities, programs, and recipes for herbs, vegetables, and flowers.

HERB COLORING BOOK (Mineola, NY: Dover Publications) #23499-1

Very reasonably priced. The lovely designs may be copied and then reduced or enlarged for stencilling and other projects. May be available from herb book dealers listed on page 293.

THE HERBAL WEAVING HANDBOOK by Nancy J. Quinn-Simon (Carlyle Herb Farm, Dept. PFHA, 2110 Carlyle NW, Massillon, OH 44646; 216-832-1934; $4.45 ppd.; Ohio residents add $0.24 sales tax)

Topics in the book include basic techniques; how to construct a lap loom from an old picture frame; double, country rag, vertical, and Victorian herb weaving; recommended herbs and flowers and sources. Color brochure ($1.00) includes lovely handwoven herbal weavings, the handbook, and a kit. This book is appropriate for all ages.

HONEYSUCKLE SIPPING: THE PLANT LORE OF CHILDHOOD by Jeanne R. Chesanow (Camden, ME: Down East Books)

A new, wonderful collection of childhood memories about games played using garden and backyard plants; a joy to read!

A KID'S FIRST BOOK OF GARDENING, WITH GREENHOUSE AND SEEDS by Derek Fell (Philadelphia, PA: Running Press; $14.48 ppd.)

Includes a section on herbs, along with several interesting projects to stimulate "the growing bug."

LET'S GROW! 72 GARDENING ADVENTURES WITH CHILDREN by Linda Tilgner (Pownal, VT: Garden Way Publishing, 1988)

Shows parents how to share their gardening hobbies with their children; includes recipes, charts, garden plans, plant experiments, a potpourri garden, and so on.

NATIONAL GARDENING ASSOCIATION'S GUIDE TO KIDS' GARDENING by Lynn Ocone and Eve Pravis (Burlington, VT: National Gardening Association, revised 1990)

Topics include planning and designing a garden.

REGENERATION: YOU AND YOUR ENVIRONMENT (A GUIDE FOR TEACHERS) (Emmaus, PA: Rodale Press)

Nice kit; great projects.

THYME FOR KIDS by Leanna K. Potts and Evangela Potts

Wonderful primer on herbs for children, including seeds, instructions, and recipes. Available from authors, 717 Glenview, Joplin, MO 64801; $9.45 ppd.

Also, write to the National 4-H Council (7100 Connecticut Ave., Chevy Chase, MD 20815) or ask your County Cooperative Extension Office about local 4-H programs

MAY

Herb Groups and Organizations

A word about THE HERB SOCIETY OF AMERICA, *the prestigious and oldest herb organization in the United States. Membership is by sponsorship and for those who have demonstrated knowledge of herbs and community service involving herbs, such as the establishment and maintenance of public herb gardens. Since education is one of the primary purposes of the HSA, it offers to the general public a large selection of publications, including the latest herb books. (For the latest book list, send $0.50 and a SASE to* The Herb Society of America, 9019 Kirtland-Chardon Rd., Mentor, OH 44060.) *Some of their own publications, which are available at quantity discounts, are* TRAVELER'S GUIDE TO HERB GARDENS (in USA and Canada), *$4.75 ppd.;* THE BEGINNER'S HERB GARDEN, *$3.65 ppd.;* JUDGING HERBS: A HANDBOOK FOR HORTICULTURAL JUDGES, *$2.45 ppd.; and* HERB GARDEN DESIGN *by Swanson & Rady, $17.25, paper; $31.25, cloth.*

Most of the organizations listed below offer an informative newsletter along with membership to anyone who is interested, since educating the public about herbs is one of their purposes. Always send a SASE (legal-sized, self-addressed, stamped envelope) when inquiring about membership in these organizations, or when asking to be notified of their special events or conference "proceedings" available to all. (List is alphabetical by state.)

THE HERB SOCIETY OF TUCSON, c/o Fred Zweig, 9841 E. Watson Dr., Tucson, AZ 85730

OZARKS REGIONAL HERB GROWERS & MARKETERS ASSN., c/o Jim Long, Rt. 4, Box 730, Oak Grove, AR 72660

HAWAII HERB ASSOCIATION, c/o Cooperative Extension Service, 910 California Ave., Wahiawa, HI 96786

IDAHO HERB GROWERS, c/o Rick Parker, College of So. Idaho, P.O. Box 128, Twin Falls, ID 83303-1238

IHGMA (INTERNATIONAL HERB GROWERS AND MARKETERS ASSN.), P.O. Box 281-HT, Silver Spring, PA 17575

ILLINOIS HERB ASSN., c/o Marilyn Miller, Oakdale Herb Farm, RR 1, Box 46, Bluford, IL 62814

THE HERB SOCIETY OF CENTRAL KANSAS, 11304 Valley Hi Dr., Wichita, KS 67209

THE ASSN. OF KENTUCKY HERB BUSINESSES, c/o Mary Peddie, Box 182, Washington, KY 41096

MARYLAND HERB ASSN., Maryland Department of Agriculture, Marketing Service, 50 Harry S. Truman Pkwy., Annapolis, MD 21401

MICHIGAN HERB ASSOCIATES, c/o Lois Frentz, 18664 Gainsborough, Detroit, MI 48223

THE MICHIGAN HERB BUSINESS ASSN., c/o Jean Riggs, 2460 N. Wixom Rd., Milford, MI 48042

NORTH KENT HERB SOCIETY, c/o Vivian Fletcher, 3601 Remembrance Ave., Grand Rapids, MI 49504

WESTERN MICHIGAN HERB SOCIETY, c/o Donna Strudwick, 2444 Estes, Muskegon, MI 49441

THYME FOR HERBS CLUB, P.O. Box 3603, Joplin, MO 64803

NEW HAMPSHIRE HERB SOCIETY, P.O. Box 142, Warner, NH 03278

ADIRONDACK HERB ASSOCIATION, c/o Jane Desotelle, RR 2, Chateaugay, NY 12920

NORTH CAROLINA HERB ASSN., c/o Dick Tippett, Rasland Farm, Rte. 1, Box 65, Godwin, NC 28344

OKLAHOMA HERB GROWERS & MARKETERS, c/o Doris Bankes, Rt. 1, Box 847, Ramona, OK 74061

POCONO MT. HERB SOCIETY, c/o Shirley Young, 80 Village Dr., Stroudsburg, PA 18360

TEXAS HERB GROWERS & MARKETERS, c/o Evelyn Harris, P.O. Box 780, Tyler, TX 75710

VIRGINIA HERB GROWERS & MARKETERS ASSN., c/o Andy Hankins, Virginia Cooperative Extension Service, Box 540, Virginia State Univ., Petersburg, VA 23803

In addition, there are hundreds of local herb groups around the country. Attend their fairs, garden tours, or plant sales, and don't hesitate to ask for membership information. If the membership is limited for some reason or another, then you'll know it's time to start another herb study group in your area! We would be happy to add other groups to this listing in future printings of this book. Please notify the author at Box 428, Washington Crossing, PA 18977. Additional herb organizations are named in many of the periodicals listed below; you will learn of their endeavors by inquiring about or subscribing to their newsletters.

Herbal Periodicals (Newsletters, Journals, Magazines)

The prices given are current as of this writing, to the best of our knowledge: send a legal-size, SASE to the publication you are interested in for the latest information.

AMERICAN HERB ASSN. NEWSLETTER, *Kathi Keville,* P.O. Box 353-P2, Rescue, CA 95672

$20/year; medicinal herbs. The AHA provides a DIRECTORY OF HERB SCHOOLS AND CORRESPONDENCE COURSES IN THE USA; *$2.00*

BU$INESS OF HERBS, *Paula Winchester,* Northwind Farm Publications, Rt. 2, Box 246/HT, Shevlin, MN 56676

$20.00/6 issues. A must for herb businesses!

COUNTRY THYME GAZETTE, *Theresa Neff,* P.O. Box 3090-HT, El Segundo, CA 90245

$11.50/6 issues. Stresses California and Southwest herbs and uses.

FLOWERLETTER, *Sunny O'Neil,* The Victorian House/HT, 600 N. Main St., Mt. Vernon, OH 43050

$12.00/4 issues. Dried floral crafts.

HERB COMPANION, *Linda Ligon,* Dept. HT, 306 N. Washington, Loveland, CO 80537

$21, USA; $28, Canada/6 issues. Lovely color magazine.

HERB JOURNAL OF THE WESTERN RESERVE HERB SOCIETY, c/o Kathleen Gips, 152 S. Main St., Chagrin Falls, OH 44022

$8.00/4 issues.

HERB MARKET REPORT, *Richard Alan Miller,* Organization for the Advancement of Knowledge, 1305 Vista Dr., Grants Pass, OR 97527

$12.00/12 issues. Each issue features an herb or spice as a cash-crop .

HERB QUARTERLY, *Linda Sparrowe,* P.O. Box 548, Boiling Springs, PA 17007

$24.00/4 issues.

HERB, SPICE, AND MEDICINAL PLANT DIGEST, *L.E. Craker/J.E. Simon,* Co-operative Extension of the U.S. Dept. of Agriculture, University of Mass., Amherst, MA 01003

$8.00/4 issues.

HERBAL CRAFTS QUARTERLY, *Grace Wakefield,* Tom Thumb Workshops, Rte. 13, P.O. Box 357-P2, Mappsville, VA 23407

$14.00/4 issues.

HERBAL GAZETTE, *Betty Wold/Barbara Downs,* Rt. 1, Box 105, Checotah, OK 74426

Send legal-size SASE for sample. Aimed at southern Midwest readers.

HERBAL GRAM, P.O. Box 201660, Austin, TX 78720

$25.00/year. Scientific research.

HERBAN LIFESTYLES, *Chris Utterback,* 84 Carpenter Rd., N. Hartford, CT 06057

$18.00/year.

INTERNATIONAL HERB GROWERS AND MARKETERS ASSOC. NEWSLETTER, P.O. Box 281-HT, Silver Spring, PA 17575

Top-notch newsletter for businesses.

LINES FROM LOIS, *Lois Wyeth,* The Peaceable Kingdom, 8375 Rapid Lightning Rd., Sandpoint, ID 83864

$10.00/5 issues. A business-related newsletter of superior quality. (Space does not allow a listing of all the promotional newsletters from herb businesses, but this one is of exceptional quality and for all nature lovers!)

OZARKS HERBALIST, *Jim Long,* Rte. 4, Box 730/HT, Oak Grove, AR 72660

$10.00/4 issues.

POTPOURRI PARTY-LINE, *Dody Lyness,* Berry Hill Press, Dept. P2, 7336 Berry Hill, Palos Verdes Peninsula, CA 90274

$15, USA; $18, Canada/4 issues. The latest in dried floral and fragrance crafting. Sample copy, $3.95.

POTPOURRI FROM HERBAL ACRES, *Phyllis V. Shaudys,* Box 428-HT, Washington Crossing, PA 18977

$18.00/4 issues. Includes the current Fall through Summer series, whenever ordered. A networking continuation of the material in this book, as well as in The Pleasure of Herbs.

JUNE

Herbal Weddings

CAPRILANDS HERB FARM, *Adelma Simmons,* Silver St., Coventry, CT 06238

Brochure, $0.50. Book, "Wedding Herbs for a Happy Household"

COPE'S POSIE PATCH, P2, *Jean Cope,* 3482 Gingham-Frederick Rd., Tipp City, OH 45371

For many years Jean has been offering customized wedding accessories by mail; brides can choose the varieties and colors of the herbs and flowers used for over fifteen offerings of everlasting creations for the wedding and reception. Send a legal-SASE for the wedding brochure.

THE PROPER SEASON, *Betsy Williams,* 68 Park St., Andover, MA 01810.

Catalog, $2.00. Betsy has been doing fresh or dried herbal weddings locally for several years. Her wedding workshops at IHGMA conferences are extremely popular. From her catalog you can order her booklet "Planning a Fresh Herbal Wedding," as well as wedding herbs in bulk or in favor-size boxes, with the meanings of the herbs included. Betsy recently began offering 3-day workshops on herbal weddings.

RASLAND FARM, *Sylvia Tippett,* NC 82 at US 13, Godwin, NC 28344

Color catalog, $2.50. Custom-designed herbal wedding bouquets, arrangements, and wreaths through the symbolism of herbs and flowers. Samples in catalog.

THE ROSEMARY HOUSE, *Bertha Reppert,* 120 So. Market St., Mechanicsburg, PA 17055

Catalog, $2.00. Bertha does herbal weddings locally. Her catalog offers numerous herbal wedding and shower accessories, favors, herbal rice, and much more. Her BRIDE'S HERBAL: WEDDINGS AND OTHER PARTIES (1989) is $13.50 ppd. This is a one-and-only of its kind, packed full of great ideas, projects, tips, instructions, and recipes!

Ribbons, Laces, and Bridal Accessories

HOME-SEW, INC., Dept. HT, Bethlehem, PA 18018

LION RIBBON CO., The Romance Collection, 100 Metro Way, Secaucus, NJ 07096

Wholesale.

TREASURE MASTERS, For Those Moments to Remember, 1 Treasure Lane, Derry, NH 03038

Wholesale.

June Books

AN HERBAL CELEBRATION COOKBOOK (Herb Guild, c/o Karen Seidlitz, 29604 Schwartz Rd., Westlake, OH 44145; $10.00 ppd.)

THE LANGUAGE OF FLOWERS. For details see **FEBRUARY**, *Victoriana Books*

STALKING THE HEALTHFUL HERBS by Euell Gibbons (Putney, VT: Alan Hood & Co., $16.95 ppd.)

A VICTORIAN HERBAL. For details see **FEBRUARY,** *Victoriana Books*

Mail-Order Roses

LOWE'S OWN-ROOT ROSES, 6 Sheffield Rd., Nashua, NH 03062

Catalog, $2.00.

ROSES OF YESTERDAY AND TODAY, 802 Brown's Valley Rd., Watsonville, CA 95076

Catalog, $2.00.

WAYSIDE GARDEN CATALOG, Hodges, SC 29695

Catalog, $1.00, refundable.

JULY

Vinegar-Making Supplies

ALFRED KNOBLER CO., Moonache, NJ 07074. 201-641-2600, inquiries.

Wholesale supplier of fancy vinegar bottles.

ASTER PLACE HERBS, *Dick Margulis*, RD 1, Box 24B, Poland, NY 13431

Wholesale listings of many supplies for small businesses. Bottles, corks, etc. $2.50, refundable with order, brings quarterly listings and updates.

THE CAROLINA BIOLOGICAL SUPPLY CO., Burlington, NC 27215 *or* Gladstone, OR 97027

Ask for their catalog #58 (biology/science materials). Bottles, corks, large flowers presses, etc.

GAZZELE'S FINE FOODS, P.O. Box 980, Canby, OR 97013-0980 (503-266-4140)

Quality wine vinegars. Price list available upon request.

LAVENDER LANE, *Donna Madora Mitchell*, P.O. Box 7265-HT, Citrus Heights, CA 95621-7265

Catalog, $2.00. Also offers jars for jellies and creams or salves.

MAYERS CIDER MILL, 699 5-Mile Line Rd., Webster, NY 14580 (1-800-543-0043; ask for Lorraine)

Vinegar bottles. Wholesale to businesses. Supply tax or Federal ID number.

NORTHWESTERN BOTTLE CO., 1816 Walton Rd., St. Louis, MO 63114 (314-426-7000; David Reed)

Ask for their catalog; inquire about warehouses near you where you can purchase their 10-ounce Flint Glass Woozy Bottle, Item #1016139, in quantities smaller than their $100 minimum.

Preservation of the Harvest Sources

ACTIVA PRODUCTS, P.O. Box 1296-P, Marshall, TX 75671-0023

Glycerin and silica gel, retail and wholesale, plus instructive booklets on using both.

NICHOL'S GARDEN NURSERY, 1190 No. Pacific Hwy., Albany, OR 97321

Silica gel.

DR. MICHAEL'S HERBS, 5109 No. Western, Chicago, IL 60625

Retail catalog, $1.00. Glycerin.

SILICA GEL is available in most garden centers. One of my readers suggests that reasonably priced glycerin is available from horse-supply stores; such glycerin must be used only for floral preservation, not edible purposes.

July Books

CHEF'S HERB FESTIVAL COOKBOOK (International Herb Growers and Marketers, P.O. Box 281-P2, Silver Spring, PA 17575)

CULINARY USES FOR HERBS AND SPICES by Pat Bourdo (Woodland Herb Farm, 7741 No. Manitou Trail West, Northport, MI 49670; $9.50 ppd.)

Delicious salt-free recipes!

FLOWER-DRYING WITH A MICROWAVE: TECHNIQUES AND PROJECTS by Titia Joosten (New York: Sterling, 1989)

GOURMET VINEGARS: HOW TO MAKE & COOK WITH THEM by Marsha Peters Johnson (Culinary Arts Ltd., P.O. Box 2157-PH, Lake Oswego, OR 97035; $5.95 ppd.)

AUGUST

Books on Edible Flowers

COOKING WITH EDIBLE FLOWERS (AND CULINARY HERBS) by Jim Meuninck

Video. Visits several famous herb and flower gardens and chefs; 60 minutes; $29.95. This, and many other herb-related videos available from The Seeker Press, P.O. Box 2899-P, West Lafayette, IN 47960; free catalog.

COOKING WITH FLOWERS by Jenny Leggatt (New York: Fawcett Columbine, 1987)

Available from Wood Violet Books (see page 00).

THE FORGOTTEN ART OF FLOWER COOKERY by Leona Woodring Smith (New York: Pelican Publishing)

Available from Wood Violet Books (see page 293).

GUIDE TO COOKING WITH EDIBLE FLOWERS by Jay and Pamela North (Paradise Farms, P.O. Box 436-P, Summerland, CA 93067; $7.00 ppd.)

LIST OF 84 SAFE EDIBLE FLOWERS, researched by Dr. Sinclair Philip of Sooke Harbour and Ron Zimmerman of the Herbfarm (The Herbfarm, 32804-PS, Issaquah-Fall City Rd., Fall City, WA 98024; ask for #3622-PS; $3.50 ppd.)

Along with the list, you will receive a full-color catalog of many unusual herb

products, such as pennyroyal soap for dogs, fresh bay wreaths, a fragrant Sleep Bunny, wedding tea, and so much more. Some of their flyers contain exotic recipes that feature fresh herbs and flowers. The Herbfarm is famous for its excellent cuisine; reservations at the restaurant are needed months in advance.

PROFITS FROM YOUR BACKYARD HERB GARDEN by Lee Sturdivant (San Juan Naturals, Box 642-HT, Friday Harbor, WA 98250; $11.95 ppd.)

Includes a section on preparing flowers for the market and keeping them fresh.

RECIPES FROM A KITCHEN GARDEN by Renee Shepherd (Shepherd's Garden Publishing, 7389 West Zayante Rd., Felton, CA 95018; $9.20 ppd.)

When you order this and Renee's Seed Catalog, ask for her flyer, "Edible Flower Recipes."

Other August Books

THE BASIL BOOK by Marilyn Hampstead (Parma, MI: Long Shadow Books, 1984)

Available from author, Fox Hill Farm, Box 7-P2, Parma, MI 49269-0007; $8.50 ppd.; autographed upon request.

HEAVENLY HERBS...ENJOY THEM! by Lane Furneaux (Dallas, TX: Ladybug Press)

Available from author, 7348 Lane Park Ct., Dallas, TX 75225; $7.95 ppd.; autographed upon request.

SEPTEMBER

Sources of Potpourri Supplies

MARI-MANN HERB CO., No. End St. Louis Bridge Rd., Decatur, IL 62521

Fragrance crystals. Write for retail/ wholesale details.

HERB GARDEN FRAGRANCES, *Rosella Mathieu* (see **JANUARY**, *Other Sources of Essential Oils*)

LAVENDER LANE, *Donna Madora Mitchell* (see **JANUARY**, *Other Sources of Essential Oils*)

Books on Potpourri

A BEGINNER'S GUIDE TO MAKING POTPOURRI by Donna Metcalfe (Good Scents, P.O. Box 854-P, Rialto, CA 92377; $4.00)

A COMPLETE GUIDE FOR MAKING POTPOURRI by Sylvia Tippett (Rasland Farm, Dept. HT, NC 82 at US 13, Godwin, NC 28344; catalog, $2.50)

CRAFTING WITH POTPOURRI MAKES SCENTS by Donna Madora Mitchell (Lavender Lane, P.O. Box 7265-HT, Citrus Heights, CA 95621-7265; $8.50 ppd.)

POTPOURRI: THE ART OF FRAGRANCE CRAFTING by Louise Gruenberg (Norway, IA: Frontier Cooperative Herbs, revised 1990)

(Available from Frontier Cooperative Herbs, Box 69-P2, Norway, IA 52318; 319-227-7991; $10.45 ppd.; inquire about wholesale rates). A real bargain of a book!

POTPOURRI...EASY AS ONE...TWO...THREE by Dody Lyness (Palos Verdes Peninsula, CA: Berry Hill Press; $6.95 ppd.)

A textbook guide for classes. Available wholesale.

POTPOURRI, INCENSE AND OTHER FRAGRANT CONCOCTIONS by Ann Tucker Fettner (New York:Workman, 1977

Available from Wood Violet Books (see page 293 for address).

POTPOURRI PARTY-LINE, a newsletter edited by Dody Lyness.

*Features fragrant floral crafts. See **MAY**, Herbal Periodicals, for ordering information.*

Sources of Deer's-tongue

APHRODISIA, 282 Bleecker St., New York, NY 10014

FRONTIER COOPERATIVE HERBS, Box 299, Norway, IA 52318

NATURE'S FINEST, Jen and Mike Mescher, P.O. Box 10311, Dept. MP, Burke, VA 22015

OCTOBER

Wreaths and Wreathmaking Supplies

FRONTIER COOPERATIVE HERBS, Box 69, Norway, IA 52318 (319-227-7991)
Cones

HEARTFELT FARMS, *Cheryl Taylor*, P.O. Box 1513-P2, Salem, VA 24153

Catalog, $2.00, refundable. Large pine cones, completed apple or eucalyptus cones, or kits to make them.

THE HERBARY, *Shirley Lokar*, Dept. HT, 3550 New Hudson Rd., Orwell, OH 44076

Wreathmaking discs for fast, easy production of herbal bases. SASE for list.

McFADDEN'S VINES AND WREATHS, Rt. 3, Box 2360-HT, Butler, TN 37640

Catalog, $1.00. Tiny Carolina and Canadian hemlock cones and natural wreath bases of all kinds and shapes.

MERRY MEADOW FARM, P.O. Box 8061/ P2, Cranston, RI 02920

Sturdy wreath display and shipping box, with see-through top. Sold in lots of 40. Sample for $5.00.

MOUNTAIN FARMS INC., Box 108-P, Candlewood Isle, New Fairfield, CT 06812 (203-746-1842)

Large assortment of cones of all sizes, barks, berries, pods, shells, and wreath- and potpourri-making supplies.

*WREATH BASES are also available from florist supply centers, from some of the sources listed in **FEBRUARY**, Everlastings Seeds and Plants, and from many craft outlets and catalogs (see **NOVEMBER**, Herb Craft Supplies). Fresh bay and balsam wreaths are listed in **DECEMBER**, Balsam Products and Fresh Wreaths.*

Books on Herb Wreaths

COUNTRY WREATHS FROM CAPRILANDS by Adelma Simmons (Emmaus, PA: Rodale Press, 1989)

FRAGRANT WREATHS AND OTHER BOTANICALS by Grace Wakefield (Tom Thumb Workshops, P.O. Box 357-P2, Mappsville, VA 23407; catalog, $1.00)

WREATHS OF ALL SORTS by Bertha Reppert (The Rosemary House, 120 S. Market St., Mechanicsburg, PA 17055)

THE WREATH BOOK by Rob Pullen (Sandy Mush Nursery, Rte. 2, Surrett Cove Rd., Leicester, NC 28748)

Over 100 wreaths designed at the nursery. Also available from Wood Violet Books (see page 293).

NOVEMBER

Herb Craft Supplies

If you want wholesale catalogs, most companies require your tax identification number, written on your business letterhead. (Many of the herbal firms mentioned throughout the book offer both wholesale and retail catalogs.)

BOLEK'S CRAFT SUPPLIES, P.O. Box 465, Dover, OH 44622

Catalog, $1.50.

CENTURY FLORIST SUPPLIES, Co., P.O. Box 32562, Detroit, MI 48232-2562

Catalog, $5.00. Drieds, ribbon, silk, wreath bases, craft supplies, all retail by mail.

COAST WHOLESALE FLORIST, P.O. Box 10, San Francisco, CA 94103

Color catalog, $3.00.

A LITTLE BIT CRAFTY, 135 Duggan Rd., Central Point, OR 97501 (1-800-422-3501)

$25 minimum. Free catalog to businesses; $5.00, refundable with order; charge to others.

MONK'S HILL HERBS, *Madeleine Siegler,* Dept. HT, RFD 2, Winthrop, ME 04364

Her own Spice Necklace is available from her at $12.00 ppd., retail.

STAR AND CRESCENT HERBS AND SUP-PLIES, 11253 Trade Ctr. Dr., Rancho Cordova, CA 95670 (800-824-7994, out-of-state; 800-321-0251 in CA)

Wholesale.

November Books and Periodicals

If you are starting an herb business, you will want to subscribe to THE BUSINESS OF HERBS and join the IHGMA (see **May**, *Herb Groups and Organizations for information). My own newsletter, POTPOURRI FROM HERBAL ACRES is an excellent networking tool for businesses. Subscribers can have a free plug ("Herb Blurb") each year, and my "Networking Column" is helpful if you need to locate resources. I have also compiled a "Source List" of herbal craft supplies, from the tips readers have sent in over the years ($3.00 ppd.). To order the "Source List" or to receive my brochure, write Pine Row Publications-HT, Box 428, Washington Crossing, PA 18977. You will also find sources listed in THE CRAFT SUPPLY SOURCEBOOK by Margaret Boyd (Augusta, GA: Betterway Pub., 1989) (available from author, P.O. Box 6232-HT, Augusta, GA 30906; $17.45 ppd.). Includes "naturals."*

BU$INESS OF HERBS, newsletter (*see* **MAY**, *Herbal Periodicals*)

CREATIVE CASH: HOW TO SELL YOUR CRAFTS, NEEDLEWORK, DESIGNS, AND KNOW-HOW by Barbara Brabec

Send legal-size SASE to Barbara Brabec Productions, P.O. Box 2137/HT, Naperville, IL 60565

HELP FOR YOUR GROWING HOME-BASED BUSINESS by Barbara Brabec

Send legal-sized SASE to Barbara Brabec Productions, P.O. Box 2137/HT, Naperville, IL 60565

HERB GAZETTE, Betty Wold (*see* **MAY**, *Herbal Periodicals*)

HERB, SPICE, AND MEDICINAL PLANT DIGEST (*see* **MAY**, *Herbal Periodicals*)

HERBS: 1001 GARDENING QUESTIONS ANSWERED by the Editors of Garden Way Publishing (Pownal, VT: Storey Communications, 1990)

HERBS WITH CONFIDENCE by Bertha Reppert (Mechanicsburg, PA: Remembrance Press, 1986)

Autographed copy upon request, $11.00 ppd.; Dept. P2, 120 S. Main St., Mechanicsburg, PA 17055. Bertha provides a brochure describing her own lecture offerings.

LIVING WITH POTPOURRI by Kate Jayne and Claudette Mautor (White Plains, NY: Peter Pauper Press)

Available from Sandy Mush Herb Nursery, Dept. HT, Rt. 2, Surrett Cove Rd., Leicester, NC 28748; autographed copy, upon request; $8.50 ppd.

THE NATIONAL HOME BUSINESS REPORT, edited by Barbara Brabec

Send legal-sized SASE to Barbara Brabec Productions, P.O. Box 2137/HT, Naperville, IL 60565

NATIVE HARVESTS by Barrie Kavasch (New York: Random House, 1979)

(Autographed copy available from the author; P.O. Box 255-HT, Bridgewater, CT 06752; $9.45 ppd.)

OZARKS HERBALIST, Jim Long, Rte. 4, Box 730/HT, Oak Grove, AR 72660

$10.00/4 issues.

THE POTENTIAL OF HERBS AS A CASH CROP by Richard Alan Miller and THE HERB MARKET REPORT, a monthly newsletter

Both available from Oak, 1305 Vista Drive, Grants Pass, OR 97527; book, $13.20 ppd.; newsletter, $12.00/year

PROFITS FROM YOUR BACKYARD HERB GARDEN: HOW TO GROW AND SELL CULINARY HERBS AND EDIBLE FLOWERS TO LOCAL GROCERS & RESTAURANTS by Lee Sturdivant (San Juan Naturals, Box 642-HT, Friday Harbor, WA 98250; $11.95 ppd.)

"SPEAKING OF HERBS..." by Betty Wold
A book of herbal lectures. Available from the author (see **Author's Directory***); $12.95 ppd.*

Free Herb Handouts

I have written each of the following, which are useful as handouts for your lectures or customers. For samples and ordering information, send a legal-size SASE to Pine Row Publications, Box 428-PSO, Washington Crossing, PA 18977: "Herb Growth/Use/Harvesting/ Preserving Chart for 59 Herbs"; "Herbal Fragrances for Your Home" *(recipes, tips, and product sources); and* "Sensational Herbs to Grow" *(descriptions, culture, and sources).*

DECEMBER

December Books and Periodicals

CHRISTMAS SCRAPBOOK by Bertha Reppert (The Rosemary House, 120 S. Market St., Mechanicsburg, PA 17055; $5.00 ppd.)

GROSSE ILE HERB SOCIETY COOKBOOK (Dept. HT, 27921 East River Rd., Grosse Ile, MI 48138; $10.50 ppd.)

HERBAL CELEBRATION COOKBOOK (c/o Karen Seidlitz, 29604 Schwartz Rd., Westlake, OH 44145; $10.00 ppd.)

HERBAN LIFESTYLES, a newsletter (Chris Utterback 84 Carpenter Rd., N. Hartford, CT 06057; $18.00/year)

POTPOURRI...EASY AS ONE...TWO...THREE by Dody Lyness (Palos Verdes Peninsula, CA: Berry Hill Press; $6.95 ppd.)

Fragrance Oils

GINGHAM 'N' SPICE, LTD., *Nancy McFayden*, P.O. Box 88-HT, Gardenville, PA 18926
Oils and fragrance products. Wholesale (on business letterhead) or retail catalogs, $2.00.

Balsam Products and Fresh Wreaths

MAINE BALSAM FIR PRODUCTS, P.O. Box 123-HT, West Paris, ME 04289
Wholesale/retail for SASE.

MERRY GARDENS, *Mary Ellen Ross*, Camden, ME 04843
Catalog, $2.00

SUNRISE CO. EVERGREENS, P.O. Box 163-HT, Milbridge, ME 04658
Catalog free. Wreaths.

UNDERWOOD HERBS, RR 2, Chateaugay, NY 12920
Wholesale price list upon request.

Fresh Bay Leaf Wreaths

BAY LAUREL FARM, *Glory Condon*, Dept. HT, West Garzas Rd., Carmel Valley, CA 93924
Brochure, $1.00. Wholesale/retail.

HERBFARM, 32804-PS Issaquah-Fall City Rd., Fall City, WA (98024)
Free catalog. Retail.

TAYLOR'S INC., Dept. HT, 3038 E. Mohawk, Phoenix, AZ 85024
Fresh bay leaf stems, in $100 lots (602-992-7967).

Herb Calendar for the New Year

HARTMAN'S HERB FARM, Old Dana Rd., Barre, MA 01005
Retail or wholesale.

Index

Numbers in italics indicate illustrations appear on that page.